THE NEW EVERYDAY

Views on Ambient Intelligence

010 Publishers, Rotterdam, The Netherlands

THE NEW EVERYDAY

Views on Ambient Intelligence

Emile Aarts & Stefano Marzano

CONTENTS

INTRODUCTION

CULTURAL ISSUES IN AMBIENT INTELLIGENCE

Stefano Marzano

For decades now, people have been predicting the imminent advent of the 'smart home', with all sorts of functions capable of being activated and controlled remotely and automatically. Now, there are signs that it may soon be about to happen. And it looks as though it may be smarter than we expected, encompassing more than just the home – a smart environment, including our home, cars, clothing, work, public spaces… Our living spaces may soon be filled with a diffuse technology penetrating many new areas of our lives. Within the next decade, we may find that any non-interactive objects or systems around us have been replaced by almost invisible, intelligent interactive systems – an 'Ambient Intelligence' that could soon form a natural part of our everyday lives.

Far-reaching implications

The implications of this development would be far-reaching for individuals, businesses and society as a whole – and not only in the prosperous, post-industrial West. It could help release us from a host of mundane activities and leave us time to lead more fulfilled lives. It could also create exciting opportunities for many companies and even whole industries to form unprecedented and fruitful partnerships. And, by injecting new intelligence into how we think and operate, it could generate models, systems and services that are customizable for use in many different contexts around the world.

Caution

But, although Ambient Intelligence would seem to offer enormous opportunities, we know technology itself is neither good nor bad; it is how we use it that makes the difference. We only have to look to the Industrial Revolution and its consequences to see how some promising ideas, when applied indiscriminately, can bring hidden problems in their wake. It was the unquestioning assumption that 'more is better' that led to some of the issues we face today, from the complexity of VCRs and 15-programme washing machines to global warming and inequalities of wealth and welfare. We should be careful not to just replace that old mantra with a new one of 'smarter is better'. Perhaps we shall discover that we don't want 'everything intelligent' or 'everything done for us'. It may be 'good for us' to struggle to do certain things. We may not want a toaster that talks, or a juicer with e-mail access. We have a duty to take out a metaphorical insurance policy for future generations. Ambient Intelligence could lead to great opportunities, but it will need to be guided. We need to take a clear cultural position which seeks to apply these exciting new technologies in ways that will contribute to achieving balance and equilibrium – the equilibrium between People, Planet and Profit. If developed within such a framework, how might Ambient Intelligence affect our lives?

Bye-bye, boxes

Much of today's material technology is still obtrusive in our homes and offices, in the shape of grey and black boxes – televisions, computers, appliances… These are set to disappear, as the technology becomes incorporated in our material environment, in the traditional objects we have surrounded ourselves with for millennia, such as tables, chairs, walls and ceilings. As technology becomes hidden within these static, unintelligent objects, they will become subjects, active and intelligent actors in our environment. At the same time, the immaterial world of our interactions with them – services, games, entertainment, information, communication – will become more prominent in our lives. And this is surely closer to what we want: knowledge, excitement, entertainment, education, productivity, social contact – without the obtrusive prominence of the technology that delivers them.

This means that in advanced societies the living space of the future could look more like that of the past than that of today. Through the ages, our homes have contained the objects that are most relevant to human life – chairs, tables and beds, for instance. We have walked on floors, sheltered from the elements under roofs and behind walls. Although these may take different forms in different cultures, climates and times, their basic form is timeless, and our distant descendants will still use them. But the technological boxes of today – the TV, radio, telephone and computer – are temporary. While their function is timeless – entertaining and informing, helping us to remember and communicate   their form is not, since that form does not relate to our physical or psychological needs. These functions will therefore be incorporated into the objects we can't do without. Screens will retreat into walls, windows or ceilings; discreet microphones will pick up our commands wherever we are, all integrated in relevant objects or invisible in the environment.

In less advanced societies, of course, the form taken by Ambient Intelligence is likely to be somewhat different. But the virtue of such technology is precisely that it is highly customizable, in terms of the technologies involved and the cultural forms it can take. Moreover, it could enable developing countries to avoid some of the problems that an over-emphasis on matter, as represented by the black and grey boxes, has caused for advanced societies, such as market saturation, pollution and depletion of resources. The new miniaturized or invisible technologies of dematerialization could allow them not only to leap-frog those developmental problems but also to surmount the limitations of time and space, and enjoy an enhanced quality of life in the context of their own cultural values.

Intelligent service

How might this ambient technology manifest its intelligence? Looking back in history, we see that people, in their unquenchable need to survive, have always been thirsty for more knowledge, power and mobility, and have always tried to make use of the intelligence around them – from other human beings through animals to plants and even microbes. But the more we have learned, done and seen, the more we have come to realize that pursuing our own desires at the expense of others is unethical. In a sense, digital intelligence could allow us to pursue our own fulfilment without depriving others of their right to do the same.

This technology will recognize us, notice our habits, learn our likes and dislikes, and adapt its behaviour and the services it offers us accordingly. It could generate new paradigms of relationships and behaviours at an individual and group level, as well as new likes and dislikes. And, by operating in a network that links us through the Internet to the rest of the world, it can combine information from disparate sources to supply us with what we need. Ambient Intelligence devices will also show their intelligence by communicating among themselves, and, as a system, communicating with us in the ways that are most natural to us – talking, gesturing, touching and showing.

Why now?

Why should this be about to happen now? Partly because the enabling technologies are now available. We have a much better understanding of the relevant technologies and how we can interact with them than we did only a few years ago. An equally important factor is the global zeitgeist: people think they are ready for it. Are they?

We live at a time when many of our traditional certainties are being challenged. What does it mean to be human? What makes an experience real? What is ethical behaviour? Where is the borderline between the natural and the artificial? How can we evaluate different cultures? In a very real sense, we are living in a new Renaissance. In the European Renaissance of the fifteenth and sixteenth centuries, people were exploring the boundaries of the world as they had known it until then. Their discoveries turned many traditional assumptions upside down. The fact that Columbus did not sail off the edge of the earth, for instance, was a great shock to most people. At the same time, the existence of a whole New World out there created great excitement, inspiring many adventurers to follow him. More powerful perhaps was Copernicus discovery that the earth was not the centre of the universe, shaking the very foundations of the established worldview as embodied in the teachings of the Church and the associated feudal system of government. The effects of this discovery were far-reaching, and can be seen in many of the social and political upheavals of the following centuries.

Perhaps it is not too far-fetched to think that the development of Ambient Intelligence may change the course of history in the same way. Certainly, during the past few decades, we have discovered that the previous 'world order' has become inadequate. On the industrial front, we have discovered that the Industrial Revolution, with its emphasis on quantity as *sine qua non* of progress, has let us down. The ozone layer, global warming, environmental pollution, not to mention corporate crises of trust and the superfluity of product features and functions that confuse rather than delight, have all shown us that another way might be preferable. Environmentalist and anti-globalization protesters are but one expression of this discontent. Similarly, on the political front, the past half-century has seen the collapse of fascism, imperialism, colonialism and communism, and, with the demolition of the Berlin Wall, the end of the old power-bloc oppositions. Are we currently seeing the rise of a new opposition between fundamentalist Islam and the West? It is clear, at least, that old orders are no longer secure. If Ambient Intelligence is part of this change, it will make its contribution by injecting new intelligence into the system that constitutes our ecology: us, as human beings, in our environment. Just as, in the past, civilization grew incrementally as a result of knowledge, communication and insight, so Ambient Intelligence will allow us to benefit more widely and deeply from the accumulated wisdom of the past and the collective wisdom of today, thereby taking us one step further in civilization.

Moreover, the insights Ambient Intelligence may help us to gain may very well change what it actually means to be human, and indeed all of the questions we asked in the old context (Is this ethical? Profitable? Desirable? Authentic? Responsible? Sustainable?…) may need to be redefined. These questions, and others, will help us to decide how best to guide the development of Ambient Intelligence. As we explore the new world of Ambient Intelligence, we need to think hard about the long-term consequences of what we are doing.

New opportunities

Ambient Intelligence can, to a degree, be thought of as an enabling and an extension of the Internet. This amorphous, networked technology is already breaking down the barriers of time and space. Information that, only a few years ago, would have taken us weeks to locate, can now be found in a matter of minutes, or at most hours. We can find and communicate with people on the other side of the world, often with long-lost friends, effectively allowing us to time-travel. And we can instantaneously avail ourselves of online services without leaving our desks. Perhaps we can understand what Ambient Intelligence might mean by imagining that range – and then imagining it expanded, customized and localized to our specific situation.

That specific situation might be in an advanced, post-industrial society, in a developing country or somewhere in between. The capabilities of Ambient Intelligence to overcome limitations of time and space could open up new opportunities for societies around the world for whom distance is a problem. For example, why shouldn't we try to develop global technological and organizational platforms that can be locally contextualized, using local people, environments and infrastructures, so that a system used for one purpose in advanced societies can be used in a modified form in developing countries? The specific application may be different, but the generic issue would be the same. If this 'multiple use' could be built in at the design and development stages, it could also be economically viable.

Take Web-based education, for instance. In the developed industrialized world, it is an interesting alternative to bricks-and-mortar education. But given the existing physical infrastructure of schools and colleges in developed countries, it is not vital. However, in the remoter parts of Brazil or Africa, where schools are few and students far apart, the introduction of Web-based education could be a relatively inexpensive way of raising educational standards rapidly. The same technology could also be adapted to provide an Ambient Intelligence service in the industrialized world for older people, in the form of online health monitoring or home diagnostics or a shopping and delivery service for them, or for others who have too little time for conventional shopping or food preparation.

In one case, we overcome the distances of the students from schools, and help to narrow the educational gap between the developed and the developing world. In the other, we solve another distance problem – the distance of the consumer from the hospital or shop, as well as the gap between those who are fit and healthy in society and those who are less so. In both cases, the technology is the same, but the group served is quite different. If we know how to look, we can see many more instances of shortage and deprivation that could be relieved in this way, both in the developing world, and closer to home – many people, for instance, find too little time to spend with family members and friends, or in relaxation, and as a society we often have too little time to devote to the welfare of our fellows.

The more we think along these lines, the more possibilities emerge. Speech technology, for instance, saves people the bother of writing, typing or reading. It also gives people whose vision is impaired access to normal channels of communication. But what about the millions around the world who have plenty of time, and can see and hear perfectly well – but who simply can't read or write? How could speech technology help them? Once the technology has been developed, such ideas do not need to be dismissed on the grounds of affordability.

Over to you

Clearly, there is no single 'right' approach to making the Ambient Intelligence vision a reality. In terms of practical implementation, new technologies will require different business models to come together, as electronics companies collaborate with others from widely different industries. New disciplines will need to work together to redefine their assumptions about our most fundamental needs. What is required is a commitment on behalf of all to continue to question what kind of world we want to live in and how we want to live and communicate within it, and then to address those questions as a group. Only by facing up to these crucial questions will we be able to guide the development of Ambient Intelligence in responsible directions and avoid repeating the mistakes of the past.

As a global society, we have a collective duty to those who come after us to ensure that this new concept, which could mean so much to humanity, is guided consciously along paths that (as far as we can judge) are responsible. It would be easy to let it just drift and evolve aimlessly. Yet conventions, once established, are very hard to change. Let us take the trouble now to take out an 'insurance policy' for future generations. Let us make sure, through reflection upon the issues, wide discussion and collaborative experimentation, that the conventions and concepts that evolve within Ambient Intelligence can stand the test of time.

TECHNOLOGICAL ISSUES IN AMBIENT INTELLIGENCE

Emile Aarts

From the age of the box to Ambient Intelligence

To date, the consumer electronics industry has existed in 'the age of the box'. Companies have concentrated on providing functions through stand-alone hardware, such as televisions, stereo systems, video recorders and DVD players. Each function or benefit has come packaged in its own box and, over the years, these boxes have accumulated in our living rooms and around our homes.

This no longer has to be the case. Technologically, electronics can now be integrated into any conceivable physical object: into clothing, furniture, cars, houses, offices, and so on. And devices can be connected together into meaningful systems, making it possible for us to access content and services in a variety of ways. In an Ambient Intelligence world, these two possibilities come together to form digital electronic networks of intelligent devices that are integrated into their surroundings and provide information, communication services and entertainment wherever they are. They will present themselves very differently to our contemporary handheld or stationary electronic boxes, being embedded into the environment around us and allowing much more natural and human interaction. These ambient intelligent environments will be context-aware (i.e., sensitive and responsive to our presence and moods), personalized, and able to adapt to and even anticipate our wishes, needs and behaviours.[1]

Trends in technology

Several technological trends point towards the emergence of this new paradigm of Ambient Intelligence.

Computing visions

On the occasion of the fiftieth anniversary of the Association of Computing Machinery in 1997, computer scientists from all over the world were asked for their opinions about the next fifty years of computing.[2] Their reactions were strikingly consistent in that they all foresaw a world of distributed computing devices that supported people in a non-obtrusive way. Weiser's work on ubiquitous computing, for example, proposes a computer infrastructure that enables any person to have access to any source of information at any place and time.[3] Such a world can be conceived as a huge distributed network consisting of thousands of interconnected embedded systems that support users and satisfy their needs for information, communication, navigation and entertainment.

Tremendous efforts are currently being poured into developing concepts for this distributed computing vision; one of the most ambitious being MIT's Oxygen project.[4] Most of these approaches aim to increase people's professional productivity: Dertouzos claims that the Oxygen technology might multiply productivity as much as threefold.[5] Yet in focusing on productivity, the efforts may be neglecting the opportunities in the personal and home domains, i.e., improving the quality of people's lives, through entertainment, leisure and the enhancement of their relationships.

Rapid change

Many of the technologies involved in information processing systems are changing rapidly. In accordance with Moore's Law, data density on integrated circuits is continuing to double every eighteen months. Storage capacity, CPU speed, memory, wireless transfer speed and battery energy density are all showing similar rates of change. In terms of Ambient Intelligence, more functionality is becoming possible, at lower cost.

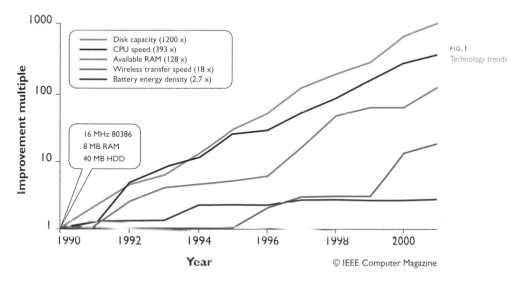

© IEEE Computer Magazine

FIG. 1
Technology trends

Display, connectivity, storage and interaction

Other innovations in the domains of displays, storage and connectivity also point to the potential of an ambient intelligent future. The introduction of blue laser and Digital Video Recording (DVR) technology will make it possible to develop consumer devices that can record several tens of hours of video material, enabling time-shifted television-viewing. Poly-LED technology has made it possible to construct the world's first matrix-addressable display on a foil of a few microns in thickness, leading to flexible ultra-thin displays of arbitrary size. LCD projection allows small invisibly built-in units to display very large high-definition images on white walls. Advances in semiconductor process technology have made it possible to separate the active silicon area from its substrate and to put it onto other carriers, such as glass, thus allowing active circuitry to be integrated into any conceivable material. In digital signal processing, it is now possible to apply audio and video watermarks that enable conditional access to, and retrieval and copy protection of, audio and video material. Compression schemes such as MPEG4 and MPEG7 enable effective transmission and composition of video material. Recent developments in speech processing and vision introduce interaction technology for the development of conversational user interfaces, in a first step towards natural interfaces. And these are but a few recent developments.

First steps in the market

In the latest consumer electronics product offerings, the embryo of Ambient Intelligence can be seen in the variety of single-point, 'box' solutions for a range of applications, including imaging (digital cameras), geographical navigation (GPS), audio replay (MP3), personal mobile communication (mobile phones), time management (PDAs) and personal TV systems like TiVo. At the component level, programmable integrated circuit platforms, small storage modules, large and small flat colour display devices, and a variety of short- and long-range wireless interconnectivity solutions are being introduced to the market. Gradually, over the next decade, consumer products will increasingly be Web-connected, allowing much more powerful functionality to be added through services on the Net. We can already witness the emergence in the market of some of the concepts related to Ambient Intelligence, closely linked to the emerging interactive digital television and personal communication waves. A number of existing products prefigure the possibilities of Ambient Intelligence, including Streamium, the world's first micro hi-fi system that offers one-button access to personalized digital audio content via broadband Internet, and the i-Pronto, a three-in-one electronic programme guide (EPG), Pronto remote control and browser able to adapt and evolve in new, unprecedented ways to suit the user's wishes, needs and tastes.

Key elements of Ambient Intelligence

The five key characteristics of Ambient Intelligence, summarized in Table 1, have different technological requirements.

Embedded	Many networked devices are integrated into the environment
Context-aware	These devices can recognize you and your situational context
Personalized	They can be tailored towards your needs
Adaptive	They can change in response to you
Anticipatory	They can anticipate your desires without conscious mediation

The first two elements are to do with digital systems and integration into the environment, and are dominated by hardware aspects – they concentrate on the 'ambient' in Ambient Intelligence. The other elements have to do with the adjustment of the system in response to the user and the exhibition of 'intelligent' behaviour. They can all be viewed as systems adjustments, but on different timescales. Personalization refers to adjustments on a short timescale, for instance, to install personalized settings. Adaptation involves adjustments resulting from changing user behaviour detected by monitoring the user over a period of time. Eventually, when the system 'knows' the user well, it can detect long-term behavioural patterns and make appropriate adjustments.

Ambient: moving electronics into the background

The first cornerstone of Ambient Intelligence is expressed in the word 'ambient', which relates to the embedded and context-aware qualities. There are three overriding considerations with regard to this new distribution of technology in the environment. Firstly, the distributed components form a system based on a non-centralized communications network. Second, the distributed electronics are ubiquitous, i.e., their capabilities are available everywhere and at all times. Finally, this distribution is invisible to the inhabitants of the environment and non-obtrusive.

The notion of ubiquitous computing, as introduced by Marc Weiser and which forms an important part of the background to Ambient Intelligence, calls for large-scale distributed processing and communication architectures. Ubiquitous computing expands the distribution of storage and computing until a huge collective network of intelligently cooperating nodes is formed.

The nodes in a ubiquitous computing system may be external or internal. The external nodes, often called terminals, take care of input and output and interact directly with the environment and the user. Examples include sensors and actuators, interactive screens, displays, and input devices for speech, handwriting and tactile information. These terminals will be small and handy, which introduces the need for low-power electronics. This issue will become even more pronounced when people start to carry the devices with them, perhaps as 'wearables', as electronics become integrated into clothing.[6] The internal nodes predominantly refer to computing elements that carry out certain network functions, such as data processing, storage and routeing. Here too, low-power issues will play an important role, as will storage capacity and speed. The internal nodes are servers, routers, processing units, storage devices and all kinds of environmental communication units. Most of the information handling will take place in the internal nodes, and they have to provide the service quality that is needed to operate the network smoothly.

The communication in a ubiquitous home system should meet certain requirements. First, it should support interoperability, i.e., the terminals should be easy to add, replace or remove. Furthermore, it must support multiple media, including graphics, video, audio and speech. There is also the issue of wireless communication. Most appliances should connect wirelessly to the network without mediation. This introduces the need for network protocols that can handle authentication, partial information and multiple media in a secure way.

As the only existing truly ubiquitous computing system in the world, the Internet will play an important role in the disappearance of electronics into our surroundings. Wireless Web access via handheld devices will allow users to access information on the Web at any time and any place. The development of the Semantic Web in combination with all kinds of high-level applications, such as content-aware media browsers, will further enhance the Internet as an interactive large-scale distributed computing environment.

Intelligence: moving the user into the foreground

If the technology can be moved into the background, the challenge of developing interface concepts that support people with easy, intelligent and meaningful interaction must be addressed. After fifty years of designing computers that require users to adapt to them, we must now enter the era of designing equipment that adapts to users. This requires the design and implementation of application scenarios that place users in the centre of their digital environment. This concept is often referred to as 'human-centric computing'.[7] Ambient Intelligence seeks to achieve human-centric computing by making people's environments intelligent.

Ambient intelligent environments will exhibit their 'intelligence' in two important ways: through the social nature of the user interface used, and by the extent to which the system can adapt itself to its users and environment. The social character of the user interface will be determined by the extent to which the system's behaviour accords with the intuition, habits and context of its users. Self-adaptability will depend on how well the system can understand context and learn through interaction with the user. The combination of human communication modalities (such as speech, handwriting and gesture) and the system's ability to adjust to user needs (i.e., to 'personalize') plays a major role in the design of novel applications and services. Ultimately, the self-adaptive capabilities of the system should be used to detect the user's mood and to react accordingly.

New Ambient Intelligence scenarios can be developed by following an approach of user-centred design. Within this design concept, the user is placed at the centre of the design activity and, through a number of design cycles in which the designer iterates concept design, realization and user evaluation, the final interaction design is created. Many interaction designers follow the argument put forward by Reeves and Nass in The Media Equation,[8] that the interaction between man and machine should be based on the very same concepts as that between humans, i.e., it should be intuitive, multi-modal and based on emotion. This proposal is simple in its nature but at the same time extremely difficult to achieve. It requires new approaches to interaction technologies and computational intelligence.

Key enabling technologies

Philips has identified 21 enabling technologies that are key to the realization of the Ambient Intelligence vision. These enabling technologies derive from careful analysis of the five key features of Ambient Intelligence. They are:

- User-centred Design
- Ambient video
- Ambient displays
- Ambient audio
- Ambient lighting
- Ambient vision
- Speech
- Smart materials
- Smart dust
- Ambient computing platforms
- Middleware
- The Semantic Web
- Computational intelligence
- Data and content management
- Pervasive wireless
- Wearable technology
- Networked storage
- Context awareness
- Ubiquitous communication
- Mobile peer-to-peer computing
- Trust

These technologies, and combinations thereof, cover all the technological aspects of Ambient Intelligence. Many of the technologies, such as audio, video, lighting and computing platforms, belong to longstanding technological domains. The various technologies are not explored in their entirety in this book, but only in their relevance to Ambient Intelligence.

The known and the new

Ambient Intelligence shares some characteristics with a number of paradigms proposed over the past decade, including Xerox PARC's ubiquitous computing paradigm, IBM's pervasive computing paradigm and MIT's Oxygen project. Even earlier, visionaries working at the crossroads of artificial intelligence and multimedia proposed ideas about intelligent man-machine interaction.[9] The film industry has also contributed to the development of similar ideas, as in Paul Verhoeven's *Total Recall* and Stanley Kubrick's classic, *2001: A Space Odyssey*.

Yet Ambient Intelligence differs fundamentally from these proposals. Whereas earlier paradigms focused on productivity in business environments, Ambient Intelligence focuses on using consumer electronics to bring a new kind of interaction with technology into our homes and personal domains, thus enhancing our experiences and lives. Whereas the increased productivity paradigms largely retain the 'desktop metaphor' graphical user interface developed by Xerox PARC in the 1970s, Ambient Intelligence requires a new metaphor or interaction paradigm, enabling natural and social interaction within ambient intelligent environments. As the technology enabling the computer to disappear becomes available, the success of Ambient Intelligence will depend on the development of concepts that make it possible for us to interact in a natural and intelligent way with our digital environments — and with each other.

1   E. Aarts, R. Harwig and M. Schuurmans, 'Ambient Intelligence', *The Invisible Future*, ed. P. Denning (New York, McGraw Hill, 2001)

2   P. Denning and R.M. Metcalfe, *Beyond Calculation: The Next Fifty Years of Computing* (New York, Copernicus, 1997)

3   M. Weiser, 'The Computer for the Twenty-first Century', *Scientific American* 265(3) (1991), 94-104

4   M. Dertouzos, 'The Future of Computing', *Scientific American* 281(2) (1999), 52-55

5   M. Dertouzos, *The Unfinished Revolution* (New York, HarperCollins, 2001)

6   S. Mann, 'Wearable Computing: A First Step Toward Personal Imaging', *IEEE Computer* (February 1997), 25-32

7   T. Winograd (ed.), *Bringing Design to Software* (Reading MA, Addison Wesley Publishing Company, 1996)

8   B. Reeves and C. Nass, *The Media Equation* (Cambridge MA, Cambridge University Press, 1996)

9   N.P. Negroponte, *Being Digital* (New York, Alfred A. Knopf Inc., 1995)

NAVIGATING THIS BOOK

The New Everyday is the result of contributions from an extremely diverse group, including technology researchers, designers, social scientists and marketing and business experts. We explore the subject of Ambient Intelligence in a wide-ranging way, although, of course, we cannot be completely comprehensive. As such, the book is a 'work in progress' and an invitation to the public to join the debate about an appropriate way forward. It is divided into eight parts, six of which examine major design and technological issues relating to different aspects of Ambient Intelligence. The seventh explores wider implications for business, and the final section introduces examples of projects that are beginning to explore the possibilities of Ambient Intelligence.

IDENTIFY, UNDERSTAND, ATTUNE

Part 1 deals with the main focus of Ambient Intelligence: people. What exactly will people want, accept or need? And how can we find that out? Chapters 1.1, 1.2 and 1.3 explore the macro issues – how the study of social and business trends, cultural diversity and human personality can help us understand the basic non-physiological parameters within which Ambient Intelligence will need to operate. Chapters 1.4, 1.5 and 1.6 examine the practical question of how we can ensure that the design of Ambient Intelligence systems is attuned to people's preferred ways of interacting with technology.

TOUCH, RELATE, INTERACT

Part 2 considers how we might communicate with an Ambient Intelligence system. As human beings, our communication is formed by our senses. Using these, we have constructed a number of languages of greater or lesser explicitness – speech and writing, of course, but also gesture, facial expression and body language. Chapters 2.1, 2.2, 2.3 and 2.4 explore how we can use these same modes of communication with our Ambient Intelligence systems. Chapters 2.5 and 2.6 look at how, using sensors and smart materials, the system will inconspicuously 'sense' who we are, what our situation is, and then process and use that information intelligently. Part of the problem lies in the complexity and diversity of a comprehensive Ambient Intelligence: the challenges relating to computational issues, especially regarding efficiency and communication, are discussed in 2.7 and 2.8. Finally, Chapter 2.9 considers how our Ambient Intelligence system will be able to go beyond itself to make use of the Internet – the Semantic Web – to resolve problems or carry out tasks.

EVOLVE, LEARN, REMEMBER

An important aspect of intelligence is learning and applying what has been learned. In Part 3, we consider how an Ambient Intelligence system will learn about its users and adapt to their needs, wants and preferences over time. This will require the system to be able to adapt and be flexible over the long term (3.1), to reason and predict (3.2), and to cope intelligently with huge volumes of data and content (3.3). But it will also mean that the system will need to know how to communicate with us in ways that we not only understand, but also enjoy (3.4).

MOVE, ACCESS, LIBERATE

The convenience of mobile communication is clear, and life for many of us is already unthinkable without our mobile phone. Intelligence that is truly ambient will therefore need to be available when we are on the move, either within the home or outside. In Part 4, the first two chapters explore the practical issues of creating an unobtrusive technology for people in a dynamically changing context, and the essentials of pervasive wireless technology. Chapters 4.3 and 4.4 look at the possibilities of integrating electronics into clothing and textiles. The technological issues involved in being able to access information from anywhere are dealt with in Chapter 4.5, while Chapter 4.6 considers how we can make a mobile tool (such as a mobile phone) able to decide where it is, what its own situation is, and what the situation of the user is – and then act intelligently in accordance with that information. Finally, Chapter 4.7 examines how we can communicate most conveniently through our Ambient Intelligence system with people in other locations.

COMMUNE, INTEGRATE, TRUST

People are essentially social creatures, and any system that aims to improve our quality of life must take this into account. In Part 5, we explore applications of Ambient Intelligence within communities and their possible effects (5.1). We also examine how whole environments, including the exteriors of buildings and other public spaces can be made 'intelligent' (5.2); and how Ambient Intelligence can help us achieve a balance between work and other aspects of life (5.3). The technological requirements for interactions between communities are dealt with in Chapter 5.4, while the security concerns involved in linking Ambient Intelligence systems are explored in Chapter 5.5.

TRANSFORM, GROW, BECOME

Ambient Intelligence is not just about material comforts, convenience and pleasure, or even enhanced social contact. It is about helping people develop their full potential so that, in interaction with others and with the world, they become (so to speak) more human. In Part 6, we first consider how individuals can play a significant role in shaping an increasingly networked society (6.1); and in Chapter 6.2, we look at how Ambient Intelligence can help to deepen relationships and personal experiences. Other chapters deal with how we can make our interactions with Ambient Intelligence more 'poetic' (6.3), and how we can learn from them and imbue them with 'stories' from our own imagination (6.4).

PARTNER, BRAND, CREATE

This part of the book explores the implications Ambient Intelligence will have for business. In Chapter 7.1 we consider how Ambient Intelligence can make a contribution to the development of a sustainable society. This is followed by a discussion of whether people are actually ready for Ambient Intelligence and how we can close the gap between awareness and acceptance of new technologies. Significant changes also await those involved in creating Ambient Intelligence systems, such as designers and developers: the shifts in focus for their disciplines and others are examined in Chapters 7.3 and 7.4. Chapter 7.5 sets the scene for branding, marketing and business, with a sketch of the new business landscape within which Ambient Intelligence will develop. There will be radical implications for marketing and branding, and some of these are dealt with in Chapters 7.6, 7.7 and 7.8. An illustration of how these various factors come together is given in Chapter 7.9, which deals with the issues involved in selling wearables. The final two chapters explore how the traditional relationships between businesses and customers and businesses among themselves will change in a world of Ambient Intelligence and propose new models for business and customer partnerships.

FIRST STEPS

Many of the chapters described above refer to a number of projects carried out at Philips (or in which Philips has played a leading role), illustrating the principles of Ambient Intelligence in practice. This final part of the book briefly introduces twenty-four examples of projects ranging from concept work to research work to finished product. Each project has its own colour code. Within each chapter of the book, coloured tabs on the edge of the page indicate the projects relevant to that chapter, allowing the reader to easily refer from chapter to project description. Within the projects, the related chapters are given as a list, enabling reverse navigation. A matrix indicating the relationships between chapters and projects can be found at the beginning of the First Steps section.

IDENTIFY, UNDERSTAND, ATTUNE

Ambient Intelligence should be a technology for people. How can we identify what people will want, accept or need from it? Could the study of social and business trends, cultural diversity and human personality help us understand the basic parameters within which it will need to operate? And how might we make sure that Ambient Intelligence systems are attuned to people's preferred ways of interacting with technology?

1.1 THINKING THE FUTURE

Josephine Green

How do you think about the future when it is so elusive and unpredictable? How do you pin down something that is constantly evolving and being made? And how do you do this at a time when companies have to think about their future more than ever?

The old ways of doing things, successful in the Industrial Age, are less relevant today. Each company has to find its own, new ways of creating value for itself, people and society in the Knowledge Age. This involves thinking about the future, difficult though that is. Given the increasing invasiveness and power of technology in our lives, thinking about the future is a particular responsibility of Philips: the big question for us is how we can think about and envisage meaningful and relevant technology solutions that can enhance people's personal, social and environmental future quality of life.

Any technological development makes sense only if it contributes to improving people's quality of life. How well it does this depends on how well it coheres with their ways of living and fits in with their values and needs. But how can we hope to determine what those future values and needs will be five or seven years from now? We can't. We can, however, try to understand what is happening in society, in cultures and in people's daily lives, so that we can envisage socially and culturally relevant and meaningful future qualities of life. Such qualities, grounded in research, can then inspire designers, technologists and marketers to envisage human-focused solutions for Ambient Intelligence.

Society, cultures, people

Over the past decade, Philips Design has taken a highly structured approach to this challenge. A multi-disciplinary team of sociologists, psychologists, anthropologists and designers have been conducting systematic research into societies, cultures and people. This multiple focus, using multiple methodologies, is enabling us to gain insights into the complexities of the changes affecting society, business and people's personal lives. We basically explore the deeper layers of transformation in society as it migrates from the Industrial to the Knowledge Age, while at the same time researching present and emerging socio-cultural values, both in advanced industrialized nations and in developing countries such as India and China. Our insights are reinforced or inspired by our study of popular culture as manifested around the globe through music, art and fashion. We also investigate the behaviour of people, generations and genders in their everyday contexts. Essential for the creation of a supportive Ambient Intelligence, we are now increasingly involving users, both in research and in creating ambient intelligent solutions. This, in brief, is the theory. But what about the content, which is ultimately what inspires our thinking and innovation processes?

Societal shift

We are experiencing a critical period in history, migrating from one set of beliefs, technologies and economic models to another. This development was anticipated and explained by Alvin Tofler.[1] Humankind has been (and is) experiencing three different 'Ages': the Agricultural, the Industrial and the present Knowledge Age. For societies moving from the Industrial to the Knowledge Age, everything seems to be changing. The Industrial Age was based on the mass production of material goods, supply chains, 'mass man' and 'mass woman', and identity defined in terms of ownership, status and possession. The Knowledge Age is based on the digitalization of almost everything: software and intellectual property blocks, networks delivering value, self-referential and autonomous individuals, and identity defined increasingly in terms of access and usage.[2] Ambient Intelligence is a response to this changing world, but should be seen as part of a larger, long-term 'shift' within western and, increasingly, global society.

Representing complexity

Each of these 'Ages' represents a different set of beliefs, values, technologies and economic models; and although the Industrial and now the Knowledge Age predominate in the western hemisphere, evidence of all three ages co-exists in developing countries. Understanding and thinking about the future on a global and regional level will inevitably be highly complex. To make content and insights more 'manageable', we have therefore clustered the values and needs emerging from our research into six 'societies'. These societies represent sets of values, attitudes and concerns that we believe will be guiding many people's lives during the coming decade. They serve as narratives or scripts to help us think about human-focused futures, going beyond the paradigm of efficiency, productivity and performance often associated with technology, towards 'softer' values relating to relationships, communities and enhancing the emotions and senses.

These 'societies' present the needs emerging in the Knowledge Age and their relevance to Ambient Intelligence. Further elaboration of these societies in relation to the various developing regions lies outside the scope of this book.

The Mosaic Society

Linear lifestyles that follow established norms and accepted patterns of behaviour are giving way to more individualized ways of being and living. We are beginning to create our own 'mosaic' lives, made up of a kaleidoscope of simultaneous or sequential relationships, careers or lifestyles. Furthermore, the availability of more information, and the way it accelerates many activities and empowers individuals, is leading to the blurring of time, space and activities. Instead of finishing one thing before moving on the next, we are doing many things at the same time. We are exploring different ways of doing things – and indeed different things to do. This offers the feeling that there are many opportunities to take advantage of, but also creates a feeling of stress and information and/or technology 'overload'. People are caught between the enthusiasm of the new opportunities and the desire to effectively juggle their work, their family and their leisure. In this 'conflict', we are beginning to question whether the belief in more and more of everything is necessarily a recipe for growth and happiness.

As our lives get more complex, we will become increasingly intolerant of complexity and reject anything we find too complicated. Anything that simplifies our lives will be welcomed. We need to think about how Ambient Intelligence can help simplify and personalize our lives as we look for ways to cope with complex situations and juggle with our multiple lives, options and commitments. How can it help us be empowered and not overpowered by the many choices and possibilities available? How can it allow us to access information, commu-nication and entertainment in a non-intrusive and natural way through intuitive interfaces that are customized to my life, tastes and preferences? How can it ensure through seamless integration and connectivity that I can get this where and when I want? And how can I stay in control? Early examples of this customized and simplified solution can be seen in the i-Pronto (a universal remote control that allows the user to customize the interface), and in the research and development of wearable technology.

23

The Collective Society

The advancing individualism of the western world seems to be slowing down, and there is a growing attention to relationships and the need for others. Life is complex and insecure, and the decline of old forms of belonging, such as local communities, church, family and nation state, means that we are searching for alternative forms of belonging and support. As we 'elect' communities based more on shared beliefs and values than geography, so our identities become more fluid as we participate in different groups, locally, globally, physically and virtually. These emerging fluid networks mean that the personal and the social is in a constant state of becoming. Different from the past, however, is the desire to go beyond the acceptance and adoption of group values to influencing the evolution of communities by expressing one's individualism: an influential as opposed to an adaptive behaviour. Psychologists have long known that human beings need to interact with others, because it is only by doing so that we can truly become ourselves. Like families at their best, these groups provide us with a place where we can exercise our individuality and even take the lead.

How, then, can Ambient Intelligence bring us together and enrich our (connected) community? As members of this 'society', we will clearly welcome tools that allow us to share and communicate with others, that will encourage us to undertake social interaction and express our views to others as dynamically as possible. A good example is Living Memory (LiMe), which allows physical communities to develop and exchange knowledge and content.

The Discovery Society

Human beings seem to have an unquenchable thirst for knowledge. Traditionally, we have undertaken our learning sequentially (first schooling, then work), and in a fixed order (topic A before topic B). Today, factors such as the hyperlinked Web, the compacting of time, and the increased background knowledge everyone can now access mean that we are not so easily satisfied. We're increasingly inclined to question more, pushing against the boundaries, challenging accepted ways of thinking. Serendipity and lateral thinking are becoming more accepted alongside logic and rational thought as respectable modes of developing insight. More generally, a trial-and-error approach to learning will become normal, with both left and right brain functions being applied. The rapid pace of change also means that a single learning phase will no longer be adequate for a whole lifetime, and we shall need to continue learning throughout our lives.

In terms of Ambient Intelligence, we shall therefore be looking for tools that give us access to knowledge and enable us to share our own with others. How can they help us turn information into knowledge? How can they encourage us to think out of the box, to explore our creativity and to indulge our inclination to play? A good example of this is Pogo, which enables young children to co-create stories using physical and virtual tools.

The Experience Society

In the past, people have tended to view entertainment and enjoyment as quite separate from their daily life of work, business, learning or even shopping. We are however increasingly integrating and expecting pleasure and enjoyment in our daily activities. Now that many of our physical needs have been satisfied, we are turning our attention to satisfying emotional, aesthetic, sensory and even spiritual needs, with moments of entertainment and experience no longer seen as extraordinary events but part of everyday life. Entertainment itself is changing. From theatre and concerts to cinema and TV, it has tended to involve one-way communication only, requiring the audience to be passive. Now, the interactivity made possible by the Internet and by the digitalization of broadcasting is encouraging us to take a more active part, engaging in 'experiences' rather than consuming 'products' or services. As we move beyond consuming to experiencing, we are also looking to co-create or 'customize' the experience according to our own mood and moment.

The Experience Society begs the question of what is 'useful' and what is 'useless' in today's society. If we are increasingly giving space to our emotions, then maybe something that talks to our emotions and spirit is just as 'useful' as a functional artifact. The ornament of Gothic and Renaissance buildings, which aspired to speak to the senses and spirit has been replaced by efficiency, cost and functionality. Against this background, technology has become 'trapped' in a paradigm of efficiency and productivity. Suppose Ambient Intelligence could provide us with tools that go beyond this, to help us experience more through our senses and allow us to 'create' experiences that we could change over time: tools that could introduce moments of magic and surprise, helping us to enhance mundane events with 'experiential' moments, stimulating our imagination and feeding our soul? Nebula is a good example of this direction.

The Care Society

Increased mobility, the fragmentation of family life, and the breakdown of national, local and community safety nets will mean that we will feel a need to take responsibility for our own welfare. Popular confidence in the ability or will of governments or other institutions to care for and protect them is waning. Greater availability of information allows people to scrutinize the basis of 'expert opinions' and reach their own conclusions. It is also bringing to light abuses of power that would have remained hidden in the past. We will be searching for reassurance.

We will therefore want technology to look after us rather than us having to look after technology. We will welcome tools that allow us to monitor the health or food intake of ourselves or our loved ones, that allow quick links to emergency services, or 'tag' our children so that we know where they are. In short, we will be undertaking our own 'risk management'. Transparency will be important: we have had enough of decisions taken about us by experts 'behind closed doors'. Examples here are wearables for children and the elderly and monitoring systems.

The Sustainable Society

The Industrial Age was based on the idea that 'more is better' and progress was mainly measured in economic terms, related to GDP and income per capita. Products were made in increasing quantities, while quality – in terms of effect on the environment, or the health or social welfare of employees, for instance – was ignored. Thanks in part to the greater availability of information, we are now more aware of the environmental, and, increasingly, also the social and economic consequences of what we do. We are beginning to understand that everything is interdependent and that we need to view everything holistically. We are beginning to see that negative environmental and social effects are not isolated but are related to our everyday pattern of production and consumption. We are beginning to see ourselves as not only living in the present, but as being connected with both our predecessors and generations to come. This is leading to a radical reassessment of the old paradigm. People are asking whether the pressure to do more and more is wise. They are searching for a better balance between material prosperity and frenzied activity on the one hand, and emotional well-being and harmony on the other – not only on a personal level, but also at a collective and global level. This implies that we shall also expect our governments and corporations to behave in a way that takes account of their effect on all their 'stakeholders'. We will be looking for a more humane capitalism.

In terms of Ambient Intelligence, all this means that we shall be looking for tools that help us live in an environmentally-friendly way: managing our domestic or mobile energy use, facilitating recycling, and minimizing the use of materials and non-renewable resources (e.g., through the use of the Internet or shared services). In this context, we can search for new business models around access and sharing rather than single ownership, and we can look to a built-in future-proofness through updating and upgrading software (as in Philips' Nexperia solution). Ultimately, through new technologies and Ambient Intelligence, we need to think not only about a 'greener' world but also about new patterns of production and consumption that will allow us to live well today without compromising the quality of life of future generations. We also need to think about how the benefits of Ambient Intelligence can be shared with people in societies other than advanced Western societies: it may be able to save them from taking the same developmental pattern we have taken in the West – with all the unfortunate consequences, with hindsight, are now clear.

FIG. 1
Changing cultural and
economic framework

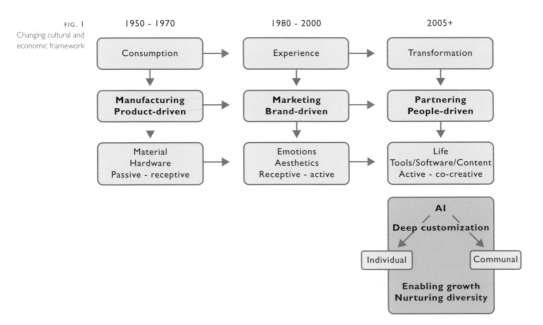

We will want Ambient Intelligence to be a socially responsible technology that nurtures us along the path of sustainability; technology that can tell us when too much is too much, and that can help redefine how we do things and what we mean by 'quality of life'. Today, for instance, we're obsessed by technological innovation: could Ambient Intelligence help us to become equally interested in introducing necessary or desirable social innovations?

Philips' People and Trends research not only provides 'scripts' or 'narratives' to inform our thinking. It also gives us a dynamic view of the cultural and economic framework we are moving in: it shows where we are coming from and, potentially, where we are going, and how that affects our values, needs, businesses and societies (see Fig. 1). The 1950s, 1960s and 1970s were manufacturing and product-driven: we were primarily concerned with consuming material goods and hardware. We wanted to 'own' and 'possess' in order to define our identity and status. Our approach to consumption and consuming was passive. Products were king. As we have become more sophisticated and autonomous, and markets have become saturated with 'stuff', we have become more marketing and brand-driven, more concerned with satisfying the less tangible aspects of our life (e.g., emotions and aesthetics) and in engaging in experiences. In this phase, the markers of our identity are our ability to define aesthetic and cultural icons and to 'manifest' our hard and soft emotions. Brands, as containers of cultural icons, are king.

Our research is now showing, however, that the continued self-referentiality and diversity of people, together with the new technologies, are moving us towards a more networking and people-driven future, less about the consumption of material goods or experiences and more about life itself. *People* are now king. As we become more concerned with personal growth, self-actualization and transformation, our ability to 'access' and 'use' the new technology tools, software and content rather than 'own' them will define our identity.

It is in this future 'people-driven' framework that Ambient Intelligence comes into its own. It is about creating 'open tools' that can be customized by the individual and that respond to personal tastes, habits and needs, going beyond 'mass customization' to a 'deep customization' between the technology and the individual or group. Such an 'intimate technology' evolves through its constant relationship with the user. It allows us to reconsider the concept of obsolescence, in that growth now depends on upgrading the software, not discarding the product. Understood in these terms, Ambient Intelligence can facilitate both individual and community empowerment and growth anywhere in the world by respecting and adapting to social and cultural tastes, habits and aspirations. Perhaps, as we progress with Ambient Intelligence and the concept of an 'open' system, we will no longer have to concern ourselves with what people will want in the future: users themselves will define what they want and how they want it. Meanwhile, our People and Trends research continues to explore and understand differences between people and cultures and to involve those people, both in the research itself, and in the creation of the Ambient Intelligence roadmap. In the end, it is the vision of a socially relevant and meaningful technology for people and a socially responsible technology for society that inspires our thinking and our society, culture and people research for Ambient Intelligence.

1.2 UNDERSTANDING HUMAN CULTURES

Karen Reddering, Liesbeth Scholten

From research in conducted China, India, Europe and the USA, for its Delphi project, Philips Design has gained cross-regional insights into societal change and human values which can help define preferable futures for the world. These insights reveal the challenges for people in the future, as well as the challenges for intelligent technology as defined by the Ambient Intelligence vision.

Social challenges: the intelligence is in the dialogue

Inequality is a major issue in Western and Asian cultures. The gap between the 'haves' and 'have-nots' is widening, despite the increase in global connectivity and improvements in living conditions. Combined with the ageing of societies in most parts of the world, and the fact that technological developments, especially in the area of Ambient Intelligence, are much faster than people's awareness and acceptance, this implies some major challenges in attempting to create preferable futures. These challenges are predominantly in the areas of knowledge, leadership, diversity and affinity:

- How can we build up knowledge, and at the same time enable enough simplification so that it is shared and applied? In India, for example, where there is a first-rate educational system, there is also a high illiteracy rate (approximately 35%), and many people lack access to education.
- How can we create leadership in harmony with cooperation? The Chinese, for instance, are facing a paradox. They put a strong emphasis on sovereignty, seeing China as the centre of the world, not needing to follow any other nation, but they are also craving recognition from the rest of the world, and realize they need to cooperate internationally to achieve some of their targets.
- How can we foster diversity and still achieve cohesion? This is a key issue in Europe, where the struggle between unity versus cultural diversity is visible in many ways. It is also important for India, the world's largest democracy, with its enormous diversity of religions and languages.
- How can we enjoy affinity and closeness while keeping an open mind? People's natural tendency to form affinity groups based on culture, nationality or background, in combination with the unequal distribution of opportunities and wealth in the world, can lead to exclusivity, with benefits only available to a few.

These challenges reveal a huge need for dialogue. Problems and needs cannot be solved in isolation, or from one perspective only, but require a mindset open to differences in culture, values, resources and restrictions. These differences make it difficult even to understand the problems and needs in another country, let alone to develop solutions.

Intelligent technology

It is all about understanding difference. In the 80s: efficiency; in the 90s: innovation; in 2000: diversity. Serving diverse needs and diverse people. It is about recognizing gender difference, cultural difference, language differences; understanding that not everybody is a white Christian with perfect sight.

Jeremy Myerson (Europe)

[The need for] meaning and purpose in life is common to everyone, the only difference is that technology changes the way it gets gratified.

John Perry Barlow (USA)

These societal challenges can also be seen as the challenges for intelligent technology, technology for people. How can we build knowledge systems that are simple enough? Who should take leadership – the user or the system? How can we make adaptive solutions that can cope with the diversity and unpredictability of human needs and desires? And how can we achieve affinity between intelligent systems and ourselves? What will make us trust technology?

One way may be to explore how human intelligence can be used as a role model for Ambient Intelligence; how the nature of relationships between people can guide us in designing the relationship between people and intelligent systems. The essence of human intelligence lies in curiosity, the tendency to investigate, to ask questions, to doubt and to wonder. This is the challenge for Ambient Intelligence: to learn to ask; to value the unknown.

A first question that arises is how 'intelligent' technology can really be compared to human intelligence. Opinions on this vary greatly, and even seem regionally determined. The attitude towards technology in the United States is very different from that in Europe, for example. In the US, there is a strong belief in technology and consequently also a fear that intelligent technology might become more intelligent than people.

We have to watch out for stupid technology cheerleading, so common in the US today. Here, some people really believe that Machines will exceed human intelligence to a point where we as humans will no longer understand what they are doing, how they are doing it and even what their purpose is. We are talking about the end of humanity and US scientists are cheering. We must never forget the human in the story.

Christopher Locke (USA)

In Europe, the attitude towards intelligent technology is much more sceptical. Europeans believe technological intelligence is inferior to human and social intelligence. Real meaning is given through communicating and exchanging ideas, through emotions, interaction and intuition. It is this serendipitous, sixth-sense quality of social intelligence that makes it so different from technological, 'constructed' intelligence. When Europeans talk about intelligence in people, they often mean the human ability to look beyond the existing representations, explanations and interpretations to find new and relevant meanings.

The distinction … is between syntax and semantics. For a machine, all that matters is syntax. The meaning does not matter … all that matters is the form and its capacity to change that form into another form. For humans, what matters is not the syntax but the semantics, the meaning, what lies inside. Even if machines are able to imitate humans perfectly, it is unlikely, I think, that they will have a concept of semantics in a way that human beings do. Meaning lies not in our heads or in the structure of our language or in the structure of our problem-solving capacities. Meaning lies in the social world. It is the social world that imputes things and phenomena with meaning. And in so far as machines don't live in a social world, they cannot have meaning.

Kenan Malik (UK)

Both the believers and sceptics will be most benefited by the development of an intelligence that is supportive of human needs and desires. The real challenge is probably to fully understand for which purposes the qualities of human intelligence are essential. This brings us back to opening the dialogue. How can we learn what makes people and relationships flourish, and what support people want from their environment, from technology, and from people? What is the relationship between quality of life and Ambient Intelligence?

POGO

HICS

OPEN TOOLS

LIME
AND PL@NET

Leadership

As long as technological intelligence is still in its infancy, its chances of being accepted as an intelligent system are best when it is positioned as a tool at the service of one or more users, asking questions before offering solutions, listening instead of talking. Intelligence and respect are not granted automatically; they have to be earned and proven. Ambient Intelligence could earn the label 'intelligent' by asking the right questions and finding meaning through dialogue. Both the questions and the answers will vary by situation and by culture, what is known, what is new and what is relevant.

Knowledge

Ambient Intelligence can be used as a tool to connect people virtually, i.e., to connect their minds. Knowledge is mostly in people's heads, and we cannot strive to know everything about everybody. Ambient Intelligence can be an infrastructure for making connections to other people's minds, ideas and emotions, and systems can derive knowledge from the connections made.

Ambient Technology and Social Progress: A Critical View

Dick van Lente and Ernst Homburg

Ambient Intelligence is usually presented by the electronics industry as its next great gift to humanity: a whole new range of possibilities in information provision, communication and entertainment, accessible anywhere at any time, and perfectly adjusted to the users' individual needs. A critical understanding of this technological promise requires that we analyze the cultural and economic sources from which it springs, the ideas about ambience and individual needs on which it is based, its promised effects and possible alternative uses.

Dick van Lente

Professor at Erasmus University Rotterdam, 'Historian'

The primary source of Ambient Intelligence is, like all industrial innovation, the pressure of competition, which in the electronics industry is particularly severe. In response, the industry searches for needs that people with sufficient purchasing power might have in the future. Technology that would respond 'intelligently' to individual needs and connect people to the electronic services that satisfy these needs would seem to be a logical and profitable answer from the industry's point of view. There are, however, three important problems with the Ambient Intelligence paradigm in this form.

In the first place, the industry assumes that the devices that will surround future consumers will 'learn' from people's behaviour in such a way as to adapt to them and anticipate their needs. In view of the fact that communication between humans is multi-layered and ambiguous, and therefore often full of misunderstandings and failed attempts to 'learn' from each other, it is very unlikely that electronic systems will ever learn to interact with people in a 'natural' way. Moreover, in the utopian projections put forward by the industry – such as the automatic switching on of a video connection to the children's playroom as soon as the mother enters the home – assumptions about human needs are made that differ considerably from ideas people generally have, both about their relation with technology and with their fellow humans. Most parents, for example, will prefer to make their own choices about having a look into the children's room, and would be quite annoyed when the technology chose for them.[1]

Secondly, while some features of Ambient Technology are based upon naïve ideas

Ernst Homburg

Professor at University of Maastricht, 'Historian'

Nothing is more important than the knowledge and information you gather in your life. By connecting Indian villages to the developed part of India, we can be much cheaper than building roadways. We connect people faster with IT solutions that could be multilingual, multicultural and give opportunities to the local people. My point is not we connect just by IT but by means of ideas, new ways of thinking (the old way is doing things by yourself).

Osama Manzar (India)

Affinity

The World Wide Web has demonstrated that when more users become involved in such an intelligent infrastructure, without a central point of control, trust becomes an issue.

... the connective network necessary underneath all of this is something whose behaviour and dynamics we do not understand or control, so it could be generating its own kind of opposition.

Peter Schwartz (USA)

about human psychology and social life, others are superfluous: they are either taken care of by present technological systems – the Internet, DVD, mobile telephones and so on – or are so far out (like projecting a sunset on one's windowpane) that only the very few who don't know what to do with their money will care to buy it. Geared as it seems to be to the affluent, much of Ambient Intelligence looks like superfluous 'gadgets for the rich'. The impressive technological advance it represents – making electronic systems practically invisible and ubiquitous – does not contribute to cultural or social progress.

The last point raises a third problem, which is basically of a moral nature. If 'improvement of the quality of life', which is the alleged social goal of these efforts, is not in fact realized, it seems a great waste of human energy. Meanwhile it is clear that there are many real needs in the world today to which Ambient Intelligence could be a useful response. Ambient Intelligence seems to offer possibilities to monitor environmental changes more extensively than is now possible, creating a firmer basis for environmental policies. Facilitating communication could reduce transportation and therefore pollution – an old ambition that new technology might help come true. Easy access to information and culture might be a boon for the lonely and disabled, which requires an effort to make these technologies cheaper. Cheapness would also be a goal for teaching aids, especially in the third world, which could provide for real needs in terms of professional training, instruction in family planning and general education: we are often reminded by experts in underdeveloped countries that a lack of education is at the basis of problems in public health, environment and ethnic conflicts.

Work aimed at these goals will require some public financing because it is directed at public problems or the needs of the poor or not so wealthy. On the other hand, these are needs that are worthy of the efforts of the teams of very intelligent people that work in the research laboratories of the electronics firms. They are likely to provide a more certain market than the hype among the wealthy that Ambient Intelligence now seems to aim at, even though it may be a less profitable market in the short run.

POGO

HICS

OPEN TOOLS

LIME
AND PL@NET

1   E. Aarts, R. Harwig and M. Schuurmans, 'Ambient Intelligence', *After Cyberspace: When Computing Becomes our World*, ed. P.J. Denning (ACM Press, 2001)

Understanding enough of what happens 'inside' technology is often the key to accepting its results. People are more easily trusted than systems. Many people still prefer to tap into other people's knowledge – and their social and emotional intelligence – than to consult an apparently all-knowing computer. Human relationships enable us to build up understanding and trust. Will technology have emotional and intuitive intelligence in the future? Will bioengineering make it possible to combine the strengths of human and artificial intelligence seamlessly, and what will that look like? In the nearer future, one step towards overcoming distrust and creating comfort with intelligent technology is to create a sense of affinity or familiarity between intelligent technology and people, to let them get to know each other. The challenge here lies in creating true cooperation, through a dialogue in which people and technology move forward together. This requires good listening and interpretation skills, learning from each other and learning from mistakes.

Diversity

In the development of Ambient Intelligence, the creation of affinity between systems and people is mainly explored through personalization, adaptivity, anticipation and responsiveness to people and their needs. These are complex and ambitious objectives, requiring technology to interpret human behaviour and thinking. One pitfall here is to tailor the solutions too much to static individual characteristics. Personalization of an offering is usually not tailored to the individual, with all their complexities and changes, but to a profile, a simplified version of that person. This can work very effectively as a tool to make 'best guesses' based on knowledge gathered about a person, but any profiling mechanism (even when advanced and dynamic) essentially puts people 'in a box', labels them, categorizes, characterizes, or (in the worst case) stereotypes them. People do not easily trust technology to support them, because they know its actions are based on a set of assumptions that might be incorrect or inappropriate.

This becomes even more complicated in the face of the diversity of human cultures. When we travel and experience other cultures, we are often faced with our own lack of knowledge. We lack the background information that could explain why behaviours are different, why ethical principles are sometimes the opposite of our own, and why some problems are not solved in the way we would solve them ourselves. When we make an effort to investigate other cultures, people and values, it becomes apparent that even the act of investigating, the research methodology, is culturally determined. As an example, when asking questions about people's hopes and dreams, interviewing men and women together in India will not shed much light on what the women feel and think. How topics are to be introduced, questions asked, and answers to be interpreted also requires insight into the cultural context and, of course, the language.

Choice

In understanding cultures, people, their needs and how to develop meaningful technology for them, the first challenge is open-mindedness: not to make too many assumptions, to display genuine curiosity about people's needs, wishes and feelings, and to allow for wide diversity. While there is a need for a wide range of available choices, the problem may be in the complexity of choosing. Instead of reducing available options to a customized set, Ambient Intelligence could focus on how to assist the process of making a choice – how to offer a cohesive set of choices and a choice process, a dialogue – allowing for the variation people might want and for the unpredictable.

The European view on choice is changing from valuing an abundance of choices towards balanced diversity. New principles are emerging beyond materialism. Immaterial values, the time to think and dream, are becoming more important. In this context, an intelligent reduction of possible options will be valued. The opposite is true for China, which is shifting from a regulated society towards a society of more individual choice and freedom. The Chinese have learnt to rely on themselves and not on their government, but the concept of freedom is relatively new to them. One way of exploring this concept is through materialism: the Chinese value the availability of choice, and the opportunity to make their own choice; it reinforces their sense of individual freedom.

Development levels: mixing low-tech and high-tech

In a dialogue about the value of Ambient Intelligence for various cultures and regions in the world, taking differences in levels of development into account is critical. In practice, the solutions for improving the quality of life will be a mix of low-tech, high-tech and human solutions, depending on the situation.

That is a great thing, this multiplicity of cultures. It is a very, very important, very precious scenario. I don't think, for instance, there are many parts of the world where you can simultaneously be in the now and 2000 years ago. I work in rural areas where the production process of the crafts people that I work with is exactly 2000 years old: the casting process, smelting, forging techniques… but I also work with IT. It is not just me, a huge number of people are working simultaneously, and also these artisans come to Delhi to sell their things… That is a great approach to this business of layered cultures, multiple cultures which gives you the opportunity to be in multiple times simultaneously, at multiple speeds…

Jogi Panghaal (India)

In China and India, labour is very cheap, and so there is often a tendency to use people rather than technological solutions. In this context, Ambient Intelligence can be seen more as a tool for professionals who provide services to consumers. Being supported by a system will enable a higher standard of professional service.

The best way to support people's needs is sometimes through simple products, and sometimes through highly advanced systems. Sometimes these needs are best met by people.

This hospital spent millions on sign systems with coloured lines and pictograms. And in the end, nothing worked at all. And they asked people: 'What will make you find your way around this hospital?' And people said: 'Somebody to show us, a human'. So the hospital asked for volunteers and everyday now you can go to a section of this hospital and there are twenty volunteers who take you by the arm and help you to find your way. Problem solved. With a complete absence of obtrusive technology.

Jeremy Myerson (Europe)

As a system that reflects an understanding of people's needs, providing smart solutions to improve the quality of life, Ambient Intelligence does not have to be built exclusively on intelligent technology. The intelligence is in finding the appropriate mix between low-tech appliances, advanced technology and services rendered by people. What is appropriate can only be discovered by asking questions in a dialogue, with genuine curiosity.

POGO

HICS

OPEN TOOLS

LIME
AND PL@NET

Note: All quotes in the text are taken from interviews conducted by the Philips Design Delphi research project into Human Futures (2002)

1.3 HUMAN PERSONALITY

WHAT AMBIENT INTELLIGENCE WILL NEED TO UNDERSTAND ABOUT US

Slava Kozlov

Sometimes I think, sometimes I am.

Paul Valéry

In an Ambient Intelligence environment, digital technologies will sense what we want, and then deliver appropriate solutions. But to intelligently guess the intentions of users and then provide relevant solutions, Ambient Intelligence systems will not only need to be technologically sophisticated, they will have to understand us very well, and have adequate user models. There are a number of advanced models of personality available in contemporary psychology, anthropology, social sciences and other human disciplines that can be of use. Specifically, the multiplicity of the Self, a model that sees personality as consisting of multiple identities, could be a highly interesting and fruitful concept in the design of Ambient Intelligence.

Postmodern complexity

We live in an ever more complex 'postmodern' world.[1] Two of its defining characteristics are globalization and the resulting omnipresence of multiculturalism. We encounter many different cultures and lifestyles at close quarters every day, either in person or on TV or the Internet. These cultures are creating a kaleidoscope around us at an accelerating pace. We don't watch them from afar, we develop our own pluralist culture, not merely tolerating cultures, but eagerly blending them into our lives.

As society changes around us, we are constantly having to learn new things and acquire new skills from various sources. Privileged sources of knowledge no longer exist, and fuzzy dynamic concepts are replacing previously stable and accepted models of the world in a situation Bauman describes as 'liquid modernity'.[2] We no longer have ready-made role models or templates: they are either absent or there are too many to choose from. Life does not follow a predefined path: instead, our 'life-site' is constantly 'under construction'.

These profound changes are affecting how we form our identity, how our personalities are constructed, function and manifest themselves. Recent findings show that we are becoming more complex, more flexible, and are constantly changing.[3]

I-positions

The once commonly held view that our personalities have a single, stable Self is being questioned. Personality is now seen not as a one-dimensional entity consisting of a core Self, but rather as a product of ongoing 'dialogues' between many 'I-positions', or narrating voices, which together make up our identity.

Each of these I-positions is characterized by a different set of attachments – to our body, to people, objects, events, past memories and future plans. I-positions have their own life-stories, their own value systems and ways of acting them out.[4]

The Self can then be seen as a motivated story-teller who tells stories in order to construct both external and internal realities and share them with others and with itself – because it is telling its stories from various standpoints. To quote Dennett, 'Our fundamental tactic of self-promotion, self-control, and self-definition is... telling stories, and more particularly concocting and controlling the story we tell others – and ourselves – about who we are'.[5]

When we listen this 'story', and analyze its contents and the way it is told, we can detect the 'narrator' who is telling the story at that moment (i.e., the 'centre of narrative gravity', in Dennett's words). 'Like the biological self, this psychological or narrative self is yet another abstraction, not a thing in the brain, but still a remarkably robust and almost tangible attractor of properties, the "owner of record".'[6]

A careful analysis of modern self-narrating strategies shows that our stories are not only told by many different I-positions, but that those I-positions may adhere to different value systems. That means that we can no longer talk about the value system of an individual: what we see is the existence of multiple, and often conflicting value systems within one personality.

These I-positions, or sub-identities, are shaped throughout our life, in response to certain physical, cultural and social contexts, and may evolve over time.

Ambient Intelligence and I-positions

To be able to respond to people sensitively, Ambient Intelligence systems will need to take the complexity of personalities into account. Designers of such systems will therefore need to consider this model of the multiple Self. Even the simple understanding that a single individual can exhibit varying behaviours and 'voices' at different times can lead to the design of a system that can recognize such differences and react accordingly.

The manifestations, or enactments, of these I-positions may be more strongly evident in some contexts than in others. Contextual triggers may be spatial (different 'heres') temporal (various 'nows'), interactions with people (real or imaginary), or social institutions (rules, roles, rituals, etc.).

OPEN TOOLS

Digital products or systems that can be 'deep customized' – changing and evolving with their owners over time

People who speak several languages, for example, tend to adopt different I-positions in each language, depending on the physical and social contexts in which they are spoken. These I-positions were shaped as the language was being learned and can be detected through the vocabulary used, the tone of voice, and, more broadly, by the 'language games' played (the language-specific rule-governed linguistic interactions). They may also be revealed in non-verbal expressions and body language. But even within a monolingual context, the speech patterns people use are very contextually determined and vary greatly. Within one conversation, we may switch from serious business discourse to irony and humour, using language with double or multiple meanings.

In some cases, Ambient Intelligence systems will need to able to define and interpret the smallest nuances of meaning and be equipped to 'understand' how people construct meaning within a given context.

Recognizing multiple I-positions and their patterning

Ambient Intelligence should therefore not only be sensitive to physical but also to personal context. When reacting in response to the natural speech and movements of its users, Ambient Intelligence will need to recognize who is talking (or more generally interacting) with whom, in what mood, and even why they are talking at all. Ideally, it should be able to define a whole set of various I-positions in such contexts, as well as remember the typical ways they pattern in their occurrence and narrative form. Equipped with interconnected and personalized interfaces, Ambient Intelligence should be able to do this, and react appropriately to different personality modes, modifying its interfaces and functionalities as appropriate.

Coping with irrationality

Despite the importance of context in determining meaning, one of the most interesting discoveries in recent studies of personality is that not all shifts in I-position can be directly linked to changes in context. Shifts often happen unpredictably and chaotically: we tend to attribute this to human *irrationality*. In such cases, the path followed by the Self's centre of narrative gravity can be compared to the 'strange attractors' of the chaos theory.[7] Again, Ambient Intelligence systems will need to be able to deal with fluctuations in narration and behaviour that do not seem to be relatable to changes in context.

Internal dialogues

We should not see personality, under this model, as being a set of 'subselves', with one member of the set being dominant at any one time. On the contrary, it seems that at any moment, our behaviour can be described as the result of complex 'polyphonic' interactions among all (or at least many) of our various I-positions. They constantly interact together, among themselves and with other agents, whether nearby or distant. In this light, the Self becomes a multi-voiced entity with multiple I-positions that, moreover, conduct inner dialogues. Such a model of personality implies that Ambient Intelligence systems will require a high degree of sensitivity, ideally becoming smart partners in these endlessly unrolling inner dialogues.

Time

One of the most useful features of an Ambient Intelligence system in this respect may well be its ability to monitor and 'remember' the interactions it has with its user over time. It would thus be able to detect users' 'voices' and moods and be able to understand what is 'meant' or implied. Having available the history of its interactions with its users' multiple I-positions, the system will be able to interact with those users in a highly personalized way that evolves over time.

Transformation

Finally, and perhaps the most intriguing of all possibilities, Ambient Intelligence may contribute to the 'guided transformation'[8] of its users, i.e., helping them to learn and achieve a greater degree of self-actualization, while the system itself learns from the user.

To be able to reconfigure and adapt itself, Ambient Intelligence will need to be sensitive to signals from the user, using several feedback channels simultaneously. It will also need to actively stimulate these feedback-generating mechanisms, sharing with its users the guesses it makes about their intentions, goals and preferred ways of achieving them. In this way, system and user co-create the end result.

At the same time, Ambient Intelligence could also provide its users with valuable insights about their own behaviours and the strategies they use to form meaning. By providing smart tools for self-reflection and the co-creation of imagined selves, the system helps users understand the patterns of interactions exhibited by their own multiple I-positions. In that way, it furthers and participates in the self-development, or transformation, of its users. This capacity for helping people discover new aspects of themselves and thus develop their personalities in new directions could potentially become one of the most valuable propositions of Ambient Intelligence.

1   S. Sim (ed.), *The Routledge Companion to Postmodern Thought* (London, Routledge, 2001)
2   Z. Blauman, *Liquid Modernity* (Cambridge UK, Polity Press, 2000)
3   A. Juarero, *Dynamics in Action: Intentional Behavior as Complex System* (Cambridge MA, MIT Press, 1999)
4   H. J.M. Hermans and H.J.G. Kempen, *The Dialogical Self* (New York, Academic Press, 1993)
5   D. C. Dennett, *Consciousness Explained* (Harmondsworth, Penguin Books, 2000), 418
6   Ibid.
7   A. Juarero, op. cit.
8   B. Joseph Pine and J. Gilmore, *The Experience Economy* (Cambridge MA, Harvard Business School Press, 1999)

1.4 INVOLVING PEOPLE AS CO-CREATORS

Christina Lindsay

I now have my Pronto opening and closing my garage doors and turning my sprinklers on and off.

Loran, Pronto Website

So I made a telephone directory and put in my favorite places (Domino's, Little Caesars, local Chinese take-out). Now I don't have to get up and get the phone book and look them up, they're in my Pronto.

John, Pronto Website

My brother-in-law received a toy Chevy S-10 pickup truck last Christmas. It had an IR remote to turn it on, set the alarm, and make it move. I created a new device on my Pronto, learned the codes and had fun controlling it without him figuring out what was going on.

Sneaky, Pronto Website

The makers of Pronto were surprised that people were so inventive in finding new uses for it – because it was actually marketed as a hand-held touch-screen customizable remote control for centralizing the operation of audio-visual equipment in the home. No more and no less. Pronto is in fact what designers refer to as an 'open tool', a product sold with downloadable software so that users can change the user interface if they wish. As the remarks quoted above show, some people went far beyond the expected changes, inventing new uses, developing and distributing the software free of charge so that others could implement them, too.[1] Of course, users have always adapted and transformed technologies to suit their needs, the Pronto experience augurs well for Ambient Intelligence, because, if it is to achieve its full potential, it will require just such a proactive stance on the part of users: people will need to become actively involved in co-creating, customizing and even training their Ambient Intelligence technologies.

Ambient Intelligence is much more than a question of embedding technology into objects. It involves human culture in its broadest sense: different value systems, individual likes and dislikes, sustainability, codes of ethics, conduct and communication. However, it is not only at a societal and cultural level that we need to understand people. To be successful and add value to people's lives, Ambient Intelligence has to be perceived by users as being relevant, meaningful and understandable. To comprehend what this means and to design technology to meet these criteria, we need to get closer to people, understanding their lives, values and needs. We need to learn what's important to them and why, what they do and where they go, how they behave, what problems they have that need to be solved, how they relate to technology now and how they want to in the future, what their dreams and desires are, and so on. How can we best obtain this information and what is the role of the users in this?

Finding out about users

There are many ways of finding out about people. Most, however, do not address the depth or breadth of the complexity of people's lives. The pyramid (Fig. 1) serves to illustrate the relationship between research methods, the kinds of information obtained through using them, and the relationship of the designer to the user in the process. The pyramid represents the fact that methods at the lower layers are used much more often in design research today than those at the top. The layers are merely illustrative and should not to be taken as rigid divisions.

The pyramid gives an overview of the research methods available to find out about people's lives. The methods in all layers of the pyramid have their strengths and limitations, but in order to provide the knowledge needed to develop Ambient Intelligence systems, the methods at the upper layers need to be further developed and used.

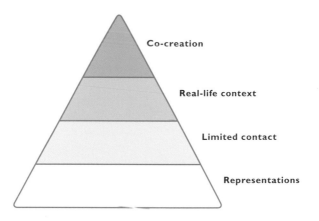

FIG. I
The pyramid of user-based design methodologies

Representations
At the lowest level, designers use two methods to understand users. The first is to draw up 'user representations'. These are based on generally accepted views of how people and technology interact, plus quantitative, statistical data concerning the demographics of particular consumer segments. However, the missing element here is, of course, the voices of users themselves: all individuality is absent. The second method is known as the 'I-methodology': designers simply design with themselves or their friends in mind.[2]

Limited contact
At the next level up, designers or researchers have limited contact with users, usually through a short interview or questionnaire, often administered by phone or mail. The interaction is usually one-way, with people being asked set questions. Usability studies often follow this procedure. Although providing slightly more individual input than the user representation method, this approach is still very limited in that it is based on a single encounter at one point in time, and on the designer's (rather than the user's) agenda.

Real-life context
Moving up the pyramid, at the next level, the information gathered about users is more qualitative. It entails a shift from general information about groups to specific information about individuals. Users and researchers enter into a ongoing dialogue. Over time, researchers discover more and more about users' everyday lives. Instead of remaining in the laboratory setting, researchers move out to observe users in their own contexts, in the home or workplace. Approaches of this type include 'empathic design' (which encourages designers to leave their studios and enter people's lives),[3] 'contextual design' (which stresses the importance of context),[4] and 'cultural probes' (which are used to obtain a view of what is important to the user). Using the techniques of ethnographic observation, they all seek to look at people's lives from the outside in (and sometimes from the inside out), paying special attention to the significance of contextual factors (in the broadest sense). These approaches certainly deliver insights into people, in effect providing us with snapshots of their everyday lives. But there is a price, both literally and figuratively, to pay. To obtain this more detailed and complex

information, lengthier research is needed, requiring a substantial commitment of time from both designer and user, thus adding to the cost of the design project.

Is this a worthwhile investment? Yes: it provides us with information not only about people but also about how they interact with technology in their daily lives. Does it provide enough information for us to successfully develop Ambient Intelligence technologies? No. It provides us with a view of people's lives mainly from the outside. We need to get *into* their lives, their homes and their thoughts. We need people to tell us what's important to them. We need to see what they do, to understand why they do it, and to witness their experiences. We need to know how they really interact with technology and what it means in their lives.

Co-creation

At the fourth level in the pyramid we therefore propose a method that seeks to involve users even more actively in research and design: 'co-creation'. Under this approach, instead of being seen purely as a source of information, the user becomes a valued colleague of the researcher and designer. Such an approach has been tried primarily in the field of software development, where it is called 'participatory design'.

The first step towards co-creation is to make users co-researchers. Having people research and analyze (along with us) their own lives makes it possible for us to look at people's lives from the inside, supplementing our own view from the outside. We take not only the user's home and work context into account but also the total context in which they do things, focusing on the combination of individual, time, place and activity. In this way, we begin to understand what people consider to be relevant, meaningful and understandable.

But this is still designing *for* people. What about designing *with* people? This is then the next step, the user as true co-developer. Involving users in the actual design process provides us with different kinds of information, as well as making good on our commitment to put people at the centre of the process, both literally and figuratively. This approach acknowledges that users are already often creative in finding solutions to their existing problems.

Ambient Intelligence and co-creation

Ambient Intelligence requires the active participation of people, because the use and usefulness of Ambient Intelligence technologies is created through the synergy of the user and the technology. By bringing people into the creative process, we learn much more about how people can and will interact with these technologies. We would be working directly with them to incorporate this experience and expertise into our designs, to dynamically and cooperatively develop new technologies that would form a valuable part of their everyday lives. And the co-creation of Ambient Intelligence systems does not end when they reach the market. The user must co-create its use — the ultimate user involvement.

Challenges

The methodologies belonging to the lower three layers in our pyramid have been well established. The details of how and when to implement co-creation still have to be worked out. Many questions arise — for instance, about its practicability (How do you persuade users to make the necessary commitment? How do you protect and respect intellectual property rights? How much time will it all take?); its feasibility (Can we find enough people who can think conceptually? Are people able to discuss technologies that don't yet exist?); and its ultimate value (How can we use the knowledge we gain in our designs? What value does it add? How do we make a good experience for all involved?)

Some answers so far

At Philips Design, we have started to apply some of the basics of co-creation in our work. We now regularly involve people in researching their own lives, keeping diaries, performing and reporting on certain tasks, taking photos, collecting objects, buying magazines and cutting out pictures that interest them, drawing pictures and maps, and telling us stories.

HiCS

In HiCS, a project exploring a new business model of global-local sustainable solutions for people with reduced access to food, we made use of the concept of 'context of use' and are involving users and stakeholders in concept creation workshops. The users documented their own relationships to food through keeping diaries, taking photos, collecting objects, drawing maps and telling stories.

Pogo

In the development of Pogo (a system providing children with a set of tools with which they can collaborate with each other in the creation of stories), detailed information about the users was included in the design process. Considerable initial research was conducted with children: watching them play, watching them create stories, watching them use technology. From these observations, an initial design was made and tested with the aid of the children. In the design of a new interface, the children became, if not true co-creators, then at least an essential element in the design process.

Living Memory

When should users be involved in the design process? The Living Memory project (LiMe) provides one answer. In this project, which aims to provide communities with an informal, accessible and intuitive interface to a computerized store of community knowledge, people in a specific community were involved after a working prototype had been developed and placed in the community. Community members were actively involved in testing the system (both hardware and software), and contributed ideas for immediate improvement and future development.

Conclusion

To develop technologies that are relevant, meaningful and understandable, we clearly need to investigate and understand the complexities of people's everyday lives. By working with people as co-creators, we will be able not only to access a deep store of knowledge and experience, but also to apply people's expertise in solving the problems and meeting the needs of their own lives. The challenge for designers is to develop methodologies that yield valuable, useful and inspirational knowledge, while remaining cost- and time-effective for all involved.

I-PRONTO

HOMELAB

MIMÉ

POGO

HICS

LIME
AND PL@NET

1   C. Lindsay, *Designing Users: The Pronto Story* (PhD dissertation, Cornell University, N.Y, forthcoming 2003)
2   M. Akrich, 'The Description of Technical Objects', *Shaping Technology/Building Society: Studies in Sociotechnical Change*, ed. Wiebe Bijker and John Law (Cambridge MA, MIT Press, 1992), 205-224
3   D. Leonard and J. Rayport, *Spark Innovation through Empathic Design*, e-book (Cambridge MA, Harvard Business School Press, 2002)
4   H. Beyer and Karen Holtzblatt, *Contextual Design: A Customer-centered Approach to Systems Designs* (New York, Morgan Kaufmann, 2002)

1.5 USER-CENTRED DESIGN

Boris de Ruyter

User-centred Design (UCD) emphasizes that a system's purpose is to serve the user, not to use a specific technology. The user's needs should dominate the user interface, while the needs of the interface should dominate the design of the rest of the system. UCD integrates knowledge about users and their involvement into the design process.

Four principles

There are generally three phases in the design of an interactive system: concept development, implementation of a prototype and evaluation through user testing. To bring UCD into the design process, the following four principles have been formulated.

User involvement	Knowledge about users (in the form of guidelines or models) should be used.
Empirical measurement	Empirical validation of the design assumptions is required.
Iterative design	Iterations should take account of insights gained on the basis of Empirical Measurement throughout the conceptualization and implementation phases.
Multi-disciplinary teams	Different disciplines should be called on for knowledge about users, technologies and the context of use that can be combined to determine requirements for interactive systems.

User Involvement and Empirical Measurement are predominantly content-related, while Iterative Design and Multi-disciplinary Teams are predominantly process-related.[1] Fig. 1 shows how these various elements fit together.

FIG. 1

The role of user-centred design in the design process

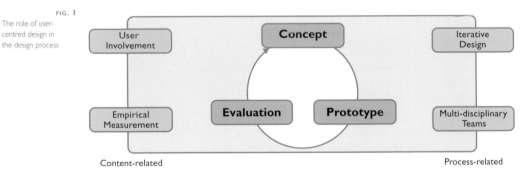

Underpinning of the content-related principles

The theoretical underpinning of the principle of User Involvement is provided by Cognitive Engineering, while the methods and tools required to be able to apply the principle of Empirical Measurement are provided by Usability Engineering.

Cognitive Engineering

Cognitive Engineering is defined as the discipline involved in applying theories and models developed by cognitive psychology to support the design of interactive systems.[2] In an empirical study, Murata and Iwase demonstrated that the design and implementation of an interactive system based on knowledge stemming from the discipline of Cognitive Engineering results in a superior system.[3] Despite such evidence, some have argued that cognitive psychology deals with scientific problems while Cognitive Engineering should deal with the problem of design.[4] This argument is based on the unrealistic objective of satisfying all UCD principles (i.e., the content- and process-oriented requirements for the design process) by bringing knowledge from cognitive psychology into the design process.

The main problem in bringing knowledge from cognitive psychology into engineering practice can be explained by the lack of ecological validity of research findings. This stems from the fact that research in the area of cognitive psychology is often 'abstract' in trying to stay away from the application context to avoid the influence of these contextual settings. Effects such as prior domain knowledge for a given application could influence the research findings, while these are very difficult to detect. Hence, many research findings from cognitive psychology are very difficult to transfer to the application reality and so are limited in terms of their applicability to real-world problems.

This lack of ecological validity has been acknowledged by psychologists, and the discipline of applied psychology was established to formulate an answer to this problem. Applied psychology is the study of the basic principles of psychology together with the application of these principles to various real-world problems. By focusing on real-world problems and the application of psychology principles, the applicability of research findings to real-world problems increases.

User modelling

User modelling is one area in which psychology principles are applied to real-world problems, and which is relevant in building interactive systems. User modelling combines current theories of human cognition and uses them to model human performance in a manner applicable to the design of interactive systems. These models enable quantitative predictions of performance to be made with less effort than is needed for the current methods of prototyping and user testing, both of which tend to be expensive and time-consuming. User modelling has two significant advantages. First, it is straightforward enough for interactive systems designers to use without extensive training in psychology. Second, it can be used for fast iterative testing of a system without an actual prototype and without costly user testing.

Currently, interface designers frequently test early versions of their designs on users in a qualitative and iterative process, but this approach can be slow and costly, and it is not always easy to find the appropriate class of user. In *The Psychology of Human-Computer Interaction*,[5] Card, Moran and Newell argue that engineering models for usability should be devised that provide quantitative predictions of how well people will be able to perform tasks with a proposed design. In recent years, a number of models have been constructed and validated in both academic and corporate settings. Three highly regarded user models are EPIC, ACT-R/PM and GLEAN3.

The EPIC model consists of a production system (acting as cognitive processor) and a series of individual processors, each of which handles one aspect of the total perceptual/motor/cognitive system. Each processor works in parallel with the other processors. This model is used for predicting performance in complex tasks involving concurrent cognitive, perceptual and motor activity. However, it can only model routine tasks.

GLEAN3 runs on the GOMS model, currently being designed and tested at Carnegie Mellon University. GOMS stands for Goals, Operators, Methods and Selection Rules. The GOMS model is a description of the knowledge that a user must have in order to carry out tasks on a device. GOMS can predict learning time, execution time and procedural aspects of usability (these concern the amount, consistency and efficiency of the procedures users must follow).

I-PRONTO

HOMELAB

PHENOM

WWICE

EASY ACCESS AND LISY

TOONS

SPICE

GLEAN3 is a GOMS model simulation tool. It is basically a simplified version of the EPIC architecture for simulating human cognition and performance. However, GLEAN3 uses the GOMS language to represent the procedural knowledge rather than the technically more difficult production-rule representation native to EPIC.

ACT-R/PM is based on the ACT-R model. In *The Atomic Components of Thought*,[6] Anderson states that in ACT-R declarative knowledge (things we are aware that we know) is represented in chunks. Production rules specify how to retrieve and use such declarative knowledge to solve problems. This is procedural knowledge. ACT-R primarily provides models of the learning and performance of subjects. However, ACT-R has a very weak perceptual-motor processor. Recently, the more responsive ACT-R user models and the parallel perceptual-motor processors of EPIC have been combined in the ACT-R/PM model.

While user models can result in very usable interactive systems, further empirical testing will highlight remaining interaction problems.

Usability Engineering

Usability Engineering analyzes user requirements and tests usability for the conceptualization, implementation and evaluation of interactive systems.

User requirements analysis

There are several methods for analyzing user requirements. One widely used method is the construction and analysis of usage scenarios. Usage scenarios are short narratives of envisioned real-life situations that describe a specific user group in a specific contextual setting interacting with specific devices to fulfil specific tasks and intentions. They illustrate the usage, functionality and purpose of new devices and services in daily life.

These usage scenarios are analyzed using a design space analysis method, such as 'Questions, Options and Criteria'(QOC).[7] In this method, the Questions identify key issues in the design space around the artifact to be developed. The user and technology requirements that stem from the usage scenarios are used to generate design Criteria. Finally, Options are technological solutions developed in answer to the Questions and evaluated on the basis of the Criteria. QOC allows the systematic exploration and recording of design possibilities, and stimulates the generation of several alternative design options. A QOC session consists of several steps: (a) generating questions, followed by supplying options and design criteria; (b) relating options and criteria in a diagram; and (c) weighing the relations between options and criteria.

Usability testing

Usability testing measures the quality of the interactive system. Methods range from observational studies and interviews to controlled (mostly task-driven) experiments. Traditional testing focuses on productivity-oriented quality measures. However, networked information, communication and entertainment systems require other measures, such as satisfaction and enjoyability. Usability testing therefore measures the extent to which the interactive system can be used in a specific context to achieve specific goals with effectiveness (i.e., whether users are able to complete a task successfully), efficiency (i.e., how much time, physical and cognitive effort it takes them), and satisfaction (i.e., the users' level of comfort with and attitudes to the system).

Since usability testing is about measuring quality, the measures need to be assessed with standardized instruments, without which it would not be possible to set design criteria or to improve the usability of an interactive system in a systematic way.

Challenges

Given the Ambient Intelligence ambition to create electronic environments that are sensitive and responsive to the presence of people, with an emphasis on satisfying user needs, user knowledge is paramount. Yet today's adaptive systems already have difficulties in obtaining basic knowledge of user preferences. Cognitive Engineering faces the challenge of establishing methods of acquiring more user knowledge in real-world situations. This knowledge will enable sensitive environments to perform intelligent adaptation and anticipate user needs. Building sensitive environments that exhibit some form of intelligent behaviour requires substantial knowledge of the people and their habits in such an environment.

The implementation of Ambient Intelligence systems raises many questions. What is the key qualification of such a system? Is it the amount of processing power in the environment? Is it the amount of digital content that can be stored in the environment? Or is it the amount of bits we can transport over a network? None of these will give us a measure for evaluating the success of Ambient Intelligence. The key criterion for these systems will be found in the effect that they have upon the user. Most of the time, this effect is labelled as the user experience. However, this is a vague qualification and difficult to measure. The 'operationalization' of the user experience is one of the bigger challenges for Usability Engineering. Traditional usability measures such as efficiency need to be replaced or augmented with measures of user experiences. Usability Engineering will need to focus on methods for gathering the user requirements and usability criteria involved in the design and evaluation of Ambient Intelligence systems.

I-PRONTO

HOMELAB

PHENOM

WWICE

EASY ACCESS
& LISY

TOONS

SPICE

1   J. Long and J. Dowell, 'Cognitive Engineering Human-Computer Interactions', The Psychologist (July 1996), 313-317
2   D.A. Norman, 'Cognitive Engineering', User Centred System Design, ed. D.A. Norman and S.W. Draper (Hillsdale NJ, Lawrence Earlbaum Associates, 1986), 31-61
3   A. Murata and H. Iwase, 'Effectivity of Cognitively Engineered Human Interface Design', Proceedings of the 20th Annual Conference of the IEEE Engineering in Medicine and Biology Society, vol. 20, no. 5 (1988)
4   Long and Dowell, 313-317
5   S. Card, T. Moran and A. Newell, The Psychology of Human-Computer Interaction (Hillsdale NJ, Lawrence Erlbaum Associates, 1983)
6   J. Anderson and C. Leviere, The Atomic Components of Thought (Mahwah NJ, Lawrence Erlbaum Associates, 1998)
7   A. MacLean, R.M. Young, V.M.E. Bellotti and T. Moran, 'Questions, Options, and Criteria: Elements of Design Space Analysis', Human-Computer Interaction, vol. 6 (1991), 201-250.

1.6 EXPERIENCE DESIGN

Lorna Goulden, Paul McGroary

In its various incarnations and evolutions, the concept of Ambient Intelligence has been with us for some time; research into the topic has been carried out for a decade. However, most of this work has focused predominantly on solving core technology issues. There is a large gap yet to be bridged between the growing wealth of advanced technological knowledge and the successful development of truly appropriate and ultimately commercially acceptable solutions. Some fundamental questions have yet to be answered. Do people really want their environment to be intelligent, and if so, just how intelligent would they like it to be? As Irene McWilliam puts it, 'there is a fine line between what is perceived as helpful and useful, and what is considered intrusive, overbearing and overly complex'.[1]

Considering these issues, what kind of relationship should people have with such intelligence, and where will this intelligence lie – in the system that delivers it, in the technology that enables the system, in the method of access and control of the system, or simply with the person using it? Perhaps the answer lies in an appropriate combination of the above, and the real intelligence resides in the dynamic flow of how we place the emphasis of this relationship over time: our experience. But what is experience? How will it contribute to a vision of Ambient Intelligence? And can it really be designed?

Experience design

The term 'experience design' has become widely used in the design world. Although definitions and approaches differ, in essence they all focus on the quality of the user experience and often signify a shift away from a focus on increasing and improving functionality towards more culturally relevant solutions. At Philips Design, for example, there is an increasing focus on the quality of a person's experience during the whole period of engagement with a brand. That experience begins with the first impression, the company's brand identity, and flows throughout the total life of a product in every aspect of usability, cultural relevance and durability, to the memory of the complete relationship.

A core element of the Philips Design research programme has been based on developing an experience design methodology that combines aspects of design, technology and business to advance the innovation and development of electronic products, systems and environments. This has enabled a necessary yet natural evolution of long-established design processes to consider, amongst other things, the uniquely complex and yet still relatively undefined requirements of ambient intelligent solutions development.

This presents quite a challenge when considering that an experience is not something that is fixed or identical for everyone, but rather something that is unique and individual. The world we perceive and the way that we perceive it are both developed over time through experiences, and in turn colour those experiences. As a result, we cannot presume to develop solutions that dictate the experience someone will have; instead we have to anticipate and design towards these anticipated experiences.

The Experience Creation Cycle

Three key activity phases are described in the Experience Creation Cycle outlined by Philips Design: the Envisionment, the Experience Concepts and the Experience Centre (Fig. 1). Each phase describes different methodologies of design research and development involved in the creation of what we call 'experience solutions'.

NEBULA

GARDEN

AURORA

HOMELAB

MIME

POGO

CONNECTED
PLANET

LIME
AND PL@NET

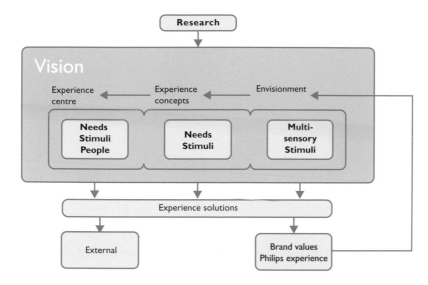

FIG. 1
The Experience
Creation Cycle

Envisionment

In this stage, the focus is on developing and understanding potential cause and effect cycles and the experiential qualities of multi-sensorial input and output from a mainly context-free perspective. Creative designers and technical experts work closely together. Rapid-prototyping is carried out with a focus on innovating in the realm of specific interface elements. For example, typography, animation, 3D graphics, sound, music, speech, tactility and form are all explored both individually and in how they relate to one or more of the other elements.

Experience Concepts

In the Experience Concept stage, human needs, values and emerging sociocultural trends are the key inputs to a design process that generates initial ideas for experience solutions. Our approach has been to expand our knowledge of traditional time-based disciplines, such as interaction design, to include a more developed understanding of time and events in a way that can be applied across all fields of design. Additional inspiration is provided by research into broad topics such as space, time, perception, memory, emotion, communication and entertainment. A structure is applied to this research that aims to promote a deeper understanding of the relationships between people, space and enablers over time, as the foundation ingredients of any experience, in order to establish the context from which to develop design ideas into experiential concepts. Fig. 2 shows the keys elements of our approach and how we view them relative to the key aspect of time.

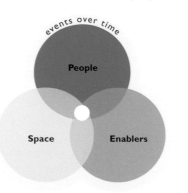

FIG. 2
Key elements when designing
for experience

People

All my knowledge of the world, even my scientific knowledge, is gained from my own particular point of view, or from some experience of the world without which the symbols of science would be meaningless.[2]

Maurice Merleau-Ponty

Putting people first is the essence of our approach. To contribute to the nature of the relationship of people to space and technology in the future, be it intelligent or otherwise, we must first understand the values and culture of those in this relationship.

No two people have exactly the same experience or interpret in exactly the same manner. Feelings about experiences vary greatly from culture to culture and change substantially as we age. Is it therefore possible to actually design experience? Maybe not; perhaps we can instead aim to develop an 'experience landscape' which provides the necessary stimuli to enable people to create or augment their own experiences. The actual experience itself is a personal interpretation and a distinctly individual choice.

Only by creating personal connections with people and by offering the experiences that they will enjoy, appreciate and pursue can we hope to create a truly lasting, qualitative approach to the design of Ambient Intelligence. Through this approach, people's experiences and actions, rather than technological capability, become the guide for innovation.

Space and place

Thirty spokes coverage upon a single hub;
It is on the hole in the centre that the use of the cart hinges.

We make a vessel from a lump of clay;
It is the empty space within the vessel that makes it float.

Thus, while the tangible has advantages,
It is the intangible that makes it useful.[3]

People will encounter Ambient Intelligence in a certain space or place. It is therefore necessary to understand the dynamics and boundaries of this environment. We must consider what effect the environment has on our senses and perception, and how this experience may be improved through the introduction of Ambient Intelligence solutions. Colour, light, micro-climate, form and aesthetics, sound and smell are the traditional tools of the designer. But what tools could Ambient Intelligence bring to the design of space or, equally importantly, what tools must be developed for its implementation to be a success?

Elements such as pattern, texture, reflection, heat, sound and smell can have a profound psychological effect on our perception of space. But what of immersion, transition, virtuality and ubiquity? What are the new enablers of Ambient Intelligence and how will they affect our perception and experience of the environments in which we live, work, travel and rest?

Enablers

In itself technology is not a force either for good or bad. Whether it works positively or negatively depends on what we decide to do with it – because not everything that is possible with technology is actually desirable. It is therefore important that we make the right choices.[4]

Stefano Marzano

Current developments in technology, the Internet and consumer electronics indicate that we now have the capability to bring very new tools to the offering. Roadmaps clearly suggest that

NEBULA

GARDEN

AURORA

HOMELAB

MIME

POGO

CONNECTED
PLANET

LIME
AND PL@NET

technology will no longer be a limiting factor. For Ambient Intelligence, the key components are sensors, actuators, interactive screens, displays, input devices for speech, handwriting recognition and tactile feedback.

Materials will also play a leading role. Recent developments in materials science have created new vehicles for the expression of sensory qualities in the form of so-called 'smart' materials. These are materials with the ability to respond to sensory stimuli and to adapt to changes in their environment.

Such developments in materials and technology provide several possibilities however; we should not neglect nor underestimate design tools as enablers. Product, interface, interaction, CAD, multimedia, graphics, interior, architecture, theatre and exhibition design have much to offer in the implementation of experience.

The success of Ambient Intelligence lies in the appropriate use of technology and materials, software and hardware, traditional and new disciplines of design. These enablers must be manifest in ways which people find relevant and meaningful within their own timeframe and culture.

Time

Now lasts approximately 0.3 seconds. This is the time it takes the workings of the brain to find a synchronous rhythm which we experience as the present.[5]

Joke Brouwer

As cognitive research into the phenomenon of time progresses, it becomes increasingly clear that time is built into natural and technological processes at different speeds. It is not an objective, continuous reality but rather a subjective response. It is personal, and therefore an emotional experience, controlled by social rhythms.

French architect and city planner Paul Virilio differentiates between 'extensive' and 'intensive' time.[6] Extensive time is the time of durability and presence, the time of archives and memory. Here time and space are continuous. Intensive time is very different. In intensive time, more and more appears to fit into a second. It is the time of acceleration, of e-mails and surfing. We may not be able observe it directly, but we are aware of it and its impact on the space we inhabit and how we choose to live.

In considering how people may experience or mark the passing of time, Philips Design focuses on three different types of event: the one-off, the repetitive and the constant event. Since the atrocities of 11 September 2001, few would deny that a one-off or singular event can have a lasting effect on the lives of many. There are, of course, other rather more personal one-off events that mark the passage of our lives: the birth of a child, marriage, graduation, moving house... repeated or patterned events can also influence our perception of time. The seasons, day and night and the personal rituals we develop, such as a morning cup of coffee or our regular route to work, are all examples of how we can be considerably influenced by patterns of time. And, finally, there is constant or learning time. This is a process of gradual reward for time invested. Take learning a language or learning to ski. At first, these are painstakingly and noticeably laborious, but after some time the skill improves, less time is required, the activity begins to flow and the experience improves.

The notion of time is key to the design of experience. It is vital that our approach and application of time goes beyond the particular instance of an experience. As suggested earlier in this chapter, ease and duration of interaction, together with cumulative experience, play a pivotal role in how Ambient Intelligence will be accepted.

Experiential prototype

With a more developed understanding of the mechanisms and issues of the context in question, this knowledge is applied to a creative process during which various methods such as brainstorming, experience story writing and idea generation are carried out. As a concept begins to take shape, design and technical experts again collaborate to develop working prototypes. Much iteration is required as different design issues are tackled but also as a means of evaluation and feedback. Such feedback loops with the intended audience guide and influences the emerging experiential prototype.

An experiential prototype is a working demonstration of a design concept where features and behaviours are simulated. Such prototypes serve as a means of communication and dialogue about what the concept does and how it might appear and be used were it to be developed for the market. The emphasis is on the quality of interaction and experience and less on the pure functionality and technology of the solution. Much attention is given to how the user interacts with the prototype from their initial impression to particular details that may at first seem to bear little relation to the functioning of the concept. These details can, however, greatly influence the relationship and level of eventual acceptance of the solution. For example, how different technologies are integrated within the product or collection of products, how they might appear and behave, wires, antennae, screens, buttons, batteries, and so forth. The choice of materials used, how they feel, textures, colours, weights, etc. How intuitive and natural is the interaction? Details such as animation timing, quality of audio and style of typography need to be addressed. How does the solution fit into the intended environment and how might it adapt or wear with use over time?

A series of breakthrough design research projects have recently been carried out at Philips Design that articulate this approach to experience concept development, creating results that can be directly experienced by people, as in the Noah's Ark, LiMe and Pogo projects. With the increasing diversity of Ambient Intelligence possibilities, we can apply this experience design approach as a means to make the more innovative, yet complex and abstract ideas physical and understandable. By turning the intangible concept into a tangible working prototype, we present the opportunity for people to experience the proposed result first hand. In this way we provide the means to test early ideas with a variety of targeted end-users.

Experience Centre

At the Experience Centre stage, experiential concept prototypes need to be developed to a level robust enough to be placed into real environments. This could be in a café or hotel, aeroplane, train or car, in the home, hospital or workplace, depending on the context of the proposed solution. This allows developing experience solutions to be tested in real time, with real people, in real space, providing 24/7 feedback and the possibility of monitoring the true effects of usage and how people's experience develops over time. This is particularly valuable in the domain of Ambient Intelligence, enabling co-design and development, adaptive and emergent behaviour observation (of both the Ambient Intelligence system and the people using it), and a greater understanding of the actual appropriateness and potential longevity of a developing solution.

The practicalities and cost of developing these robust prototypes should, however, not be underestimated. They need to be developed far beyond the level of the experiential concept and there needs to be constant aftercare to monitor and repair any technical problems which must be anticipated in developing innovative ambient intelligent solutions. Technical failings

NEBULA

GARDEN

AURORA

HOMELAB

MIME

POGO

CONNECTED
PLANET

LIME
AND PL@NET

can seriously impact the experience and eventual acceptance of a solution, but in the controlled environment of an Experience Centre they can also give valuable indications of the range of issues that may arise and the level of impact they may have.

A 'parent-child' approach to implementing complex technology combinations is also proposed to encourage the inclusion of fragile emergent technologies. The approach relies on the durability and reliability of long-established, off-the-shelf 'parent' technologies to be partnered with the more unreliable emerging 'child' technologies. This makes it possible to get new technologies into the environment possibly years before traditional development cycles might allow, and can provide invaluable feedback to guide the development cycle in appropriate directions for business application.

Recent technological developments have already had a massive impact on the way we innovate and the offerings we take to market. Should such advancement continue, Ambient Intelligence would undoubtedly have a massive role in steering its development. But how will we offer it to the end-user? Through existing sales and distribution channels? Or is it prudent to assume that we will require new mechanisms through which we can achieve a meaningful and lasting relationship with our consumer. Users, increasingly sophisticated and demanding, are placing less emphasis on the products they buy and more emphasis on the experiences those products and environments provide. This is where the Experience Centre approach can play an important role.

By way of example, let us look at the pharmaceutical company Boots, based in England. Although not directly adopting an approach of testing Ambient Intelligence scenarios, there are parallels in the approach that they have implemented. Boots recently underwent substantial changes. Traditionally known as 'the nation's chemist' the company has reinvented itself as the company of well-being. Boots has successfully repositioned itself: in addition to providing products; it now offers advice and services to enhance personal well-being. They have invested substantially in one-stop 'experience' centres that offer everything from conventional and complementary medicine, to relaxation and beauty treatments. Lessons learnt, the company claims, have helped them integrate services into a cohesive offering that makes the best use of the brand, at the same time more completely meeting the needs of their customers.

In addition, together with Granada Media plc, the Boots Company plc have created a joint venture company to form a new Internet business called Digital Wellbeing Limited. The Website *www.wellbeing.com* commits to providing the user with clear views on the areas that touch and affect their health and beauty. By all accounts, Boots customers have strongly endorsed these new services and in particular the method of delivery. Sales have increased, particularly where service users become both more frequent visitors and heavier purchasers of Boots products.

Is it feasible for the consumer electronics industry to adopt a similar Experience Centre approach as a means of implementing the Ambient Intelligence vision? Could this provide the much-needed pathway essential to bringing Ambient Intelligence to the world and the way that we live in it? We believe so.

1 I. McWilliam, 'The Design Perspective on Ambient Intelligence', *InCA* (http://idsa-sf.org, Spring 2001)
2 M. Merleau-Ponty, *Phenomenology of Perception* (London, Routledge & Kegan Paul, 1992)
3 Lao-Tzu, *Tao Teh Ching* (written in the sixth century BC)
4 S. Marzano, *The Culture of Ambient Intelligence* (Philips Design, 2002)
5 J. Brouwer (ed.), *Machine Times* (Rotterdam, NAI Publishers, 2000)
6 P. Virilio, *The Clairvoyant in the Age of Total Transparency* (http://www.cyberhobbit.de)

TOUCH, RELATE, INTERACT

How might we communicate with an Ambient Intelligence system? Will we be able to use natural, human modes of communication – speech, sight, hearing and gesture? Suppose it could 'sense' who we are: would it then be able to interact with us intelligently, as if it 'knew' us? How will the various parts of the system talk to each other? And who else might they be talking to?

2.1 TOWARDS A NEW SENSORIALITY

Marion Verbücken

The senses

Sensory stimulation (i.e., the stimulation of sight, touch, sound, taste and smell) is a key element in determining our experience of the world. The man-made artifacts in our environment, from buildings and products to communication networks and transport systems, are created with sensorial qualities in mind. As new technologies providing new sensorial qualities emerge, they become incorporated into our culture and can have an impact both on how we experience our environment and on how we interact with it. The experience of walking among the shimmering glass towers of New York is radically different to that of walking among the stone buildings of a medieval town. The introduction of plastic into our production processes led to a whole new category of cheap and disposable products, but also to objects that were comfortable, hygienic, flexible and more durable. More recently, 'high-tech' combinations of materials have resulted in clothing that regulates body temperature, toothbrushes with composite ergonomic handles and car seats that mould themselves to the shape of our bodies. These developments affect all of our senses, from sight to smell, sometimes obviously and sometimes in a more subtle, peripheral way.

Senses and memory

It is a paradoxical but common experience that different persons at the same time have both a similar and a different experience of the same environment. That we participate in the activities of daily life proves that we have a common world. But we can also say that we have different worlds that even we ourselves perceive differently due to differing attitudes to the same things.[1] The way we interpret our various sensorial inputs is crucially built upon our memory and expectation – it is not only based on our sensory apparatus, but also on how this apparatus is conditioned to respond. Our personal, emotional experiences and anticipations, our physical, sensory experiences and our cultural experiences all work together to form one overall, integrated experience. As we experience and act in this world, we go through cycles of awareness, anticipation, reflection, recombination, reaction, exploration and adaptation. The artifacts with which we interact, and those interactions themselves, have an enormous influence on how we perceive the world. In turn, the perceived experiences affect our interactions. As a result, our interpretations change as time goes by.

Ambient Intelligence proposes a world in which our interactions with products will become increasingly intuitive, using technologies that are sensitive to the way we communicate, the way we talk, feel, touch and use our body language. These technologies make new interactions possible by providing new sensorial points of contact between our environment and ourselves. In turn, these can allow us to increase our control and understanding of the material environment, and of our creative and productive interaction with it. We need to provide people with intelligent enablers that feed the senses and brain with entertainment and information. At the same time, we need to increase our freedom in many fields, enabling us to multitask, play, connect, care, create, explore, discover, manipulate, learn – to be whoever we want to be, to be human.

Ambient Intelligence centres on meaningful experiences and is therefore devoted to generating experiences which are both physically and mentally in harmony, allowing a fluid, empowering interplay between mind, body and the surrounding natural or man-made environment.

NEBULA

AURORA

PML

CDS

MIME

POGO

Homo digitalis: a new sensorial culture

We are moving towards a highly sensorial culture that will be strongly focused on all our senses. Society is becoming characterized by a demand for more intensive experiences and deeper meanings. Many of today's young adults have grown up in a context which allowed them extensive freedom to try things, to learn things, and in which there was ever more to discover. In the daily reality of these younger members of society, changes follow each other rapidly, and the innovations of our information age have dramatically influenced the environment in which they have grown up. As new phenomena are introduced, there is no time to gradually adjust to them, and fear is absent. Why read a user guide? Just press a button and see what happens. They have learned to be curious and anxious to discover new things from their parents, school, society and culture. Self-expression is stimulated and media are there to be edited and fed back into the world; their favourite occupation is to explore and try out new things. Their world has to be experienced as real, either through extreme realism or by trying to get as complete a picture as possible, so that even digitally simulated worlds need to look realistic.

Digital media, multimedia, information and communication technologies are not only changing our world but also our very selves, our behaviours and how we think. On the one hand, we may be in the process of losing traditional qualities associated with skills such as traditional writing and concentration, but we may be becoming better at dealing with multiple issues simultaneously, and in lateral rather than linear thinking. We are learning to communicate in different ways, perhaps more easily, informally, openly and directly. The 'Homo digitalis', equipped with a multimedia brain, is rapidly replacing the 'Homo analogus'. On the Internet, we see and hear images and sounds and come together in new spaces such as chatrooms and newsgroups. Nobody has the last word, and discussions are never-ending. We experience the fact that we can't know everything about a given subject or keep everything under control, and that we have to live with many uncertainties. In e-mails, we express our emotions with 'smileys' and other emoticons. Images still say more than a thousand words and have become increasingly important in our multimedia-dominated age. Computer animations, image manipulations and display screens in our architectural and domestic environments are mixing reality and unreality. These different ways of communicating and signifying are changing our perception of the world, in which nothing seems impossible and everything is constantly evolving.

Towards a mixed reality

Digital communication networks are being developed globally, already allowing us to meet each other, interact and exchange information and even money and wares in a 'virtual space'. This space is currently represented by Websites, Internet chatrooms and communities, and online gaming environments. Some of these gaming environments, globally accessible and never sleeping, have hundreds of thousands of players using them at any one moment, and generate such a high financial turnover that they are wealthier than actual countries.

Not so long ago, virtual reality technologies were expected to make these virtual spaces more immersive, allowing us to 'build' environments inside them in which we could move around and carry out activities. However, wearing the bulky headsets, strange gloves, body suits and other visualization equipment required for full immersion is not very desirable. In many cases, it is also self-defeating to try to build an entirely new reality experienced through unfriendly suits and helmets, when the world we already have is so rich in experiential potential, and our sensory apparatus is so finely attuned to it.

It's wonderful to be able to explore a particular country or its architecture through digital media; we can take a virtual reality walk on any remote tropical island, highly realistically. But it isn't real. What is there to do on a virtual island if you can't smell the air, or play in the sand?

How can you feel excitement if there is never any threat and when everything is only pixel-deep? What is a world without all its sensorial emotions and pleasures? And why would we want to live in a virtual world when we have the real one? Our virtual space need not be a place in which to build artificial alternative worlds, but rather a tool that has the power to offer new solutions that could make life more enjoyable, richer and perhaps more meaningful. The challenge lies in the creation of authentic virtual realities.

However, the current digital means embedded in our physical reality are also clearly lacking. With the advent of digital media, Amazon.com now not only sells paper books, but also e-books to read on screen. Yet, books have a certain value that can't be expressed digitally. We don't just read books: we feel them, smell them and dream with them. Handwritten letters have more sensorial aspects than e-mails. These virtual spaces and their virtual realities are becoming more and more immersive. A hundred years ago, people were easily immersed by the cinematic experience of a flat, black and white, silent projection of a train drawing into a station. Today we use surround sound, special effects in the creation of ever more realistic Dinosaur movies, and ever more complex technology and equipment. How far do we have to go technically to achieve a degree of immersion with which we will be satisfied? In the end, it is the engaging quality of the experience that is key. As Tztom Toda puts it, 'Reality is not what is presented to us but must be formed within us'.

Due to miniaturization and dematerialization, technologies are continuously shrinking. They will soon have minimum mass, use minimum energy, provide maximum functionality and will be wireless. They will therefore easily be 'swallowed' by other objects, surfaces or surroundings. As human beings, we are only interested in the experience these devices can provide. One consequence is that we no longer need to physically collect data (compact discs for example) because we can access a virtual data collection. Another is that we no longer need to be assigned a workstation in the office because our laptop can plug in to the wireless office space from anywhere.

But what is the result of this miniaturization? We still need to use physical touch, speech or gesture recognition, since we are not yet able to activate or operate with our minds. This means that whilst creating the digital world, we can't discard the material world. We need to seriously consider how we will experience and interact with this new mixed reality.

We can take advantage of new materials and technologies to create moments of contact with our environments which relate to our conflicting needs for increasingly fast and efficient sensorial experiences on the one hand, and for engaging, meaningful, rich and poetic experiences on the other. We can create a multi-dimensional space in which people can experience and interact using different modalities and means simultaneously.

The new sensoriality of Ambient Intelligence

Ambient Intelligence builds on these trends and proposes a scenario in which technology is seamlessly and unobtrusively embedded into many aspects of our environment, enabling us in our daily tasks and routines in intelligent, meaningful ways. This places a greater emphasis than usual on the experiential qualities of our interactions with such technologies, and necessitates the extension of the concept of sensuality into the immaterial. To quote Tony Dunne, we have arrived at a point where we must consider the 'sensuality of the immaterial'.[2] We need to create new touch points and moments of contact with our new mixed reality environments which make use of all of the different aspects of our sensoriality to richly bring the world of Ambient Intelligence, in both its material and immaterial aspects, to the user.

Traditional knowledge and new technologies and processes are being used to customize, extend and modify the physical properties of materials, and to invent new ones that are liquid, transparent, invisible, flexible and smart. Materials are made of molecules that can be

'genetically' manipulated or combined with other types to obtain different qualities. These contemporary smart materials, or mutant materials, are augmented with the power of change and have the ability to perform or respond. They automatically react and adjust to their environment or to their wearer. Technologies are heading for futures in which computers are designed from a bio-molecular basis, and the design or engineering of artificial life forms will be common. We are now standing on the threshold of this evolution. Many technologies and materials are under development; sometimes, we don't even know their vehicle or purpose yet. What will their sensorial qualities be? How will we feel, 'think', hear, smell and act with them?

New skins
The skin or surface of an object is the point of interface with users, and conveys the identity of the thing as well as containing its controls. Much new work is going into developing skin materials that can be both sensitive and responsive. Touch screens can be seen as the embryo of this work that will eventually lead to fully sensitive skins. Future skins will incorporate other sensors including touch, heat and light sensitivity, and different display technologies including foldable displays and electronic inks.

New materials
Apart from the skins of objects, the material of the object itself will also contribute to the new sensoriality. Materials with memories, with electro-mechanical properties that enable them to harden or soften, contract or expand, and to change texture depending on the situation will open a new world of responsive and sensorial objects.

New horizons
Context awareness and other new technologies will enable objects to be more responsive to their situation, both physically and culturally. Things will be able to 'place themselves' within your field of view and field of interaction. With the adjustment of their other physical properties, objects will be able to propel themselves into the foreground of your attention or retreat to the periphery of your world. The dynamic of this background–foreground positioning will constitute a new interactive quality.

New responsiveness

We can create systems that respond in real-time so that we can engage fully in an interaction. Further, we can develop systems that learn how to respond; self-organizing systems and neural networks that can bring different sensorial qualities into play under different conditions.

The automotive industry is moving from steering to power steering to drive by wire. It's now possible to make your car 'drive' like a saloon or like a sports car, depending on how it's programmed.

New perspectives

We use technology to enhance our senses and give us new perspectives on the world. An example is enhanced vision, where infra-red cameras on cars coupled with a windscreen display can visualize details from the night-time environment that are hidden from the naked eye. Another example is the cochlear implant developed for people with impaired hearing.

New spaces

Apart from purely virtual spaces, the new sensoriality will also be exhibited as a new mix of space and capability. With wireless networking and short-range communication proliferating, Bluetooth space and LAN space are becoming realities, and with new devices enabling people to interact with these spaces, they will become more real and exhibit sensoriality. 'Warchalk' markings in London advertise the fact that wireless access is available. Games like Electronic Arts' 'Majestic' mix digital experience with real life. Physical Mark-up Language (see Chapter 8.10, First Steps, PML) will enable all devices within a space to become responsive to media playing there, whether video, audio or interactive game.

New presence

Some of the new sensoriality enabled through Ambient Intelligence will involve projecting the self into remote locations – telepresence. Currently rudimentary, through the use of audio and increasingly video, new techniques will enable people to commune virtually with more of the sense of presence familiar to the real world.

Illustrations

One project that strongly focuses on sensorial, virtual and physical, spatial and environmental qualities is Nebula, an interactive ambient projection system designed to enrich the rituals of the bedroom. Nebula uses an intuitive, natural and playful way of physical interaction in a virtual space, through simple body movements and gestures. Another example is Aurora, an interactive light surface that enables people to draw with light using their finger as paintbrush, to leave messages, for entertainment or decoration. Pogo, an interactive system for children to learn through play, is another project highly focused on sensorial interaction. All Pogo's objects have a strong tactile value that makes children want to play with them and gives them different sensorial pleasures in an intuitive way.

Our major challenge in the coming years is to bring people's sensorial experience and technology closer together, to create a more human way of interacting using natural gestures and emotional sensorial qualities, and to give them choice: to interact or not, to connect or disconnect. The more people feel part of the experience, the deeper the experience becomes. We have to rethink the nature of the human senses and the environment in relation to the new reality and create an environment that responds to the subjectivity of our moods, wishes and lifestyles.

1   C. Norberg-Schulz, *Genius Loci: Towards a Phenomenology in Architecture* (New York, Rizzoli International Press, 1980)
2   A. Dunne, *Hertzian Tales* (Royal College of Art, 1999)

2.2 AMBIENT VIDEO, DISPLAYS, AUDIO AND LIGHTING

Our interactions with Ambient Intelligence will ideally take place through modalities that are essentially human – i.e., our senses. Here, we explore some of the technologies that will affect what we see and hear in an ambient intelligent environment.

AMBIENT VIDEO
Geert Depovere

Video is soon likely to become one of the most natural and personal channels through which people will communicate with others at a distance and distribute information. The displays used will apply intelligence to provide us with optimum image and audio quality, in line with our own personal preferences, and regardless of the source of the video material, the type of displays, or the lighting conditions in the room. Video cameras, initially used only for communication purposes, will later become an unobtrusive way of enabling devices to interact with us (for example, to adjust settings depending on our presence, location, mood, and so on). In addition, in an ambient intelligent environment, we might expect people to be able to watch any type of video content on any available video display (including 3D displays), communicate with people either elsewhere in the home or outside it, and use displays as 'windows' to the outside world or as paintings.

Better quality
Optimizing displays to take account of the viewer's position
Studies have shown that viewers' preferences regarding the degree of sharpness enhancement or noise reduction applied to video and audio output depends on their position in relation to the screen and their distance from it. Ambient Intelligence displays will be able to take account of this by making use of video signals from a small camera within them to determine the position of the viewer relative to the screen. (The displays will normally contain such a camera anyway, to enable people to communicate by video with others.) Once this position is known, video settings can be optimized for the viewer, and the size of subtitles adjusted, for instance.

Information from the same camera can also be used to discern which part of the screen the viewer is actually looking at. This is useful in the case of very large screens, which viewers sit relatively close to. To get the necessary very high resolution, they require a great deal of processing power. Knowing which part of the screen the viewer is looking at will allow the system to economize on power by providing high resolution only for the specific part of the screen being looked at. When eye tracking is available, this can also be used for high-resolution near-eye displays or head-mounted displays.

Optimizing the relation between the display and the ambient lighting conditions
The quality of the image seen on a display varies depending on the lighting conditions under which it is being viewed. The relationship between the display and these conditions can be optimized in two ways. The display can adapt to the lighting conditions, on the basis of information about the degree of illumination and its colour point received from an integrated

NEBULA

AURORA

WWICE

EASY ACCESS
AND LISY

PMI

CDS

MIME

Q4 PLUGGED

SMARTMIRROR

TOONS

sensor. However, it is very difficult for displays to adapt to certain lighting conditions. In an ambient intelligent environment, the display will be able to communicate with the lighting system itself, so that it can be adjusted to create optimum viewing conditions on the display in question.

Customizing displays to viewers' personal preferences

People have different preferences with respect to the settings of their TVs. Some people prefer highly saturated colour settings, for instance, while others prefer settings that give a more natural impression. Such individual settings can already be stored in high-end television sets, but in an Ambient Intelligence environment, the display may be able to recognize you and to implement your personal TV settings. This recognition could be accomplished using the camera system described above, or some personal device that you carry with you (e.g., a mobile phone), which would communicate your preferences to the display. Ideally, your settings (expressed in terms of perceptual attributes, such as colour, sharpness, brightness, contrast, etc.) would be able to be implemented on all other displays in the system, so that you can always see images with your preferred settings.

Greater realism

Bigger screens

In real life, we focus our eyes on part of the scene before us, but see the rest of the scene indistinctly around that area. Current TV images 'focus' our eyes for us, cutting out the indistinct part of the scene. This means that the bigger the screen, the further away we have to be in order to view it without turning our heads. In a future broadcast standard, there might be a fixed area in the middle of the screen, decoded with a very high image quality, with a lower quality coding outside that area. With such a standard, small TVs (with a narrow viewing angle) could display only the middle part of the scene, whereas large screens (with large viewing angles) would display the entire scene, and create a more realistic effect.

The ideal size of the screen may vary depending on what it is used for. For instance, if used as a 'window' or as a painting, size is not an issue. However, if used to provide communication between two groups of people (e.g., videoconferencing), it will need to be large enough to provide a life-size effect, and the distance viewers sit from the screen will need to feel natural (i.e., about as far as you would sit from your neighbours while having coffee with them).

Ambient 3D video

Throughout the history of television, there has been a drive to provide the most natural viewing experience possible. Black and white became colour, but 3D has so far remained elusive. Nonetheless, the advancement and popularity of 3D video games and the convergence of TV and PC applications in broadcasting (e.g., time-shifted viewing) and DVD, as well as the convergence of monitor and TV screen formats, suggest that the introduction of 3D displays into home networks is only a matter of time.

3D displays are currently being developed on several different principles: multiple layers (e.g., stacked LCDs), stereoscopy (e.g., head-mounted displays, liquid crystal shutter glasses), direction multiplexing (where the light emissions from 2D images are directed exclusively to one eye, e.g., using lenticular screens), volumetric 3D (whereby light is generated in a volume) or even holography. Since dedicated content and rendering hardware is usually required to drive each of these types, use in an Ambient Intelligence context (in which any content should be viewable on any display) is not yet possible.

However, 2D compatible 3D displays are already available. These can be switched between the two modes. An example is the ViRex LCD display, in which alternating columns are coated with different polarizers. With polarized glasses, and stereo views on the alternating columns, this display serves as a stereoscopic display. Without glasses and 2D content, the display acts as a regular LCD. Typical applications for the 3D mode would include gaming and viewing 3D movies (e.g., on 3D-DVD).

In due course, dedicated autostereoscopic displays (3D displays that do not require the use of glasses or other headgear) will be introduced into the home. Although these could be used to watch 2D video, it would be an attractive option if incoming 2D video could be augmented to 3D. This is possible, because most video sequences contain many implicit cues to depth: sharpness, shadows, dynamic occlusion by moving objects or people, implicit depth probabilities, etc. A video home server could provide sufficient calculation power to make these implicit relations explicit by calculating the depth value per pixel. This reconstructed depth information could then be sent as metadata with the original video stream.

One implementation might be a 2D video base layer combined with a depth-enhancement layer. The rendering engine of any 2D and 3D display could exploit this enhancement layer. In 2D mode, it could be used for depth-specific enhancement, or to provide different views of the same scene, depending on the viewer's position ('motion parallax'). This implementation would also provide the flexibility required to render 3D information on most autostereoscopic 3D displays. On the basis of the video image and corresponding depth map, different views could be rendered through image morphing, a basic feature of any 3D PC graphics card. The convergence of video and graphics is therefore likely to become one of the facilitators for the introduction of combined 2D and 3D ambient video.

Design and implementation issues

A number of issues will need to be considered when designing and implementing video processing within an Ambient Intelligence system.

Energy

Portable displays will need to have ultra-low power consumption, because video processing requires considerable processing power. Both algorithmic design and implementation architecture (e.g., dedicated hardware vs. software on a programmable general-purpose processor) can dramatically affect power consumption.[1]

Standards

Since an Ambient Intelligence system will have to deal with video content from many outside sources, it will need to cope with many different video coding and transmission standards. Software implementation of the video-processing functionality is not only cost-effective, allowing sharing of processing and memory resources, it is also flexible, enabling the system to cope with evolving standards.

Distributed resources

Processing and storage resources required for video processing do not need to be physically located where they are functionally needed, but can be distributed throughout the system and called upon when and where required. Mobile devices, for instance, might store data on nearby stationary devices, or request those devices to perform processing. The architecture of the whole video-processing chain, from sources to displays, therefore needs to be studied. Efficient video compression techniques will also be a key factor.

Cost-effectiveness and robustness

Processing power and energy resources in the system may be limited or fluctuate, and the video-processing functionality and quality may also vary over time, due to changing user requests, for example. If processing is implemented on programmable platforms, scaleable video algorithms, together with dynamic resource management, may serve to improve cost-effectiveness and robustness. Scaleable video algorithms allow a run-time trade-off between resource usage and output quality. The resource management is responsible for making the trade-offs.[2]

Variety

Video will be entering the home from many different sources, in an increasing variety of formats, each requiring different processing in order to obtain the best quality. New methods for broadcasting and storing video signals have also emerged. Display technologies are also increasing in number, each requiring different processing of the video signals to provide an optimum image. The traditional convergence between standards for capturing, broadcasting, storing and displaying video signals will be difficult to retain. There is consequently a good argument for uncoupling source format from display format and performing conversion. Some high-end TVs already incorporate video format conversion.

AMBIENT DISPLAYS
Toon Hultslag

We are already surrounded by displays – in our houses, cars, offices and public places. As Ambient Intelligence systems become widespread, displays will play an even larger role in our lives. But what sort of displays will they be?

Technologies
The four most important types of displays surrounding us today are the Cathode Ray Tube (CRT), the Liquid Crystal Display (LCD), the Plasma Display Panel (PDP) and the upcoming Polymer Light Emitting Display (PLED). Other new technologies include Low Temperature PolySilicon (LTPS) and Liquid Crystal on Silicon (LCoS).

Cathode Ray Tubes (CRTs)
Cathode Ray Tubes are the displays we are familiar with from our traditional TV sets and computer monitors. CRT produces images among the brightest and clearest produced by any displays currently available. Invented in 1879, CRT technology is still changing significantly today, although CRTs are still very large. Work is currently in progress to make the CRT less bulky, so that a 32-inch CRT will fit on a bookshelf 32cm deep. However, 'cost innovation' will be the most important R&D activity in safeguarding future CRT sales.

Liquid Crystal Displays (LCDs)
LCDs are commonly found in laptop computers, digital clocks and watches, microwave ovens, CD players and many other electronic devices. They are also starting to be used in televisions and computer monitors. LCDs are thinner, lighter, require much less power and generate less heat than CRTs. They are ideal for hospitals because, unlike CRTs, they do not emit electro-magnetic radiation and therefore do not interfere with other high-tech medical devices. They are also easier on the eyes because they do not refresh their screens in the same way, and their flicker is less noticeable. In active-matrix LCDs (in which, unlike passive-matrix LCDs, each pixel is individually addressed), the image is clear, with high contrast. LCDs generally have a narrower viewing angle than CRTs, giving a less clear image when viewed from the side.

NEBULA

AURORA

WWICE

EASY ACCESS
AND LISY

PML

CDS

MIMF

Q4 PLUGGED

SMARTMIRROR

TOONS

However, within the past decade, several solutions have largely eliminated this problem (e.g., the use of in-plane-switching, compensation foils and a multi-domain approach). Colour and motion artifacts in LCDs can still be improved. In addition, active-matrix LCDs can also be made in flexible form, using plastic instead of glass. This opens up the possibility of displays of almost any shape, and displays so flexible that they can be rolled up. Philips has already demonstrated early prototypes of these.

Today, LCD screens are still relatively small, due to a manufacturing problem. For a resolution of 1024 x 768 (e.g., for a typical notebook computer), some 2.4 million transistors are needed. Larger screens require many more. But the more transistors used, the more likely it is that some will be misplaced or malfunction, resulting in 'bad pixels', forcing manufacturers to reject many of the panels that come off their assembly lines and therefore raising prices. However, at current rates of development, costs are expected to halve within the next five years, making LCDs a contender for a preferred display technology for many Ambient Intelligence applications. LCD TVs (15-30 inches) are now on the market and 40-inch prototypes have already been produced.

Plasma Display Panels (PDPs)

Invented in 1966, today Plasma Display Panels with 32 to 63-inch screens are used as large-screen TV displays or as monitors for business presentations. PDPs enjoy a number of benefits over other types of displays. They are thin – only about 10cm thick, and allow very large screen sizes. The image is very bright and clear and the viewing angle is extremely wide – over 160 degrees. Energy consumption, however, is rather high, since the differential lumen efficacy in PDPs currently on the market is poor. Philips has recently improved lumen efficacy substantially, while maintaining consistent brightness, cutting power by up to half. The images produced by the best PDPs now equal or exceed the picture quality produced by CRTs.

Price is currently a barrier to the more widespread use of PDPs, although it is falling rapidly. The stage seems set for a contest between PDP and LCD, even at larger screen sizes (e.g., 40-60 inches).

How does a PDP work?

PDPs basically light up millions of tiny coloured fluorescent lights to form an image. Each pixel is made up of three fluorescent lights – red, blue and green. Combining and varying the

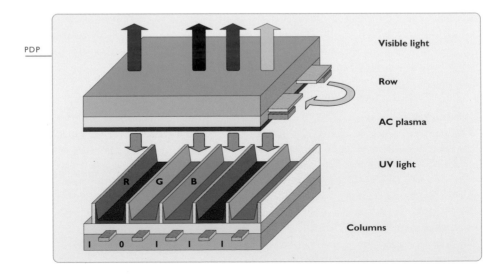

PDP

Visible light

Row

AC plasma

UV light

Columns

NEBULA

AURORA

WWICE

EASY ACCESS
AND LISY

PML

CDS

MIMF

Q4 PLUGGED

SMARTMIRROR

TOONS

intensities of the different lights produces a full range of colours. The 'lights' are formed by a mixture of xenon and neon gas contained in hundreds of thousands of tiny cells that are partially lined with phosphor. These cells are laid out in a grid structure, positioned between two plates of glass. One set of electrodes (row or display electrodes) are aligned horizontally, another (column or address electrodes) vertically, forming a basic grid. The display's computer gets the electrodes to give the right charge in the right place, one cell at a time, thousands of times in a fraction of a second. When the gas in the cells is charged, it is ionized and emits UV photons that heat the phosphor to create light, which is then visible on the display.

Polymer and Organic Light Emitting Displays (PLEDs/OLEDs)

The most recent display technology to reach the market uses natural or artificial polymers that emit light when an electrical charge is passed through them. This technology is variously known as LEP (Light-Emitting Polymer), OLED (Organic Light-Emitting Diode), PLED or PolyLED (both Polymer Light-Emitting Diode) (see Chapter 2.5, Smart Materials). Small PLEDs are currently being used for instrument panels and in shavers, mobile phones, DVD players, digital video cameras, personal digital assistants and car stereos. Prototypes for larger displays (13-inch OLED and 17-inch PLED) have recently been introduced. It is still unclear whether they pose a challenge to LCDs, although PLEDs at only 1mm thick, already enjoy a significant size and weight advantage.

PLEDs are expected to rapidly become more widely used, first in portable devices and later in consumer appliances more generally. An important potential future advantage is that the displays can be inkjet-printed, which is likely to cut manufacturing costs considerably. Moreover, PLEDs are thinner and weigh less than other displays because they do not require backlighting. This also cuts heat generation and power consumption (they use only 2-10 volts) and eliminates the need for environmentally undesirable mercury lamps. Compared to LCDs, PLEDs are also very bright, have high contrast and a wider viewing angle than LCDs (160 degrees). PLEDs are also stronger than LCDs (polymers are used in car bumpers and bullet-proof vests). And like LCDs, PLEDs open up the prospect of flexible displays: it should become possible to put them on plastic 'substrates', so that they can be made in almost any shape.

How does a PLED work?

PLEDs work by passing a current across a layer of polymer, which then emits light. The display itself consists of a layer of polymer (in colour displays, three different polymers deposited by inkjet printing) sandwiched between a transparent layer (the column electrodes) and a layer of metal (row) electrodes. The electrodes can be arranged in a passive matrix

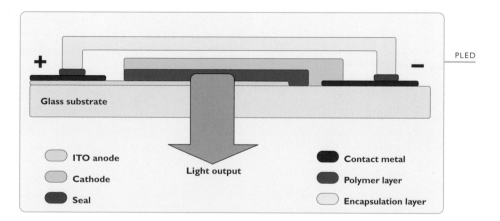

PLED

Glass substrate

ITO anode   Contact metal
Cathode   Light output   Polymer layer
Seal   Encapsulation layer

(with pixels addressed a row at a time), or in an active matrix (with pixels addressed individually). At the front is a glass plate onto which everything is fixed, and the whole is sealed at the back with an encapsulation layer, resulting in a display that is less than 1mm thick (including glass and encapsulation).

The columns and rows form a matrix which can be addressed passively (electrically activated, row by row): DC voltage pulses are applied across selected row and column electrodes to generate light flashes 'one line at a time'. Alternatively, by adding an additional active matrix structure on the glass substrate, it can be addressed actively. Finally, encapsulation with a hermetic seal is applied, or an encapsulating layer stack is deposited.

Other developments
Projection TV
CRT-based projection TV suffers from a number of problems, including poor colour convergence and brightness, compared with non-projection displays. New technologies that eliminate some of these problems are now becoming available. Texas Instruments' Digital Mirror Device (DMD) technology, for instance, uses small moving micro-mirrors the size of a pixel to produce the light-valve action needed. Several other companies, including Philips, are using Liquid Crystal on Silicon (LCoS). This is an active-matrix LCD micro-display with all the necessary silicon on the back. For very large screens, a light is reflected off the screen through a magnifying lens and onto a much larger viewing surface.

3D television
Real 3D for mass markets might be the next important innovation to come from the display industry. But there is a chicken-and-the-egg problem here: a 3D display requires 3D content, and 3D content requires a 3D display. This problem can only be solved gradually, but some 3D content is already available in graphics (e.g., video games), and quasi-3D content can be constructed from 2D video streams (see Ambient Video above). Time will tell which display principle will be most attractive for 3D television, but direction-multiplexing displays will probably be available first in mass applications, because of the low cost of the display. The super-high resolutions possible with LCD will allow multiple views to be created easily.

Which display where?
How will the technologies described above be used in an Ambient Intelligence setting?

In the home
For TV-type functions, LCDs will almost certainly replace CRT for smaller sizes. New Advanced Television (ATV) broadcast standards will stimulate high-resolution displays, favouring LCDs over PDPs because these still suffer from resolution problems. It remains to be seen whether there will be room for both of these technologies for large-screen televisions (from 40-70 inches). If LCD does replace CRT in televisions, it will be difficult to push aside: it is already very thin, it offers very high resolution in all screen sizes, and the price may well drop. Beamers, expensive and widely used in offices, are the ideal display illumination source for large and/or scaleable surfaces. In an Ambient Intelligence context, using Polymer Dispersed Liquid Crystal (PDLC) technology, windows could become a white projection screen at the touch of a button (the noise made by the projector remains a challenge, however).

On the move
LCDs are completely dominant in the notebook market. Possible new technologies in this field include flexible displays that could be drawn out of the top or side of an attaché case,

NEBULA

AURORA

WWICE

EASY ACCESS
AND LISY

PML

CDS

MIMF

Q4 PLUGGED

SMARTMIRROR

TOONS

or laser-projection-based technology that can be incorporated into a mobile apparatus to provide a portable beaming facility.

Currently, the displays in most mobile phones are LCDs. However, this could be seriously threatened by OLED/PLED in the next few years. Flexible devices, based on these technologies might also penetrate the market soon.

AMBIENT AUDIO
Ronald Aarts, Carel-Jan van Driel

In an Ambient Intelligence environment, where audio will feature prominently as a means of communication, interaction and content distribution, loudspeakers will need to merge into our surroundings in unobtrusive shapes and sizes. Sound will need to be directed to the user, and it will need to be of high quality. We will also want to enjoy the same excellent experience of unobtrusive audio when on the move.

Since audio perception depends heavily on the individual listener, as well as on the set-up of the loudspeakers, the room and the listener's position with respect to the loudspeakers, the system will need to use its intelligence to take account of all these factors.

'Disappearing' speakers
A number of unobtrusive loudspeakers have already been developed. Figure 1 shows a new-generation speaker, using technology developed by NXT, which consists of electro-dynamic transducers attached to panels. This lightweight, flexible speaker can reproduce high- to mid-range frequencies, and can be used in a wide variety of applications, including multimedia, plasma TVs, home stereos, architectural acoustics and consumer electronics products. The panels blend invisibly into the room, and the detachable frames allow people to insert their favourite prints.

FIG. 1
Panel loudspeaker

Preserving sound quality in unobtrusive speakers
In many Ambient Intelligence applications, large loudspeakers would simply be inconvenient or obtrusive. But small loudspeakers typically have poor low-frequency bass response (i.e., a significant portion of the audio signal is not reproduced sufficiently).[3] This poses a problem, because the bass portion of an audio signal contributes significantly to overall sound quality.

A traditional, conceptually simple way to increase the perceived sound level in the lower part of the audible spectrum (below the loudspeaker's resonance frequency) is to amplify the low-frequency part of the audio spectrum. However, in the case of very low frequencies, the loudspeaker's mechanical limitations will limit the distance the loudspeaker's cone can vibrate, leading to distortion and possibly loudspeaker overload, while physically increasing the perceived sound level will force the loudspeaker to radiate sound in a frequency range for which it is not equipped.

Fortunately, psychoacoustic theory can help us resolve this problem. People can perceive pitch at frequencies that are not actually contained in the audio signal, either because of non-linearities in their cochlea ('difference tones') or a higher-level neural effect ('virtual pitch'). This effect can be exploited in a system that uses simple, non-linear processing, replacing very low frequencies by higher frequencies, which will still be perceived at the same pitch as the original. Philips' Ultra Bass system, applying this principle, uses non-linearities in a controlled manner, and restricted to only the lowest frequencies. The resulting advantages include high perceived sound level, reduced power consumption due to increased efficiency, and less disturbance to neighbours due to the fact that higher frequencies are better absorbed by the surrounding structures.

Directed sound

Ideally, sound should be directed to exactly where it is wanted – the ears of the listener. The I Limited Digital Sound Projector is a slim panel that connects directly to a DVD or CD player. By producing tight, focusable beams of sound, the Sound Projector beams the separate sound channels around the listener's room. Reflected off walls and other surfaces, these beams finally reach the listener from the left, right, front and rear.

Position-independent stereo

The ideal stereophonic sound reproduction system can exactly reconstruct the wavefront from a given sound scene over the area occupied by the listener's head. The use of two separate loudspeakers, however, imposes restrictions on the reconstruction of the correct acoustic field. Depending on the placement of the speakers relative to the listener, such a system is able to provide a well-defined image (mainly at low frequencies) for a listener who is centrally located between them.

Philips Research has conducted research into how to increase the 'sweet spot' area (the position with the best sound quality) in a stereophonic set-up, and this has resulted in a 'position-independent' stereo sound system. The basic idea is that the directivity pattern of a loudspeaker array should have a well-defined shape. Optimal digital filters are designed and applied to individual drivers of linear loudspeaker arrays to obtain a directivity pattern of a specific shape. This shape has to be adapted to the time/intensity trading mechanism of the human auditory system by means of psychoacoustic experiments within a wide listening area.

Improving the effect

In an Ambient Intelligence environment, we will require the quality of the audio produced to be high. A number of techniques can help to achieve this.

Incredible Surround Sound

Incredible Surround Sound is a convincing stereo base-widening system developed to improve sound reproduction in applications with closely packed loudspeakers.[4] A filter is derived, using a simple model that assumes ideal loudspeakers and an acoustically transparent subject's head. This system appears to be very practical to implement and tolerant towards head movements.

Multichannel audio

Since the advent of Digital Versatile Disk (DVD) and Super Audio CD (SACD), multichannel audio has become popular in consumer sound systems.[5] It is also possible to convert

NEBULA

AURORA

WWICE

EASY ACCESS
AND LISY

PHIL

CDS

MIME

Q1 PLUGGED

SMARTMIRROR

TOONS

two-channel stereo to multichannel sound reproduction using a three-dimensional representation ('space mapping'). Using Principal Component Analysis, we developed an algorithm that produces a vector indicating the direction of both the dominant signal and the remaining signal. These two signals are then used as basis signals in the encoding. This has two advantages compared to existing multichannel techniques. First, it reduces a problem associated with channel cross-talk, thereby improving sound localization. Second, better sound distribution to the surround channels is achieved by using a cross-correlation technique, while maintaining energy preservation. In this way, it remains backward- and forward-compatible with ordinary stereo. Furthermore, the preservation criterion ensures that all signals present in the two-channel transmitted signals are produced at a correct power level, so that the balance between the different signals in the recording is not disturbed.

On the move
In an Ambient Intelligence context, as users move around, portable or even wearable audio devices will increasingly be used, perhaps even communicating with other devices and systems to bring added functionality.

Background
The physical properties of the listener's head and outer ears modify sound as it travels from the source to the eardrums. This propagation of sound from multiple sound sources to each ear is described by what are known as Head-Related Transfer Functions (HRTFs). These vary from individual to individual, and particularly affect the localization of sound in the front back and vertical dimensions. If multichannel audio is filtered with the listener's own HRTFs prior to headphone sound reproduction, a very accurate emulation of the multichannel loudspeaker system is achieved.

3D headphones
Headphone virtualizers commercially available today are not optimized for the individual listener's head, and most listeners experience large localization errors. To solve this, Philips Research has introduced a system requiring a calibration procedure that listeners can easily carry out themselves. The system consists of ordinary headphones into which microphones have been mounted, and gives the user the same listening experience as a multichannel loudspeaker system.

In this system, the headphones are connected to a Digital Signal-Processing unit (DSP). During calibration, the DSP is connected to a multichannel loudspeaker set-up. A noise signal is played through each of the loudspeakers and registered by the microphones. The DSP then computes how the sounds should be processed prior to headphone reproduction, so that exactly the same sound is generated at the position of the microphones, i.e., close to the ears. When the calibration is complete, listeners can manually choose between loudspeaker or headphone sound reproduction, experiencing the same sound with either.

Wearable audio
Headphones are not entirely suitable in environments where users need to hear other sounds as well, or when their use is considered anti-social. Speakers worn on the body could instead provide directional sound without covering the ear. They must, however, be easy to wear and as inaudible to others as possible.

The MIT Soundbeam Neckset, a patented research prototype originally developed for hands-free telephony, has been modified for audio input/output from the wearable. It consists of two directional speakers mounted on the user's shoulders, and a directional microphone placed on the chest. A button on the Neckset activates or deactivates speech recognition. Spatialized audio is rendered in real-time and delivered to the Neckset.

Nomadic Radio: wearable audio messaging and awareness

Nomadic Radio was developed at MIT as a unified messaging system using spatialized audio and speech synthesis and recognition on a wearable audio platform. Communication and location awareness may also be added. Messages such as hourly news broadcasts, voice mail and e-mail are automatically downloaded to the device throughout the day. A combination of speech and button inputs is used to control the interface. Text-based messages such as e-mail, calendar reminders, weather forecasts and stock reports are delivered via synthesized speech. Users can select a category, such as news or e-mail, and browse messages sequentially, saving or deleting them from the server. The various elements would work together as a system, so that, for example, the user might be listening to a news summary, when the news fades and a voice message reminds the user of a meeting later that day. The user's location might also enable the system to provide relevant messages, so that, when in the vicinity of a particular room, the user may hear a voice message left by a colleague, or be reminded of a meeting elsewhere.

AMBIENT LIGHTING
Albert Comberg

Quality of life

Whereas in the past the main purpose of light generation was simply to improve visibility (and so, for the most part, to raise productivity), today we increasingly want light to contribute to our quality of life by adapting to our given situation. The possibilities and benefits are many. One example might be an airplane cabin in which the lighting simulates sunrise as we land after crossing several time zones, thereby relieving some of the symptoms of jetlag. At home, the lighting could adapt to create a suitable 'mood', depending on whether we are having friends over for dinner or settling in to watch television for the evening.

In the context of Ambient Intelligence, the key issue will be to develop lighting solutions that adapt to the needs and desires of their users. The many types of electric light sources available today, combined with tremendous progress in micro-electronics, make this increasingly possible.

Manipulating light

Two basic possibilities exist for light manipulation. Either the light source itself can be manipulated, or the path of the emitted light can be influenced, for instance, by using lenses, mirrors, gratings, electronic light shutters or paints. The two possibilities can of course be combined. Here we will restrict ourselves to the first: the light source, or lamp. The straightforward way to manipulate a lamp's light output is to manipulate its electrical power input. Both brightness and colour can be controlled in this way.

Colour

We already have gas discharge lamps that allow for relatively pronounced colour shifts in operation, for instance, by applying a DC bias to the electrodes, which leads to a de-mixing of the lamp's gas filling, thereby causing a colour change. An alternative method is the switching of a multitude of lamps exhibiting intrinsically different primary colours. Finally, pulse operation is another elegant solution, and is the preferred solution for light emitting diodes, or LEDS (see Chapter 2.5, Smart Materials).

Brightness

Brightness control is commonly achieved by dimming the lamp. Gas discharge lamps need a ballast (because of their specific current voltage characteristics, they cannot be connected directly to the mains). Depending on the type of lamp, the light can be dimmed by modulating the output of the ballast. The ballast and the lamp have to be matched to each other: an inadequate combination would result in unreliable operation or shorten the life of the lamp, or both.

Another type of gas discharge lamp called the dielectric barrier discharge lamp allows for extremely flat discharge vessels, and so can be used for 'light tiles'. Moreover, depending on the output modulation of their ballast, these lamps can generate either a homogeneous light emission or various fancy patterns of light. Yet another, still emerging technology for 'light tiles' consists of large-area light sources made of luminescent polymers, also known as polymer LEDs (see Chapter 2.5, Smart Materials).

Controlling light

The most simple control device for electric light sources is still a simple on/off switch. In the past, these switches had to be operated manually. Today, they can be activated automatically by electronic sensors and computers programmed to learn and to anticipate the user's habits and needs. The operation of the whole illuminating system can be controlled in the same way. This allows a range of other possibilities, including End-of-lamp-life-alert (i.e., a message is sent to the user when it is time to replace the lamp), and reduced electricity consumption.

Developments

In the past, light source development has mostly concentrated on increasing the efficiency of light solutions. With the advent of Ambient Intelligence, lamp development will increasingly focus on the lighting system as a whole. Consequently, the system features and compatibility of existing light sources will be further optimized. In addition, other new technologies, such as large area light sources or high brightness LEDs, will be developed, enabling new all-digital electrical driver concepts.

NEBULA

AURORA

WWICE

EASY ACCESS
AND LISY

PML

CDS

MIME

Q4 PLUGGED

SMARTMIRROR

TOONS

ICD+

NEW
NOMADS

1 J.M. Rabaey and M. Pedram (eds), *Low Power Design Methodologies* (Boston, Kluwer Academic Publishers, 1996), Chapter 11
2 C. Hentschel et al., 'Scalable Video Algorithms and Dynamic Resource Management for Consumer Terminals', *Proceedings of International Conference on Media Futures* (Florence, 8-9 May 2001), 193-196
3 E. Larsen and R.M. Aarts, 'Ultra Bass', *J. Audio Eng. Soc. 50 (3) (2002)*, 147-164
4 R.M. Aarts, 'Incredible Sound', *J. Audio Eng. Soc. 48(3) (2000)*, 181-189
5 R. Irwan and R.M. Aarts, 'Multichannel Sound', *Proc. 19th Int. Conf. AES* (June 2001), 139-143

2.3 AMBIENT VISION: INTERACTION, ADAPTATION AND MANAGEMENT

Radu Jasinschi, Jan Nesvadba

Ambient Intelligence provides people with an easy, natural and customized way to interact with the devices in their environment, all of which are linked to form an intelligent system. Visual information processing has a fundamental role to play in this. By being able to 'see', the system can not only facilitate interaction with users, but can also ensure that such interaction is highly adapted to their tastes and preferences, without any effort being required on their part. In addition, the system can make use of the visual information received from its various 'eyes' by coordinating and managing that information intelligently.

Interactivity

Interaction with people can be facilitated by visual means in various ways. At the most basic level, the system can detect the presence of someone, or perhaps several people, in the room. This will cause it to switch certain devices on. Similarly, when it discerns that the room is 'empty', the devices will be switched off. Actions can be triggered on the basis of a proximity metric, which will differentially switch devices on or off, or adjust their settings, depending on how close the user is to them. In this way, 'active' intelligence will effectively follow the person around the room, or adjust to provide optimum 'service' wherever the user is located.

Adaptability

By recognizing the user's appearance (facial or bodily characteristics) and identifying the user on that basis, the system will be able to perform customized actions that are of specific interest to the user. And by distinguishing facial expressions and other indicators of mood, the system will be able to establish whether the user finds those actions satisfactory or not. Since the system will also be able to recognize, interpret and process generic human visual commands, such as hand gestures, the user will be able to gesture in order to indicate any desired adjustments to settings (e.g., volume control).

Ambient Intelligence devices do not only use visual information to adapt to users. They also adapt to their surroundings, actively sensing or 'seeing' visual characteristics of the environment, and changing their set-ups accordingly. These environmental characteristics may include physical properties, such the layout of furniture, the position of walls, and so on, as well as ambient lighting conditions, or the position of a light source. By taking account of such factors, a video projector will be able to make sure that the image it projects on to a wall will always look perfect, regardless of the angle of the wall. By calculating the relative orientation of the direction of the central beam and the surface of the wall, it will be able to decide if the screen is on the slant relative to the beam, adjusting the dimensions of the projected image accordingly so that is rectangular rather than trapezoidal, for instance (current work on this specific problem is often referred to as 'automatic keystone correction').[1] The system will also be able to adapt to take account of the lighting in the room, automatically adjusting screen illumination.

Management

Ambient Intelligence systems deal with information within the system in a coordinated and goal-directed way. This applies equally to the visual content that is acquired, processed, stored and transmitted by and between devices (e.g., a video presentation during a business meeting, or multimedia information such as commercial TV shows or personal video). By incorporating management functions into ambient vision, we open up the possibility of people being able to interact with the content, and to indeed be immersed in it.

These three aspects of Ambient Intelligence vision – interactivity, adaptability and management – are coordinated by a set of high-level processes that take into account the physical characteristics of these devices, user profiles as they evolve over time (including preferences and tastes), and visual content information.

How the visual information is sensed and processed

The process whereby visual information in the environment is acquired and interpreted consists of four elements:

- Sensing
- Information processing
- Coding and representing
- Storing and transmitting

Sensing and information processing generally relate to the interactivity and adaptability aspects mentioned above. Coding and representation, and storage and transmission relate more to the management of visual information.

Sensing

Visual sensing works through video cameras on the devices or distributed in the environment. These cameras may be static or active (i.e., able to move to some degree).

Information processing

Visual information processing includes the processing of low-level, mid-level and high-level visual information (see over), the perception and interpretation of 3D images, and the recognition of the distinction between natural and synthetic visual information (e.g., between a real face and a digital animation of a face).

Coding and representation

The efficient coding and representation of video information is a prerequisite for successful storage and transmission of video content within an Ambient Intelligence system. Earlier standards (H.261, MPEG-1 and MPEG-2) concentrated on reducing low-level video signal redundancy using spatial coding techniques, and on reducing temporal redundancy by time coding blocks of motion. They also exploited the static and dynamic characteristics of the human visual system to reduce redundancy even further. More recent standards (e.g., MPEG-4 and MPEG-7) tackle the coding of mid-level visual information and the semantic indexing of low- and mid-level information, respectively (see over for the various levels of information).

Storage and transmission

The management of visual information (and more generally multimedia content) for distributed storage and transmission can already be implemented using advanced set-top boxes, DVD+RW, TV sets and a high-speed connection. Advanced set-top boxes that perform the smart segmentation, indexing and storage of this information are currently being researched in projects that include Video Scout[2] and AVIR.[3]

Low-level information

Low-level information includes the basic visual attributes of colour, motion, shape, texture and stereo depth. This is information that is contained purely in the image itself (the image plane) and each attribute is generally processed independently. Typical low-level features include the edges of images, contours (i.e., a coherent combination of edges, such as the boundaries of someone's facial features),[2] optical flow (the way image pixels are displaced between successive images in a video sequence), structural texture patterns (e.g., the patterns on a leopard's skin, or on grass)[3] or stochastic texture patterns (e.g., random patterns of dots).

Mid-level information

Mid-level information represents the visual information in regions, processing and clustering information about individual attributes or combining them, in a process known as 'visual information fusion'.[4] Examples of the sorts of regions represented in mid-level information include the colour of someone's face or the depth map of their body. In order to achieve this level of representation, it is necessary to decide which parts of a face, body or object have a 'similar' set of values for a given visual attribute (i.e., which bits 'go together'). Information from various attributes needs to be combined within the regions (e.g., optical flow and the contour of a human body).

High-level information

Finally, high-level information deals with the semantic visual information which results from combining various pieces of mid-level visual information. A typical example of high-level vision is the recognition of an object, such as recognizing a face as belonging to a particular person, or recognizing an object as a chair.[5]

Three dimensions

When we see a scene in three dimensions, we are able to deduce a great deal more information from the scene than when we view it in two dimensions.[6] It will therefore be desirable for our Ambient Intelligence system to be able to 'see' in 3D. To do this, it has to extract 3D information from 2D images, in a process known as 'visual reconstruction'.[7] This process is not based solely upon 2D visual data, but also on certain assumptions about the world. For example, to compute the depth (i.e., distance away) of points on a 3D object, we have to use at least two stereo cameras that are horizontally aligned. Each of these stereo cameras generates a separate 2D image of a different viewpoint of the 3D scene. If we assume that the cameras taking these images are at the same height from the ground, we can assume that the corresponding points on the same line in each image refer to the same point on the 3D object, and that the depth value computed on this basis is directly proportional to the actual distance of the object from the cameras. These assumptions, used in the visual reconstruction process, are not based on the particular scene being imaged but on prior information about the world.

Natural vs. synthetic visual information

Natural visual information is 'as seen in the real world', while synthetic information is generated via computer graphics. The latter is increasingly common in TV programmes, films and games; and synthetic and natural information are in fact frequently combined in TV programmes and films. Since synthetic visual information is much easier and more compact to process, store and transmit than natural visual information, it will be possible to provide Ambient Intelligence systems with attractive visual interfaces that mimic human behaviour and emotion.

Examples

Examples of visual information processing that are relevant to vision within an Ambient Intelligence context include:

- Face and body recognition, including facial expression recognition, and hand/body gesture recognition[8]
- Geometric modelling of 3D objects, such as human head/body 3D meshes modelling,[9] and the use of projective geometry for representing planar surfaces[10]
- Dynamic tracking of points or objects in 3D scenes,[11] with the use (if necessary) of articulated models to represent partially rigidly moving objects, such as human hands or legs[12]
- Layered mosaics and surfaces that can be used in application scenarios that include immersive environments combining natural and synthetic visual information[13]
- Dynamic depth computation of moving objects in 3D space via multiple views, where each view is obtained by a single CCD camera[14]
- Bio-informatics,[15] such as identifying a person by their fingerprints or iris

By combining all these aspects of visual information – sensing, processing, coding and representation, storage and transmission – we are able to build systems that enable ambient vision.

Four projects

The principles and tools described above are currently being applied in a number of projects. Four of the most significant of those that deal with the 'interactive' aspect of Ambient Intelligence vision are Virtualized Reality,[16] Smart Rooms,[17] DigitEyes[18] and EyesInTheSky.

Virtualized Reality

The aim of Virtualized Reality, a project being carried out at Carnegie Mellon University, is to generate full 3D scene information by combining the output of a given number of cameras regularly distributed over the nodes of a hemispherical dome. These cameras are synchronized to a common signal, and they compute a stereo depth map. Besides the cameras, the system consists of digitizers, video switches, real-time (video-rate) stereo machines and graphics machines. The graphics machines synthesize different views of the 3D scene.

Smart Rooms

MIT's Smart Rooms project aims to achieve real-time generation of interactive virtual spaces (graphics). The output of stereo cameras processing real-time video data is mapped onto simple graphics (blob) models that interact with the user; the user and/or other (virtual) objects are also described in terms of blob models. This system has an interface that requires no head-mounted displays, data gloves, or the like.

DigitEyes

DigitEyes is a complete system for tracking hand movements. It uses a full kinematical model of the hand, using visual data provided by a static camera. Each joint is tracked by image registration. A template defined by an image of each finger part is used to match the projection of the corresponding real finger part. This is achieved by minimizing a residual error measure between successive frames. A graphical interface of a 3D mouse is used to generate a synthetic model of the hand as it is being tracked. All this is realized in real-time.

EyesInTheSky

Philips Research's EyesInTheSky project is a system that enables the automatic detection, classification and tracking of intruders or moving persons in a secure facility equipped with a number of CCTV cameras, plus the storage and retrieval of security video information. The project has three main components:

- ViewSpace, a library that enriches the CSS security system's graphical user interface with Pick & Click: the operator clicks on a location on the map and the nearest PTZ (Pan-Tilt-Zoom) camera is turned to view that location
- Briarcliff Intruder Tracking Engine (BITE), which allows an operator to select a target and direct a PTZ camera to automatically follow that target
- Video Content Analysis (VCA), which automatically determines which individuals and events appear in a live video stream. It will annotate and index the security video as it is stored, and allow retrieval based on event queries. It will also trigger an alarm when one of a designated set of events occurs.

Integration of vision with audio

We have been considering vision here, but we should not forget that, in human beings, hearing and vision are normally integrated to form a coherent perception of a scene. In automatic sensing, the traditional approach has been to analyze separately the visual and auditory input provided by sensors or sources of information, largely due to the different fields of expertise required. However, as comprehensive as an exclusively visual or exclusively auditory system may be, it can only cover a subset of the environment. The information on which high-level meaningful descriptions are based is therefore inevitably to some degree impoverished. However, an intellectual and intelligent semantic description of the environment cannot be drawn from isolated instances from isolated perceptual domains, but only from consideration of the time-spatial correlation between instances from various domains. The fact that an Ambient Intelligence system can combine information from various domains in this way is one of its great strengths.

Content immersion

Finally, we conclude by considering content immersion. Immersive environments aim to replicate the experience of 'being there' in a real or synthetic 3D world by allowing one or more users to interact with this environment and possibly with other users as well. This is achieved by combining visual, audio and tactile information. The visual information, which can be either natural, synthetic, or a combination of both, seeks to replicate 3D environments. The user (wearing interactive goggles) can see and navigate within this 3D space. In the case of natural visual information, planar, circular or cylindrical panoramas are used to represent the 'static' part of a scene, while foreground objects are superimposed on this background, and can thus move independently of it. In the case of synthetic visual information, computer graphics are used and combined with VRML (Virtual Reality Modelling Language). Finally, the natural and synthetic information is combined using texture mapping of natural and synthetic material in VRML. Such environments offer the exciting prospects of, for example, surgeons being able effectively to be present in an operating theatre far away, scattered families and friends getting together and interacting, though miles apart, and people being able to take an active part in remote 'live' entertainment experiences. Could it be that the 'holodack' of Starship Enterprise (or at least some early precursor) is closer to reality than many people think?

1   R. Sukthankar, R.G. Stockton and M.D Mullin, 'Smarter Presentations: Exploring Homography in Camera Projector System',
    Proc. of IEEE ICCV 2001 (2001)
2   R.S. Jasinschi et al., 'An Application and System for the Integration of Multimedia Information in Personal TV Applications', *Proc. of IEEE
    ICASSP 2001* (Salt Lake City, 2001)
3   M. Barbieri et al., 'A Personal TV Retriever with storage and Retrieval Capabilities', *Proc. Workshop on Personalization on Future TV (8th
    Conference on User Modeling, UM2001)* (Sonthofen, 13-17 July 2001)
4   I. Essa, *Analysis, Interpretation, and Synthesis of Facial Expressions* (PhD thesis, MIT Media Laboratory, 1995)
5   H. Voorhees, *Finding Texture Boundaries in Images*, M.I.T. A.I. Laboratory Technical Report, AITR-968, 1987
6   J. Clark and A. Yuille, *Data Fusion for Sensory Information Processing Systems* (Boston, Kluwer Academic Publishers, 1990)
7   S. Ullman, *High-Level Vision: Object Recognition and Visual Cognition* (Cambridge MA, MIT Press, 1996)
8   D. Marr, *Vision: A Computational Investigation into the Human Representation and Processing of Visual Information* (San Francisco,
    W H Freeman & Co., 1983); B.P.K. Horn, *Robot Vision* (Cambridge MA, MIT Press, 1986)
9   O. Faugeras, *Three-Dimensional Computer Vision* (Cambridge MA, MIT Press, 1993)
10 J. Rehg, *Visual Analysis of High DOF Articulated Objects with Application to Hand Tracking* (PhD thesis, Carnegie Mellon University, 1995); K.
    Rohr, 'Towards Model-Based Recognition of Human Movements in Image Sequences', *CVGIP: Image Understanding*, 59(1), 94, 115 (1994)
11 E. Puppo, 'Variable Resolutions Triangulation', *Computational Geometry*, Vol.11, No. 3-4 (1998), 219-238
12 Faugeras
13 M. Isard and A. Blake, 'CONDENSATION – Conditional Density Propagation for Visual Tracking', *Int. J. Computer Vision*, Vol. 29, No.1, 5,
    28 (1998)
14 D. Metaxas, *Physics-Based Deformable Models Applications to Computer Vision, Graphics and Medical Imaging* (Boston, Kluwer Academic
    Publishers, 1996)
15 J.Y.A. Wang and E.H. Adelson, 'Representing Moving Images with Layers', *IEEE Transactions on Image Processing Special Issue: Image
    Sequence Compression*, Vol. 3, No. 5, 625, 638 (1994); R.S. Jasinschi and J.M.F. Moura, 'Nonlinear Video Editing by Generative Video',
    Proceedings of IEEE ICASSP (1996)
16 T. Kanade, P.J. Narayanan and P. Rander, 'Virtualized Reality: Constructing Virtual Worlds from Real Scenes', *IEEE Trans. On Multimedia*,
    Vol. 4, No. 1, 34, 47 (1997)
17 A.K. Jain, R. Bolle and S. Pankanti (eds), *Biometrics: Personal Identification in Networked Society* (Kluwer Academic Publishers, 1999)
18 T. Kanade, P.J. Narayanan and P. Rander, 'Virtualized Reality: Constructing Virtual Worlds from Real Scenes', *IEEE Trans. On Multimedia*,
    Vol. 4, No. 1, 34, 47 (1997)
19 http://vismod.www.media.mit.edu
20 J. Rehg, 'Visual Analysis of High DOF Articulated Objects with Application to Hand Tracking', (PhD thesis, Carnegie Mellon University,
    Technical Report Computer Science Department CMU-CS-95-138, 1995)

2.4 USER-SYSTEM INTERACTION BASED ON SPOKEN DIALOGUES

René Collier, Eric Thelen

Part of the Ambient Intelligence scenario is an environment in which technology is invisible to people, yet so powerful that it can support highly intelligent applications. If technology is no longer tangibly present, our interaction with it will often have to be hands-free. In that case, the use of natural language, especially speech, will be an attractive solution. Additionally, because we perceive many applications to be smart, we will be tempted to communicate with them using speech. To be able to implement realistic speech dialogue, we need to understand two major aspects of natural language interaction – speech recognition and speech synthesis – and how they can be combined to create dialogues between systems and their users.

The architecture of a Spoken Dialogue System

An interactive dialogue system consists of a number of components. The system starts by receiving a speech signal from the user as input, and ends by producing speech output that expresses the system's response to the user's input. Figure I shows the processing steps involved in creating a dialogue between user and system that users find satisfying.

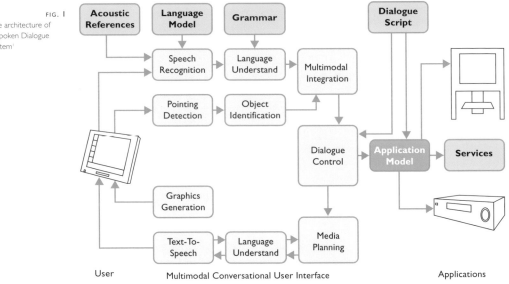

FIG. I
The architecture of a Spoken Dialogue System[1]

First, the system records and digitizes the input, i.e. (the speech signal). There are various techniques for making sure this is received as clearly as possible, such as focusing several microphones on the position of the speaker ('beam-forming') or eliminating extraneous noise by using acoustic echo-filtering techniques. The features required for speech recognition are then extracted from this signal and fed into a Speech Recognition module for decoding. The significance of the features is found by comparing them to three sources of knowledge: an inventory of acoustic reference models of speech sounds (Reference Models), a list of words that the system can recognize (Lexicon) and information about the likelihood of particular word sequences occurring in a given context (Language Model). The output of the Speech Recognition module is a set of hypotheses as to the correct transcription of the spoken utterance. These hypotheses form the input to the Language Understanding module, which interprets the utterance on the basis of language rules (Grammar), specifically compiled for the application in question. At various points during processing, the system takes into account what it knows it can do (System Knowledge) and what the system knows about the user (User Model). The core element in the system, the Dialogue Manager, which has overall control of the interaction, now takes all the information gathered about the input utterance, interfaces with the application and then initiates the system's response. Depending on the current status of the interaction, this response may be a question (to get more information from the user) or a confirmation (giving the user positive feedback).

From this point on, the output speech is prepared, in line with any rules on what would be appropriate (Output Planning), put into a relevant context, so as to make it easier for the user to understand (Context Generation), put into words, following grammatical rules (Language Generation), and finally presented to the user through a text-to-speech (speech synthesis) engine.

Then it is the user's turn to process this information (by means of his own 'dialogue manager'), and to initiate the next turn in the user-system interaction by replying.

Problems posed by variability and fluency

Common problems in recognition and synthesis arise from the fact that the physical speech sounds that we produce and perceive are far more variable than our phonetic intuition makes us believe. Every language has a finite set of basic sound units, or phonemes (about forty), but each phoneme is realized in a highly context-sensitive way. For instance, the phoneme /k/ is quite different in 'keep', 'cool' and 'car', and different again in 'beak', 'book' and 'back'. In automatic speech recognition, these six different [k]-like sounds have to be traced back to the same underlying phoneme /k/, which in speech synthesis has to be turned automatically into six different speech sounds, depending on context. An additional problem is posed by the fact that speech (unlike writing) leaves no pauses between words, let alone between sounds.

Speech recognition

Initial attempts at automatic speech recognition in the 1950s were limited to differentiating numbers spoken in isolation. Since then, speech recognition technology has made considerable advances, in part due to the availability of greater processing power and memory, but especially to improved algorithms and methods of speech analysis.[2]

As speech recognition has been applied in increasingly complex contexts, the number of words included in recognition vocabularies has necessarily increased significantly. Early systems were trained to recognize whole words, generating statistical models for them. However, this method becomes less practical when large vocabularies are involved. For that reason, it was decided to construct acoustic models of words from smaller acoustic units – the 'phonemes' mentioned above. Then, given an inventory of phonemes in the language in question, adding a new word to the recognition vocabulary is simply a question of introducing the word, along with its pronunciation expressed as a sequence of phonemes. Alternative phoneme sequences (i.e., pronunciation variants) can be added for words that have varying pronunciations (e.g., in different dialects).

Vocabularies are usually defined in relation to a particular task or application. However, some contexts are so general (e.g., dictating e-mails about any topic), or so changeable (e.g., interactions relating to TV programming information) that a more complex approach is required.

HOMELAB

EASY ACCESS
AND LISY

SMARTMIRROR

CONNECTED
PLANET

SPICE

In the Ambient Intelligence home, speech recognition will migrate into more 'real-life' situations like these, and more attention is consequently being paid to the robustness of speech recognition systems. Breadth of vocabulary is only one problem. These systems will also have to be able to cope with extraneous noise affecting the input signal, recognize the speech of a wide range of speakers (even those with a strong accent), be able to allow for spontaneous speech (with hesitations, pauses, repetitions, irrelevant remarks, etc.), and they will also be subject to limitations of computing power and memory (e.g., in miniaturized applications).

Recognizing variation

Speech is a communication medium that allows an enormous amount of flexibility (prosody, emotion, etc.) and variability (speaker, usage scenario, etc.). Most speech recognition systems today rely on statistical models, very often based on the Hidden Markov Model (HMM) concept.[3] The models are trained using data that is representative of the specific task to be performed. To allow for variation, the training data covers as much of the variation expected in the real-life situation as possible. In addition, the system can keep learning at any time and adapt by continuously updating its models on the basis of what it encounters.

Speech synthesis – formant synthesis

The goal of speech synthesis (or automatic speech generation) is to mimic as closely as possible the production of human speech.[4] Early attempts used mechanical means to achieve this, but from the 1950s onwards, electronic solutions became dominant. As noted above, the phonemes of a given language vary greatly, depending on the context in which they occur. This variation is largely predictable, so that in principle it is possible to describe it by means of a (relatively large) set of speech production rules. These rules can be used to drive a hardware or software speech synthesizer, which contains signal-generating components equivalent to the workings of the speech organs. The resulting sound patterns may then approximate natural speech. This approach is known as 'formant synthesis' (formants are regions of high spectral energy; they appear as dark horizontal bars in the lower parts of Figure 2 (a, b, c).). However, implementing this approach in a working system that can deliver very high-quality synthetic speech has turned out to be far more difficult than anticipated. Even the best systems are deemed unsatisfactory for commercial applications.

Speech synthesis – diphone synthesis

The physical properties of speech sounds change constantly, depending on their context, as each sound merges with the sound preceding it and the sound following it. This process of mutual adaptation between adjacent sounds is called 'co-articulation'. Getting the rules of co-articulation right is the most difficult task in modelling the variability in speech production. The idea therefore arose that, rather than continually trying to improve the accuracy of this modelling, it might be possible to actually record all the intricate transitions between sounds and then string these tiny fractions of natural speech together into words and sentences. This led to what is known as 'diphone synthesis'.[5] A diphone extends roughly from the second half of one sound into the first half of the next, thus capturing the essence of the transition. Since, in principle, every phoneme in a given language can be followed by every other phoneme in that language, the number of diphones needed is approximately the square of the number of phonemes, which amounts to some 1,600 for English. When this approach was first tried, it turned out to deliver fairly good speech quality with little effort and without the need to understand much of the complex process of speech production.

Subsequent efforts were focused on refining this basic way of working, for instance, by allowing for larger units than diphones (triphones, demi-syllables). Since diphones are very

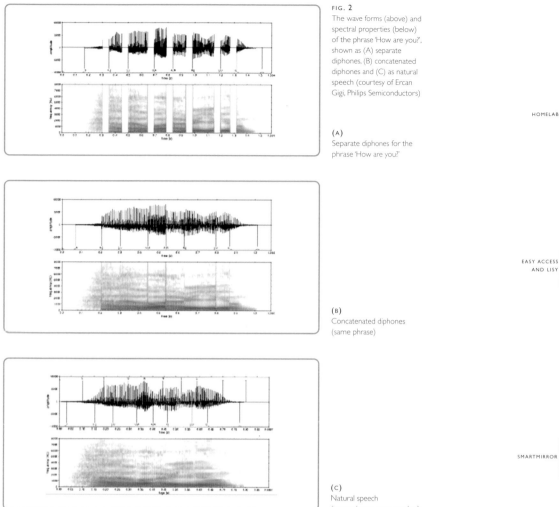

FIG. 2
The wave forms (above) and
spectral properties (below)
of the phrase 'How are you?',
shown as (A) separate
diphones, (B) concatenated
diphones and (C) as natural
speech (courtesy of Ercan
Gigi, Philips Semiconductors)

(A)
Separate diphones for the
phrase 'How are you?'

(B)
Concatenated diphones
(same phrase)

(C)
Natural speech
(same phrase, same speaker)

short, there are dozens of them in an utterance of average length, and this may give rise to many
audible discontinuities at the boundaries between diphones. To remedy this, attempts have
been made to maximize the size of the speech units to be concatenated. This approach (called
'unit selection') requires a very large database of natural speech and fast search algorithms.

Synthesizing natural prosody
Whatever the form of synthesis chosen, the sequence of speech sounds needs further adaptation
in order to give an utterance a natural course of pitch and the right accentuation.[6] The rules
of prosody that take care of this form a separate module in the system. It was hoped that
unit selection would make these prosodic adaptations superfluous, but it has not yet been
convincingly demonstrated that this is the case.

Text-to-speech conversion
Speech synthesis as described so far is a form of 'sound generation', a way of producing an
acoustic signal with speech-like properties. However, to be useful, this technology needs to be
able to work from text input, so that the system not only mimics sound production but also

the complete process of reading a text aloud. Automatic Text-To-Speech conversion (TTS) of this type requires additional knowledge of the relationship between spelling and speech (no trivial matter in languages with complex spelling systems, such as English). A complete TTS system will therefore require a pronunciation dictionary and some insight into the syntax and semantics of the sentence. However, in a spoken dialogue system, the sentences to be produced are generated by the system itself, so that their linguistic properties are known. This procedure is called 'concept-to-speech conversion'.[7]

Application scenarios

In our vision of Ambient Intelligence, the user interfaces will allow intuitive, efficient and enjoyable interaction with intelligent systems. But when do people consider a system to be intelligent? This is particularly relevant if we want to integrate the recognition of single utterances into an interactive dialogue system. Users experience a system as intelligent not only if it accepts natural language input rather than just specific command words, but also if it allows the user to take the initiative in the interaction instead of simply prompting the user to respond to specific questions. In addition, systems are seen as intelligent if they adapt themselves to the user's interests and interaction preferences, working cooperatively with them to help them accomplish specific goals, and finally, if they also make use of additional sources of knowledge to meet the needs of the user. Such considerations will need to be taken into account in any complete interactive dialogue system.

If speech is to be an interaction modality, then this also implies that users will not need to worry about the location of the microphone(s) or about how to activate the recognition system. The intelligent environment will be listening continuously and be able to distinguish between remarks that are part of a normal conversation and remarks addressed to the system as part of a desired interaction. Ideally, all Ambient Intelligence applications would be available at any time through the same interface, which would mediate between what the user wants and the functionality provided by all the applications. The use of speech as an interaction modality with any individual application would need to provide some specific user benefit over the use of a non-speech interaction modality.

In conclusion, let us look at three examples of specific applications making use of a spoken interaction:

- Via consumer electronics devices, people today have access to a vast amount of audio/video content. They usually know what they want and can describe it in their own words. But getting what they want using the user interface of the device or service in question is often a problem. Programming the VCR is a popular example of this: setting the timer takes a while, since date, time and channel information have to be entered sequentially. Advanced devices already offer access to Electronic Programming Guides (EPGs), which enable people to select the shows they want to record. But to find the desired show, they have to browse through the information offered by the EPG, which also takes time, since only so much information can be displayed on the screen at any one time. In that case, a speech user interface would enable intuitive and direct access to the desired content. The VCR could be programmed by simply telling it what should be recorded. 'I'd like to record the James Bond movie tonight' or 'Record the movie with Julia Roberts on Channel 2'. In some cases, after evaluating the situation through its dialogue manager, the system might respond with a question in order to clarify possible alternatives. Thus, in the examples above, the system might simply respond with 'OK', or it might ask, 'There are two James Bond movies tonight: *Moonraker* and *Goldfinger*. Which one would you like to record?' or 'There is no movie with Julia Roberts on Channel 2, but *My Best Friend's Wedding*, starring Julia Roberts, is on Channel 5. Would you like to record that instead?'

- Whether it is a question of holiday pictures or MP3 files, users want to archive their personal content, and they want to be able to access the stored content later on, quickly and conveniently, without having to navigate through long lists of items or through hierarchies of archive folders. If speech were used as an interaction modality, an acoustic signature (e.g., a short spoken description) could be attached to each item as it is stored. Retrieval would then be possible by means of spoken queries. For example, a potential signature for a holiday picture might be 'Aunt Helen at Lake Tahoe'. People could then retrieve this picture from the archive by instructing the system to 'Show me all the pictures of Aunt Helen' or 'Show me the pictures I took at Lake Tahoe'.

- Imagine a proactive personal electronic assistant (or companion) with which users communicate using speech interaction. Your assistant knows you and your preferences, your schedule and your personal interests. It suggests to you what to do and discusses potential consequences with you. It learns from the feedback you give it and adapts to your preferred style of interacting.

Assistant:	*Your training session at the gym starts in 30 minutes. You need to leave in ten minutes or you'll be late.*
You:	*OK. Anything else before I go?*
Assistant:	*There's a movie with Gwyneth Paltrow on TV tonight: do you want to record it?*
You:	*Yes, please.*
Assistant:	*There's hardly any milk in the fridge: you won't have enough for breakfast tomorrow. If you leave now, you'll have time to call in at the supermarket before you go to the gym.*
You:	*OK, I'm on my way…*

Vision and outlook

The success of spoken dialogues in the man-machine interface will depend not only on the quality of the various technological components that make up the total system, but also on the naturalness of the dialogue itself. In human conversation, information exchanges rely on a mix of modalities, of which speech is only one, alongside facial expression, gestures and other channels of communication. All of these will need to be integrated seamlessly. Another determinant of future success will lie in the acceptability of speech as a means of interacting with an intelligent environment. Psychological and social barriers to the 'public' use of this technology are still largely unknown.

1 See, e.g., B. Souvignier, A. Kellner, B. Rueber, H. Schramm and F. Seide, 'The Thoughtful Elephant: Strategies for Spoken Dialog Systems', *IEEE Transactions on Speech and Audio Processing*, 8(1) (January 2000), 51-62,

2 See, e.g., L. Rabiner and B. Juang, *Fundamentals of Speech Recognition* (Prentice Hall, Englewood Cliffs 1993); V. Steinbiss, H. Ney, X. Aubert, S. Besling, C. Dugast, U. Essen, D. Geller, R. Haeb-Umbach, R. Kneser, G. Meier, M. Oerder and B. Tran, 'The Philips Research System for Continuous-Speech Dictation' *Philips Journal of Research*, Volume 49(4) (Eindhoven 1995), 317-352

3 F. Jelinek, *Statistical Methods for Speech Recognition* (Cambridge MA, MIT Press, 1997)

4 T. Dutoit, *An Introduction to Speech Synthesis* (Dordrecht, Kluwer Academic Press, 1997)

5 J. van Santen, R. Sproat, J. Olive and J. Hirschberg (eds), *Progress in Speech Synthesis* (New York, Springer-Verlag, 1997)

6 E. Keller, G. Bailly, A. Moneghan, J. Terken and M. Huckvale (eds), *Improvements in Speech Synthesis* (Chichester, John Wiley, 2002)

7 R. Collier and J. Landsbergen, 'Language and Speech Generation', *Philips Journal of Research*, Volume 49/4 (Eindhoven, December 1995), 419-437,

HOMELAB

EASY ACCESS
AND LISY

SMARTMIRROR

CONNECTED
PLANET

SPICE

2.5 SMART MATERIALS

Stefan P. Grabowski, Hans Nikol

New materials or material properties are rapidly being applied in devices to meet increasingly ambitious requirements such as miniaturization, cost or power efficiency. Materials development will therefore play a key role in advancing the practical implementation of Ambient Intelligence. Below, to illustrate the progress being made, we look at just three of many different areas in which new materials are likely to play a significant role.

Lighting

Lighting will play an important role in Ambient Intelligence, both because light is key to providing a personalized 'ambience' and because new lighting concepts may enable new types of display. Two related developments are of particular interest here: inorganic light-emitting diodes, and organic light-emitting diodes, consisting of light-emitting polymers or evaporated small molecules.

Inorganic light-emitting diodes

A paradigm shift, enabled by new materials, is about to take place in the field of lighting.[1] Light-emitting diodes (LEDs) emit light through the movement of electrons in a semiconductive material when a current is passed through it. When an electron recombines with a positive charge, it emits a quantum of electromagnetic energy in the form of a photon of light. The colour of the light depends on the semiconductor material used. Light-emitting diodes, in allowing the direct, controlled conversion of electrical power into photons, bring us close to the 'final frontier' of light generation.

Light-emitting diodes also have a number of advantages over conventional incandescent lamps. They last much longer, as they don't have a filament that burns out. They are also much more efficient, because, unlike conventional bulbs, they generate relatively little heat, so that more of the electricity used goes to generating light, and less energy is required for the same amount of light. And they allow light of all colours of unsurpassed quality to be mixed and controlled in time and space. It is therefore not surprising that lighting architects, designers and artists are increasingly taking advantage of these digital, low-voltage and easily programmable light sources.

The present status enjoyed by LEDs is the result of a remarkable development in the past ten years. Red LEDs of good quality (using gallium arsenide phosphide as the semiconductor material) and (poorer) green LEDs had existed for some time, being widely used as 'pilot lights' in many consumer electronic and electrical goods to indicate that the power is on. But scientists were anxious to produce really good bright blue and green LEDs as well, so that, with the three primary colours and white light, the full spectrum of colours could be produced. It was also highly desirable because blue light has the shortest wavelength and a blue laser diode (which involves the same basic principle) would make it possible to store more data on a CD or DVD and make laser printers sharper. This was proving elusive, however, because of the instability and difficulty of processing of appropriate semiconductors to produce light of the right frequencies. Then, in the early 1990s, a Japanese engineer, Shuji Nakamura, managed to produce blue LEDs using as the semiconductor a material – gallium nitride (GaN) – that had earlier been abandoned by generations of LED engineers as being too difficult.[2] A layer of this material, only a few nanometres thick, processed on a sapphire substrate in a quality only enabled by the most advanced deposition tools, is sandwiched between two electrodes. When a charge of a few volts is passed through it, blue light is emitted. Researchers expect that within a few years its internal yield will approach 100%, which is as good as the best red LEDs.

The next step is to partially transform some of this blue light into red and green with the help of luminescent materials (phosphors). The mixture will then result in white light. The size of the chip on which the semiconductor and other materials are deposited in an LED is typically only 1mm^2, which means that those materials will need to be controlled to the nearest few nanometres. This is because even the tiniest deviations will be immediately visible to the human eye, which is extremely sensitive to colours. However, this process is manageable, since it is possible to control the size of the powder grains deposited on the chip. The use of phosphor materials related to some of the hardest materials known to science (nitrides), or use of sophisticated ultra-thin coatings on phosphor grains (Fig. 1), will make it possible to keep light conversion at an even quality with a surface temperature on the chip of up to several hundred degrees Celsius, which is necessary to enable high driving conditions. That will enable a single LED to be powered by a few Watts, making LEDs suitable for general (i.e., ambient) lighting.

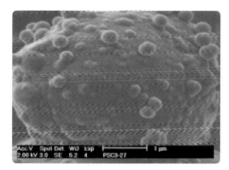

FIG. 1
A grain of phosphor with 'moth-eye' coating to enhance light output and stability: typically, some 10,000 of these grains are deposited on an LED chip

Source: T. Jüstel, P.J. Schmidt (Philips Research)

The tiny size of such inorganic LEDs is very relevant for Ambient Intelligence. The light outputs per unit of these point sources has increased dramatically over the past five years. Single LEDs with up to 10W have been achieved recently, which means that only two or three LEDs are now needed to replace one halogen lamp, and the limit has not yet been reached.

Organic LEDs

Equally exciting, but further away, will be the extension of solid-state lighting to large surface areas. The inorganic LEDs just described are chip-based, and since the size of the chip determines the price, they are currently inappropriate for large areas. However, a completely different class of materials – semiconducting organic molecules or polymer chains – also emit light when a low voltage is passed through them. What makes these materials particularly interesting is that they will do this when deposited on virtually any sort of substrate, including glass, plastic or even plastic foil.

Polymer LEDs were first demonstrated 12 years ago, and then had an efficiency of 0.02%. Today, their efficiency has been increased by almost three orders of magnitude, and organic LEDs – also known as electroluminescent lighting (or EL) – are already being used in displays in commercial products. It was long believed that 25% internal efficiency would be the limit for this class of materials, due to the physical boundaries of the optical transition. However, a few years ago, it was shown that by adding certain dopants (i.e., small, controlled, amounts of other molecules), some involving transition metals such as iridium, this level of efficiency can be increased significantly.

Light-emitting polymers need to be ultra-pure, a quality that can be checked with advanced analytical methods (e.g., nuclear magnetic resonance). Layers can be deposited using ink-jetting methods (although the robust printing process required for the commercial production of light-emitting polymers is quite unlike the commercial inkjet printers used as a computer peripheral). Alternatively, organic molecules can be evaporated or transported to the substrate by means of what is known as an organic vapour phase deposition. As organic materials are much more sensitive to ambient conditions (air, water) than the materials used in inorganic LEDs, their application poses a real challenge. However, remarkable progress has been achieved in the past few years using sophisticated packaging methods. Today, organic LEDs can exhibit lifetimes of several tens of thousands of hours.

FIG. 2
A flexible display based on light-emitting polymer. Electroluminescent foils can be produced in a similar way

Wallpaper lighting

Transparent and flexible displays using organic LEDs have also been demonstrated (see Fig. 2). These materials will ultimately enable whole walls to be evenly illuminated with light tiles or lighting foils, in effect creating wallpaper lighting.

Smart windows

Transparent organic LEDs will also be able to cover whole windows, allowing for an even level of lighting, both day and night. This development will be facilitated by a recent discovery. In reverse bias, organic LEDs can act as solar cells. In a clever approach, this feature has been used to construct LED devices with a built-in photosensor. When light shines on the LED, photocurrent is generated that can be used for signal processing (e.g., for controlling the light level). This combination shows how materials can be designed in an intelligent way to integrate several functions. It is the concurrent engineering of materials and processing methods that makes this possible.

Nanotechnology

Miniaturization is crucial to Ambient Intelligence, since the technologies involved will need to be non-intrusive and capable of being embedded in the environment. With feature size further decreasing, we shall soon be entering the realm of nanotechnology. Nanotechnology describes the science of particles that have at least one dimension below approximately 100 nanometres (nm). It has already had considerable impact on modern technology and is likely to revolutionize materials science. Such small particles exhibit completely new and exciting size-dependent properties. Materials scientists, physicists, chemists and engineers alike are working intensively to find ways of utilizing these properties.

Smart windscreens

Smart windscreens with nanoparticle films can change colour depending on how bright the daylight is. The windscreens are covered with a film of nanometre-sized particles of titanium dioxide and nickel hydroxide. In sunny weather, electrons are transferred from nickel hydroxide towards titanium dioxide, which results in a darkening. When the sun is clouded, a reverse reaction occurs and the windscreen becomes transparent again.

Self-assembling structures

These 'dwarves' are also beginning to play a significant role in electronics. Faster computers require smaller features: it is anticipated that by about 2010, the feature size in computer chips will be about 10nm. Using current semiconductor technology (which uses lithography and etching processes almost exclusively), it will become increasingly difficult and costly to reduce feature sizes still further using this top-down approach. Consequently, research is being carried out into bottom-up approaches, whereby nanomaterial building blocks are used to assemble larger functional structures. These building blocks are nanocrystals, small molecules, nanowires and carbon nanotubes (carbon nanotubes are rolled-up layers of graphene which have a diameter in the nanometre range and a length of up to several micrometres. In contrast to nanowires, which have the same shape but are crystalline semiconductors or metals, carbon nanotubes are hollow).

The bottom-up approach has several advantages. The building blocks are small, new functionalities arise due to quantum effects, and device properties can to a large extent be tailored. For example, the emission colour of semiconductor nanocrystals can simply be changed by varying their size. Furthermore, the building blocks can be made to self-assemble into larger structures. By functionalizing the particle or substrate surface, ordered arrays and deposition on selected areas can be achieved without the need for manipulation at the nanometre level. Examples are shown in Figures 3 and 4.

FIG. 3
A 'forest' of self-assembled carbon nanotubes

Source: P.K. Bachmann, V. van Elsbergen,
C. McGrath, G. Zhong, G. Gärtner, M. Caron
and D.U. Wiechert (Philips Research)

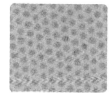

FIG. 4A
A self-assembled array of cadmium selenide nanocrystals

Source: H. Weller (University of Hamburg)

FIG. 4B
A cross-array of indium phosphide nanowires (length of scale bar = 2 mm)

Source: Y. Huang, X. Duan, Q. Wei and
C.M. Lieber, 'Directed assembly of one-
dimensional nanostructures into functional
networks', Science, 291 (2001), 630

Mini-memories

Several nanoelectronic devices have already been demonstrated, some of which have excellent properties. Single-electron transistors (SETs), for instance, can be used for memory applications.[3] They work by storing only a single electron per bit. Compared to conventional non-volatile FLASH memory or DRAM, where 10^3 and 10^5 electrons are needed to write a bit, respectively, this means an immense reduction in current flow and thus power consumption. SETs are non-volatile, but allow many more read/write cycles than FLASH memories at a higher storage density.

Molecular electronics

The device building blocks in molecular electronics are molecules, and device properties can be tuned by modifying the molecules. Using this concept, electronic switches and molecular random access memories with bit-retention times exceeding 15 minutes have been demonstrated.[4]

Most promising candidates

However, the most promising candidates for nanoelectronic devices at present seem to be nanowires and carbon nanotubes. The superb field-emission properties of carbon nanotubes are especially interesting, and have led to the successful demonstration of field-emission displays (Samsung Electronics, for instance, recently demonstrated a prototype of a 32" full-colour field-emission display).

Both carbon nanotubes and nanowires have the advantage of having one dimension in the micrometre range, which makes it easier to electrically contact these tiny structures. Nanowires can be made from various sorts of material, they can be doped to achieve different electrical properties, and junctions to different materials can be prepared, even within the same wire, with such junctions being able to be radial or along the wire axis, opening up various new device design options. Several have so far been demonstrated: LEDs[5] and lasers[6] on nanowires, carbon nanotube and nanowire field-effect transistors,[7] and logic gates based on both carbon nanotubes and nanowires.[8] Most of these devices are still the subject of long-term research, although their present performance is in some cases already better than their standard counterparts: the performance of carbon nanotubes transistors, for instance, is better than that of the best silicon transistors which will be used in the next-generation computer chips.[9]

Challenging goal

Such new concepts will only result in real products, however, if self-assembly (i.e., positioning and contacting) into complex, robust logics is feasible. Casting it in terms of the history of silicon CMOS technology, we may say that the field-effect transistor is here, but what we still need is the integrated circuit. If that can be achieved – and it is a very challenging goal – we will no doubt be on the eve of a new revolution in electronics, opening the way for the next-generation Ambient Intelligence scenarios.[10]

Sensing devices

Nanotechnology challenges the dimension limits of chemistry, i.e., the size of single molecules. The enormous progress in analytical methods makes it possible to follow molecular processes, often in real time. Sensing devices, which will become important to collect information in Ambient Intelligence scenarios, are benefiting dramatically from these developments. Biochemical sensors are already revolutionizing pharmaceutical and medical research. DNA and increasingly even more highly complex and sensitive proteins can be screened in parallel in compact biochip architectures in a matter of hours (Fig. 6). The next step may be expected to be sensors for clinical use (e.g., for measuring critical protein markers). In fact, relatively simple sensors are already being applied at the bedside (known as 'point-of-care devices') or in the home (e.g., the glucose sensor and the pregnancy stick). Scenarios have been developed as to how to 'export' biosensors to the consumer market for monitoring health and fitness parameters. Consumer devices will need to be even more robust than devices for clinical use, and they should preferably also be non-invasive.

FIG. 6
Motorola's e-sensor
for DNA analysis

The manufacturing of sensing devices is benefiting greatly from advances in surface structuring methods such as microcontact printing, where resolutions of 200nm have already been achieved. For example, instead of conventional lithography, little rubber stamps print patterns of self-aligning polymers on a surface which can subsequently be used as a substrate for building up pixelated layers of biological material such as DNA or proteins. 'Lab-on-a-chip' architectures can supply the necessary reagents for analysis using microfluidic principles.

Electronic nose

An initial device of potential relevance for Ambient Intelligence might be an electronic nose. This nose would be able to sense odours and create an electrical signal that can then be used in a certain Ambient Intelligence scenario. Electronic nose sensors are currently being investigated at several universities and institutions. Most of the systems being studied make use of electrically conductive polymers which change their electrical behaviour when they take up odour molecules (e.g., exhibiting increased resistance if sandwiched between two electrodes).

Conclusions

The three rather different areas illustrate how materials and materials research will influence device development on a timeline starting now and stretching ten years or more into the future. Many other exciting developments, such as passive integration, energy management or storage options, will make important contributions to the implementation of Ambient Intelligence, and these, too, will be influenced by developments in materials science in similar ways. If we look back only ten to fifteen years in some fields, we can see that dramatic progress has already been achieved. Looking into the future, if only some of the promise of materials research can contribute to Ambient Intelligence, exciting times lie ahead.

1   T. Jüstel, H. Nikol and C. Ronda, Angew. Chem. Int. Ed. (1998), 37, 3084
2   S. Nakamura and G. Fasol, The Blue Laser Diode (Berlin, Springer, 1997)
3   K. Yano et al., 'Single-electron memory for giga-to-tera bit storage', Proceedings of the IEEE 87 (1999), 633
4   M.A. Reed et al., 'Molecular random access memory cell', Applied Physics Letters, 78 (2001), 3735
5   M.S. Gudiksen et al., 'Growth of nanowire superlattice structures for nanoscale photonics and electronics', Nature, 415 (2002), 617
6   M.H. Huang et al., 'Room-temperature ultraviolet nanowire nanolasers', Science, 292 (2001), 1897
7   R. Martel et al., 'Single- and multi-wall carbon nanotube field-effect transistors', Applied Physics Letters, 73 (1998), 2447; S.J. Tans et al., 'Room-temperature transistor based on a single carbon nanotube', Nature, 393 (1998), 49
8   A. Bachtold et al., 'Logic circuits with carbon nanotube transistors', Science, 294 (2001), 1317; V. Derycke et al., 'Carbon nanotube inter- and intramolecular logic gates', Nano Letters, 1 (2001), 453; Y. Huang et al., 'Logic gates and computation from assembled nanowire building blocks', Science, 294 (2001), 1313
9   S.J. Wind et al., 'Vertical scaling of carbon nanotube field-effect transistors using top gate electrodes', Applied Physics Letters, 80 (2002), 3817
10 See also Scientific American, September 2001; P.G. Collins and Ph. Avouris, 'Nanotubes for electronics', Scientific American (December 2000), 62-69; M.A. Reed and J.M. Tour, 'Computing with molecules', Scientific American (June 2000), 86-93; Physics World, 13 (June 2000)

2.6 SMART DUST

Marcel Pelgrom, Raf Roovers, Henk Jan Bergveld

Ambient Intelligence originates in part from the quest for the next generation of computing in the home. From its earliest stages, the concept of distributed computing was seen as the natural way of transforming the basic concepts of parallel and networked computing into revolutionary experiences for people.

In its extreme form, computing is literally distributed throughout the home. A large number of computing devices ('nodes'), spanning the total computing function, are located at various places in the living environment – on or in walls, objects or clothes, for instance. The fact that the nodes are distributed means that sensor functionality can be added to them. They then become a computing and sensing network capable of perception. As a part of an entire system, this will assist people in their living environment or daily work, in accordance with the Ambient Intelligence vision.

Smart dust

Until now, this fully distributed concept has failed, due to the excessive power requirements for both communication and computing. That means that intensive computing for Ambient Intelligence purposes needs to be centralized in layers where mains power is available. The sensing function (with some dedicated logic) can remain distributed and is often referred to as 'smart dust', 'electronic paint' or 'intelligent wallpaper'.

Nowadays, smart dust is approached from two angles: communications and computing. Kris Pister's group at Berkeley, one of the foremost research teams in the field of integrated smart sensors,[1] focuses on the communication approach. The challenge is to reduce size and weight while extending the capabilities of single devices. State-of-the-art sensors are less than a cubic millimetre ($0.1 cm^3$) in size. Powered by hearing-aid batteries, they can transmit data about temperature, humidity or other environmental conditions over distances of tens of metres. The more computational approach is concerned with multi-node performance. Leaving the communication and energy problems to be resolved by others, these investigations focus on increasing the added value of networked computing.[2] In this chapter, we look at the boundary conditions imposed by energy and transmission limits.

Functionality

For the purposes of Ambient Intelligence, we can distinguish three categories of computing devices, based on their function and power needs.[3]

The 'watt node'

The Ambient Intelligence home will have at least a 'head-end' and computing-intensive server in the home. It will be the main gateway through which cable, optical and other connections enter the home. The amount of energy in this unit will be of the same order of magnitude as in present high-end consumer appliances or PCs. Power will be provided by mains connections (hence the name 'watt node'). Typical data throughput would be in the order of 100 MB per second.

The 'milliwatt node'

Many terminals in the Ambient Intelligence environment will need only limited functionality, providing speech, control or display interfaces for smaller objects in the home, for instance. These 'milliwatt nodes' will take their energy from rechargeable batteries, or from a power connection from the host function. The devices in question, such as advanced cellular phones or PDAs, are linked to individuals. The challenge here is to get maximum functionality per unit of energy.

The 'microwatt node'

In addition to the above, a large number of small and extremely simple devices – 'microwatt nodes' – will be spread around the environment, forming a network of 'smart dust'. These devices have only very limited functionality per unit: their contribution derives from the fact that they work together as a whole. Smart dust devices comprise a sensing function, a control mechanism, a means of communication and a power supply.

Smart dust devices are typically used to gather information whose density is relatively low, such as information about the following:

- Environmental conditions (temperature, humidity, light intensity, vibration, etc.)
- Security (presence of individuals, fire, smoke and gas alarm)
- Communication by gesture or sounds
- Health-related information (body temperature, sunlight intensity, sufficient lighting for reading)

The functionality of the microwatt device is determined by its major boundary condition: the device must be self-supporting throughout its life-cycle. Unlike the 'watt node', it has no wired connections; and unlike the 'milliwatt node', there is no room for any sort of battery (except for temporary energy storage). Moreover, smart dust devices are so numerous and are potentially located in hard-to-service places, so that replacement becomes impractical. This means that the power needed for operation must either be present from the start, or be supplied throughout the device's lifetime from external sources. This makes power management a dominant boundary condition.

Figure 1 shows in diagrammatic form the basic architecture of a microwatt node smart dust device. The sensor itself might be of various sorts: for example, a diode for light or temperature measurements, a structure for detecting vibrations or an electro-chemical interface for gas detection. A sensor typically provides its information in the form of several numbers per second. The signal from the sensor is first amplified and converted into bits by the analog interface. The digital logic and memory store then process the converted signal, and add some identification and security bits.

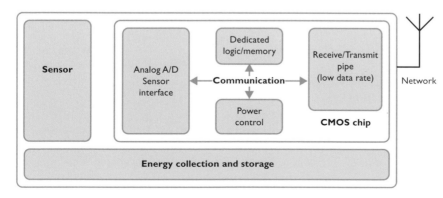

FIG. 1
Architecture of a smart dust device: the sensor sends data to the analog interface, which converts it into digital form and sends it to the digital logic and storage for processing. It is then sent to the transmitter, which sends it to the network via a wireless connection. Energy is collected, stored and supplied as required to the various components

The processed signal is then passed to the transmitter, which sends it by wireless connection to the Ambient Intelligence network of which the smart dust device forms a part. The intelligence of this network will use the sensor's information to perform its functionality. More complex smart dust devices also include a receiver to accept instructions from the network. A power control mechanism feeds the relevant parts of the smart-dust device with energy. As the sensor probably does not operate continuously at full strength, and as the energy in a microwatt node is not enough to power continuous operation, the power control unit also determines the 'duty cycle' of the device (e.g., that an active period of one second will be followed by a stand by period of 15 minutes).

All the functions (except the energy storage) shown in Figure 1 can be put on a single silicon IC (or chip). However, full integration is not really necessary, since it is the power suply and the size of the sensor itself that mainly determine the physical dimensions of the entire device.

How much power do smart dust devices require?

The power requirements reported in the literature for the various sensor types suggest that they will not give rise to a power bottleneck. However, since many smart dust devices will operate under some form of duty cycle management, the sensor type will need to be able to react sufficiently quickly to a start-up sequence.

As smart dust devices form part of a larger and more complex system, it is almost inevitable that they will use information coding and digital transmission protocols for the exchange of information. In the analog interface, the analog-to-digital converter will transform the sensor data into bits. The power requirements of an analog-to-digital converter depend on the bandwidth and resolution (i.e., accuracy) of the sensor signal.

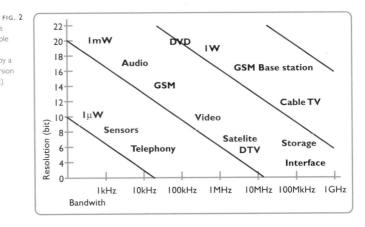

FIG. 2
The power needed for the analog interface depends on bandwidth and resolution (or accuracy). For simple sensors (10 bit 10 kHz), the power is only 0.1 mW. This is 1000 times less than the 100 mW required by a mobile phone (GSM) for its analog-to-digital conversion (based on 5 pJ/conversion: state-of-the-art for 2002)

Figure 2 shows the trade-off relationship between power and bandwidth/resolution for analog-to-digital conversion. Many sensor systems have a bandwidth of between 1 and 100 kHz, the lower boundary being mainly due to the expected duty-cycle constraints. With a modest resolution (8-10 bits), the expected power consumption during operation of the smart dust device will be in the order of 0.1 mW.

In the digital logic of the system, two aspects need to be considered: the energy needed for operation, and static power consumption. The trade-offs in power consumption for various types of digital hardware have been discussed extensively in the literature.[4] For the same task, for instance, programmable solutions consume two to three orders of magnitude more power than dedicated hardware, which means that programmable solutions are only appropriate if they offer clear benefits in terms of flexibility. But the smart dust systems being proposed currently do not need this degree of flexibility.

Another source of digital power dissipation is the static power consumption due to leakage.[5] In an advanced IC process, a circuit of 100,000 gates (such as a simple microcomputer) consumes 50µW of static energy. So even without any activity, this power is needed. On the other hand, in the watch industry,[6] digital circuits operate at a performance level which is 10,000 times lower than advanced microprocessors. These circuits are used for very simple operations (clock, alarm, timer, etc.) and need only 10µW.

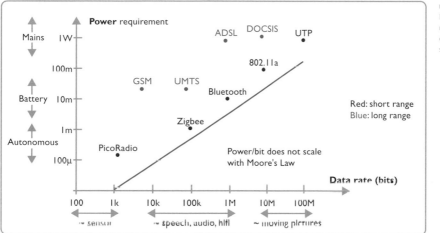

FIG. 3
Data rate vs. power requirement in communication systems

Whatever function the smart dust device performs, communication will always be required. In Figure 1, communication is carried out through a wireless (RF) link. Transmission in some form is essential, but if full interaction with the network is needed, a receiver will also be required. Figure 3 shows the relationship between the rate of data transmission and power consumption. The actual or expected relation is indicated for a number of communication systems. As can be seen, the higher the data rate, the more power is needed. Short-distance systems require less than long-distance systems. There is no system currently in existence that can really provide adequate communication at the level of power available in the microwatt nodes. Some new developments (e.g., PicoRadio)[7] set very ambitious targets, but are in line with other short-range communication systems. Assuming that a smart dust device needs to send a data stream of 1kbit per second, extrapolation in Figure 3 indicates that 0.1mW power would be needed for communication during the active phase of the duty cycle.

Besides wireless transmission of data, there are two other interesting options for communication. One of these is optical communication, which is currently being explored. In principle, this method would allow virtually zero-energy communication to and from smart dust devices. However, it requires the network to send a strong light beam to the device, which is problematic. The second possible method of communication is similar to that used by identification tags. To transmit their data, these tags absorb different amounts of energy from the electromagnetic field generated by the tag reader. This method could result in a very low communication energy budget. However, for it to be feasible, a major improvement in tag reader sensitivity is needed. In addition, the rather strong electromagnetic field emitted by the tag reader may give rise to environmental and health objections.

The above list of ingredients for a smart dust device shows that various trade-offs have to be taken into account when building such a device. Nevertheless, it is clear that communication in particular will consume a considerable amount of energy. But even if this were not the case, power constraints imposed by leakage currents in the digital circuits would prevent smart dust devices from being able to carry any substantial computing power. The exact duty cycle to be used is, of course, still open, and will be application-dependent. Taking all the above considerations into account, we can say that when active, a smart dust device will consume 0.2 mW, while only 10-50 µW will be used when it is on stand-by.

What sources of energy are available for smart dust devices?

Energy from the environment

The energy supply for smart dust is definitely a critical matter, since the device's functionality is determined by the energy available. It is sometimes supposed that smart dust devices will draw their power from the environment. However, a quick scan does not result in any suitable candidate: [8]

- Vibration energy can be transformed via piezo material into electrical energy (0.05-0.5 mW/cm^3). But vibration energy is not available in all locations
- Acoustic noise results in roughly 1 µW/cm^2 at 100 dB noise (making any conversation impossible), so the disadvantage for the living room environment is clear
- Thermoelectric transformation, from heat to electricity, at 1-10 µW/cm^2/°C gradient, is rather impractical because in most environments such a temperature difference is not available
- Direct sunlight generates 1kW/m^2 of power, but even advanced solar cells yield only 10mW/cm^2 electrical power. Indoor conditions reduce this even further to 10µW/cm^2. That means that a solar cell of 1cm^2 is needed to power 0.2mm^2 digital logic in standby mode.

Since none of these power sources can deliver the continuous power needed to operate the transmitter, the most practical solution is to have a duty cycle, with solar cells charging batteries during standby time which then operate the smart dust device during the active period.

FIG. 4
Possible set-up for energy system of a smart dust device[9]

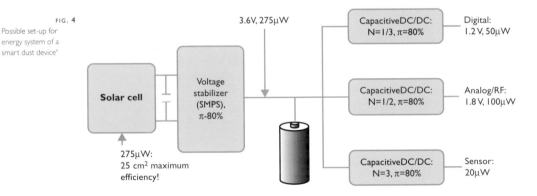

Batteries

What type of battery would be most suitable? Ideally, we would like a battery that provides sufficient power but is also as small as possible and will last as long as possible. Primary batteries have better energy densities than secondary batteries but, unlike secondary batteries, are not rechargeable. A popular rechargeable 0.1-cm^3 battery (with roughly the size of an electronic watch battery) would be able to fuel an electronic dust device with a sensor, basic digital functionality and a transmitter, for one month. For comparison, the same battery can power an electronic watch, which needs no communication power, for several years. It also needs to be borne in mind that batteries lose charge over time due to internal leakage. And, in the case of certain rechargeable batteries, the power budget will also be affected by the fact that they require some circuitry for voltage conversion, safety and regulation purposes.

A possible energy system for a smart dust device (of the type shown in Figure 1) is shown in Figure 4. Although to reach real smart dust dimensions, further optimization of the power supply will be needed, this system illustrates the general concept.

In this example, power is acquired by a solar cell of $25cm^2$, supplemented by a rechargeable battery. Using the previous data, some 2-5 cm^2 of solar cell is needed to make up for leakage during stand-by. Applying duty-cycle operation, the remaining area of the solar cell is used to charge the battery. This energy is used in the active phase of the duty cycle, where the sensor analog interface, digital circuit and transmitter are operating. With the limited efficiencies of energy collection and conversion, a ratio between active and standby mode of 1 to 100 is sufficient. Further optimization would allow to reduce the solar cell to approximately 10 cm^2.

The voltage stabilizer is some form of Switched-Mode Power Supply (SMPS), which ideally ensures that both the solar cell and the battery run at optimum efficiency.

Since the various parts of the system (Figure 1) have different voltage requirements, the battery voltage is converted to the lower levels required by the sensor itself, the digital logic and memory, the analog interface and the transmitter (and receiver, if any) by voltage converters.

The digital logic and memory will benefit from low supply voltage, as this will keep its operating power consumption low. Depending on the specifications to be met by the analog interface and wireless part (the transmitter), the supply voltage for these parts is likely to be higher in order to accommodate sufficient signal-to-noise ratio in the communication chain.

Conclusion

The concept of smart dust certainly seems feasible and attractive from most perspectives. Various research groups have shown samples of acceptable size and cost levels. However, the major stumbling block at the moment lies in providing the energy required for the communication link. If we extrapolate from today's technologies, we can envisage only a limited improvement in performance. For real smart dust, with many thousands of tiny devices scattered around our living environment, we will need to achieve a more fundamental breakthrough in this respect.

1 J.M. Kahn, R.H. Katz and K.S.J. Pister, 'Next century challenges: Mobile networking for "smart dust"', ACM/IEEE International Conference on Mobile Computing and Networking (Seattle, 17-19 August 1999)
2 IBM System Journal, Special Issue on Pervasive Computing, Vol.38 (4) (1999)
3 R. Roovers, 'Ambient Intelligence', Workshop (February 2002)
4 J. Rabaey, 'Wireless Sensors networks', International Solid State Circuits Conference (2002), T.A.C.M. Claasen, High Speed: Not the Only Way to Exploit the Instrinsic Computational Power of Silicon, International Solid State Circuits Conference (1999)
5 ITRS Process Technology Roadmap (2001)
6 Datasheet EM Electronic EM6680 (2002)
7 J. Rabaey, 'PicoRadio Networks – Opportunities and Challenges', Focus2000 (Berkeley, 26-27 June, 2000)
8 H.J. Bergveld, 'BMS for Microdevices', Workshop (July 2002); 'Ambient Intelligence', Workshop (February 2002)
9 H.J. Bergveld, W.S. Kruijt and P.H.L. Notten, Battery Management Systems – Design by Modelling (Kluwer Academic Publishers, in press)

2.7 AMBIENT COMPUTING PLATFORMS
A VERY LARGE-SCALE INTEGRATION (VLSI) PERSPECTIVE

Jef van Meerbergen

Ambient computing

Ambient computing is the third phase of computing. The first phase began with mainframe computers in the 1960s and 1970s. During the 1980s and 1990s, the second phase, we saw the breakthrough of the personal computer or PC. In the new millennium, we have witnessed the arrival of embedded systems and ambient computing. Computing is still present in our lives, but it is increasingly hidden in the background, embedded in our environment.

Post-PC

The driving force behind this evolution has been the continuous progress in integrated circuit (IC) technology, as expressed by Moore's Law, which states that the number of transistors doubles every process generation or every 18 months. While this driving force is common to all three phases of computing, there are major differences, and even discontinuities and disruptions, between them. Each phase is characterized by different design criteria, different constraints and cost functions. During the PC phase, architectures were optimized for performance, mainly obtained by higher clock speeds. This led to excessive power dissipation and expensive packages and cooling systems. In contrast, cost aspects are more important for the embedded systems of the third phase. Consequently, these systems are designed for the largest computational efficiency, i.e., performance per watt.[1] These third-phase systems are also called 'post-PC' or 'post.com' systems.[2] As a further consequence, the introduction of ambient computing requires breakthroughs in architectures and design technology.

Computational efficiency

The computational efficiency of most popular programmable processors can easily be calculated from their data sheets. The results are shown in Figure 1.

FIG. 1

The intrinsic computational efficiency of silicon compared with the computational efficiency of programmable processors

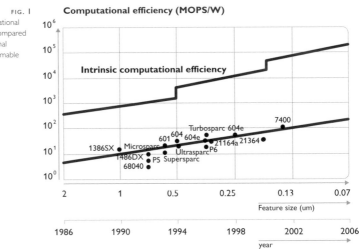

The computational efficiency is expressed in MOPS (Million Operations Per Second) per watt, where each operation is a 32 bit-wide RISC (Reduced Instruction Set Computer) type operation. The horizontal axis represents the different technologies on an equivalent time axis. The lower of the two red lines represents the average increase in computational efficiency of programmable processors. The upper red line shows the intrinsic computational efficiency (ICE) obtained by an architecture that fully matches the application. The difference between the two lines represents the 'overhead' of a programmable architecture due to the controller (the part of the processor that controls the transfer of data from a computer to a peripheral device and vice versa through instruction selection) and also to storage of data and programs. There is a clear gap of two to three orders of magnitude.

Processors

Between the two extremes represented by these lines, we find other types of processors, such as programmable digital signal processors (DSPs) and ASIPs (programmable processors with application-specific instructions). There is a relationship between the processor type and the tasks mapped onto it. The following types can be distinguished, in order of decreasing programmability:

- Programmable RISC-type central processing units or CPUs: These are used for control type of functions or handling of events that determine the mode of operation or the configuration of the system.
- Programmable DSPs: These are used for signal or media processing with medium throughput requirements with sampling frequencies in the kHz range (typically, telecom, voice and audio processing).
- ASIPs. These are used for high-throughput processing with sampling frequencies in the MHz range (typically, video processing).

For these processors, the area of the processor core in a sub-100 nanometre (nm) process is below one mm^2. A complex system can contain 50 to 100 of those cores, and so the system-level architecture is a heterogeneous multiprocessor, i.e., a carefully chosen combination of different types of processor, ensuring that the overall computational efficiency of the system is sufficiently high.

Platform-based design

This begs the following question: how can we obtain a sufficiently high computational efficiency whilst avoiding a disproportionate design effort as a result of growing complexity and diversity? The answer is platform-based design. Applications that are closely related can be grouped into application domains to which a unified design approach can be applied. An example is the digital video domain, which includes set-top boxes, digital television, interactive TV, Web TV, etc. Different designs can be derived from the same platform by reusing key components or processor cores. A platform is therefore defined as a set of hardware and sofware modules, configured in a prescribed communication structure and tailored towards a particular application domain.

Communication infrastructure

This communication infrastructure is very important. If 50 to 100 cores are cooperating, then communication is a much larger problem than computation. To have the correct data operands (operands express the things that are being manipulated) available in the right place and at the right time is much more difficult than the pure computation itself. One solution is to use on-chip busses, as shown in Figure 2.

FIG. 2
Bus-based communi-
cation with central
memory

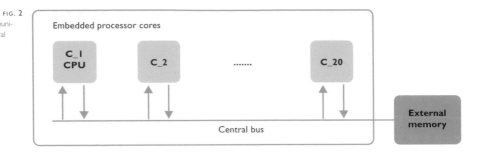

Figure 2 shows a central CPU, a number of additional processor cores and a large external memory, all connected via a single bus (i.e., a collection of wires through which data is transmitted from one part of a computer to another). The communication takes place via external memory and the synchronization is handled by the CPU. Four phases can be identified. First, the sender processor sends the data to the external memory. Next, once this transfer is completed, the sender informs the CPU that the event has occurred by means of an 'interrupt'. In the third phase, the CPU informs the receiving processor that the data is ready in the memory. Finally, the transfer from the memory to the receiving processor begins.

This concept has some important advantages: it is relatively simple, it supports task-level parallelism and it allows processor architectures to be tuned to tasks, which in turn improves computational efficiency. However, the communication via external memory and the fact that the same data is transported via the bus twice has a negative effect on the computational efficiency. The interrupt rate should not be higher than a few kHz, to avoid overloading the CPU: consequently, the number of processor cores should be limited, and the level of granularity of the tasks mapped onto them should be coarse. For video applications, for example, this means that tasks should be defined at the field or frame level, not at the line or pixel level. Furthermore, the software development can become a bottleneck, since scheduling the activities of the central resources (CPU, bus and memory) can become difficult, especially when real-time constraints have to be met.

Hardware

In addition to the software issues, there are also hardware issues, due to deep sub-micron effects that have important consequences for the VLSI design. Two aspects are especially important. First, the delay of a circuit will no longer be dominated by the gate delay (the time required for an electrical signal to propagate through a basic logic circuit or gate) but by the interconnect delay (the time taken to travel between gates). That means that VLSI designers, who have been used to delays becoming shorter as new processes become available, will now be faced with the opposite situation. Long connections and busses running from one end of the chip to the other end are no longer possible. Second, the size of the isochronous zones (i.e., areas for which the same clock can be used) are shrinking because it will become increasingly difficult to control the clock skew (i.e., the difference in path delays between a clock signal and its loads).

Conclusions

The scaleability of busses is limited. The next step is to use multiple busses, as in the Nexperia DVP platform. Bus-based subsystems communicate via bridges, which can be seen as an *ad hoc* solution for what is really needed, a Network-on-Silicon (NoS). A network consists of routers (small switch boxes) and links (connections between routers). Connections between processors go via one or more routers. This way, long connections are implemented by multi-hop communication. The network will provide packet-switching as well as circuit-switching services. However, on-chip networks need to be much more predictable than their off-chip counterparts. At the level of end-to-end services over the network, guaranteed throughput services are needed if, for example, many video streams have to be communicated. This makes the software development of the higher application layers much easier, especially in relation to real-time constraints.

Another element of predictability can be found at the deep sub-micron level. Timing issues at this level can be managed by a predefined routing strategy, which chooses the layer, width and pitch of the wires, and which limits the length to, for example, 2-3mm. This way the whole layout problem becomes manageable with a limited design effort up to clock frequencies of 500 MHz. Future platforms for ambient computing will look like the platform shown in Figure 3.

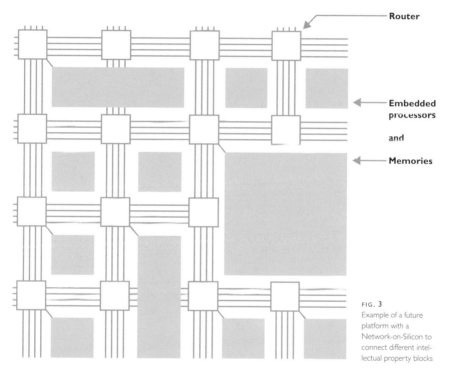

Router

Embedded processors

and

Memories

FIG. 3
Example of a future platform with a Network-on-Silicon to connect different intellectual property blocks

1   E. Roza, 'Systems-on-chip: What are the limits?', *Electronics & Communication Engineering Journal* (December 2001), 249-255
2   H. de Man, 'On Nanoscale Integration and Gigascale Complexity in the Post.com World', Keynote speech, Design, Automation and Test in Europe 2002 (Paris, March 2002)

2.8 MIDDLEWARE FOR AMBIENT INTELLIGENCE

David P.L. Simons, Rob T. Udink

For Ambient Intelligence to work well, people need to have natural and seamless access to services and content, anytime, anywhere. By facilitating high-level communication between all the elements in the system, 'middleware' is a key technology that will help make this possible.

As Ambient Intelligence environments are developed, more and more devices will become interconnected in a network. They will be of many different types. Some will have quite limited functionality (e.g., a sensor detecting the presence of someone in a room); others will make intelligent use of services provided by other devices in the network (e.g., offering music to fit the mood of people walking through the house). To provide the user with the appropriate experience, all these functionalities and applications will have to cooperate in the network. They not only have to be connected, they will need to communicate meaningfully with each other and share each other's resources. And they will have to work without disturbing the operation of other devices in the network.

An additional complication is that most people will not buy their Ambient Intelligence systems all at once, but will build them up over time, bringing together different devices and software services from various manufacturers and suppliers.

Middleware
Middleware will ensure that everything works together in spite of the diversity in the system and the changes that take place in it over time. The literature contains many definitions

FIG. I
Devices in a network are linked by a network stack consisting of three layers. Middleware facilitates communication horizontally between devices and vertically within devices

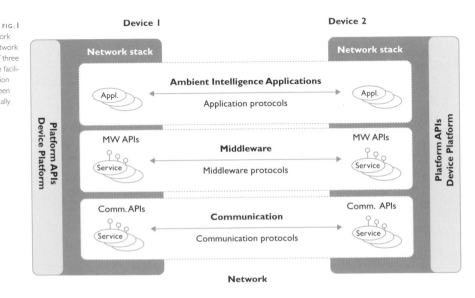

of middleware;[1] for our purposes, however, we define it as 'those networked services that allow multiple networked and distributed applications to co-exist and co-operate'.

Figure 1 shows how middleware relates to the rest of the system. It shows two devices connected in a network. Each has its own platform (i.e., internal realization), along with aspects designed to enable it to participate in the network (known as the network stack). We can think of the network stack as consisting of three layers. One deals with the basic communication between the device and other devices through a wired or wireless infrastructure. Another layer consists of the software relating to different Ambient Intelligence applications. The third (intermediate) layer is middleware, which abstracts away from all the peculiarities of the underlying communication layer and allows all the Ambient Intelligence applications to co-exist, communicate and work together. Each layer will span all networked devices, each of which implements all or part of that layer. 'Horizontal' communication between entities in the same layer but on different devices (peer-to-peer) is facilitated by protocols. 'Vertical' communication between entities from different layers within the same device is facilitated by application programming interfaces (APIs).

The focus of middleware in Ambient Intelligence systems is different from the focus adopted in more general frameworks. In the latter, middleware is often directed towards maximizing overall efficiency by distributing functions. In Ambient Intelligence systems, however, distribution is not a goal but is inherent (certain functions are located in particular devices and have to be performed there) and needs to be dealt with for that reason. Moreover, the focus in other middleware approaches tends to be on APIs, whereas our main focus in Ambient Intelligence systems is on protocols. Current middleware services tend to be concentrated at the level of infrastructure; Ambient Intelligence systems, by contrast, will require middleware services that exhibit greater intelligence. We expect middleware services to evolve in that direction, with lower-level services being aggregated and general concepts being extracted from the application layer.

Interoperability

How will middleware enable devices in a heterogeneous networked system to work together to achieve the behaviour required by each Ambient Intelligence application in that system? It will depend on the type of products in question, and that, in turn, will depend on the types of business models prevalent in the market. For instance, some products may be self-contained devices, with applications and services embedded in them; others may be general-purpose devices, for which software applications can be downloaded separately; and software may also be a product in itself.

Different standards supporting different business models will co-exist. The issue for middleware is whether interoperability of APIs or protocols is required. Several types of middleware are currently available, each addressing interoperability at different levels, and influenced by the business models adopted by their proponents. The best-known are UPnP (Universal Plug and Play), Jini (from Sun Microsystems) and HAVi (Home Audio Video interoperability). UPnP focuses on making sure that self-contained devices can communicate with each other using an agreed protocol. Jini is designed to ensure that applications bought separately from a general-purpose device will work on that device. HAVi allows for both possibilities: it allows separately purchased devices to communicate with each other (as in UPnP), but since devices can also exchange application codes, it also ensures that the exchanged code can be executed on any device in the network.

Heterogeneity

Middleware will also need to deal with the great diversity within Ambient Intelligence

PHENOM

WWICE

STREAMIUM

EASY ACCESS
AND LISY

PML

CAMP
AND MADS

OPEN TOOLS

networks. Given the wide diversity of devices (cheap/expensive, mobile/stationary, dedicated/general purpose, etc.) and that each will have to carry at least part of the middleware layer of the network stack, middleware itself will have to be scaleable to fit types, even performing middleware tasks for their 'poorer' peers when required.

Middleware will abstract from the heterogeneity of platforms and communication layers, so that devices can share resources and functionalities across the network, regardless of the type and characteristics of the underlying platforms (e.g., different run-time environments) and communication layers (e.g., differences in physical media or connectors).

Even the middleware itself in the system will be varied, with different devices operating different middleware solutions. Special bridges and gateways will thus be needed to translate between different solutions. Coexistence and cooperation will be the watchwords, not uniformity.

Dynamics

The state of the network will be continually changing in often unpredictable ways. Some devices will be removed and new ones introduced; mobile devices will be linked to the network via different connections at different times, depending on the user's location; stationary devices may be on or off, or change their configuration, depending on the services available. Network connections may be temporarily or permanently unavailable (e.g., because they are in use or out of order). Services may vary in their availability, as they are added or removed from the system; they may also migrate from one device to another, depending on applications, users and devices. The content in the system will change as it is added, deleted, modified, relocated or replicated throughout the system. And, of course, people themselves are dynamic: they move around and change habits and preferences.

Middleware is vital in detecting and dealing with such changes. It supports the 'lookup' and discovery of devices, services and content, to obtain an overview of what is available. It monitors and manages network connections, and supports context awareness by determining the locations and identities of devices and end-users. It also keeps devices informed of relevant changes, such as the removal or addition of devices and applications. But middleware should not hide these dynamics completely: essential changes still need to be conveyed to applications.

Middleware services for Ambient Intelligence

What specific services will middleware need to provide in an Ambient Intelligence system? These services will not normally be located on one specific device but will be distributed over several cooperating devices (with due account necessarily having been taken of issues of interoperability, heterogeneity and dynamics – including appropriate protocols and APIs).

Device abstraction

Middleware will abstract from each device the functionalities and resources it has available (and which can be used by other devices) and enable other devices to use them. Examples include storage, data processing, capturing (e.g., of images and sounds), rendering (e.g., of images on displays or sound through speakers). These abstract services will need to be generic enough to be used and provided by as many devices as possible, but not so generic as to exclude the use of a device's specific functions wherever appropriate.

Resource management

Sharing resources and functionality in this way means that various services will often be competing for use of the same device or resource. Middleware provides resource management to deal with these conflicts. In the Ambient Intelligence context, this will be mainly about resolving interference between applications or services, and informing users about relevant issues, choices and consequences. It will also allow the reservation of resources so that applications can use them in the user's absence.

Stream management

In Ambient Intelligence systems, various applications will make use of audio and video streams. These streams will be from different sources, varying in bandwidth and latency; they may pass through different media, each with its own transport characteristics; multiple streams may need to be synchronized; the coding and encoding abilities of various devices may vary and need to be resolved (e.g., by stream transcoding); in the event of disruptions, alternative paths or sources and destinations may need to be found; and quality-of-service (QoS) guarantees will need to be provisioned. All this will need to be managed, a task that will fall to middleware.

PHENOM

WWICE

STREAMIUM

EASY ACCESS
AND LISY

PML

Content and asset management

Key elements in an Ambient Intelligence system are the content (e.g., audio, video, still images and text) and other digital assets (e.g., digital rights, public and private encryption keys and electronic banking data). Given the rapid growth in storage capacity, people will have huge collections of such material, and will need help in managing them. Middleware will play an important role here. Assets will need managing during their entire lifetime: from creation or acquisition, through storage and retrieval, sharing and publishing, modification and annotation, to archiving, deletion or transfer to another person. Assets may need to be distributed, stored in various places or synchronized, so that users can access them anytime and anywhere. In addition, royalty liabilities on material covered by digital rights will need to be managed.

Personalization

People will want to personalize their Ambient Intelligence systems by expressing preferences (the behaviour they prefer from applications and services and their own preferred mode of interaction with them) and enabling the compilation of a personal profile (personalized selection of content, possibly based on their past history in terms of content previously accessed). Middleware will enable applications and services to share personalization data across the system and access it anywhere.

Communities and collaboration

People tend to socialize in communities (families, friends, colleagues, etc.) to share experiences, information and objects, and do things together. Middleware will support such communal behaviour by providing 'virtual' meeting places that allow participants to be aware of the presence of others, and enable natural interaction and collaboration, regardless of location. It will need to be able to deal with community dynamics, facilitate collaborative activities, and ensure that all participants are kept up-to-the-minute on the interaction, wherever they are.

Distributed multimodal user-interaction

People will be able to interact with their Ambient Intelligence systems in natural and appropriate ways, including by speech, touch and animated graphics, besides keyboards and menus. They will also be able to combine several of these modalities – in different ways, at different times and at different locations – making optimal use of the set of interaction mechanisms of the devices around them at any given moment, multimodal interaction thus being distributed over several devices. This complex situation will be facilitated by middleware, which will also take into account the user's context, preferences and profiles.

Context awareness

Ambient Intelligence systems will be sensitive and responsive to the presence of people and devices. To make the system context-aware in this way, middleware will need to furnish applications with knowledge about the context of the users and the system itself. Sensors – detecting the location, motion, presence and identity of individuals and devices, as well as the date and time – will provide information, the implications of which can then be reasoned out and the resulting model (the 'sensor-based context') made available by middleware. In addition, by monitoring the courses of action users have taken in the past and that have led to the current state of applications, middleware can also provide the required 'application context'.

Security

Various aspects of security must be dealt with throughout the system: privacy (of special interest to users), safety (important to vendors), ownership of content (vital for content

AMBIENT INTELLIGENCE IN EUROPE

Technological developments alone are not enough to bring about positive social and economic change. Instead, it should be combined with changes in public policies and a continuous effort both to better understand people's reactions to these developments and to widely expose their possible benefits to society as a whole.

The EU has set an ambitious objective for Europe by 2010: to become the world's most competitive and dynamic knowledge-based economy, capable of sustainable economic growth, with more and better jobs and greater social cohesion. Two main EU initiatives will help achieve this goal: eEurope, which aims to deliver an information society for all, and the Sixth Framework Programme for Community-supported Research and Development (FP6), which includes an important IST project and will begin in 2003. The crucial role of information society technologies in achieving EU objectives for the knowledge society is reflected in the project's budget of € 3.625 bn.

This renewed effort in IST research is essential to ensure European leadership in the technologies at the heart of the knowledge society, and to enable all European citizens and companies to benefit from that leadership. Today, we are still far from taking full advantage of the possibilities that IST can offer. Only 5-10% of the world's population have access to IST applications and services. Costs, complexity, unavailability and unreliability often impede the further development and broader deployment of the knowledge society, and the digital divide is widening. Even in developed countries, only a fraction of the possibilities of IST are actually used, despite recent progress in the uptake of Internet and mobile technologies. As we begin to understand the advantages and limitations of current technologies, research should target new avenues that will not only extend the scope, functionality and efficiency of IST applications and services, but will also make these available, in the most natural and trustful way, to all citizens, wherever and whenever they need them.

In this vision, technology should be invisible, embedded in our surroundings and present whenever we need it. Interacting with it should be simple and effortless. It should enable every patient to be treated in the comfort of their own home and

Erkki Liikanen
Member of the European Commission (Enterprise and Information Society)

providers) and access rights (a concern of service providers). Security solutions appropriate to the Ambient Intelligence framework are still in their infancy.

Conclusions

Middleware will become the vital glue between intelligent and adaptive Ambient Intelligence applications and the underlying networked set of devices. The aspects of interoperability, heterogeneity and dynamics must be properly addressed in line with underlying business models, and supported by standardizations. Middleware will provide services that can be shared by applications and that satisfy their common needs, enabling users to access content and services from anywhere at any time.

1   P.A. Bernstein, 'Middleware: A Model for Distributed System Services', *Communications of the ACM*, vol. 39 no. 2 (1996), 86-98; A. Tanenbaum and M. van Steen, *Distributed Systems: Principles and Paradigms* (Englewood Cliffs, Prentice Hall, 2002)

PHENOM

WWICE

STREAMIUM

EASY ACCESS
AND LISY

PML

CAMP
AND MADS

OPEN TOOLS

should bring personalized learning resources to every child. It should lead to a world where every engineer and scientist has the power of global computing resources at their fingertips. This will help us to better predict and manage natural disasters, and to design and manufacture products more efficiently. Technology should enable every business to be connected to worldwide trading communities and every individual to work in the best, most efficient conditions.

This is the world of Ambient Intelligence that will gradually but surely emerge from research in IST. It puts people at the centre of the development of future technologies, aiming to design technologies for people and not to force people to adapt to technologies. Ambient Intelligence also provides a clear opportunity for European industry to build on and strengthen its leading position in areas such as mobile communications, consumer electronics, home appliances and micro-electronics. It will help to reinforce the competitiveness of all industrial sectors.

This vision is not an impossible dream. Key steps forward have already been taken in mobile and wireless technologies, with the 2.5 and 3G mobile systems which provide 'anywhere access' to applications and services from a non-PC platform and for the ordinary person in the street. Wearable mobile devices that incorporate interfaces making use of our senses, speech and gestures are currently under development. Cars already contain many IST devices that we use without even knowing it, just by turning the steering wheel, activating the brakes or touching the accelerator.

Sustained research is needed to accelerate progress in key areas such as advanced interfaces, broadband, and mobile and wireless communications, as well as distributed and embedded computing technologies and knowledge-handling techniques. This research must push the limits of miniaturization and minimize the costs and power consumption of microelectronic components. It should explore new materials, such as organic and flexible material for displays and sensors, so that they can be placed anywhere and take any shape. Finally, these technologies must be integrated into innovative applications and services that genuinely address user needs.

The EU objectives are ambitious, but the will is there and the strategy is clear, based on a close relationship between innovative and forward-looking research and policy initiatives to promote the wide adoption of the Information Society. In implementing these fundamental, long-term changes, our success will depend largely on a sustained, step-by-step effort and commitment.

2.9 THE SEMANTIC WEB

AMBIENT INTELLIGENCE AND THE INTERNET

Warner ten Kate, Herman ter Horst

The Internet Computer

Ambient Intelligence systems link many different devices within a variety of networks, distributing content and functions so that they can be accessed anytime, anywhere. This makes connectivity a key factor in the implementation of Ambient Intelligence. And with its portfolio of technologies and global distribution, the Internet is a natural place to start looking for ways to enhance this connectivity. Designed as a global network to connect computers (or, more precisely, to connect computers on local networks), the Internet is all about the connections between machines: configuring and maintaining the network, implementing communication protocols between the processes they host, and exchanging information. It is, like an Ambient Intelligence system, essentially a collection of interlinked devices, with functions distributed across them and shifting between them as appropriate. Arising as it does from the tradition of computing, it has also had the separation of functions and the places where they are hosted built into it from the start. Terminal-mainframe, client-server, proxying, and peer-to-peer systems all differ mainly in the way functions are hosted, and they reflect a gradual evolution in the direction of a decentralized and distributed system, in which the ultimate stage will be 'ubiquitous computing'.[1]

In fact, one could put it thus: 'In the future there will be one computer – it's called the Internet'. This reflects the prediction that the devices themselves will become invisible to us, while the functions will remain accessible to us at all times, wherever we are. To all intents and purposes, it is as if there is only one single device. The Internet offers an infrastructure that could make this a reality. It remains to be seen how, in terms of architecture (or, more likely, interoperable architectures), this experience of there being 'one computer' will be achieved. But it is clear that the separation of functions from the places where they are hosted will be a significant factor.

A simple model of how this might work is shown in Figure 1. Like an ordinary computer, the Internet Computer will have peripheral, physical devices close to the user. For the purposes of Ambient Intelligence, we can make a distinction within these peripheral devices between sensors, input devices and output devices. Sensors provide the system with information about the user's current situation to help it shape the interaction in an appropriate way. Input devices are the means by which the user 'talks' to the system (e.g., a remote control), while output devices (e.g., a display) are the means whereby the system 'talks' to the user. The intelligent processing (such as adapting the interaction to fit the user's situation) is hosted by the Internet Computer.

FIG. 1
The Internet as one computer

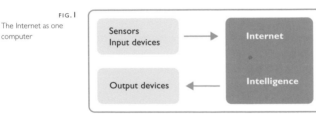

106

What happens in a typical situation is summarized in Figure 2.[2] Sensors provide information to the system to the effect that a given user – let's call him Bob – is in the room and that there is someone sitting in an armchair. On the basis of this knowledge about the context, the system, applying rules learned previously, reasons that Bob's current situation can be classified as 'alone and relaxing'. The system then consults Bob's profile, which it has available, to see what Bob likes in this situation. It sees that Bob enjoys listening to classical music, and therefore formulates a query to its database to compile a suitable play list. The content is then retrieved from various content providers (this process being facilitated by the use of metadata and ontologies that define the vocabularies used to express the metadata). The system has meanwhile ascertained which devices are available in the room and what their capabilities are. Matching the media content to the devices, the system then generates an appropriate way of presenting the content, for example, sending it to an Internet radio in the room. As part of its creation of an appropriate 'alone and relaxing' context, the system also instructs the lighting in the room to adopt a suitable setting.

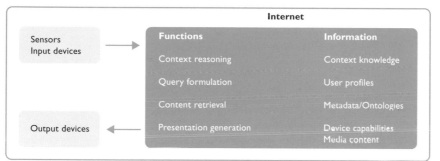

FIG. 2
Example of networked functions

Towards a more dynamic and intelligent Internet

In order to provide this Ambient Intelligence functionality, the Internet will need to change, and certain changes are already under way. One of these changes is actually a paradigm shift, as the Internet changes from a network of existing documents to a network of services that can provide new documents created dynamically in response to people's specific needs and wants at any given moment. Another of these changes is that the Internet is supporting more intelligence: this development, known as the Semantic Web, is intended to provide solutions for machine-understandable semantics of Web data, and for the support of reasoning by means of information on the Web. These two changes are shown schematically in Figure 3, with Ambient Intelligence through the Internet and the Web being seen as the result of the combination of both greater dynamism and greater semantic understanding than currently exhibited by the Internet.

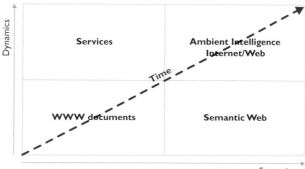

FIG. 3
Web ingredients for Ambient Intelligence

An important part in both developments is played by XML (short for Extensible Markup Language).[3] This is a generic language for exchanging structured information.

The World Wide Web and the concept of hypertext

To understand why it is important, it may be useful to briefly recall the nature of the World Wide Web. The Web is based on the notion of documents linked in a hypertext system. A 'web' is seen as a coherent set of 'nodes', or meaningful units of information (i.e., documents). These nodes are connected by 'links', specific relationships. These links are from one specific point in a document (e.g., a word or phrase) to another specific point in another document, these points being called 'anchors'. (Links can also be between anchors within the same node/document).

All the information about the links (where to, where from) is contained within the document itself. And in order for these documents to be readable on any system around the world, the document (including information about links, etc.) is encoded in such a way that, when interpreted by a 'browser' on the user's own computer, it is readable and will function as intended. To this end, the document is 'marked up' with codes added 'in line', i.e., within the lines of text, the most usual code being HTML (HyperText Markup Language).

Since the documents linked in the Web are stored on different computers, they have a unique 'address', the URL (short for Uniform Resource Locator). This is a string of easily understandable code that specifies the name of the resource (i.e., the document), the computer (IP address or domain name) where the resource is located ('hosted') followed by the path that needs to be followed within that computer to find the resource, and finally the communication protocol that needs to be used to access the document (e.g., http or ftp).

The above description represents the World Wide Web as we have grown to know it over the past few years – based on the concept of static documents, essentially text-based, and hosted at a specific location. However, as more and more information is being integrated – not only text, but also data and other media; not only information on the Web, but also information within companies – the need has arisen for a more generalized and more flexible approach.

New language

This has resulted in a more general markup language. The new, more generic language for exchanging structured information, known as XML (Extensible Markup Language), is a simple way of encoding both text and data so that content can be processed with relatively little human intervention and exchanged across diverse hardware, operating systems and applications.

There are two fundamental differences between HTML and XML. First, XML separates content from form in a much more rigorous way. Whereas HTML mostly consists of tags defining the appearance of text, in XML the tags define the general structure and content of the data, with the actual appearance being specified by a specific application or an associated stylesheet.

Second, XML can be extended *ad hoc*. Whereas the HTML standard tagset is defined by the World Wide Web Consortium (W3C, the international consortium of institutes and companies involved with the Internet and the Web whose aim is to develop open standards), in XML tags can be defined by individuals or organizations for some specific application. The result is a dedicated markup language.

Several such languages have now been specified by the W3C. Examples in the domain of presentation and interaction include XHTML (for text-based documents), XForms (for user interaction), SMIL (for media-related semantics), and SVG (for graphics-related semantics).[4]

New identifier

Similarly, a generalized, more extended version of the URL has been developed: the URI (Universal Resource Identifier). This makes it possible to additionally identify documents or other resources that are not necessarily even on the Web.

Dynamic documents – Web services

XML allows for a high degree of flexibility. By defining communication in terms of the data structure that is exchanged, the processing of the data can be specified separately, so that even the choice of programming language (e.g., Java, C, Lisp) is left open.

As noted above, the Web started off as a means of exchanging and presenting text-based documents. Users ask a server to provide a certain document, identified by its URI. The document and its URI are static. And almost all interactions take place through the exchange of text documents. Increasingly, with the rise of Web services, people are not simply linking with a document, but with an application. They are not looking for a specific document; they are looking for a service. They submit a query or data by means of a form, for instance, which is then processed by an application 'behind the scenes'. In effect, the link (i.e., the resource's URI) is extended with an additional string of code representing the query that is being submitted. The application generates a new text document containing the answer to the query. In other words, the document is dynamic, created 'on the fly' in response to a specific query.

The notion of Web Services provides a standardized mechanism for describing, locating and communicating with online applications. The most commonly referred to specifications are UDDI, WSDL and SOAP.[5] Each adds a component to the overall framework: UDDI (Universal Description, Discovery and Integration) offers a unified way of finding services in the form of a directory, much like a telephone or business directory; WSDL (Web Services Description Language) specifies the messages exchanged during a session, where an XML schema is usually used to define the vocabulary; and SOAP (Simple Object Access Protocol) specifies a communication protocol for the actual exchange, centring around the specification of the envelope in which the protocol's messages are carried. Development is ongoing, and alternative and additional solutions are being proposed. DAML-S, for instance, is an ontology being designed to help people find services.[6]

Semantic Web

If our Ambient Intelligence systems in the home and elsewhere are to be able to make use of the Web in reaching their conclusions, the content on the Web will need to be made understandable not only to humans but also to machines. The Semantic Web is the notion of having data on the Web defined and linked in such a way that it can be used by machines not just for display purposes, but for the automation, integration and re-use of data across various applications. The W3C, in collaboration with many researchers and industrial partners, is developing standards to enable this. Typically, the data and other resources will be identified through a URI, and therefore their scope is not strictly limited to the Web.

The Semantic Web requires knowledge to be represented in such a way that machines can reason on the basis of that knowledge. In other words, it seeks to make reasoning explicit. This contrasts with the current situation, where reasoning processes remain largely hidden (e.g., within Java programs). One of the main problems in the field of knowledge representation and reasoning involves the trade-off between expressive power and reasoning efficiency. If many ways to express knowledge are allowed, then reasoning may become very complex, or even intractable. In designing a formalism for knowledge representation, a prime concern is to keep computational complexity within bounds. This problem is compounded when that knowledge is distributed on the Web.[7]

PHENOM

WWICE

MIME

OPEN TOOLS

LIME
AND PL@NET

As currently envisaged, the Semantic Web consists of a layered system of languages (see Figure 4).[8] At the bottom are XML and URI: these provide the basic mechanisms for resource identification and document exchange. The next layer up is RDF (Resource Description Framework). This is a language that allows descriptions of a variety of data, for instance, providing metadata about audio and video content, or keywords about documents, etc.[9]

The next step is to add simple reasoning capabilities, so that on the basis of the metadata described by the RDF it is possible to infer other facts. This is the level of the ontology, an ontology in this context being a taxonomy providing definitions of classes of objects and the relations between them. The language currently being developed for this level is OWL (Web Ontology Language).[10] At the simplest level, an ontology can specify, for instance, that two keywords are synonyms. At a more complex level, it can specify, for example, that

100 billion devices

We have all experienced Moore's Law: every year a more powerful PC for the same price as last year's. If cars were computers, we would be able to buy a Rolls Royce today for the price of a small Volkswagen several years ago. Unfortunately, the comparison ultimately fails, because it would also mean the car would shrink each year, and no one wants a 50cm Rolls Royce.

But with an embedded computer, this is precisely what you do want: the same computing power, cheaper and smaller each year. Trace this trend back five years and you see a price/performance improvement by a factor of 1000. At that rate, the rules of the game in an industry change radically, as we saw in the transition from the mainframe industry to the PC industry between 1980 and 1995. What will happen by 2010, when we have had another improvement by a factor of 1000? Will we be surrounded by all kinds of embedded, hidden, ubiquitous or ambient computing devices that will improve our way of life? Who will have won the game by then? And who will have solved the challenge in the right way?

Egbert-Jan Sol

VP Technology, Ericsson

Netherlands

Director/Architect, LM Ericsson

(Eurolabs Deutschland)

Columnist, Computable

There is a problem with shrinking electronics. Not the micro-electronics, but the housing, the power supply, the connectors, and so on become the costly and problematic components. With 5-axis Numerical Controlled machining technologies, all kinds of plastic moulds can be made with dual curved surfaces resembling biological shapes. But energy consumption and battery life still remain a challenge. Connectors can be largely avoided thanks to wireless communication, such as infrared, Bluetooth, and more recently OFDM and UWB radio.

In the field of communication technologies, a trend similar to Moore's law is accelerating the development and use of embedded devices. While the price/performance improvement of micro-electronics accelerated over the past few decades, communication bandwidth was kept – in part, artificially – scarce. Over the past decade, technological developments in executing complex communication software protocol stacks, advanced DSP chips, as well as deregulation have all created an environment in which every computer with Ethernet/IP/TCP is gradually becoming connected to every other computer, and soon to every other computing device as well. The surge of the Internet and the growth of the peer-to-peer networks are the beginning of a price/performance improvement in the cost of bandwidth that is predicted to go faster than Moore's law.

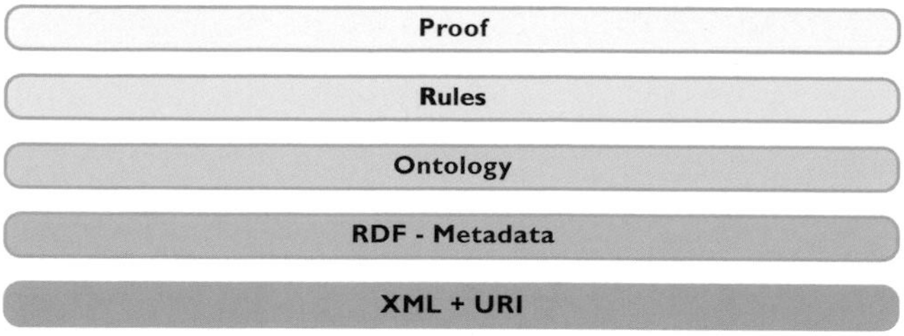

Proof
Rules
Ontology
RDF - Metadata
XML + URI

FIG. **4**
The layering of Semantic Web languages

content exists in different genres and can be obtained from different providers. Such information, recorded in a 'machine-understandable' way, will make it easier for a computer to navigate its way through the Web more intelligently when, for example, looking for the answer to a specific query.

These reasoning capabilities are expected to be further enlarged at the next layer, where rules are added, so that further inferences can be made on the basis of the descriptions themselves, such as information about user preferences. The top layer deals with validation and proof that the correct information has been identified and can be trusted. The intention is to publish proofs of inferred conclusions on the Web so that others can check the reasoning, and thus their truth.

Semantic Web technology can facilitate the development of intelligent, Web-based systems. In particular, there is a natural connection between Ambient Intelligence and the Semantic Web. Processes that look for specific media content on the Web, or for specific Web services, could benefit from Semantic Web ontologies. Sensor technology could be combined with Semantic Web technology to enable systems to adapt to the user's context. Other specific procedures for representing knowledge and reasoning could be realized with the help of Semantic Web languages.

Conclusion

The Internet will play an important role in the development of Ambient Intelligence. In particular, the separation of functions from their hosting is significant in allowing the Internet to behave as if it is a single computer that can be accessed from anywhere. Work on the development of interfaces for this distributed environment is now well advanced, XML providing a basic format to specify the data structures that are exchanged. By defining communication in a data-oriented way and by making data 'machine-understandable', the Web becomes a flexible environment that will enable our Ambient Intelligence systems to make use of the vast amount of information available to serve us even better.

1   M. Weiser, 'The Computer for the Twenty-First Century', *Scientific American* (September 1991), 94-104
2   H. ter Horst, M. van Doorn, N. Kravtsova, W. ten Kate and D. Siahaan, 'Context-aware music selection using knowledge on the Semantic Web', *Proceedings of the 14th Belgium-Netherlands Conference on Artificial Intelligence* (BNAIC, Louvain, 2002)
3   Extensible Markup Language (XML) 1.0 (Second Edition), W3C REC (2000), W3C Technical Reports and Publications, http://www.w3.org
4   W3C Technical Reports and Publications, http://www.w3.org
5   The Universal Description, Discovery and Integration Project, http://www.uddi.org/; Web Services Description Language (WSDL) 1.1, W3C Note (March 2001) and Simple Object Access Protocol (SOAP) 1.1, W3C Note (May 2000) in W3C Technical Reports and Publications, http://www.w3.org
6   DAML Services, http://www.daml.org/services/
7   In this connection, it is relevant to note that the OWL is based on the area of description logics, where powerful reasoners have been built. See further, below, and I. Horrocks, U. Sattler and S. Tobies, 'Practical Reasoning for Very Expressive Description Logics', *Logic Journal of the IGPL*, vol. 8, no. 3 (2000), 239-263
8   Adapted from T. Berners-Lee, Semantic Web on XML, Sheet from Talk at XML2000 (Washington DC, June 2000), http://www.w3.org/2000/Talks/1206-xml2k-tbl/slide10-0.html
9   W3C Technical Reports and Publications, http://www.w3.org
10 Ibid.

PHENOM

WWICE

MIME

OPEN TOOLS

LIME
AND PL@NET

LEARN, REMEMBER, EVOLVE

We expect Ambient Intelligence systems to learn about us, adapting to our needs, wants and preferences over time. How might they do this? Will they be able to cope with the masses of information involved? And more importantly, will they be able to draw conclusions from remembered details to reason and predict intelligently? As creatures of emotion, how can we be sure our technology will leave us free to become ourselves?

3.1 DEEP CUSTOMIZATION

Anton Andrews, Monica Bueno, John Cass

What would it be like to create tools that could evolve with their owner, shaping themselves to their specific and particular habits and needs?

The Ambient Intelligence vision proposes a world in which people are meaningfully empowered by digitally enabled environments and devices. These products and the services they provide would enable us by being adaptive, personalized, interconnected and embedded in our lives. In bringing this vision to life, it becomes necessary to probe the potential meanings of these keywords. Currently, the economy is increasingly focusing on supplying experiences, services and solutions rather than commodities.[1] This is matched in industry and design by a move away from thinking about isolated products towards designing patterns of relationships and behaviours which guide these experiences.[2] Socio-cultural developments indicate a need for solutions that provide simplicity, flexibility and sustainability, and a technology for people should allow people to choose and shape those features of products and services which they themselves perceive as desirable, meaningful and appropriate.

Investigating the adaptive and personalized delivery of functionality and services to the end-user, and the impact of this on both the user and the brand, enables us to contribute to an understanding of what it means to be a 'digital' brand, and how this would affect the long-term relationship between the brand and users. As a result of this investigation, Philips Design proposes 'Open Tools', a strategy for personalization and customization in Ambient Intelligence that is based on a dialogue between the user and adaptive tools in the delivery of content, functionality and service.

Open living

In the past few decades, daily life has undergone subtle yet substantial changes. The stability and reassurance we once found in well-structured, predictable routines can no longer be taken for granted. Our approach to living, commerce, technology and the use of services is increasingly complex and 'open': we relocate, job-hop, freelance, we carry out many activities in parallel, we travel in different ways for work and leisure, and we interact with and freely choose between various content, media and service schemes.

Yet in attempting to navigate this open lifestyle, we are currently limited to choosing between unwieldy multipurpose devices such as the PC, or numerous dedicated products and services that are fixed in their application potential and have a short lifecycle, needing frequent replacement. Manufacturing-led mass customization techniques provide a wider range of choice at purchase, but are not sustainable. A truly personalized offer should be constantly open to dialogue and negotiation with the user regarding its purpose and abilities.

Simplicity, flexibility and sustainability

Open living requires new tools, and so new design strategies. A brief look at some relevant sociocultural, technological and business trends helps define the drivers for creating these tools and strategies.

Sociocultural trend analysis indicates a growing desire for simplicity, flexibility, trust and sustainability. In the face of our increasingly complex and changeable living and working habits and environments, we need less confusion and more simplicity. Simultaneously, we are showing a preference for solutions that are sensitive to our specific values and choices as individuals. We require flexible solutions that allow us to perform our activities across dynamically changing contexts. There seems to be a desire for more security, trust and reassurance, mirrored by a drive towards more social interaction and knowledge exchange and longer, more sustainable relationships worth investing in.

Technologically, the combination of digital networking, software and open standards and platforms means that devices are becoming able to access any number of distributed resources, services or functionalities. The affordance of these devices will increasingly be determined as much by their software as it is by their physical properties and hardware. Tangible products, such as mobile phones, already deliver their services through large, intangible, networked systems maintained by provider companies. This system architecture itself is becoming flexible and open-ended, and is non-proprietary, making use of open standards allowing products, content and services of different origins to work together.[3] Consequently, devices are being designed with less constraining hardware and more upgradeable and adaptive software, and recent advances mean that now even the chips can be reconfigured.[4] Together, these developments allow the creation of 'future-proof' tools which will be able to evolve as necessary.

Current business trends reveal an increased interest in selling highly personalized and customized experiences to end-users in appropriate contexts. These interests are fuelled by a desire to increase the longevity of customer brand interaction and ensure brand fidelity and continuing returns over a longer period. The delivery of such 'holistic' experiential solutions for the end-user implies new partnership models for businesses, especially between the vendors of devices, networks, software and content.

These trends can be condensed into three key objectives for the design of a framework which delivers meaningful services, functionality and content in an intelligently personalized and adaptive manner: simplicity, flexibility and sustainability.

Simplicity
We require tools that provide simplicity in the face of increasingly complex and changeable living and working habits and environments. We need tools that can help us navigate and make sense of the growing density of our informational environments and the increased speed and reach of our mobility.

Flexibility
We require tools that are flexible in that they allow us to improvise and move freely and creatively across situations and environments involving digital elements, and that respond usefully to the effort we invest in them.

Sustainability
We need tools that are sensitive to our current needs whilst leaving control firmly in our hands, and that provide sustainability, longevity and reassurance by becoming truly customized to our unique situation over time.

A new design strategy for deep customization
Current mass-customization techniques do not satisfy these key needs. Due to manufacturing limitations, they have until recently been based on allowing a selection at purchase from a limited range of options and are therefore defined by short consumption lifecycles. Examples include customizable Dell computers, Nike shoes and mobile phone clip-on covers.

The Internet and software-based devices such as mobile phones have gradually allowed richer customization services to emerge, for example Websites providing new screen graphics, new types of ringtones, logos or extras for mobile phones. In 1998, Philips launched the Pronto family of 'universal' remote controls. These remotes allow users to freely create and customize their own interfaces, and come packaged with a software application for that specific purpose. The Pronto can be made to control virtually anything with an infrared eye in it, and user communities in which people swap interface designs and application ideas or even 'home-grown' application software have formed. By putting the tool and its 'destiny in life' firmly in the hands of the user, the Pronto has become a success.

Based around this idea and the framework of Ambient Intelligence, the Open Tools strategy takes current customization trends one step further towards truly meaningful solutions, proposing the in-depth customization and adaptation of tools through their use.

Open Tools

The Open Tools strategy describes a new paradigm for deep customization in the delivery of content, functionality and services. The strategy answers the key needs of simplicity, flexibility and sustainability by making use of the new possibilities afforded by digital, networked services. It aims to provide people with tools which can become truly customized to their unique environment, needs, desires and patterns of use over time. In an increasingly complex world, Open Tools aim to be 'open-minded', to achieve a greater connection between the end-user, the tool, the desired experience and the brand.

Open Tools are defined as digitally enabled product-service combinations designed to offer the user a range of latent functionality that can develop through their use, becoming customized to any user's specific requirements over time. An Open Tool becomes what you make of it!

Open Tools are conceived as digital service units that allow an ongoing interactive dialogue between the user and their preferred services, functionalities and content. They provide personalized solutions based on longevity, allowing a sustained dialogue between the user and the brand over time. Open Tools contain 'latent' potential bound by a designed set of rules. They allow the user to negotiate and develop functionality within these boundaries. Through use, the user causes the tool to become specialized to specific functions. Over time, new potential or specialized functionality can emerge. This process may be explicit, with the user making adjustments to the tools, or implicit, with the tools themselves responding to their use and context. These adaptations empower the user and encourage further investment in the tool.

The paradigm consciously takes into account the possibility of both users and third parties contributing to the customization of their devices in unanticipated ways. Consequently, an Open Tool has the potential to become specialized to specific functions over time and during use in ways not anticipated at the time of design.

Open Tools in use

Open Tools channel personalized content, functionality and services from a global pool to a specific user, based on their use of each specific tool over time. Although the Open Tool is in this sense flexible and adaptable, it is still a 'tool' as opposed to an unwieldy multipurpose device. As such, it has a sense of purpose which has developed through the user's choices. As an Open Tool, however, its definition is not final, but in a constant state of becoming. To understand how such tools might enable the delivery of customized content, functionality and services to the user through a personalized set of interfaces and tools, Philips has developed a framework consisting of the interplay of three basic elements: the Open Hand, the Open Tool and the Open Space. These shape a system in which Open Tools form a personalized point of contact and a place of articulation between the user and digital resources and services.

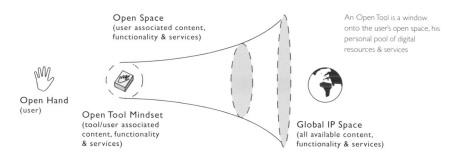

Open Space
(user associated content,
functionality & services)

An Open Tool is a window
onto the user's open space, his
personal pool of digital
resources & services

Open Hand
(user)

Open Tool Mindset
(tool/user associated
content, functionality
& services)

Global IP Space
(all available content,
functionality & services)

The Open Hand

The Open Hand symbolizes the user's unique identity. For Open Tools to be able to deliver personalized functionality and services over time and across networks as well as locally, users need to be able to identify themselves. Identification can take many technical forms, from entering a pin number to using biometric data, and allows an Open Tool to be intimately, securely and uniquely linked to one person.

The Open Tool

Upon purchase, an Open Tool will carry some object-related constraints, and will have certain basic functionalities and connectivity to services associated with it. As the tool is initially 'factory-fresh' and unused, it can be said to be 'open-minded'. As each Open Tool is used, successive moments of use form a local, tool-specific memory. The tool can remember information and content viewed, used and created, or functionalities and services used, as well as contextual information such as time, place, activity and people involved. Over time, its memory reflects the role the user wants the tool to play.

The Open Space

Each user's Open Tools connect to their Open Space, their personal pool of digital resources and services. Each Open Tool will have a unique way of accessing this Open Space depending on its own memory of use, prioritizing or disregarding relevant content, functionality and services.

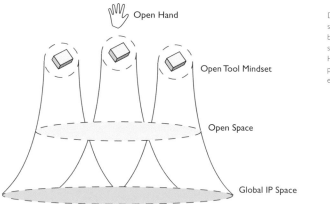

Open Hand

Open Tool Mindset

Open Space

Global IP Space

Different Open Tools form
specialized points of contact
between digital resources and
services and the user.
However, each tool retains the
potential to access the user's
entire Open Space

Over time, items of content, functionality and services will gradually form relations to those Open Tools they are used with, to each other and to the context in which they are used. These relations may be explicitly formed by the user, or implicitly formed by higher-level 'smart' software (see 7.4: Intrinsic and Extrinsic Intelligence).

Designing for potential

That which is overdesigned, too highly specific, anticipates outcome; the anticipation of outcome guarantees, if not failure, the absence of grace.[5]

William Gibson

To be able to design Open Tools, the role of the designer must undergo a radical shift in emphasis. Rather than designing the finished product, in which every detail has been worked out for a particular context or setting, the designer will be designing for potential. This involves designing for simplicity, for flexibility and for sustainability.

Designing for simplicity and transparency

Open Tools aim to provide simplicity by helping us personalize, channel and navigate our increasingly dense informational environments. It should be up to the user to determine the preferred balance between complete control and giving up some control in favour of the simplicity provided by intelligent software. Transparency and simplicity of the user interface and interaction framework will be vital in ensuring the user does not lose perspective. This imposes heavy expectations on the design of user interface and interaction frameworks for Open Tools. Users need to be clear about the potential use of an Open Tool if they are to invest in it. The tools can invite use by providing a clear and simple view of relevant possibilities and how these can be achieved.

Designing for flexibility and evolution

Through use, Open Tools unfold aspects of their potential. An important design issue here is the tension between the intuitive 'sense of purpose' a tool should provide and the possibilities for evolution of that tool offered by its digital framework. The physical properties of an Open Tool will make it better suited for use in certain contexts, whereas its digital possibilities are much more flexible. Restrictions therefore need to be designed into the system. The designer needs to be skilled in 'boundary care', giving each tool just the right amount of freedom of movement in functionality without losing its sense of purpose.

Open Tools can also allow some direct physical customization, depending on the technology available. Today, users could choose materials, colours, shapes and accessories; in the future, the design of 'smart skins' could allow the tool's surface colour, display and potentially even its shape to change in response to the context of use. As hybrid physical-digital objects, these tools are also flexible in that they can evolve by partnering with new peripherals or other products.

Designing for sustainability and longevity

The Open Tools strategy centres around a set of new interactive relationships between the user, the tool and its associated brands. The qualities of these relationships will be vitally important, both in relation to immediate operational interactions with Open Tools and in relation to time, with the emphasis on behaviour and the development of a long-term dialogue. The design of product-user, product-product and system-system relationships will crucially contribute to overall brand perception. As the main daily contact point between the user and the brand, Open Tools will carry a high responsibility in terms of delivering the right experience.

This raises the question of how we can develop appropriate design methodologies and product rationales for such evolutionary 'enhanced life' products. The designed behavioural properties of the Open Tool will determine how it reacts and responds to its environment, unfolding new experiences for its user over time. As part of a longer-term relationship, Open Tool systems can also be designed to contribute to a sense of trust by being accurate, non-intrusive and clear in their functioning and by providing security mechanisms the user can rely on.

Business implications

A strategy for personalization and deep customization such as Open Tools will also affect current business models and the brand-customer relationship. Open Tools are essentially service units which 'live' with the user. They allow brands to provide experiences and guide transformations by forging long-term customer relationships, and allow product and service co-creation to continue after purchase. They are mnemonic points of contact which form a focal point for memories of compelling experiences by providing transparent, adaptive customization as well as cosmetic customization. The Open Tools strategy is a business platform that allows brands to develop and maintain a direct, tailored, interactive dialogue with their customers over time through digital service units.

When purchasing an Open Tool, the user buys into an open dialogue with a highly personalizable device, and new business models will be able to make full use of the increased customer interaction. Similarly, these new models will involve returns over a longer period for both the user and the brand, and lead to a greater degree of customer interaction with the brand. This implies a greater responsibility on the part of the company for the products, systems and services that it manages.

Open Tools as service units may encourage access rather than ownership, since software functionalities and content need not necessarily belong to or be stored with the end-user. The physical or product aspects could also be open to business models centred on leasing rather than ownership, with instant personalized configuration occurring upon and during leasing.

Conclusion

In some ways, the Open Tool strategy is a strategy for the domestication of technology through Ambient Intelligence: just as an old suitcase reflects its passage through time and the user's journey through life, so the Open Tool becomes a mirror of the user's habits, needs and desires. It is able to reflect these in its functionality as well as in its outward interface and interaction mechanisms, both with the user and with other objects. The more the interface and interaction design of Open Tools address this 'journey with the user', the more valuable the tool becomes to them.

1   B.J. Pine and J.H. Gilmore, *The Experience Economy* (Boston, Harvard Business School Press, 1999), 165
2   N. Bolz, 'The User Illusion of the World: on the Meaning of Design for the Economy and Society in the Information Age', *Mediamatic*, vol. 9, no. 3 (1998)
3   IBM, *Autonomic Computing: IBM's Perspective on the State of Information Technology* (October 2001); Wireless World Research Forum, *The Book of Visions 2001: Visions of the Wireless World* (2001), online at http://www.wireless-world-research.org
4   R. Ball, 'Why the future for FPGAs looks rosy', *Electronics Weekly* (29 August 2001); International Conference on Evolvable Systems 2001: From Biology To Hardware (Tokyo, October 2001)
5   W. Gibson, *All Tomorrow's Parties* (London, Penguin, 2000), 133

3.2 COMPUTATIONAL INTELLIGENCE

Emile Aarts, Jan Korst, Wim Verhaegh

Electronic systems may be said to be intelligent when they exhibit three characteristics: the ability to solve problems, the ability to predict and adapt, and the ability to reason. Within computational intelligence – the scientific and technological pursuit of designing and analyzing algorithms that, when executed, give electronic systems such intelligent behaviour – there are a number of approaches that seek to address one of these three characteristics. A variety of well-known search methods are used to tackle the question of problem-solving; machine learning techniques are applied to produce prediction and adaptation; and expert systems are used to generate the ability to reason. These approaches will be described below, with particular reference to Ambient Intelligence. Since many problems encountered in the context of Ambient Intelligence are intrinsically hard to solve, we also need to address the topic of computational complexity.

Artificial intelligence

Computational intelligence can be seen as a sub-field of artificial intelligence, which Minsky describes as the science of making machines do things that require intelligence if done by men.[1] The subject (which dates back to the early days of computing science and Turing's first models for electronic computing)[2] focuses on the study of vision, natural language and speech processing, robotics, knowledge representation, problem-solving, machine learning, expert systems, man-machine interaction and artificial life.[3]

Over the years, this field has produced a number of major achievements, many of which are discussed by McCorduck[4] and Norman.[5] These include various expert systems: one using speech and dialogue technology to facilitate hotel reservations and travel planning; a computer program to assist physicians in making a diagnosis (MYCIN); and another to help geologists explore oil fields (PROSPECTOR). Artificial intelligence research has also resulted in robots that can play baseball, climb stairs or play chess: IBM's Deep Blue was the first chess computer that could compete at world masters' level. Neural networks – introduced as artificial computing models based on an analogy with the human brain – were used to produce NETTALK, the first operational neural network able to produce speech from written text. Arguably, all these achievements were the result of using sophisticated algorithmic methods that were able to make excellent use of greatly increased computational power that had become available.

More recently, several exciting new developments have arisen within artificial intelligence. One of these is the result of incorporating elements from cognitive science. For instance, the generally held belief that human intelligence does not follow a specific predetermined path to accomplish a task but merely responds to a current situation gave rise to a novel concept known as 'situated action'. This concept has been applied with great success in robotics by replacing classical path-planning by approaches governed by environmental response mechanisms. Another new development in artificial intelligence is the use of 'case-based reasoning', solving problems using commonsense understanding of the world, based on the use of ontologies embedded by agents that carry information about the meaning of fundamental everyday concepts such as time, objects, spaces, materials, events and processes.

Problem-solving

Problem-solving involves selecting from a large set of alternatives one solution that will minimize or maximize a given objective function. Usually, the set of possible solutions is not given

LIME AND PL@NET

LiMe uses agent technology to
search intelligently for relevant
information and stories

PHENOM

WWICE

EASY ACCESS
AND LISY

SMARTMIRROR

SPICE

LIME
AND PL@NET

explicitly but is rather defined implicitly by a number of variables that, within certain
constraints, need to be assigned a value. The set of possible solutions generated by such
a compact description is often exponentially large. Let us look at three classic methods
of searching through such a solution space for an optimum result.[6]

The first is known as 'branch and bound'. With this method, the solution space is recursively
split into subspaces (by setting the value of a variable, for example). This splitting is the
'branching' aspect, and results in a tree-like search pattern. The 'bounding' aspect consists of
pruning as many parts of the search tree as possible: a simple 'bound' on the value of solutions
in a given a subspace (corresponding to a subtree) is compared with the best solution found
so far, and if the bound is not even better, the subspace is pruned, and the proliferation of
solutions thus limited.

The second method, generally more efficient, is 'dynamic programming'. This is often used
if the problem is structured in terms of solution states. Basically, if values have to be assigned
to a number of variables, one variable is considered at a time. For each possible value of the
variable, a check is performed to establish the effect of choosing that value in terms of its
direct effect and the state that would result. The value that delivers the best result is selected
and the process is repeated with the other variables until all have been assigned a value.

The third classic method, called 'linear programming', is applicable if all constraints and the
objective function can be expressed linearly in the variables and if the variables themselves are
continuous. In this case, an optimal solution can be found in a run-time that is polynomial
in the size of the problem instance (i.e., not exponential).

It is often impossible to find an optimal solution within an acceptable time. In that case,
resort is made to the use of heuristics.[7] 'Local search' is commonly used to find a reasonable
solution instead. This involves making small alterations to a possible solution that has already
been found, iteratively changing it a little, and each time evaluating whether the change has

a favourable effect on the objective function. If so, the new solution is accepted and used for the next iteration. If the change causes the objective function to deteriorate, the new solution may be rejected unconditionally: this approach is known as 'iterative improvement'. Alternatively, a mechanism may be used to accept the solution with a certain probability (which is lower the greater the deterioration and which is reduced as the algorithm proceeds). This approach is called 'simulated annealing'. Local search has given good results for various well-known problems and it is easy to use in that it requires hardly any specific problem knowledge.[8] A slightly more sophisticated approach is to use what are known as 'genetic algorithms'. These allow iterated modifications to be made using not just one solution, but a population of solutions at the same time. Cross-over schemes can be defined between different solutions to generate 'offspring' from two 'parent' solutions. A rule of 'survival of the fittest' restricts the population to only the best solutions, which become 'parents' in the next iteration. In this way, good solutions are found by a form of evolution.

Not all search problems come with an objective function, i.e., they do not require 'the best' solution to be found: sometimes only a feasible solution is required. A common method that can be used in this situation is called 'constraint satisfaction', whereby a solution is sought that meets a number of constraints. By combining several constraints, the sizes of the domains from which the values of the variables are to be taken are reduced ('constraint propagation'). When domains cannot be reduced any further, a variable is selected and assigned a value from its remaining domain. Then again constraint propagation is applied and a new variable is assigned a value, and so on. The strength of this method depends on the extent to which improbable values can be eliminated by combining constraints: considerable research has been devoted to finding those types of constraints that lend themselves best to propagation.

Machine learning

Machine learning will be a key factor in making Ambient Intelligence systems capable of adapting and predicting. Machines are adaptive if they can learn a given input-output behaviour on the basis of training examples. They can predict when they are able to generalize this behaviour beyond the observed situations.[9]

The best-known method in machine learning is perhaps the application of neural networks, built on the analogy of the human brain. 'Neurons' have inputs and outputs, these outputs being linked to inputs of other neurons. Each neuron takes a weighted sum of its inputs and, depending on the result, sends a signal to its output. For communication with the outside world there are also input neurons and output neurons. During training, the input pattern of a training example is fed to the input neurons, and the weightings are adjusted so that the required output pattern is achieved. During actual application, the input pattern of a new situation is fed to the input neurons, and the output neurons are read to obtain the predicted response.

Another machine learning method is based on 'support vector machines'. Support vector machines can perform classification by generating a separating hyperplane in a multi-dimensional space. This space is usually not the space determined by the input variables, but a higher-dimensional space that is able to obtain classifications that are non-linear in the input variables. An advantage of support vector machines is that they minimize structural risk by making a trade-off between the error in the training examples and the error in the generalization.

A different way of dealing with classification is afforded by what are called 'Bayesian classifiers'. This approach makes use of classification rules that are based on probability theory. Using Bayes' rule of conditional probabilities, the classifier then uses probabilistic reasoning to arrive at the most probable classification for any new example. In other words, *a posteriori* probabilities are derived from *a priori* probabilities. An advantage of Bayesian classifiers is that they allow the use of prior knowledge. The combination of prior knowledge and inferred knowledge is an important subject in current research in machine learning.

Expert systems

An expert system is a computer program that, within specific knowledge domains, provides solutions to search problems or gives advice on intricate matters by making use of reasoning mechanisms. Expert systems can emulate human reasoning using appropriate knowledge representations, they can learn from past experiences by adjusting the reasoning process to follow promising tracks discovered on earlier occasions, and they can apply rules of thumb ('heuristics') to 'guess'.

The behaviour of expert systems can be transparent, in that they can explain how solutions are obtained. They can also be used in situations which require decisions in real-time. The performance of expert systems is typically evaluated on the basis of criteria normally applied to human task-performance, such as consistency, regularity, typicality and adaptability – all of which relate to the basic requirement that repeated and minor changes of input should produce results that make sense. The reasoning mechanisms of early expert systems were based on logical rules. More recent approaches, however, apply probabilistic reasoning and mechanisms that can handle uncertainty. The latest development is the introduction of 'semantic engineering', based on important concepts such as belief, goals, intentions, events and situations, often including the use of ontologies. The use of the 'semantic Web' is another intriguing new development, which may further stimulate the development of expert systems that can perform truly convincingly performance across a range of applications.

Much attention has recently been devoted to 'agent systems'. These are collections of small intelligent software programs that perform certain tasks collectively. They run continuously and exhibit intelligent behaviour (such as adaptability and automated search); they exhibit anthropomorphic properties in their interactions with users, through the expression of belief or obligation and even through their appearance; they act independently of human control or supervision; they are context-aware (in the sense that they are sensitive and responsive to environmental changes); they can interact with other agents and migrate through a network; and they can develop themselves to become reactive, intentional, and eventually social. The development of agent technology is a rapidly growing field of computational intelligence. Since their introduction about a decade ago, intelligent agents have been widely recognized as a promising approach to embedding intelligence in interactive networked devices, and for that reason it has a special significance in relation to Ambient Intelligence.

Computational complexity

Based on theoretical computer science, it is possible to analyze the complexity of computational intelligence algorithms. This has led to a distinction between 'easy problems', which can be solved within polynomial (i.e., non-exponential) running times, and 'hard problems', which are believed to be not so solvable. This means that some ('hard') problems may not be able to be solved successfully within a reasonable time. Indeed, if the instance size is sufficiently large, running times for certain problems may easily extend beyond a human lifetime. Such intractable problems require methods that do not perform the task optimally but rather approximate the final result. Although such approximation algorithms may reduce computational effort, if the quality of the final result is required to meet certain criteria, then for many well-known problems exponential running times are still inevitable. That is why heuristics without performance guarantees are often used. This improves running times considerably, but at the cost of final solutions that may, in theory, be arbitrarily bad.

A learning system constructs a number of hypotheses concerning a given target function

PHENOM

WWICE

EASY ACCESS
AND LISY

SMARTMIRROR

SPICE

LIME
AND PL@NET

whose precise form is unknown. How can the system decide which hypothesis is the 'correct' one? Several approaches are possible. 'Identification in the limit' works on the assumption that, presented with enough training data, a learning system will eventually be able to converge on the target function. Early work in computer science, based on Popper's theory of falsification, suggests that this may not be possible, however, the implication being that certain learning tasks are unperformable. A second approach is to apply 'Ockham's razor', which states that the most likely hypothesis will be the simplest one consistent with all training data. Simplicity here can be defined in terms of 'Kolmogorov complexity': the length of the shortest program accepted by a universal Turing machine implementing the hypothesis. The question also arises as to how many training examples a learning system needs to be presented with before it can accept (within certain limits) a hypothesis as having a high probability of being correct. This issue is addressed by the theory of Probably Almost Correct (PAC) learning. However, the theory suggests that for certain non-trivial learning tasks the number may be exponentially large, thus requiring exponential running times.

Applications

Computational intelligence can claim an important role in the development of Ambient Intelligence. Much of the intelligence exhibited by ambient systems is generated by techniques originating in the field of computational intelligence. In personal recommender systems, for instance, machine learning techniques (e.g., Bayesian classifiers, neural networks and support vector machines) are used to capture the viewing or listening behaviour of users into personal profiles. Play lists are generated using sophisticated search methods that select titles which match optimally with the profile. In collaborative recommender systems, expert systems techniques are first used to compile a collective profile reflecting the preferences of a set of users, and then sophisticated search techniques are used to compile a play list matching the collective profile. There are now collaborative recommenders that make use of the semantic Web to exploit the collective knowledge representations built by communities of Web users.

'Query by humming' is an intentional search application that allows a user to browse music databases by simply humming tunes. It applies sophisticated string-matching techniques such as dynamic programming to find approximate matches between the melodies extracted from the humming and the melodies in the music database. These techniques are extremely efficient in searching for matches, and allow online data mining. The domain of intentional search applications for media browsing is rapidly developing techniques that can effectively analyze audio and video material and generate 'metadata', information about the content at higher

EASY ACCESS

levels of abstraction, such as object types and genres. These items of information may form nodes in a data network, with the arcs in the network used to represent semantic relations between the items. Search techniques can then be used to reason within the network to respond to certain queries.

Neural networks can be used to generate metadata from media files by analyzing patterns and deducing spatial and temporal relations. They can also be used to analyze audio and video streams to extract specific features. Applications could include classification of music genres, speaker identification, scene detection and image recognition. Neural networks can also be used to select characteristic passages of speech or images as a content-addressable memory.

The uses for computational intelligence techniques in an ambient intelligent environment are abundant. One particular field of interest is context awareness, whereby systems take account of contextual factors in their reasoning. Analog neural networks, for instance, can be used as adaptive sensing devices that detect and adjust low-level signals within domestic or mobile environments to control, regulate and personalize environmental conditions, such as temperature, humidity, draft, loudness and lighting. One step further is to reason what higher-level factors may be responsible for such environmental conditions (e.g., a thunderstorm, the time of day, or the fact that the room is empty). A step beyond that might be to apply reasoning to deduce appropriate pre-responsive actions or make suggestions to the user: for instance, if it is night-time, the room is empty and the light is on, the system could suggest switching it off.

PHENOM

WWICE

EASY ACCESS
AND LISY

SMARTMIRROR

SPICE

LIME
AND PL@NET

1   M. Minsky, *The Society of Mind* (New York, Simon and Schuster, 1986)
2   A. Turing, 'Computing machinery and intelligence', *Computers and Thought*, ed. E.A. Feigenbaum and J. Feldman,
    (New York, McGraw Hill, 1963)
3   M.A. Boden, (ed.), *Artificial Intelligence* (San Diego, Academic Press, 1996)
4   P. McCorduck, *Machines Who Think* (New York, McGraw Hill, 1979)
5   D.A. Norman, *Things That Make Us Smart* (Cambridge MA, Perseus Books, 1993)
6   C.H. Papadimitriou and K. Steiglitz, *Combinatorial Optimization: Algorithms and Complexity* (Englewood Cliffs, Prentice-Hall, 1982)
7   I.H. Osman and J.P. Kelly (eds), *Meta-Heuristics: Theory and Applications* (Boston, Kluwer Academic Publishers, 1996)
8   E. Aarts and J.K. Lenstra, *Local Search in Combinatorial Optimization* (Chichester, Wiley, 1997)
9   T.M. Mitchell, *Machine Learning* (New York, McGraw Hill, 1997)

3.3 DATA AND CONTENT MANAGEMENT

Eelco Dijkstra, Willem Jonker, Hans van Gageldonk

Content plays an important role in our lives, from music, photographs and books to films, radio programmes, news broadcasts, and more. Since the invention of printing, technology has had considerable influence on the creation, storage, distribution and presentation of content. Just as recent technological advancements in multimedia and the Internet have influenced content and how it is managed, the Ambient Intelligence vision will influence it in the future. Where multimedia has introduced new ways of modelling (e.g., object orientation) and retrieving content and data, and the Internet has led to new ways of handling semi-structured data (e.g., XML), Ambient Intelligence will lead to new ways of managing data and content. But what are the key data and content management issues that will need to be addressed to support Ambient Intelligence? To answer this question, we will first address the key qualities of an ambient intelligent world from a data and content management perspective. We will then explore in more detail the kinds of data and content involved, followed by a discussion of the management issues along two lines: intelligence and ambience.

An ambient world

The ambient world is best described by means of example scenarios. Three such scenarios were developed recently in a study devoted to the relationship between storage and Ambient Intelligence. [1]

Record your life

Imagine that all the events in your life were recorded and available to you. For instance, you could carry a tiny camera and microphone somewhere on your head (other embodiments and content types would also be possible). This could support various goals, enabling you to relive your memories or recall past events that are hard to remember – when you bought your first car, what that great recipe was, what it was that guy said exactly, whether the dog was limping a bit already yesterday, or whether that suspicious-looking birthmark thing on your back had grown significantly over the last six months.

Your content anywhere

Imagine being able to access your collections (photos, music, video, etc.) from any location, whether you were in the car, at the office or in a hotel room, at any time. You could also easily allow other people, such as friends or family members, to have access to particular parts of your content collections, or share a complete collection with others. You want your privacy protected, without being continually bothered by password schemes or other irritating identification procedures.

Ambient room

Imagine a meeting room that could behave intelligently. It would be able to extract keywords and topics from the conversation and to present relevant and/or amusing associations with the topic discussed. It would also be able to show some topic history, i.e., how you arrived at a particular topic. Perhaps the associated information and content would be presented on the walls or on interactive windows. The room might also have ambient windows, transparent windows able to present any scene in high-quality 3D video. This would enable you to create a 'room with a view' that could differ every day or automatically adapt to your mood.

Key qualities

These three scenarios illustrate the key qualities of Ambient Intelligence: embedded, adaptive, anticipatory and personalized. Let us explore what these terms mean from a data and content management perspective.

Embedded

Data and content in an ambient scenario can be stored on a wide variety of heterogeneous devices that are in some way interconnected. In the 'Record your life' scenario, data and content are stored in a collection of portable registration devices as well as on a home server. In addition, input devices for the creation of content (sensors, cameras, microphones) and output devices for the presentation of content (screens and speakers) are deeply embedded in the environment.

Adaptive

The presentation of content should be adapted to the situation and the environment in which it is used. In the 'Your content anywhere' scenario, the presentation of content is the same when you are at the wheel of your car as it is when you are sitting in front of a large screen.

Anticipatory

The content offered to users should anticipate the users' intentions. In the 'Ambient room' scenario, the content depicted on the wall anticipates the information necessary and relevant for the discussion in the room.

Personalized

Content should be targeted to the specific user, based on their point of view and preferences. In the 'Your content anywhere' scenario, for example, only relevant content is presented.

In order to analyze and describe the technological requirements of these qualities for the handling of data and content in the ambient environment, we distinguish the following components:

- The content itself and metadata (i.e., data describing the content, necessary for the automatic interpretation of the content to enable personalization, adaptation and anticipation).
- The context in which the content is presented, consisting of people, locations, objects and events. Both current and historical information, such as the television-watching profiles of viewers, are required. For personal content, such as photographs or home movies, the context of the content's creation is also relevant, as it may provide data for the description of the content.
- The wired or wireless connected devices for input, storage, distribution and presentation of content. Usually, these devices have a high degree of autonomy.

For the first two components, the use of metadata describing the content and its semantics and the organization of the content and data play an important role (discussed further below). With regard to the third component, a primary problem, already encountered today, is the handling of content over a set of connected autonomous devices. We may want to play music on an audio (MP3) player (which can also be used as an independent device) via the speakers in the living room. The next step is that we don't even want to know where the music resides: it is enough to know that we have it 'somewhere' on those connected devices, and this should suffice to identify the music. For the goals of adaptation, personalization and anticipation, we need a much more elaborate system for storage and retrieval, including the data describing the content and the context. A centralized solution for this is probably impossible: each of these autonomous devices will have its own organization. This brings us the problem of integrating the data and content management of these autonomous devices in such a way that users are still served unobtrusively.

I-PRONTO

PHENOM

WWICE

EASY ACCESS
AND LISY

MIME

SPICE

LIME
AND PL@NET

Types of data and content

Before exploring the data and content management techniques needed to support the kind of ambient scenarios described above, we will elaborate on the types of data and content that play a central role in Ambient Intelligence. Three kinds of information are required to support the qualities of Ambient Intelligence: information about the content, the user and the context. Content can therefore be divided into raw content and metadata, with three subcategories of metadata: content-related, user-related and context-related.

Content

Content refers to any uninterpreted information in digital form. This includes electronic documents of any nature, such as electronic forms, text files or electronic books, as well as digital multimedia information, such as images, digital audio, video, etc.

Metadata

Consider a large collection of items, such as video films, music tracks or still photographs. To find the items we want, or to interpret an item found, we need some data describing these items: metadata. We might want to find a movie with a specific title, or want to know who is in a particular picture. Metadata often has a specific application 'in mind', such as enabling easy content retrieval, for instance.

Content-related metadata is data that describes the underlying content, in terms of features, concepts or other relevant information. Content-related metadata is mainly used for search and classification purposes. The best-known metadata standards are MPEG7 and Dublin-Core. The metadata can be derived from the content itself or be independent, from an external source. An electronic programme guide, describing the programmes broadcast by a specific channel, is independent metadata. As pattern-recognition capabilities improve, we can sometimes derive metadata with the same information as independent metadata.

User-related metadata is data that describes the user, and can be either static or dynamic. Static metadata describes the user's preferences and stable characteristics, while dynamic metadata describes the user's behaviour. Static user-related metadata is often referred to as user profiles.

Context-related metadata is data that describes the context in which the user operates. This can vary from a simple indication of the location to a complex description of the environment.

Metadata may relate the content to its contexts: to the context of creation (e.g., describing the actors in the movie or the location of the photo); to the context of distribution (e.g., describing the distributor, price, access rights, etc.); or to the context of its user (as an element of a television-watching profile of a specific person, for example).

Metadata gives meaning (semantics) to content, and is essential for intelligent retrieval and anticipatory actions. Often, the value of the content increases significantly when the right metadata is available – for instance, when you learn that the people in that unidentified photo happen to be your distant cousins. The creation of precise and useful metadata can be very time- and labour-intensive, so the automatic generation of metadata is important. This generation can be done by analyzing the content (metadata extraction), by using information from the context, or by a combination of the two. In an 'intelligent ambience', there is much available context information which can be used as metadata for the content created in this environment. Consider taking a photo in such an environment: not only are the time and location known (e.g., meeting room 3 in the WDC building, on 23 July 2003, 10:30), but also what meeting has been planned, who is expected to attend, etc. Given such information, the facial recognition process is much easier, since the set of 'candidate' persons to find on that photo is very small.

Metadata can also be used to link content to other content or other independent metadata. Once the person in the film has been identified as the actor James Dean, other movies with the same actor can be found. When a tennis player has been identified, his results in other games can be displayed.

Finally, metadata can be associated with people in the context in which the content is used. One example of this is profiling information, obtained from observing the television-watching behaviour of those persons. In an intelligent ambience, there will be many sensors, and thus many occasions to observe the behaviour of those in that environment.

In summary, the kinds of information that play a role in ambient scenarios are the actual content, the semantics of this content and the contextual information. The three scenarios show that ambient systems also need to provide mechanisms to organize and retrieve content, as well as mechanisms to learn from both content and context, and to relate content to specific contextual information.

Bridging the gap

Data and content management can be seen as the bridge between the developments in storage technology and Ambient Intelligence. This is well illustrated in *Storage in an Ambient World*, paraphrased here. On the one hand, the developments in storage technology act as an enabler for data and content management in that they allow high volumes of data to be stored on a wide variety of devices. On the other hand, they present new challenges to ways of handling data and content distributed over an environment of interconnected devices.

Two major technological trends in storage have been identified. The first is the exponential growth in storage capacity over the past decade, envisaged to continue; the second is the miniaturization of storage components, also expected to continue. The exponential growth in storage capacity will allow the capturing of high volumes of data, and the storing of digital content by consumers.

I-PRONTO

PHENOM

WWICE

EASY ACCESS
AND LISY

MIME

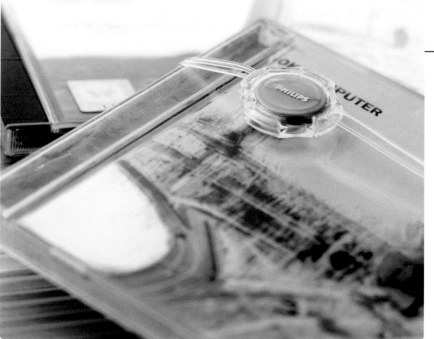

MIME

The MIME GlowTags add metadata to physical objects of emotional significance

Content management and retrieval techniques much more advanced than the current simple play list will be needed in the near future. Content organization and metadata will play a central role here. In an Ambient Intelligence context, the dimensions of intelligence and adaptive behaviour have to be added. From a content perspective, this means that semantics of content become crucial. The interaction with the content also has to be taken into account in order to learn access patterns related to specific user intentions.

The miniaturization of storage components has enabled the development of very small tags, tokens and sensors with local storage. In the Ambient Intelligence context, this allows the seamless integration of storage components in a variety of everyday objects and devices, i.e., 'embedded storage'. The result will be an environment in which storage will be present in a large heterogeneous collection of objects and devices that will all be interconnected. In order to control and manage such an environment, scaleable architectures are needed that support high degrees of autonomy of the participating components.

This holds for the system architecture, but also for the data management architecture that governs the data kept on the storage components. Particularly in the case of sensors and tags, this data also represents contextual information that can be exploited to create the adaptive and anticipatory behaviour that characterizes ambient intelligent systems.

Intelligent data and content management: find, learn and anticipate

Finding the right information in vast amounts of content is one of the most challenging issues in ambient scenarios. Contrary to traditional retrieval systems where 'right' can be clearly defined, in the scenarios 'Record your life' and 'Ambient room' the notion of what is right is not so easy to capture. Not only must content that exactly responds to the query be retrieved, but also content that is in some way related, in that the user sees a clear association between the retrieved content and the query.

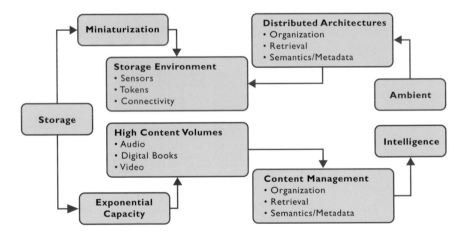

Research on associative retrieval extends traditional information retrieval research by taking user feedback and contextual information into account. Modelling user intentions and associations is core, as are new indexing techniques that allow irrelevant information to be discarded quickly. In addition, learning techniques should be exploited to update user models based on previous retrieval behaviour.

The modelling and description of the content itself are also crucial. Research on metadata representation and handling, as well as on semi-automatic generation (e.g., feature extraction) to allow content-based retrieval, is key here.

Another important characteristic of ambient systems is their anticipatory behaviour. Many scenarios envisage systems that anticipate user intentions based on their habits. As a rule of thumb, their behaviour in the past can be used to predict their wishes for the future. In order to allow systems to do so, much information must be processed and interpreted to build predictive models of user behaviour.

The central issues here are to acquire and interpret the relevant information in order to allow predictive or anticipatory behaviour. The techniques that can be applied and need to be developed are mainly statistical methods and data-mining techniques. The bottleneck is the development of scaleable techniques able to analyze huge volumes of data continuously generated by the various devices and sensors of the ambient environment.

Ambient data and content management: embed and interconnect

Many ambient scenarios envision large numbers of interacting devices that jointly produce some kind of intelligent behaviour. In order to make this work in a real-life environment, a scaleable and robust system architecture, together with a scaleable content management solution, has to be provided as the basis for any 'intelligent' layer on top.

The system architecture issues deal mainly with the question of how to design the architecture of the processing, communication and storage in a system in a scaleable way that can cope with the distributed and heterogeneous nature of the system components in ambient scenarios. The components include small devices, sensors, electronic tags, consumer electronics devices, etc. Monolithic system architectures are not adequate, and component based system design seems the way to go.

The content management issues deal with the question of how to organize and manage content in a scaleable way in an environment of distributed, heterogeneous and embedded data sources. Given the complexity of the environment, centralized solutions seem to be inadequate, and new ways of managing content in a kind of self-organizing manner have to be explored. The vision of organic databases is very relevant here. Decentralized solutions immediately bring up issues around the consistency and coherency of information, and scaleable caching, replication and synchronization techniques will therefore need to be developed.

Conclusion

The main trends in content management focus on the organization, retrieval, interpretation and targeting of content. In all these areas, content semantics play an important role, most clearly demonstrated by the interest in metadata research and closely related activities around semi-automatic or automatic content interpretation. Contextual information is also highly significant, particularly in content targeting, as can be seen from the research activities on personalized content and location-related content.

I-PRONTO

PHENOM

WWICE

EASY ACCESS
AND LISY

MIME

SPICE

LIME
AND PL@NET

1   W. Jonker, N. Lambert, G. Mekenkamp, R. van de Sluis, E. Aarts and W. Leibbrandt, *Storage in an Ambient World* (Technical Note, Philips Nat Lab, July 2002)

3.4 FLOW: THE EMERGENCE OF RICHNESS FROM SIMPLICITY

Paul Thursfield, Monica Bueno, John Cass

Everyone has experienced flow within some aspect of life. Think about how musicians can lose themselves in jamming music, or how a parent and child playing together can experience complete absorption in an activity. The suspension of time, the freedom and the sense of pleasure this gives lead to fulfilling experiences and a sense of 'flow'.

The importance of flow at Philips Design became apparent while presenting the Pogo project at the Comdex technology showcase in Switzerland in November 2001. Pogo is a system of tools for children to use at school to create stories with pictures, sound and video. The idea was to take a new approach to computer tools that would allow collaborative and expressive ways to create and tell stories. The prototype system seemed to strike the right balance between the needs of children and teachers, encouraging experimentation and fun while giving a focus to the activity. Many Comdex visitors also commented on the ease with which children could use Pogo with little or no instruction.

Members of the design team were encouraged, but also perplexed about why Pogo worked so well. It seemed unprecedented that a computer system should produce such rich results and work so well for people with no prior experience or instruction. We knew that it had something to do with focusing on the nature of activities as opposed to specifying outcomes. This enabled us to build a system that allowed very diverse results from the combination of very simple elements. People using the system were developing unexpected ways of using Pogo elements and tools in a process we named 'tool combining', which supported

POGO

Children use Pogo's collection of tools to create rich results easily and with little or no instruction

improvised actions. Although this was not exactly a revelation in itself, we realized that we didn't really know so much about how or why it happened in the first place.

How was the flow in activities facilitated, and what were the elements necessary to make this happen? This chapter will discuss the different components of flow and how design can acknowledge these.

The desire for flow

In observing many people's private and professional activities, psychologist Mihaly Csikszentmihalyi has found flow to be a universal experience sought and referred to in all cultures and walks of life.[1] Flow seems to make people feel in contact with the world around them, giving a sense of reason and purpose to their activities. Csikszentmihalyi is particularly interested in how this occurs in everyday life, and surprised that such an important effect on well-being has been given so little attention in modern society. So what are the flows that people desire and need?

The smell of bread

First, there is the flow of sensations. Sensations are the primordial level of our being. Everything we know about the world comes through our senses and the feelings and emotions we associate with them, both pleasure and pain. It is the activation and stimulation of our senses that makes us alive, gives us a sense of being and makes us what we are.

Can technology be appealing to our emotions? Certainly its power and efficiency have long captured our attention, but it has often been at the expense of sensations. Though the emotional and psychological benefits of sensations are difficult to measure, we are nonetheless aware that they play an important role in our lives. In fact, new technologies, once mature and established in people's consciousness, pass into a stage of 'cherished' sensations and are no longer seen as technologies. People no longer think of pen and paper as a technology, but measure their quality by the emotional performance of feel, colour and surface, as well as functional performance.

Design has been very successful in stimulating our aesthetic senses by creating forms with seductive attractiveness and desirable beauty, but these have often turned out to be shallow and unappealing in the long term when the surface personality has failed to turn into deeper, satisfying experiences. In *Undesigning the Bath*,[2] Leonard Koren describes how design often fails to understand how to provide a deeply satisfying sensual experience to the act of bathing because of over-reliance on form rather than the formation of experiences. Sensations are the building blocks that create the substance of experiences, and technology is in fact full of new and deeply impressing sensations – if we just release them.

Butter side down

Next are the flow of actions and the way we get things done. Actions are probably the most obvious way in which flow occurs in activities. The action/reaction premise, taught in physics classes at school, is familiar to most people. From a very early age, we learn about the multitude of results that can emerge from our actions, and develop highly tuned motor skills to get the results we are looking for. This is how we communicate with reality, bend and shape it to our purpose, and become very good at theorizing about the nature and operation of things before we have even touched them.

For the action/reaction method to work successfully, however, it must be possible to establish a logical cause and effect loop. The user performs an action and a certain reaction is clearly the result. The more latency introduced into this causal 'flow', the more difficult it becomes to rationalize the link between an action and an outcome, making it increasingly

WWICE

STREAMIUM

MIME

POGO

CONNECTED
PLANET

CAMP
AND MADS

OPEN TOOLS

LIME
AND PL@NET

ICD+

harder to utilize. This behaviour of objects is all too often missing when using the latest digital electronics and is degrading our skill and dexterity. Frequently, the numerous buttons and knobs on equipment seem to be entirely unresponsive or result in unexplainable outcomes that don't seem to relate to them. Writing with a stylus and PDA is definitely inferior to writing with a pen on paper and forces us to write in a manner that is completely unnatural. And why do touch screens only allow one finger at a time? In Pogo, children wanted to paint with more than one finger!

Appropriate tools are needed that make the best of our natural skills, respond consistently to our actions, and offer 'rich usability'. They need an 'active skin' that will serve as a seamless point of contact between us and the increasingly immaterial world of technology. In *Hertzian Tales*, Anthony Dunne refers to an 'immaterial sensuality' of technology.[3] This sensuality will add a new dimension to the behaviour of digital technologies moving them beyond mechanistic analogies and metaphors, and making them respond intimately and organically to our touch and manipulation.

How do you like your toast?

Then there is the flow of narrative that allows us to establish the relationship between things. Language lets us communicate and express ideas and meaning. We use many languages, not just the language of words. There is the language of our bodies and gesticulation, the language of expressions that show how we are feeling, and there is the language of eyes and what we are looking at. Our technologies have allowed us to further enhance this with additional languages of symbols that represent meanings, through the use of different media. Painting, drawing, writing and music are all languages we can read and in most cases understand. But these are the end products of our technology. What if we were to communicate with technology itself?

In fact, we already communicate with complex systems. We instruct many of our objects, such as thermostats, in what to do, and the system works away, carrying out our wishes. However, the bandwidth of communication is narrow and usually more mechanistic than human in its nature. The video recorder is a well-known example of this problem. Everyone knows that to make a recording, certain information is necessary, such as the time, channel and date. Yet people still find it difficult to make a recording. This is invariably a communication problem. The way we communicate and organize processes is parallel, collaborative and non-linear, and most technology is not able to cope with this very human mode of communication.

My kind of bread

Finally, there is the flow of value, that gives relevance and meaning to something. Think about how you arrange your CDs on the shelf. Perhaps they are in alphabetical order, maybe you prefer to arrange them in genres, or maybe the most recent are nearest to the player and the rest are in no particular order. The arrangement and layout is there and says something about your music habits and tastes. It has a structure and system which might only make sense to you, but which you are able to understand and use.

In many instances, this structure has as much value as the content itself. Nicholas Negroponte refers to this in *Being Digital* as the 'bits that describe the other bits'.[4] Where does something come from, who created it, should I believe it? Reputation and character can say everything about the real value of something. Context is also very important – right time, right place, right thing. Yesterday's news has little value today, but tomorrow's news today would be priceless.

Technology needs to become far more a product of the users' nurture than of the nature of its manufacture; a digital entity that can learn and respond to the habits, likes and dislikes of

WWICE

STREAMIUM

MIME

POGO

CONNECTED
PLANET

CAMP
AND MADS

OPEN TOOLS

LIME
AND PL@NET

ICD+

the user, and understands appropriateness and timing. Its value in the long term goes beyond functionality and content, as it is the product of a person's own investment and has become more part of their life as a result.

Flow experts

Humans are actually 'flow experts'. We are extremely sensitive, have great expertise in the handling of the physical world, can behave and respond appropriately to events around us, know how to interpret different meanings into language, and can make value judgments based on slippery issues such as reputation and behaviour. Can we use this innate ability to greater effect? Is it possible to imbue our technology with the equal of these skills and create simpler and richer flow in our use of it?

Designing for flow

Life is not made from atoms, it is merely made out of them. What life is actually 'made of' is cycles of cause and effect, loops of casual flow. These phenomena are just as real as atoms – perhaps even more real. If anything, the entire universe is actually made from events, of which atoms are merely some of the consequences.[5]

Steve Grand

If we wish to design for flow, what are the things we need to keep in mind? Clearly, designing for flow is quite different from designing the typical form factors of physical objects. Flow has no substance or materiality, but it pervades all activities and events, and if we wish to design for it, we need to consider new words to describe it. Potential, nature, diversity, growth and vitality are terms that are more typically associated with living things but may also be used to describe the nature of flow. In designing for flow, we need to understand these.

Designing for potential

For flow to happen, it is important that there is a possibility for it to occur in the first place. The Japanese concept of Wabi Sabi is particularly concerned with the nature of potential.

Its core theme is the idea that the greatest potential lies in nothingness, and that everything in the universe is either devolving or evolving towards nothingness. Nothingness is something that is as hard to imagine as the vastness of space, but where there is space there is the greatest possibility for something to emerge, as nothing is decided.

Technology can be full of growing potential. Who would have believed the potential that lay in hypertext, for instance, a relatively simple concept whereby the user is in fact the author of the relevance and order of reading information, rather than following the order defined by a writer. Simple things can have very large and far-reaching effects.

Designing for nature

What are the intrinsic properties and qualities that make a thing a 'something' or even a 'living thing'? According to Steve Grand, we have a 'hierarchy of liveliness' with which we discriminate things in the world. This colours our perceptions of the nature of things and therefore the way we behave towards them.

Most of our technology is a non-living entity that needs our presence to animate it. We understand most technologies from a mechanical perspective, tending to focus on how they work and what they do for us. With the advent of digital media, especially intelligent media, our relationship to technology is changing. As Reeves and Nass demonstrate,[6] when confronted with digital and interactive technologies, people tend to treat the system as they would another human, with respect, politeness and observance of social norms.

Designing for diversity

Every pebble on the beach is different; every snowflake has another pattern. Diversity is clearly a property of life, both the means and outcomes. There is no single perfect means or perfect way: there are simply different ways and means. You can take the super-express highway in your Porsche or you can take the picturesque route on bicycle, or maybe a bus tour that takes in certain sights. All are journeys, and each has different means and opportunity, but which is most fulfilling depends on the situation.

Unfortunately the benefits of industrialization and standardization seem to have crept into areas where it has far less benefit. Leonard Koren complains about 'the accelerating trend toward the uniform digitalization of all sensory experience' and the way things that normally have freedom of expression are being standardized and made into formulaic procedures of correctness. E-mail and word processing have realized great benefits, but at the same time have removed an enormous bandwidth of expression available to a person with pen and paper. How long will it be before the treasured drawings of young children also adhere to the template mentality of a drawing application?

Designing for growth

In *Origin of Species*, Charles Darwin created a theory of evolution that laid out a theory of the development of life on earth. Over time, due to the events of natural selection, species evolve, grow and die out according to natural conditions and competition. The processes of growth are known to science and have been named and categorized. How life happens, however, is still a mystery.

Learning, adapting and reproducing are all strategies used by life and could potentially benefit technology. At present, this still seems a long way off, despite the power of computers such as IBM's Deep Blue, which recently 'won' several matches of chess against world chess champion Kasparov. However, it still took a team of programmers to teach it how to deal with Kasparov's changing tactics, which were constantly adapting and testing the machine's knowledge.

Designing for vitality

What is the life-force of something? This is not just the energy that gives animation and movement to something; it is also what gives it its purpose and directs its actions. Objects have functions, systems have behaviours, and entities have motives. Functions are something that technology clearly possesses, but what about behaviour and motives?

At the moment, technology often lacks even rudimentary behaviour, and only takes on the motives of the user very temporarily. Left to its own devices, our technology would soon come to a stop, run out of power, or break down. This has led to a terrible burden of maintenance and upkeep that is fast becoming unmanageable. There are very few cases where technology attempts to become self-contained and self-sufficient; robot vacuum cleaners look after themselves and recharge when necessary, and computer viruses can be voracious in their aim to destroy information. But most of our things – the phone, the PDA, the computer – need constant care and attention, and are unable to look after themselves.

Flow and Ambient Intelligence

In the past century, 'flow' has become synonymous with efficiency of operation, unimpeded movement and consistent flawless operation and results. Regularity, predictability and perfection are goals that have been at the core of scientific progress and the Industrial Revolution, to the point where these ideals have been applied to almost every aspect of life. But here lies the flow paradox: despite all this effort, we have in many cases ended up with sterile, inhuman and humourless results that have alienated people and are entirely out of step with the living qualities of our world. A never-changing, unresponsive, repetitive, mechanistic future is perhaps not the future that many would readily welcome.

Impermanent, incomplete and imperfect

The very things that industrialization has sought to eliminate, such as irregularity, uncertainty and difficulty, are the very things that can make life interesting and worth living, because they make us feel alive and give us involvement, challenge and excitement. This is not a suggestion that everything should become a challenge, but skill of use is not fatally antagonistic to ease of use: they are simply different forms of intelligence. One is provided by the intelligence and knowledge that can be built into our technology for the benefit of the user, and the other is the intelligence and knowledge that lies within the user to be active and make their wishes known to technology. Though technology is a very effective provider of comfort and saves human labour, carrying out those duties we cannot or do not wish to do, we still have a role and say in the quality of what they do and how they behave. We still have and enjoy a certain degree of control over our technologies in terms of our relationship with them and their response.

What we will make of technology in this new century should become more about people. The kind of intelligence we put into technology and what our relationship with that intelligence will be should emerge from our needs and circumstances, and not be dictated only by the needs of manufacturing. Then maybe technology will truly become 'technology for people'.

1   M. Csikszentmihalyi, *Flow: The Psychology of Optimal Experience* (New York, Harper and Row, 1990)
2   L. Koren, *Undesigning the Bath* (Berkeley, Stone Bridge Press, 1996)
3   A. Dunne, *Hertzian Tales* (London, Royal College of Art, 1999), 85
4   N. Negroponte, *Being Digital* (New York, Alfred A. Knopf, 1995)
5   S. Grand, *Creation: Life and How to Make It* (Cambridge MA, Harvard Business Press, 2001)
6   B. Reeves, C. Nass, *The Media Equation* (Cambridge MA, CSLI Publications, 1996)

WWICE

STREAMIUM

MIME

POGO

CONNECTED
PLANET

CAMP
AND MADS

OPEN TOOLS

LIME
AND PL@NET

ICD+

MOVE, ACCESS, LIBERATE

Is Ambient Intelligence something we can only have at home, or will we be able to take it with us, on the move? How might it enable us to access whatever information we want, from wherever we are? How will we be able to communicate most conveniently through our Ambient Intelligence system with people elsewhere, liberating us from the constraints of time and space?

4.1 MOBILITY: FREEDOM OF BODY AND MIND

Evita Stoop

The Ambient Intelligence vision proposes that people will be empowered in their daily activities by technology that surrounds them, responds to them and anticipates their needs, yet remains invisible to the eye. Although this 'invisibility' – or rather, unobtrusiveness – is only one element of the vision, it provides an interesting entry point for this discussion of mobility and relevant and meaningful technology on the move. As Emile Aarts puts it, 'The elimination of this visible hardware is how we will know we are on our way to an Ambient Intelligence future'.[1] The 'disappearance' of technology is easily imagined in a home or work environment where the architectural context is relatively static and predictable. Using the infrastructure of walls, furniture and decoration as hiding places for our technology will make the home of the near future resemble the tranquil home of the past more than the technology-dominated home of today.[2]

But how can such a vision support activities and experiences on the move, when people are not restricted to one or several known spaces? How can our interaction with technology be made unobtrusive and significant in a dynamically changing context? Could mobile devices also be internalized in the infrastructure of the only static environment that accompanies people as they are on the move – their clothes or body? Could it be interesting to perceive our environment increasingly as an extension of our own personal space?

Freedom to walk and talk

Let us first look at the essence of those human values and desires that drive us to be mobile, to explore the world around us, to experience ultimate freedom of body and mind. We will then explore how unobtrusive technology can support us in our quest for freedom on the move.

The ups and downs of connectivity

… the ultimate goal of our species is omnipresence, omnipotence, omniscience: the ability to be everywhere, to do everything and to know everything.[3]

Stefano Marzano

More than ever, people are in search of freedom – to go where we want to go and know what we want to know. Today, we are not necessarily challenged by the borders that separate us from the places we want to be, from opinions we would like to express or from information we would like to obtain. Planes, trains and cars quickly take us to anywhere on earth, making us feel at home in the process. Russian spaceships have just started their first commercial flights to the moon, stretching mobility even beyond our planet. The Internet has opened up other horizons. Allowing access to a global information database and communication forum, it provides an extra dimension of freedom, crossing the borders between the real and the virtual. In this new world, there are new rules and possibilities. Now, for example, Iranian women can speak out about taboo issues on 'Weblogs' set up after a huge growth of Internet access in the Middle East. In the entertainment industry, a virtual kingdom built by millions of gamers ranks as the 77th largest economy in the real world, between Russia and Bulgaria.

But besides the benefits of these new powers and areas of freedom, we also increasingly experience the responsibilities of being globally connected. We are faced with the downsides of this multiplicity of choices, possibilities and opportunities. Today, our challenge is defined rather by what we don't want to do or know, than by what we can do. To quote Mark Taylor, we are living in a 'moment of unprecedented complexity when things are changing faster than our ability to comprehend them'.[4]

This overflow of information, possibilities and choices might leave us unwilling to be connected at all. As much as the Internet can free people by opening the gate between the real and virtual worlds, this extension of connectivity and personal presence in both worlds can also be abused. Children are now bullied not only in the playground, but also through SMS messages and e-mail; this bullying is more pervasive and harder for parents or teachers to control. We want to be continuously connected, but we also want products to know when we don't want to be disturbed. This theme has been central to the Philips Context-Aware Mobile Platforms (CAMP) project, understanding that people want specific things, in specific places, at specific moments, related to their specific individual or social situation. This is part of what the Ambient Intelligence vision understands by 'relevant and meaningful technology'.

Mobility offers an extension of choice, but we would like our choices to consist of relevant and meaningful options. In this sense, technology should be considered both as an inspiring means of increasing people's freedom to move, and as a gateway to services that support people on the move with access to information, communication, entertainment and education.

Why do people value technology-enabled mobility?

The general notion of 'freedom of body and mind' can be viewed as arising from five different motivations: productivity, showing off, caring, exploring and belonging. This helps us to construct a new definition of 'mobility' and to envision the impact technology will have on mobility in the near future.

Productivity: I feel free because I can work whenever I need to

Our private and business lives have become increasingly interrelated. We need to be accessible and connected to our information sources wherever we are, whenever pertinent and significant. In today's global economy, being mobile seems more of a given than a choice for those aiming to juggle choices, responsibilities and desires.

Mobile devices should empower the business world to connect to any relevant information or person in an efficient, effective and transparent way, increasing productivity. This is exemplified in one of the scenarios of the Connected Pl@net project. A businessman joins a meeting and instructs his device to switch into meeting mode. It will now ring discretely, but only for high-priority communication.

CONNECTED
PLANET

CAMP
AND MADS

CONNECTED PLANET

Mobile devices should empower, not over-power the business world

LIME
AND PL@NET

ICD+

NEW
NOMADS

All other messages are diverted to his secretary or his voice mail. During the meeting, he uses his Bluetooth pen to take notes on paper, which are then displayed and stored on his device. A voice message from his daughter is translated to text and he quickly writes his reply.

Showing off: I feel free because I am (perceived as) who I want to be

As Josephine Green puts it, 'Individuals explore and implement different ways of organizing and living their lives and search for new personal strategies and fulfillment in an ever more option-filled life – mosaic lifestyles'. People will always be interested in expressing their personality. As the specific aspect they want to express changes over time, even within a day, the elements that can support this expression need to become more flexible, both in functionality and in style. Mobile devices should enable this dynamic behaviour of expression unobtrusively, making the device an integral part of a person's emotional and bodily expression.

Caring: I feel free because I feel cared for

Trends related to care, safety and security point to the emerging need for devices that support us in monitoring ourselves, our loved ones, our possessions and our memories, wherever we are. Mobile solutions which are less confusing and more humane in their use and application can help us feel more confident in our use of technology. Mobile solutions can increase the experience of freedom by enabling us to take care of ourselves and others, be it to check on our children or grandparents, to monitor home security or to create cars and planes which feel like home. A French company, Novacor, is currently developing miniaturized heart-rate recorders patients wear around their necks, providing a direct link between patient and clinician. No longer hospitalized, and free to move, the patient gains both physical and mental freedom and a sense of maximum care.

Exploration: I feel free because I can go wherever I like to go

Humans have always liked to explore and discover things about our world, our environment and our inner self. As our frame of reference expands due to knowledge about other cultures, religions and our own capabilities, we search for new triggers and experiences that go beyond the known. On the move, devices should help us to explore, record, manipulate, store and share these new experiences. Our interaction with technology should address all of the human senses. Mobile solutions should fully support and motivate the person on the move, stimulating multi-sensory interaction, triggering creation and facilitating exploration and discovery.

MOBILE WINDOW
Mobile devices should
offer human interaction

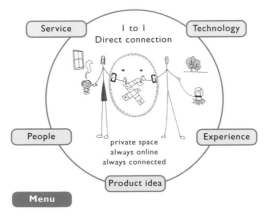

Belonging: I feel free because I am not alone

As global citizens, we travel the world and explore different cultures, both digitally and physically. As a result of the Internet and digital communication, we sometimes lose real-life contact with other people and need devices that mediate human interaction. This interaction needs to convey as much of the richness and intimacy of the intended communication as possible. Supporting our aspirations for communal belonging, mobile devices should offer dedicated solutions, enabling us to engage with the right people and exchange meaningful information and access to relevant knowledge.

People look for tools that will help them to create a sense of belonging, even in virtual communities, but without replacing the need for human contact. By valuing the different relationships between people, knowledge and environments, we can design solutions that foster social cohesion and rich knowledge-exchange on the move. As researched in the Mobile LiMe project, the creation of micro-communities that foster special relationships between a select group of people with mobile devices becomes a way to 'layer' the connectivity between community members. Not every community member is equally connected, just as not every friendship is equally important.

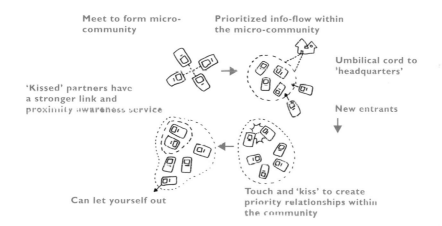

Meet to form micro-community

Prioritized info-flow within the micro-community

Umbilical cord to 'headquarters'

'Kissed' partners have a stronger link and proximity awareness service

New entrants

Can let yourself out

Touch and 'kiss' to create priority relationships within the community

MOBILE WINDOW
Micro-communities layer the connectivity between community members

Technology should also enable people to actually come together more often. Mobile communication and Internet relationships have increased global travel; people have a greater need for technological support on the move, not only because of the increased amount of travel, but also because new technology has actually enabled and motivated increased contact between people on a global scale.

Around me, on me, in me

Let us now look more closely into the 'unobtrusive' or embedded aspect of Ambient Intelligence. How can we design devices that offer us the benefits of intelligent technology without us adjusting to the product, but rather the product adjusting to us, our environment and state of mind? How can we experience the benefits of modern technology while on the move, rather than experiencing the difficulty of interacting with highly advanced technology?

Smaller is better?

One major development in technology has been the ongoing miniaturization of audio, video and computer technology. Thanks to digital technology, the dimensions of devices are no longer determined by the size of their constituent components. Many people carry an audio player, a telephone and a handheld computer in their pockets. In our enthusiasm to miniaturize,

CONNECTED
PLANET

CAMP
AND MADS

LIME
AND PL@NET

ICD+

NEW
NOMADS

we are overlooking the idea that smaller is not always better. With miniaturized products come smaller input and output elements, such as buttons and displays. We don't always seem to realize that we need those elements to be able to translate our personal wishes into the functionality of the device, or for us to obtain content from these same devices. Miniaturization and complexity conflict with ease of use.

Disconnecting physicality from functionality

As the technology offering the core functionality of devices shrinks, we can disconnect this functionality from their physicality. Once a device is so small that the size of the components does not dictate a physical form factor, we can start to think of physicality in a way that is most enabling to the total user experience. The form or shape of mobile devices can then be optimized to the specific motivations of the person, whether these are related to productivity, showing off or exploration. The physical carrier, the interface and gateway to underlying functionality, might be integrated in one of the most essential elements that people always carry with them, such as jewellery, clothing or even their own body. Alternatively, the functionality might be embedded in the environment that person moves in and accessed only when relevant.

Progressive integration

The first layer of technology integration into the personal domain will be integration into our clothes or the accessories on or around us. The Philips Design Wearables group researches and develops wearable electronics in programmes such as the ICD+ project with Levi's or the MP3 venture with Nike. The group explores intelligent fibres that can conduct electricity, sense heat, cold or sweat, display visuals or change behaviour according to the physical status (stretch, pressure) of the material. Wearables overcome the contradiction between an ever-expanding array of functionalities and miniaturization, incorporating trends in consumer adoption of technology into the fashion statement. The ritual of dress combines the functionalities of protection, thermal insulation, waterproofing and links with personal and cultural qualities of aesthetics and identity. This ritual could be evolved so that in future people will be able to assemble an outfit that connects the traditional usage of clothing with its potential new usage – information, communication or entertainment – empowering the wearer and providing seamless and efficient solutions for mobility (see Chapter 4.3, Intelligent Fibres).

In this sense, unobtrusive technology is not actually about hiding the technology, but about making it appropriate, comprehensive, more human and so less 'alien'. Using intelligent fibres, we can design solutions that distribute the technology all over the body, creating a true Personal Area Network (PAN). The 'real estate' of the body provides endless opportunities to distribute controls, such as displays, audio feedback and power sources. Natural movements, gestures and speech can all be used to control and direct an application through dedicated or shared input and output channels, such as displays, controls or sensors. Intelligent software can be applied to create a network that can learn how you prefer connecting to various people. The wearables will adapt to the user, rather than the user to the system.

From carrying separate or networked portable and mobile devices products with us, we may move towards using wearable solutions that integrate technology, and finally even into a future of completely integrated technological solutions using the human body as their physical carrier. As Stefano Marzano argues in New Nomads, 'The ultimate step will be when we have such functionalities incorporated directly into our bodies'. It will be some time before people widely accept the integration of technology into their bodies, but starting in the medical arena (e.g., pacemakers, prosthetics), people are becoming increasingly used to depending on it. In Design, Technology and the Body,[5] this area of technology is actually clustered into a new domain alongside hardware and software, referred to as 'wetware'. These developments raise new ethical, medical and infrastructural questions; the possible violation of human rights is a particularly sensitive issue.

Access versus ownership

Another issue arising from the notion of splitting the physicality of a product from its functionality and content is the possibility of not having to consciously carry it around. Instead, relevant data can be accessed when required. One way this can be executed is by designing products containing latent functionality, applications available in the device which become apparent only when the user needs and values them. Instead of bringing along several products with dedicated applications on a journey, one could have an 'access key' that knows how to unlock virtual doors to whatever may become relevant. We could describe this as a 'mobile window' through which we see things in different ways depending on what we want to look at. A mobile device then becomes an intelligent agent that helps access only the functionality specifically of interest to you. Such a product will become deeply customized to your personal needs, desires and preferences as you use it over time.

Beyond envisioning mobile devices which make use of internal intelligence, we can also think of access-concepts where the intelligence is built into our environment. Tagging technologies, for example, allow the environment to be activated if a person with a certain profile enters that space. Think of a bus stop that recognizes you and displays relevant details, billboards showing commercials related to your preferences, or fashion stores broadcasting information on clothes you have shown an interest in. Products in a car or the family television can provide personalized content to meet individual needs. As you are on the move, the personal domain currently defined by your body's contours will expand to incorporate parts of the environment. These access-related themes are elaborated in projects such as Connected Planet, WWICE2, CAMP and Pl@net.

Conclusions

As technology shrinks over time, we are challenged to design mobile devices that become a more natural part of the fabric of life. We can imagine designing new interaction models to access functionality, such as extending the personal domain into the situational context or even using the human body itself as a vehicle. The essential value of mobility, however, is the ultimate notion of freedom of both body and mind that it can support and stimulate. Mobile technology can motivate people to move more freely by providing them with the relevant tools to be productive, to express themselves, feel safe, explore and connect with others. It can also support them once they are on the move, giving them access to solutions that meet the needs of their immediate personal context.

CONNECTED
PLANET

CAMP
AND MADS

1 E. Aarts (Philips Research), speech given at the opening of the Philips HomeLab (2002)
2 Philips Design, *La Casa Prossima Futura* (Royal Philips Electronics, 1999)
3 Philips Design, *New Nomads* (Rotterdam, 010 Publishers, 2001)
4 M.C. Taylor, *Awe and Anxiety* (University of Chicago, 2001)
5 J. Thackara, 'Working with Wetware: Design, Technology and the Body', *Winners* (Amsterdam, BIS Uitgeverij, 1997)

LIME
AND PL@NET

ICD+

NEW
NOMADS

4.2 PERVASIVE WIRELESS

Neil Bird

Wireless communication already plays a significant role in our everyday lives, and with the Ambient Intelligence vision defining requirements for future wireless technologies, it will become increasingly important. Take, for example, the explosion of mobile phone use in recent years: in several countries, more than half the population now own a mobile. In the developed world, almost every household now has a television (in many cases, several) which is operated using an infrared (but nevertheless wireless) remote control. We are in the midst of a wireless connectivity revolution: technologies such as IEEE 802.11b have resulted in the increasing use of wireless LANs for computer networks, and our mobile phone or MP3 player can now be wirelessly linked to a headset using Bluetooth. For simpler applications, new technologies such as ZigBee are emerging; soon even the humble light switch will become a wireless device. In the near future, Ambient Intelligence will be a major driver for the development of next generation wireless technology. The technical challenges are considerable and diverse, but the ultimate goal is clear: these wireless links and networks must be pervasive – but not invasive.

The need for pervasive wireless in Ambient Intelligence

The Ambient Intelligence vision describes digital environments that are sensitive, adaptive and responsive to the presence of people. A number of scenarios and modes of intelligent interaction in these environments are described in this book. The technological requirements of these scenarios are diverse, from sophisticated user interface concepts to distributed sensors. Yet underlying this diversity is a common theme: the need for communication. For example, sensors in a distributed network will need to communicate their status to a monitoring device. A new user interface might rely on communication with a person's badge or ring to be able to determine where that person is and what gestures they are making. Consequently, we require a range of technologies that allow devices, objects and people to communicate with their environment and with each other. Since people are mobile and many of the devices and objects will be moveable, portable or even wearable, most of this communication will need to be wireless.

So what are the characteristics of these wireless links and networks? In answering this question, we must start by considering the types of data that need to be transferred. Table I outlines five different categories, from video and audio streaming through to the transfer of control and status messages.

There is clearly a wide range of requirements, and it is extremely unlikely that we will see a single 'one-size-fits-all' standard emerging for all devices and applications. In recent years, a number of different standards have already been defined and implemented. For the higher data rate applications, a set of standards known collectively as IEEE 802.11 exists. Developed as a wireless replacement for wired LANs, various derivatives are now emerging for high-quality multimedia transport for our wireless home entertainment networks. At the other end of the spectrum are standards such as ZigBee and Bluetooth,[1] which have been developed with specific applications in mind. ZigBee is a low-power, low-cost but relatively long-range wireless network intended for applications such as home automation, toys and games, and personal health care applications (e.g., body area networks for fitness monitoring). Bluetooth has a higher data rate capability than ZigBee, and has been developed for *ad hoc* networking. It is the technology choice for many applications including audio streaming in mobile phones and wireless headsets.

Type	Rate	Technology	Description
Video	3-6Mbit/s 2-3Mbit/s 1.5Mbit/s 784kbit/s	802.11a/g 11b (with Qos enh.) 802.11b 802.11b	DVD (MPEG2) Broadcast (MPEG2) Broadcast (MPEG2) PDA/Small screen (MPEG4)
Audio	500kbit/s 128-300kbit/s ≤64kb/s	High rate BT High rate BT BT	Surround sound HiFi (stereo) Voice
Data Transfer	≥2-3Mbit/s	High rate BT 802.11a/b/g	E.g., file transfer
Control	<100kbit/s	BT, ZigBee	Wireless remote control
Status	<100kbit/s	BT, ZigBee	E.g., sensor reading

TABLE 1
Typical wireless data

In terms of the new requirements posed by Ambient Intelligence, wireless links for the last two data categories in the table, control and status, are arguably the most challenging. These are the links that will connect the multitude of devices and objects together in our ambient intelligent environment. They will be everywhere, pervasive but hidden. It is this combination that raises so many technological challenges: how can we integrate a radio device into a tag, a token, a badge, or an everyday object such as a pen? These radios will need to be extremely small and very low-powered. With literally hundreds of these devices in our homes, changing batteries simply won't be feasible. Finally, the data rate that needs to be supported by these devices is low. Typically, messages from one device to another will be very basic: 'I'm too hot', 'Turn on', and so on. For many applications, even a few bits per second will suffice. In order to make an environment intelligent, it is not so much the complexity of messages that is important, but rather the sheer number of them.

The 'WWW' of pervasive wireless

So far, we have only considered one aspect of pervasive wireless, the 'what' – the actual data that is transferred between devices. But this is only part of the story. In many cases (if not the majority), in order to turn the data into something useful, we also need to consider the 'who', 'when' and 'where'. The 'who' is simply an identification element ('which sensor?') and is generally taken care of by the wireless network protocol. The 'when' information is generally already available. Virtually every electronic device sold today contains a clock, or at least a timing element from which time can be derived. The last 'W', the 'where', is something that we all take for granted. It is difficult to think of almost any activity that does not depend on where we are, where we want to go or where something else is. In an ambient intelligent environment, knowledge of where people, objects and devices are is therefore a prerequisite for the environment to be able to adapt and respond in an intelligent manner. This might be simple, such as displaying the football match we're watching on a display in the room we're in, or optimizing the flow of data through a network by hopping between nodes that are physically close together. When the wirelessly linked devices communicate, in many cases a key element of the data exchanged is the location of the source of the message and the location of its destination.

Let us now concentrate on two aspects of pervasive wireless: low data rate and low-cost radio devices and systems, and the issue of providing location information.

CONNECTED
PLANET

CAMP
AND MADS

OPEN TOOLS

LIME
AND PL@NET

Low-power wireless technologies

Two standards have been defined to address the need for low-power radio links: Bluetooth and ZigBee. Of these, Bluetooth is arguably the best-known, and Bluetooth-enabled products are readily available. Bluetooth is intended as a cable replacement, and supports applications such as *ad hoc* networking, hands-free audio (e.g., headsets) and the transfer of data such as screen graphics, pictures and files. However, with a data rate of 720 kilobits per second and other advanced features, Bluetooth is 'overkill' for many home control applications and many of the Ambient Intelligence requirements. The ZigBee standard has been designed to address these low data rate applications. ZigBee supports a data rate of 128 kilobits per second, and is designed to be inexpensive (between $1.5 and $2.5 by 2004). Typical ZigBee applications include static networks between simple devices, sensors, home automation and control, and data exchange. A typical ZigBee network is shown in Figure 1. The blue lines represent the wireless links between the 'slave' devices and the master device, and the red lines represent virtual connections between the slaves. All real communication links are between the master and its slaves. In this way, for example, the light switch (a slave device) can control the table lamp (also a slave device). A routing table maintained by the master keeps a record of the virtual links and allows the master to forward messages from one slave to another. The other main features of ZigBee are outlined in Table 2.

FIG. 1
Typical ZigBee network

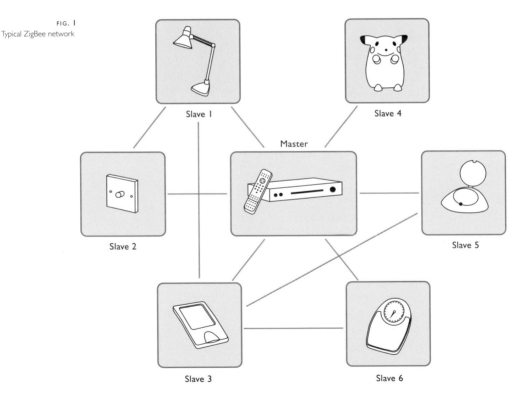

Slave 1   Slave 4

Master

Slave 2   Slave 5

Slave 3   Slave 6

Some differences between Bluetooth and ZigBee

A ZigBee network is made up of a master unit and up to 254 slaves, of which four can be time-critical devices such as joysticks. Multiple networks may be co-located, as each one has a unique ID. This is essential if several networks are active in the environment at the same time, and also in buildings such as apartment blocks, as the radio frequency (RF) signals can penetrate walls and ceilings. A piconet (i.e., a network of devices connected in an *ad hoc*

Frequency	2.4GHz global licence free ISM band operation
Data rate	250kbps over air
Data throughput	128kbps (implementation-dependent)
Operating range	10-30m
Network	Support for up to 255 devices (including 4 critical devices) Support for co-located networks
Battery life	0.5-2 years

TABLE 2
Main features of ZigBee

fashion using Bluetooth) also contains a master device which administers the network, but it is limited to just seven active slave devices. However, there can be in excess of 200 'parked' slaves, with a 'park mode' to render the slaves inactive but still synchronized to the master. Co-located networks are possible in Bluetooth, as each network has a unique hopping pattern and it is possible for devices to be registered on multiple piconets, thereby forming a scatternet (i.e., a group of independent and non-synchronized piconets that share at least one common Bluetooth device).

For ZigBee devices, the battery lifetime from standard batteries is expected to be two years or more, depending on how the device is used. In fact, for a device such as a wireless light switch, which might only be used a few times a day, the shelf life of the battery is expected to dictate the replacement interval. This low-power capability is a direct result of the design of the protocol. For short-range radios such as Bluetooth and ZigBee, it takes more power to receive data than it does to transmit it. This is critical in designing a low-power protocol such as that used by ZigBee. In a ZigBee network, the slaves are designed so that they can remain in a powered-down sleep mode most of the time, periodically waking up to interrogate the master. In contrast, Bluetooth devices do not have this level of power optimization, and are designed to be used in devices that have power models similar to mobile phones, in that they require regular charging.

These and other differences between the two standards do not mean that one is intrinsically better than the other: they are optimized for and targeted at different types of applications. What is clear is that both of these technologies have an important role to play in the realization of pervasive wireless.

Positioning

The importance of position or location information in Ambient Intelligence has been explained earlier. This translates into a need for a technology, possibly based on pervasive wireless networks, to be able to determine the coordinates of an object or person. However, it is usually not the coordinates themselves that are useful, but rather what they mean in terms of the context of the environment. In answering the question 'Where are my car keys?', the basic x,y,z coordinates are not particularly helpful. What is required is an answer such as 'They're under the sofa you were sitting on last night while you were watching the film'. With the information structured in this way, the position of the keys is immediately recognized in the context of the environment and related to the owner's actions.

Principles

Determining the position of an object using wireless technology involves three fundamental steps: range measurement, physical location calculation, and translation to a logical or contextual position. The first of these is the measurement of the distances from the object whose

CONNECTED
PLANET

CAMP
AND MADS

OPEN TOOLS

LIME
AND PL@NET

position is to be determined to a number of other fixed positions. These fixed positions could be wireless beacons that have been placed around the environment or fixed nodes in one or more wireless networks. These ranges are determined by measuring the time it takes for RF signals to travel from the object to these other fixed positions.[2] Measuring these ranges is difficult, and two main issues need to be addressed. The first is the accuracy: RF signals travel at 300,000,000ms-1, which means that the measured time delay is very short (typically a few tens of nanoseconds in an indoor environment). Very accurate timing electronics are required to measure these short intervals. The second issue is that the signals reflect off the surfaces in the room, and these reflections, known as multipath, interfere with the signal being measured, resulting in a loss of accuracy. Advanced algorithms are being developed to cancel the effect of the multipath, and their success will determine the ultimate accuracy of RF-based indoor positioning systems.

Once the ranges have been determined, the next stage is to calculate the coordinates of the object. This is done by triangulation, and a minimum of four range measurements is required to give a unique set of coordinates (unless some other information is available, for example, that the 'z' coordinate in an apartment is greater than 0 and probably less than 3 metres).

Finally, the coordinates have to be converted into something meaningful. In a car navigation system, this conversion is an integral and expected part of the system. The position of the car is first calculated in terms of longitude and latitude (by measuring the distance from the car to a number of satellites) and then overlaid on a map to show the driver which road the car is on. This overlay is clearly a useful way of presenting the data, and in a home environment a similar translation is required. However, this is more difficult in the home as objects and people move around, unlike a roadmap, which is fixed. The translation from physical location to a logical or contextual position will therefore require a considerable amount of additional information from the environment (who is where, what are they doing, and when). This is one of the challenges to be addressed by Ambient Intelligence.

Other technologies for determining location are also being investigated, such as ultrasound.[3] So which technology is the best for determining position in an ambient intelligent environment? Each has its own advantages: ultrasound travels much more slowly than RF, for example, making the range measurement much easier. It could be that different technologies are suitable for different applications. Certainly, in an outdoor situation, the GPS works well and is available all over the globe. For indoor environments, there is still much technology development required, but given the presence of pervasive wireless links in an ambient intelligent environment, the use of RF to determine position, although difficult, is certainly attractive.

Towards pervasive wireless

To sum up, the various requirements of wireless technology that result from the Ambient Intelligence concept range from high data rate links for bulk data transfer and video streaming, through to low bit rate links for automation, control and simple data exchange. These latter types of wireless links have been the primary focus of this chapter, and wireless solutions such as ZigBee are being developed with these types of application in mind. But what of the future? Inevitably, systems such as ZigBee (and Bluetooth) will benefit from developments in integrated circuits and future hardware and software improvements. These will result in incremental improvements in performance and reductions in both power consumption and cost.

We also need to look at what future requirements might be from the Ambient Intelligence perspective. Ultimately, nearly every object in our lives may have an element of wireless connectivity built in to it. Even a coffee cup may come equipped with an embedded radio. Perhaps our dishwashers will warn us that we've left a coffee cup on the dining room table,

before we switch them on. In a world where environmental concerns and efficient use of resources are becoming more important, this level of intelligence might be essential. Perhaps our health monitoring system will check how much caffeine we have had today! If we are to put wireless links into such simple objects as a coffee cup, wireless technology will need to take a quantum leap in the direction of ultra-low power, small size and low cost. Passive RF tags are about the closest thing we have in terms of cost and size, and will suffice for some of these applications. However, for other applications, they will not, because passive tags have one important shortcoming: they cannot initiate a conversation. Passive tags always have to wait until they are interrogated by a reading device. Conversely, radio (such as ZigBee) can be the first to speak, and this proactive ability will be essential in some situations, for instance, when warnings are issued ('Help! I'm too hot!').

Many groups are now starting to develop the technology for these next-generation radio devices,[4] and for the low bit rate links at least, these devices, merging the functionality of short-range radio and passive tags, will form the basis of future pervasive wireless systems.

CONNECTED
PLANET

CAMP
AND MADS

OPEN TOOLS

LIME
AND PL@NET

1   http://www.zigbee.com and http://www.bluetooth.org
2   D. Porcino and M.S. Wilcox, 'Empowering Ambient Intelligence with a Direct Sequence Spread Spectrum CDMA Positioning System', *Proceedings of the Location Modelling Workshop at UBICOMP 2001* (Atlanta, September 2001), 99-106
3   N.B. Priyantha, A. Chakraborty and H. Balakrishnan, 'The cricket location-support system', *Proceedings of the Sixth Annual ACM International Conference on Mobile Computing and Networking* (MOBICOM, August 2000)
4   J. Rabaey et al., 'PicoRadio Supports Ad-hoc Ultra-Low Power Wireless Networking', *IEEE Computer*, vol. 33, no. 7 (July 2000), 42-48

4.3 INTELLIGENT FIBRES: FORM FOLLOWS FANTASY

Clive van Heerden, Philippa Wagner, Jack Mama, Nancy Tilbury

Ambient Intelligence holds the promise of truly integrated technology. Since the advent of electric and electronic appliances, individual functionalities such as mobile phones or personal stereos have assumed specific forms that have largely remained as physical objects that clutter our environment. The vision of technology disappearing into the surrounding fabric and becoming smart enough to assist our everyday processes, from work to leisure and household chores, is tantalizingly close. The idea that form can follow fantasy, and need not be restricted to the physical presence of bulky components, holds enormous potential not only for design, but also for the creation of hybrid applications and multi-functional products. These are the products that will shape the Ambient Intelligence landscape.

Many of the technical innovations that will make electronic ubiquity a reality are ready to be applied. Innovations in display technology, nano-machines capable of moving dust through carpets, miniscule diagnostic processors capable of surviving gastric acid and analyzing our internal physiology, and textiles with potentially thousands of complex electronic functionalities embedded in their structures are all technologies on the threshold of widespread application. These technological developments are beginning to change our understanding of form, location and user interface, not to mention the scale of application. The multiplicity of these components changes the value we attribute to specific functionalities and our cultural attitudes towards redundancy. Computers become cheap enough to integrate in multiple locations, and their disposability after extremely short lifecycles will be commonplace. But before we become carried away by the trend of infinitesimal miniaturization and the promise of omnipresence, let us step back for a moment.

Technological revolution?

Are we at the dawn of a new era, a technological revolution? In identifying changes in function, design and culture, are we predicting a historical transformation comparable to the shift from steam power to electricity, or from mechanical processes to electronics? Various indicators characterize the introduction of new technology, which can be defined by the social forces that precede it and the effects that follow its introduction. It is possible and necessary to understand the effects that these 'revolutions' have had on gender relations, the organization of work, the environment and changing social trends such as the expression of sexuality, homogenization, fashion and the arts. Technology is neither the simple and direct result of a social impulse, nor does it have a simple and direct effect on the transformation of society. Many factors give rise to technological progress and similarly complex, often indiscernible changes take place in our culture. Yet we can trace major technological revolutions back to social crises. The advent of steam power and locomotive transport enabled colonization, opening up new markets and leading to mass manufacture.

In World War I, the crisis that propelled the technological developments of flight, communications and mass oceanic transport was followed by the 'kitchen revolution' that re-relegated women to a new home, equipped with electric 'labour-saving' innovations such as the Hoover, electric kettle and toaster. The massive social changes following World War II can be linked to the rise of electronics, jet propulsion, and chemical innovations like synthetics and nuclear power. Similarly, the development of satellite communications, the space race and the microprocessor need to be understood in the context of the Cold War.

Technology can light up our world or obliterate it

In each of these historical phases, driven by major social and political crises, we can see how technology can be both destructive and liberating, depending on the organization of the society within which it finds expression. Technology (e.g., in the form of nuclear power) can light up our world or potentially obliterate it. So-called labour-saving devices held out the promise of the gadget-filled home as a haven of feminine control, but can be held responsible for the relegation of female workers to domestic servility after the war, when they became surplus to economic requirements as producers.

The fabric of our environment

For thousands of years, textiles have played an important role in both social and technological developments. They were a key factor in the Industrial Revolution and in colonial expansion, as colonial wars were fought to secure materials for mass manufactured garments. The Jacquard loom which used punch cards as a 'programming method' to specify fabric decoration later led to IBM's adoption of the technique in the development of modern computing.

The New Textiles

As we enter the era of Ambient Intelligence, textiles continue to play a vital role. We can envisage textiles that transform their structure, counter allergens, shield against electromagnetic smog, apply a host of medical therapies, release fragrance, moisturize, and contain electronic networks and miniature electronic processors and communications technology. These may be textiles that can respond to human and environmental conditions, creating clothes that adapt to different temperatures, have the ability to heat and cool, to sense a host of biometric indicators through a series of integrated sensors and respond with a range of applications to enhance human behaviour. The fabric of our environment – the universe of soft surfaces and objects that will host electronic and biochemical functions – makes textiles critically important to the Ambient Intelligence discussion; from microscopic fibres carrying power and data, to multi-layered complex woven structures that sense miniscule changes in human physical and emotional condition.

Social trends

We are living in an age in which we need to understand the social trends that are impacting our everyday thoughts, habits and lifestyles. Take the move towards physical homogeneity, for instance: half the world is starving while levels of obesity increase in western cultures, and yet society aspires to approximate one type, one look, one body form, one breast size, one nose shape, etc. Similarly, we need to understand social trends like the ascendancy to full political hegemony of the gay and lesbian community in many urban centres.

We now have the technical ability to 'liberate' people from the factory or the office. The constraints of time and location are disappearing, and being globally connected to the tools of work blurs the boundaries between work and leisure. The domains of work, travel and home become meaningless as we become tied to the 'machines' of work that enable us to be connected constantly. Time is no longer divided into 'personal' and 'productive', as e-mail and the ubiquity of access points on a global scale make working an 'anytime' possibility. Whereas factories and offices were a direct mechanism for ensuring hours of productivity, less direct and more subtle technological mechanisms fuel the compulsion to work.

Filtering and redefining technology

Today, the challenge is that form follows fantasy. It is not so much that we need to make *new* technology, but rather that we need to develop methods for filtering the effects of the technology we surround ourselves with and redefine that technology in a way that enhances our everyday experience. An invention such as e-ink (printed ink technology that creates flexible dynamic displays) could result in a moving image on every surface and every bit of packaging, screaming for our attention.

Alternatively, it could be used indirectly and non-literally as material art to create changing dynamic textiles altering the colour of our apparel and our built environment. As such, the criteria for its function should not be about pixel resolution and scrolling text as the determinants for this technology, but rather our ability as people to be able to control it creatively through the intelligence of objects. Its widespread application as a material that can alter pattern and colour far exceeds its use as a replacement display technology. Ambient Intelligence gives us the opportunity to recreate our environment, such that the technological functionalities that we want or need manifest themselves only when we choose.

The key to making life-enhancing innovation to enrich our experience lies in ensuring that people maintain their decision-making ability and in creating more freedom in our 'money-rich, time-poor' society. We don't want our car to suggest where we want to go unless we ask it to. We want the environment to anticipate and respond, but not to eliminate decision-making. We would go crazy if technology with intelligent processes did away with our decision-making power. In *Being Digital*, for example, Nicholas Negroponte argued that it is technologically feasible for us to receive 15,000 concurrent TV channels that would take over an hour just to scroll through.[1] The challenge is not in creating the technology, but in creating the tools to manage it.

Intelligent fibres

What does all of this mean if technology is disappearing? To be able to make technology disappear into our environment, we have to design the technology to hide it. This is not about hiding speakers behind our living room curtains, but about integrating them into textiles and other soft materials, one of the most natural materials known to man. We walk on textiles, sleep in them, dress in them and shut the world out with them. It therefore makes perfect sense to see them as the new 'material of invention'. Understanding the limits and possibilities of all textiles, embroidered, woven, knitted, and printed, is the key to making our ambient environments work.

Mixing industries

For us to be able to realize a technological environment of ubiquitous electronic functionality, form must follow fantasy and industries must collide in this new space, generating knowledge transfer between the worlds of hard components and soft textiles to create the new 'softwear'. Taking the basics of textile mechanics and mixing silicon and silk, the matrix of warp and weft can be used to create integrated networks that carry power and data to a range of technical functionalities integrated in the fabric of apparel, furnishings and any other woven surface. Displays can be woven using phosphor-impregnated yarns, and the ability to overlay layers of functional arrays has enormous potential in continuous reel-to-reel production.

With Jacquard processes, local areas can embody specific functional components such as switches or sensors, but this requires specialization in yarn spinning. The development of yarns from filaments into complex structures to create 'cables' that are insulated and durable enough to endure the lifecycle of a textile will change the inherent use of fabrics.

Electronic lingerie?

Advances in knitting technology have produced seamless processes whereby individual items are knitted whole, with no 'cut and sew' steps in the process, and where all seams are achieved through knit structure and sonic welding. An infinite range of sensing capabilities can be integrated using conductive yarns in complex knit design, which will impact the world of lingerie, electronic sportswear, smart furnishings and automotive interiors. This revolution in 'circular and seamless' knitwear is paralleled in the non-woven and laminate industry, where structure, texture and form is brought about through complex laminates of materials that expand and contract under different conditions. Etching through these laminates can enable us to develop sophisticated networks in wafer-thin structures.

Integrating hard and soft

The work of the Physics and Media Group at MIT's Media Lab will have considerable impact on the world as it matures, not only in developments such as e-ink, but also in developing dynamic materials that can carry out complex operations at a microscopic level. Materials that can harden and soften, contract and change structure hold the promise of fabrics that transform their structure according to atmospheric conditions and sensory responses. This will give rise to new forms of product and interaction design, not to mention specialized industrial design engineering. Developments in materials are paralleled by the development of new design disciplines which fuse fashion and textile skills with three-dimensional design. This is a very specialized process, as we are witnessing the transformation of manufacturing methods in both garment construction terms and product engineering. Developments in circular knit technology, for instance, enable the development of 3D forms. The use of hardened resins will enable us to knit what had previously been injection-moulded. These processes are well-established in aerospace manufacture, where aircraft nose cones are produced in this way. Similarly, traditional fashion production methods are incorporating moulding techniques which were traditionally the preserve of product design. The combination and manipulation of materials using these techniques enables us to integrate hard and soft forms in new and innovative ways, encapsulating electronic components that can withstand the rigours of washing machines and tumble dryers.

Decomposing the phone

The challenge is to design the interaction modalities at a pace that consumers will understand and accept. Having the 'real estate' of an entire body to distribute functionalities gives us the opportunity to use gesture, motion and movement as both indirect and direct interaction. Coupling these methods with advances in context awareness will provide real benefits and help to overcome the contradiction that exists between an ever-expanding array of functions with the cultural obsession of miniaturization. The conflict we encounter using miniature interfaces and codified interactions on cell phones and PDAs can be eliminated through distributed interfaces and new interaction paradigms, but it will require users to be willing to accept the abandonment of traditional forms and interaction habits. Culturally, changing the typology of a specific set of functionalities like the telephone will take time. Consumers expect devices to change shape incrementally, and we believe that the physical form of electronic components will metamorphose from the 3D materializations of traditional forms into distributed modular and often invisible technical capabilities. As a wearable, a mobile phone can be any form when broken up and integrated into a textile; the challenge is in physical management issues and in finding and developing the user interface.

E-broidery

Development in electronic embroidery techniques, pioneered by MIT, have given rise to single threads that make new interfaces possible. Unlike circular knit, where the integration of sensing and networks requires complex engineering design at an industrial level, 'e-broidery' is an essential technology for retro-fitting electronic components. New threads and the modification of traditional equipment and unlikely partnerships between thread companies and the electronics world will enable these changes.

Practical manufacturing issues

The single biggest problem confronting wearables designers is the interconnection between hard electronic components and soft textiles. The physical rigours that clothes undergo are far greater than traditional consumer electronic appliances, and we can anticipate a cultural lag before consumers feel comfortable with washing electronic devices. It is therefore to develop robust and versatile interconnects with intuitively understood affodances in this stage of wearable development, where the issues have yet to be identified, let alone the standards.

We can anticipate a plethora of methods of integration. To use Negroponte's analogy, we are at the 'horseless carriage' stage in the design of ambient technology interfaces, but it is only through trial and error that the new language of interaction with these functionalities will emerge. It is clear that the simple application of integrating a device into a garment falls short of our expectations of 'wearability', despite the difficulties of distributed components and the integrated networks they imply. We need to develop electronic garment construction techniques to develop products that are truly wearable. This raises a number of serious issues. How do we repair and maintain these soft body area networks? The methods of manufacture, particularly those involving 'cut and sew' techniques, are not ideally suited to electronic components. Distributing power to a range of different functionalities implies the need to create network junctions in seams and fastenings. The textile and garment construction industry will need to adapt if they are to handle these materials. For instance, the fashion industry makes

156

garments in 'small', 'medium' and 'large' sizes; electronic components will need to be adapted for these industrial manufacturing processes.

What lies ahead?

Developments in producing smart materials are already underway, with fabric keyboards and responsive sensing garments making the fantasy a reality. So what lies on the horizon? Whereas the last 400 years of industrial development have been about the colonization of territory, shrinking the world through communications, transport and markets, new products and the global procurement of materials, we see the challenge of this era as developing technology that works with and in the human organism. The convergence of scientific developments in 'bio-silicone' physical augmentation, biometric sensing and communications hold the promise (or curse) of intra-body applications.

Understanding the trends in culture and in miniaturized technology will enable us to develop products that are either life-enriching or imprisoning. We need to understand the space between the human body and apparel, and between apparel and the near environment as a series of locales in which human behaviour is differentiated.

Understanding emotional and physical behaviour in miniscule detail will allow us to develop applications that are transparent and unobtrusive. We must ensure that electronic ubiquity provides us with solutions that are not frustrating, where users are not pestered and second-guessed by semi-intelligent menial functions, but instead augmented in real and meaningful ways.

How we develop these in a technical milieu where every garment has the capacity to incorporate a multiplicity of sub-miniature processors and every object in our environment is stuffed with smart electronics is a challenge. We have enough difficulty sanitizing our desktop computers from viruses; the spectre of maintaining the viral health of our 'equipment' in the age of ubiquity could prove to be a nightmare. 'Swallowable' diagnostic electronics, electronic tattoos and functional implants could provide truly hands-free environments or lead to dependence on a mammoth scale. Our challenge is to ensure the former, and guard against the latter. If we do not adopt a user-centred approach to the design and application of technology, we will end up with electronic clutter that jars our cultural sensibilities, even if it succeeds in making us dependent on it.

1   N. Negroponte, *Being Digital* (New York, Alfred A. Knopf, 1995)

4.4 WEARABLE TECHNOLOGY

Paul Gough

Lessons from history

Wearable technology offers the promise of enhancing our experiences, extending our personal abilities and ultimately mediating and enhancing our perceived reality. Before we race ahead to consider these possibilities, we should remember that this kind of technology has been with us for many millennia, in the form of clothes: a sophisticated form of wearable technology that provides us with a means of extending our body's thermal regulation. This technology has had profound consequences, enabling our species to migrate and colonize both colder and hotter parts of our planet. Clothes also perform other functions, such as protecting our modesty and as a canvas for personal expression. Glasses, devices that redirect photons in a prescribed and controllable way, thereby improving eyesight, are another example of a successful wearable technology. The portrait of Hugh of St. Cher painted in 1352 by Crivelli shows glasses very similar in form to those today, proving that successful wearable designs can last a very long time!

These examples teach us that to be successful, a wearable technology must offer value that far exceeds any inconvenience. Clothes can be inconvenient; they require washing, ironing and changing, and some, like coats, can be heavy. Yet these inconveniences are outweighed by the value of garments to people. If future wearable technology is to succeed, it needs to respect this ratio.

What is wearable technology?

Wearable technology is simply personal technology that you can carry with you. A mobile phone clipped to a person's belt with a hands-free headset is a slightly 'clunky' example of wearable technology. Other examples include heart-rate monitors, wristwatches and portable MP3 players. Wearable technology is about functionality combined with ease and convenience but, as will be shown, it will also increasingly become a means of enabling us to maintain control of our personal space.

In laboratories around the world, scientists are strapping computers to their bodies and sporting over-eye displays, inspired by research conducted at MIT. These pioneering researchers are willing to tolerate heavy devices, poor user interfaces and displays in an effort to work out which future wearable applications make sense. It is unclear whether a future with such devices will be one most people will be prepared to tolerate.

Perhaps the most extreme example of today's wearable technology is the space suit (Extravehicular Mobility Unit) used for work outside the space shuttle. This provides a complete environment for the astronaut, including ventilation, liquid cooling, physiological telemetry, and radio communication and video links. While such technology is far removed from our everyday lives, the idea of a protective 'second skin' is worth bearing in mind.

Wearable trends

One clear trend is that people increasingly want access to information, communication and entertainment on the move. We want to feel connected and in control. This is exemplified by the 'killer app' of the last decade, communication, which has led to the staggering sale of nearly a billion mobile phones worldwide and has been accompanied by the unforeseen rise in the use of the Short Message Service (SMS). Billions of SMS messages are sent every week in Europe alone, despite the poor interface offered by the typical multi-tap keyboard on a mobile phone. This illustrates how quickly a wearable technology can grow and penetrate the mass market, provided its perceived value exceeds any inconvenience.

The 'next wave' is likely to be the capturing and sharing of other media, such as still images and short video clips. This has some interesting implications. As people carry more and more technology with them (e.g., mobile phones, PDAs, portable music players and digital cameras), this becomes increasingly inconvenient, because there is nowhere to put these devices. This inconvenience is compounded by the fact that these devices do not cooperate with each other. Moreover, there is considerable component redundancy – each device has a screen, an interface and a power source. To address the first of these problems, clothes with dedicated pockets have started to appear. A more sophisticated solution to the problem was shown in the ICD+ jacket developed by Philips and Levi's.[1] Not only were a mobile phone and MP3 player integrated within the jacket, as were headphones and microphones, but the wired network within the jacket also enabled the two devices to cooperate. The MP3 would pause when a phone call came in, for example. This simple contextual awareness shows the first glimmerings of Ambient Intelligence.

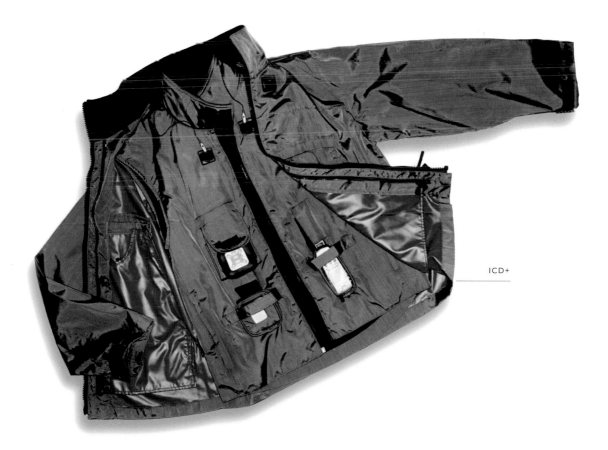

ICD+

There are a number of potential stages in the development of 'humanized' wearable technologies, as illustrated in Figure 1. We explore each of these stages below.

FIG. 1
Stages in wearable
technologies

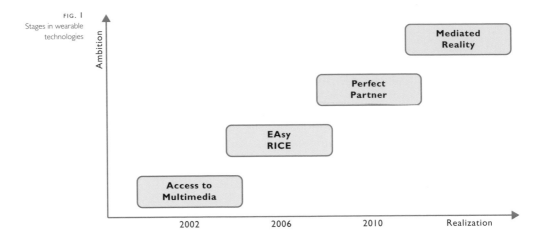

Access to multimedia

Flexible interfaces

This stage is about giving people the freedom to access and share multimedia material, unconstrained by time and place. Examples include viewing a video clip of your team scoring just after the event, or sending a picture of a coat you are thinking of buying to a friend while you're in the shop. This is broadly where we are today, with mobile phones beginning to sprout digital cameras and FM radios. Beyond this, we can see other wearable technologies emerging. Clothes have enormous space, certainly compared to the miniscule keypads and screens on mobile devices. Can we use this plentiful garment space as a display or interface? Flexible displays are currently an area of intense research. Technologies such as e-ink,[2] electro-luminescent materials, PolyLED displays on plastic, and many others are vying to be the first reliable flexible displays. One or more of these is likely to be successful, allowing us to consider integrating soft displays into apparel. This could lead to a football shirt that can show the goals from the team's latest match, shirtsleeves that display SMS messages, or children's clothes that change colour when they are 'tagged' in a playground game. Alternatively, the display could simply be used to enhance the aesthetics of the garment.

Soft interfaces

Soft interfaces are fabric or textile input devices. Imagine a sleeve you can press or brush to control the volume of your music. Pressure-sensitive fabrics are now being developed, allowing the surface of garments to act as a second skin. Again, the space a garment offers can be put to good use. As a simple example, you could have an FM T-shirt that had all the radio station names marked on the front. By just pressing one of the names on the shirt, your radio would be tuned to that station. The heart-rate monitor used by runners is another example. These devices have fiendishly complex interfaces, as everything has to be done through a few buttons and a small watch display. All the controls could be spread out on a runner's shirt, so setting upper and low heart-rate limits could be done in single presses, rather than the six or seven currently required. This 'spreading out' of interfaces can be extended to other devices, such as mobile phones, which currently use 'deep lists' due to their small screen size. Of course, the ergonomics of these interfaces need to be investigated – we are not used to stroking our sleeves or pressing a location on our shirt in this way.

The rise of modular functionality

Today, when we buy a piece of wearable technology (a wristwatch or mobile phone, for example), it is self-contained. Once people can buy a jacket with a display and soft interface, they will want it to work with at least one of their devices, but probably with all of their devices, or it will have limited value. In the future, when we drop a device into our jacket pocket, we will want to be able to use the jacket's display and soft interface for that device.

Ultimately, our clothes could become 'universal accessories'. In this scenario, a device that can be linked to clothes would still be able to be used as a stand-alone device, i.e., without the jacket. There may come a time when the devices themselves will no longer contain interfaces and screens, because displays, power sources and interfaces will be available as separate items, some integrated into clothes, others still rigid and separate, others as 'fold-ups'. Alternatively, these items will be provided by the environment. People will assemble the functionality they need from a set of components, just as we select our clothes in the morning according to what is appropriate for the day ahead.

Body-centric networking

To have clothes as universal accessories, we need a network around the body that enables the various devices to communicate and share resources.[3] The availability of conductive fibres, soft to the touch, means that garments can provide a wired infrastructure for data and power. Low-power wireless technologies such as ZigBee could also be used to connect devices. Here, fabric antennas could be used.

Washable electronics

Ironically, when we 'care' for our clothes, we actually treat them quite harshly, washing them at 40° or more, tumble-drying them at even higher temperatures. Imagine what this would do to any integrated electronics. Research has now begun into washable electronics and connectors that can survive this kind of treatment.

EAsy RICE

Once people can access multimedia on the move, the next challenge will be to provide easy access to the right information, communication and entertainment (EAsy RICE). People will be overwhelmed with content and communication options. Freedom to quickly access whatever we want will be an important requirement. This might be achieved using large, soft interfaces on clothes, but thinking beyond just repositioning and scaling the interface, context sensing may also play an important role. By context, we mean relevant information about a user and their situation. This may include location, the current activity, persons present, age, weight, sex and many other details. If a device can be made aware of aspects of the user's context, then perhaps the system can 'shortcut' the selection process or even suggest an option to the user. Someone in a railway station is likely to want to know train times, for example. Someone at a sports event might well want more details about that event; if they are actively engaged in the sport, however, they probably won't want to be interrupted.

Context based on location

One of the most powerful indicators of context is location; people's activities are often strongly related to place. Our information and entertainment needs are likely to vary according to whether we are at work, at an airport, in a shopping mall, or in a gym. There are a number of wearable technologies that could provide location and related services. The simplest and most self-contained would be a GPS device carried by the user or integrated into their jacket. The user's location could then be fed to a service (perhaps via a cellular system) that would give options tailored to the current environment. The main difficulty with GPS is that it generally cannot be used indoors. Location-based services could also be provided using short-range beacons (i.e., with a range of tens of metres). In this case, the user's body-centric network not only supports on-the-body devices but also looks to make links with services outside the body space. As the user enters a room, their personal device can listen to the transmissions from local beacons and present, if appropriate, a list of the services and resources available. Upon entering a restaurant, for instance, a beacon would transmit the menu to their body-centric network. Their personal device, which knows they don't like fish, would present them with a menu from which the fish options are missing. Such a combination of wearable technology and beacons has been well explored in projects like CAMP (Context-aware Mobile Platform).[4]

Perfect partner – the rise of intimate interfaces

The 'perfect partner' is wearable technology that proactively works on your behalf. It understands you and your context well enough to make accurate predictions of your needs, and with sufficient autonomy to take actions on your behalf to support those needs. The combination of technology will have its own defined personality or set of personalities dependent on context. It will improve its predictive capacity by observing you.

Building on augmented memory

How might a perfect partner arise? Well, wearable technology is likely to be with the user for large periods of time and so could easily observe their behaviour. With the appropriate sensing capabilities, it could determine what you watch, listen to, to whom you speak, the subjects you discuss and where you have been.[5] One immediate benefit of such a capability is that it could provide you with a powerful augmented memory system. If you wanted to know when you last spoke to a friend, it could tell you when, where, who else was there, and the subject of the conversation. So even without making predictions, a system that intimately records details could provide a beneficial service most of us could imagine using. Once details start to be collected, the system could then begin to make predictions or give advice.

Sports coach

One illustration of the concept of a perfect partner is the idea of a sports coach, i.e., sports apparel with integrated sensing, such as a sensor jacket,[6] which uses knitted material that changes its resistance as it is stretched, to determine the position and dynamics of the user's arms. This could be used to record the amount and type of exercise done, or to analyze movement and give feedback to the user about a particular exercise. Tactile feedback could be given in the garment to indicate when a particular limb or muscle should be used to complete an action. Other wearable technologies that could help in sports analysis include shoes that could determine, via accelerometers and pressure pads, how far a user has run and which analyze footfall to suggest ways of avoiding injury; sensors buried in garment fibres to analyze sweat to determine hydration and lactate levels; and fibres that release chemicals to the skin to help recovery after training.

Mediating reality

Mediating reality is about reinterpreting a user's reality and merging it with virtual objects to enhance their experiences. This could be a pair of glasses that modifies your view of the world. These glasses could change day into night, enable a historical character to walk beside you and tell you about your surroundings, or enable you to compete against a virtual training partner while running. You could read visible messages left in the air for you at specific locations or replay an incident you saw just a few moments ago. The glasses could show the path your golf ball took through the air and compare it to Tiger Woods' shot on the same hole, make the wind visible as arrows in the sky, or project today's football highlights on the wall of your train.

In a very limited way, we already mediate reality. When we wear a set of open-ear headphones, we hear the music 'laid over' the noise around us, and this can enhance our experience of the moment. With 3D audio, we can have virtual 'audio objects' at different locations around us. Some examples of visual mediation are also appearing in research labs.[7]

The real breakthrough required is a comfortable wearable display that can merge reality and virtual objects, and that can track the movement of the user's head to ensure that the virtual objects appear to hold their position in the real world. Once this has been developed, a flood of applications will become available, as the necessary processing power and basic pattern recognition software are already in place.

The rise of 'personal realities' provides interesting issues and possibilities. On the one hand, people will no longer be certain that they share aspects of reality. I might decide that I like to see the stars in the sky during the day, while you may not. On the other hand, it would be possible to transfer your view of an event to someone else so they could see it through your eyes. This is the future of wearable technology: creating personalized realities, with the user right at the centre. The role of Ambient Intelligence is to mediate those aspects of reality that enhance the user's experience and interaction, while keeping the user in control.

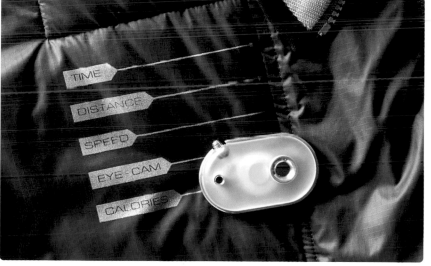

1   http://www.levis-icd.com
2   http://www.eink.com
3   K. Van Dam, S. Pitchers and M. Barnard, 'Body Area Networks: Towards a Wearable Future', WWRF kick-off meeting (Munich, 6-7 March, 2001) and 'From PAN to BAN: Why Body Area Networks', WWRF Forum (10-11 May 2001)
4   P. Rankin, 'Context-Aware Mobile Phones: The Differences Between Pull and Push, Restoring the Sense of Place', *Proceedings of the HCII 2001 Conference* (New Orleans, 5-10 August 2001)
5   T.E. Starner, 'Wearable Agents', *IEEE Pervasive Computers*, vol. 1, no. 2 (April-June 2002), 90-92
6   J. Farringdon, A.J. Moore, N. Tilbury, J. Church and P.D. Biemond 'Wearable Sensor Badge and Sensor Jacket for Context Awareness', *IEEE Third International Symposium on Wearable Computing* (18-19 October 1999)
7   S. Mann, 'WearCam (The Wearable Camera)', *IEEE Second International Symposium on Wearable Computers* (19-20 October 1998), 124-131; L. Cheng and J. Robinson, 'Dealing with Speed and Robustness Issues for Video-Based Registration on a Wearable Computing Platform', *IEEE Second International Symposium on Wearable Computers*, 84-91; B. Thomas, B. Close, J. Donoghue and J. Squires, 'ARQuake: An Outdoor/Indoor Augmented Reality First Person Application', *IEEE Fourth International Symposium on Wearable Computers* (16-17 October 2000)

4.5 STORAGE EVERYWHERE

Henk van Houten, Wouter Leibbrandt

Today, we all make considerable use of digital storage in the home: CDs, DVDs, solid-state devices, and computer hard disks and diskettes. As the quantity of 'digital content' available in the home grows – whether coming from the Internet or multi-channel TV-based services – storage will occupy an increasingly central role in the connected home. Our consumer electronics equipment itself is becoming increasingly digitalized, with digital interfaces between consumer systems also starting to emerge. As a result, digital data storage media, such as hard disk drives and solid-state memories, already familiar from computing, are now being incorporated into home entertainment and other domestic systems. Ultimately, this will lead to a situation in the Ambient Intelligence home where storage will make stored data of any kind available to users, anywhere and at anytime, in a responsive and transparent way, while the technology remains unobtrusively in the background. But what sort of technology will that be? How will the material be physically stored? More importantly, perhaps, once stored, how will we find it again, and having found it, what will we be able to do with it?

Physical storage

There are several technologies competing for the role of storage technology within the Ambient Intelligence home: hard disks, familiar from the PC; optical disc drives, familiar from CD and DVD; and solid state, familiar from digital cameras and video game consoles. As we shall see, rather than competing with each other, they are more likely to complement each other, since each has particular advantages and disadvantages.

Hard disk drives

Hard disk drives (HDDs) use magnetic fields to read and write data in much the same way that cassette tapes do. Although the read/write head on the hard disk drive never actually touches the disk, it is nonetheless so close to it that any dust on the surface of the disk may cause it to 'crash'. As a result, hard disks are usually non-removable and constitute a 'closed box system'. This, in turn, makes them unsuitable for distributing content or exchanging data. However, their performance in terms of data rate and access time is good (better than that of optical storage), and they do not require standardization, so that individual manufacturers are free to make their own improvements. Resulting technological advances mean that the bit density on hard disks is doubling each year.

Hard disks are currently optimized for computer use, not consumer electronics applications. A key difference between the two types of application is that computers require the highest possible level of data integrity: they call for the 'best effort', with speed being less important. For real-time audio and video, however, timeliness is critical: this requires the 'best you can get' in the time available. This is because, whereas a PC hard disk can take the time to recover a misread data bit in reading a file, a real-time audio or video device adopting the same strategy would produce an unacceptable delay in playback – simply dropping the bit would be better. Philips is currently developing a 'real-time' operating system and file system – at a level above the physical hard disk control – which addresses the problem of how to get data on and off the hard disk in a way that would make it suitable for streaming audio and video. Activities are currently focused on the combination of a hard disk drive with an optical drive.

Optical disc drives

Optical disc drives – such as the Compact Disc (CD) system and its successors (DVD and Blu-ray discs) – work by focusing a light beam generated by a semiconductor laser. This beam passes through a 1.2mm-thick transparent plastic substrate on the surface of the CD to focus on the information layer. The substrate protects the information layer from scratches or wear, and since the laser beam is out of focus at the surface of the transparent substrate, it is insensitive to dust or fingerprints on the disc. This property gives optical disc storage its crucial advantage over hard disk storage: it means the medium can be removed, exchanged and distributed. And since the distance between the lens and the disc is large (more than 1mm in a CD), there is no danger of the optical pick-up and the disc crashing.

DVD

The second generation of optical disc storage is the Digital Versatile Disc (DVD). From the outset, this was intended as a storage medium for the home as well as the PC, and was designed to store video, audio, digital stills and home movies as well as data files. The capacity of a DVD is more than seven times that of the CD – 4.7 GB on a single layer of a 12cm disc – and even 8.5 GB in the two-layer version. This is achieved by using a red laser instead of an infrared one (as in the CD), by using a more powerful lens, and by exploiting advances in servo technology, lasers, channel modulation coding and error correction. A recent development with distinct advantages for home use (including full compatibility) is the DVD+RW (DVD Rewritable), which enables recording in addition to playback.

DVD or HDD?

For archiving and data interchange, removable DVD storage represents easily managed, unlimited capacity. Hard disk drives, however, also offer unlimited capacity (drives with over 100 GB in total capacity are not uncommon), and they are well suited for temporary storage and time-shifting. But although HDDs are proven, reliable and inexpensive, their performance is, as noted above, optimized for PC rather than consumer electronics applications. In fact, it is not necessary to choose between the two types of storage. People will never have enough fixed storage capacity – they will fill whatever fixed storage is available and will always want to copy material onto removable storage. An attractive solution might be to combine hard disks with DVD+RW.

Blu-ray Disc

The third generation of optical storage is about to appear. The Blu-ray Disc will be a 12cm single-sided, single-layer optical disc with a capacity of up to 27 GB. The technology involves using a blue laser instead of a red one (as in DVD), plus a more powerful lens and a new disc technology. It also takes advantage of innovations in optics, media and signal processing concepts, such as the channel modulation code, the error correction scheme and the addressing method. As with all consumer products, standards will be essential in building consumer confidence and creating strong demand for optical recording. A standard for blue laser technology has now largely been agreed by a consortium of European and Japanese companies.

Taking it mobile

In the future, portable devices will be seamlessly integrated into our lives, at home and on the move. Whatever form they take (mobile phone, PDA, stills camera, camcorder, navigation system, portable health monitor or portable audio/video system), they will all need to access and store content.

I-PRONTO

WWICE

STREAMIUM

CONNECTED
PLANET

OPEN TOOLS

The storage systems of such devices may take various forms: they may use various types of 'local' storage, such as Flash cards or removable optical discs, or they may connect to a central storage 'server' on the user's belt.

Here the interplay between storage and connectivity becomes significant. When on the move, you cannot necessarily count on being connected all the time, but you will want to have access to material stored elsewhere. That means the benefits and disadvantages of storing particular material in particular locations will need to be worked out, as well as when it would be appropriate to interconnect mobile devices with local storage, and when it would be better to access content from a remote server through wireless connectivity. There will also be trade-offs between quality of service, battery lifetime, speed and picture quality.

Technologically, mobile storage is a major development area, especially because current proposed solutions are still in their infancy and cannot handle high-quality streaming audio and video: most centre around small optical discs and solid-state memory (RAM or Flash).

SFFO disc: an optical disc drive for the mobile world

Could optical discs such as CD and DVD be adapted for use in mobile applications? They could, but in this context size is a crucial factor, making the Small Form Factor Optical (SFFO) disc a natural extension to the optical storage family. The size of an average coin, the SFFO disc has a capacity (1 GB) that exceeds that of traditional CDs (650 MB). Future dual-layer versions may double the capacity again. Philips sees SFFO discs being mainly used for exchanging data between devices (e.g., a camera and a mobile phone) or for distributing content such as movies through downloading onto a recordable disc, or by disc replication from a master (as in CD-ROM or DVD-Video).

Shrinking optical technology and taking it 'mobile' raises a number of challenges, especially with respect to the mechanics involved. To read an SFFO disc you need a small optical pick-up unit with an extremely small lens and an equally tiny actuator. Blue laser technology will probably prove to be the most appropriate, as it will enable sufficiently high storage capacity on such a small disc. Once commercialized, the SFFO disc will be the natural mobile counterpart to DVD+RW in the home or office. It can achieve high enough data rates to handle multiple audio and video streams, so that data-hungry applications (such as video and gaming) will be viable on mobile handsets.

Power is also a key issue in small, portable appliances. Although much smaller than standard discs, an SFFO disc drive still needs mechanical components and will therefore tend to be

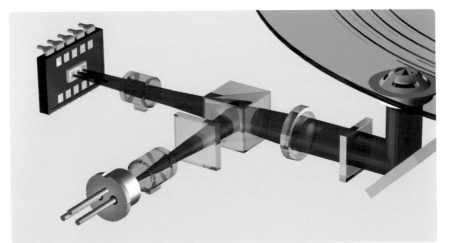

FIG. I
Enlarged view of an optical disc read and write unit, consisting of a laser, optics focusing the laser onto the disc, and a detector to read the signals coming from the disc. The complete unit measures just a few centimetres, or even less in miniaturized versions

more power-hungry than a solid-state solution, which has no moving parts. But the power consumption of SFFO discs can be substantially reduced by using clever buffering schemes, whereby discs can be read in burst mode, stopping the motor and switching off the laser when not needed. Low-power optical recording still requires a lot of research and presents a serious challenge. Other difficult areas in 'on the move' storage are reliability and playability: more sophisticated error recovery algorithms may be required, as well as more reliable mechanical components.

What about solid state?

To what extent is solid state a viable alternative technology for mobile applications? On the one hand, it uses less power, is physically smaller and, having no moving parts, is more robust than SFFO discs. On the other hand, it is generally more expensive. The current mainstream non-volatile solid-state storage technology is Flash. However, several new solid-state non-volatile memory technologies are emerging, including MRAM and ferro-electric RAM, both of which offer substantial promise. MRAM in particular is seen as the next logical step in in-field rewritable memory for two reasons. First, it is much faster than Flash and, second, unlike Flash, it is expected to be able to cope with the much smaller chip feature sizes required when, within the next few years, integrated circuit (IC) features shrink below 100 nanometres. Indeed, if we can believe Moore's Law, non-volatile, solid-state storage ICs of many gigabytes will be available at affordable prices in less than a decade from now. Solid state is therefore certainly a good contender as a storage technology for mobile applications.

Compression

So far, we have considered a range of physical media for digital storage. However, a significant role in physical storage is also played by compression techniques. Digital audio is stored on CD in an uncompressed format. One minute of top-quality audio in two channels takes about 10 MB of storage. By contrast, one minute of uncompressed digital video at standard TV quality requires over 1.5 GB of storage space. Thanks to elaborate compression techniques (known as MPEG-2), over two hours of video can now be stored on a DVD of only 4.7 GB. MPEG-2 compression relies on correlations within video frames and on temporal correlations between them to reduce the number of bits needed to describe each frame. MPEG-2 compresses material by a factor of 50, resulting in a bandwidth of about 5 Mbits per second. This is very similar to the bandwidth of about 5 MHz that was typically needed for TV-quality video; and for over a decade the general view was that no further compression efficiency was possible. This view is changing, however. New compression schemes, such as MPEG-4 and H26L, are likely to improve compression by a factor of two, and increases in efficiency beyond that are also expected. For instance, Philips is combining its 'Natural Motion' technology with advanced compression techniques to reduce the bit rate for video recording to extend DVD+RW long-play modes to eight hours or more. New layered compression techniques are also under development that will make it possible to store a full-length movie in superb high-definition video quality on a common dual-layer DVD (8.5 GB).

Although video compression rates are arguably among the most striking achievements in compression technology, other types of content are also regularly compressed. MP3 (short for MPEG-1, layer 3) is a compressed audio format, allowing storage of ten hours of stereo audio on a CD, while popular compression formats for digital photographs are JPEG and GIF. The development of new and improving compression formats is continually enabling new storage formats and enhancing existing ones.

The object of storage: the content

A powerful characteristic of digital data storage is that everything is represented on the storage medium in the same way: no matter what the material 'is' – video, e-mail, pictures, speech or scanned documents – it is all stored as bits. Traditionally, the digital content we store at home originates from some professional source (e.g., studios, broadcasters or record labels). Increasingly, however, we also digitally store self-generated content (e.g., photographs, camcorder recordings, e-mails and v-mails). The way in which we store this content is not organized according to the type of technology; it is dictated by how we regard the content. Ordinary users see a digital camera, in which they store pictures, as a completely different type of storage device from an MP3 audio player, in which they store music, although the underlying technology may be the same (e.g., solid-state memory).

The unified digital mode in which content is stored, means that people will be easily able to combine content in ways that was impossible in the non-digital past (e.g., combining still pictures with spoken text and animated graphics). Content will converge to form a rich multi-media experience. The 'place' where this interaction between users and their content takes place is known as the 'storage application'. It abstracts away from the underlying hardware within a total storage system to give people an interface where they can create the sort of rich multimedia experience just hinted at. This interface will involve a degree of complexity that we are only just starting to explore.

Indexing, navigation and retrieval

How will we find our way around all the material we have stored away? There is a considerable danger that, as the volume of stored data increases, we shall simply lose sight of it and be unable to retrieve it when we want it. For that reason, content management using 'smart storage solutions' will be absolutely essential.

One such smart storage solution is the Electronic Programme Guide (EPG). Combined with smart agent software, this will help us organize and filter content coming into our homes. By monitoring our recording and viewing habits it will draw up our 'profile' and then search for similar material and automatically record it for us. The combination of DVD+RW and HDD already offers a basic form of content management, with the HDD storing summaries of material archived on DVD and HDD. But this is only a simple example: much more sophisticated mechanisms will be needed for the sorts of applications envisaged above, whereby users can combine different types of content in new and creative ways. A prerequisite for that will be that the system can recognize what the content consists of, i.e., 'what it is about'. The more detailed the semantic knowledge that the system has of the content, and the greater the accuracy of that knowledge, the more sophisticated the applications can be. This knowledge will depend on an efficient system of screening the content and cataloguing or tagging it.

Intelligent content tagging

The 'tags' in question (also called 'metadata') are descriptors that characterize the data (e.g., in terms of its subject matter, location, etc.). In the case of material that is easily categorized by genre or subject matter (e.g., movies and news broadcasts), the tags can be automatically provided along with the content by the service provider. In the case of other material, the system itself will be able to analyze the content and generate its own tags. This will be especially useful for material recorded within the home. For example, a recording of a football match could be identified as such on the basis of factors such as the noise of the crowd in the audio, the dominance of the colour green in the video and the length of the recording itself. Both types of metadata – pre-supplied and self-generated – are likely to coexist and complement each other. Standards describing the metadata format and its link to the proper data are being established by bodies such as MPEG-7 and TV Anytime.

Synchronizing content

Content management will also need to cover synchronization. What happens if we want to modify content on one device that is stored on another and backed up on a third? Or if we want to upload new material from a friend's portable device to our own? Or synchronize our mobile content automatically with our home server, and then have our mobile system automatically load files for a trip tomorrow? Complex interactions of this sort are likely to become commonplace as the Ambient Intelligence home begins to materialize. Current strategies for dealing with them are still rather primitive, usually involving fitting every piece of equipment with some kind of removable storage for data exchange rather than using wireless links. In the future, such activities will need to be integrated into a total content management system that draws on all the physical digital storage available to us everywhere – whether within the home or outside it.

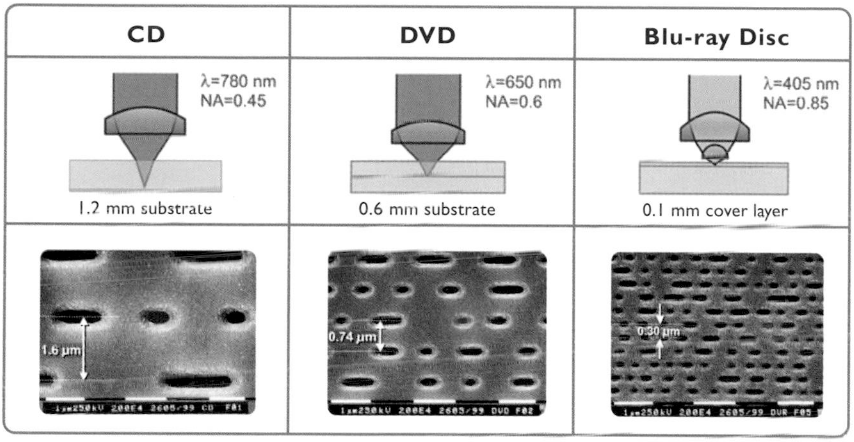

CD	DVD	Blu-ray Disc
λ=780 nm NA=0.45	λ=650 nm NA=0.6	λ=405 nm NA=0.85
1.2 mm substrate	0.6 mm substrate	0.1 mm cover layer
1.6 µm	0.74 µm	0.30 µm

FIG. 2
Three generations of optical disc systems. Progress in 'areal density', or bit count per unit area, takes big steps; a CD holds 650 MB, a DVD 4.7 GB, and a Blu-ray Disc up to 27 GB. This is achieved by reducing the spot size through shorter wavelength and stronger optics. The electron micrographs show read-only discs with replicated pit patterns

4.6 CONTEXT AWARENESS

Emile Aarts

In an Ambient Intelligence context, devices and applications will need to be aware of their context, i.e., the state of their surroundings at any given moment. Technologies are currently being developed to provide the environment with 'senses', ways of translating sensory input into meaningful information, which can then be used to adjust the functional behaviour of digital devices. This behaviour may be considered 'smart' and, ultimately, intelligent.

Early developments

Context awareness, a relatively young field of research, grew out of research into human-computer interaction and artificial intelligence. It initially centred around robotics, with sophisticated sensor technologies being used to make robots aware of their environment, and help them respond to changes in it. Particular attention was devoted to helping robots 'see'. Other early work focused on context awareness for mobile devices, simply because they frequently change location and therefore context. A context awareness technology that is now familiar to almost all of us is GPS (Global Positioning System), the technology used in car navigation systems to tell the vehicle where it is in relation to the desired destination.

With the advent of other small, personal mobile devices, additional technologies have been developed to try to make them easier to use in a more natural way. These technologies make it possible to modify the behaviour of a device depending on changes in its surroundings. For example, your mobile phone can be automatically adjusted to ring quieter or louder, and the voice reception volume turned up or down depending on whether you (and the phone) are in a quiet meeting room or a noisy canteen. As more small mobile devices have been produced, in response to market demand, technologists have been looking for ways to make them interoperable and usable anywhere. Context awareness technologies can facilitate this by determining whether there are other interoperable devices in the vicinity that are seeking to transmit information, or available to relay or receive it. Other recent applications of context awareness technologies are tagging and tracking. Luggage equipped with smart tags can detect 'where it is' and automatically be routed within complex transportation systems; and motorists visiting a filling station can pay automatically via a special tag on their key ring.

Structuring the context

It would be more interesting and challenging, however, to make a device that could take such basic sensory input and then classify and analyze it so that it could decide what was going on around it and behave accordingly. Besides the technological complexities involved, one of the first problems encountered in developing context-aware devices is to decide what aspects of contexts are relevant to a given device. Any situation involves myriad conditions, most of which may be irrelevant to the operation of a device. To select those that are relevant requires not only a deep understanding of what contexts are relevant to people, but also how devices interact with their surroundings.

A general model often used for analyzing context is shown schematically in Figure 1. This model distinguishes three dimensions of context, which can be adapted for our purposes as follows:

Self   The device itself, where it is, what state it is in, etc.

Environment   The physical surroundings of the device: how warm, humid or light it is, whether any noise can be heard (and if so, how loud it is), whether it is static or moving, whether anyone is present (and if so, who), etc.

Activity   The activities going on in the context (if any), including any behaviour or interaction.

Suppose you are driving alone in a car at 120 km per hour and your mobile phone is in your jacket on the back seat. The device might then apply the three-dimensional model of context as follows:

Self   The phone is in a jacket pocket on the back seat of a car.

Environment   The car is moving at high speed.

Activity   The user is driving the car and is alone in the car.

The phone has either been told or has learned that a phone ringing in such circumstances is distracting and potentially dangerous for the driver. It has also been told that, given that context, it should not ring, but should act in some less dangerous way, such as taking a message, or connecting to the car navigation system or in-car communication system, so that through the call can be processed through a different medium.

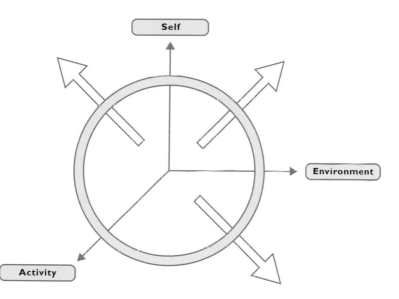

FIG. 1
The three dimensions
of context

Three phases of context awareness

The process of becoming context-aware can be broken down into three main phases. First, the device must be able to extract information from the environment, either through its own sensors, or by communicating with other devices nearby that may be able to provide information about the environment (e.g., from their own sensors). Second, it will need to have a way of representing and analyzing that contextual information within a coherent (and relevant) framework. Finally, it will need to be able to decide on the basis of its analysis of the context and its knowledge or previous experience what action (if any) it should take.

Phase 1 – Perceiving the environment

The first step in creating a context-aware system is to get information about the environment into that system in some useable form. As humans, we use our senses to start to understand what is happening around us. In electronic and digital systems, we use a variety of sensors, extremely specialized components, each of which can capture a certain characteristic from the environment and deliver information about that characteristic to a computer.

Sensors are fundamental to enabling electronic devices to be 'aware' of the fundamentals of the environment around them.

Sensor technology

Sensors are analog devices that can transform non-electrical environmental signals into electrical signals. Sensors come in many different types, depending on their effect (e.g., physical or chemical), the phenomena they measure, how they work, what they are made of, their function, their cost and their accuracy. The type of sensor deployed will depend on what the output information will be used for. Sensors used in the home for leisure purposes, for instance, may not need to be as accurate as sensors used in a car braking system.

Sensors take input, in the form of physical, chemical or biological quantities, and transform it into an electrical value that can eventually be used by a computer. Sensors can detect variations in a wide variety of parameters, including:

Mechanical	Length, area, volume and all time-based derivatives (e.g., linear and angular velocity or acceleration, mass flow, force, torque, pressure, acoustic wavelength and intensity)
Thermal	Temperature, heat, heat flow and state of matter
Electrical	Voltage, current, charge, resistance, inductance, capacitance, polarization and electric field
Magnetic	Field intensity, flux density, magnetic moment and permeability
Radiant (including optical)	Intensity, phase, wavelength, polarization, reflectance, transmittance and refractive index
Chemical	Composition, concentration, reaction rate, pH, and potential for oxidation and reduction.

Smart sensors

'Smart' sensors include an analog-to-digital converter and a microprocessor that can perform complex digital signal processing tasks. Ideally, smart sensors perform all the processing necessary to deliver clear, reliable and useful signals to the host system. This processing may include subsystems that undertake:

- Excitation control
- Amplification
- Analog filtering
- Conversion between analog and digital modes (in both directions)
- Compensation for non-linearity, noise, interference and drift
- Digital processing for signal integrity checks and signal restoration
- Digital processing for output communication.

The digital information processing within a smart sensor is designed to condense the information produced by the sensing elements.

Sensors can also be used to monitor and check data that forms the input to electronic devices. This can make an important contribution to the customization of devices to their users. Some of the sensory input devices relevant to context awareness include:

- Digitizer boards and tablets that use ultrasound or pressure techniques to digitize writing on whiteboards, drafting tables or other surfaces
- Digital pens that use a very small trackball in the tip or inertia sensors to read handwriting or recognize signatures
- Game control devices like joysticks, steering wheels, pedals, pistols and game pads that use mechanical sensors to sense movement
- Electronic gloves that transmit detailed information from all three joints of the fingers

- Head-movement trackers that use movement sensors to locate the position of the head (often based on acceleration sensors)
- Joysticks, mice and trackballs that use mechanical transduction, displacement or acceleration sensing, based on gyroscopes or optical techniques
- Speech recognition and speaker identification devices that use microphones, often positioned in arrays to track speakers
- Body movement and activity sensing devices that use six-degree-of-freedom ultrasound and inertia trackers to capture information about human body motion, such as standing, sitting, lying down, walking or running
- Galvanic skin response devices that measure changes in skin conductive properties due to sweating when someone is startled or experiences anxiety
- Electromyogramic muscle sensors that use sensitive electrodes to measure electrical signals resulting from muscle contraction
- Electro-oculogramic eye movement sensors that use motion sensing to measure eye positions
- Electroencephalogramic brain sensors that use electrodes to measure brain activity, providing information about a person's mental state
- Eye-movement trackers that use mounted or stationary cameras or infrared reflections to track the movement of a person's eyes
- Face, hand and iris recognition devices that use various biometric entities to identify faces, hands and eyes
- Electronic noses that detect people or environments through their characteristic scent.

In an Ambient Intelligence world, not every device will need to have every kind of sensor built in. Devices will be able to learn about various environmental conditions from other sources nearby. This means that the accuracy with which the context is 'perceived' may vary from place to place, depending on how many sensors can be called upon in a particular location. For example, a device may have a clock to tell it the time, a light sensor to tell it how bright it is, a motion sensor to tell it whether it is moving or not, a location sensor to tell it where it is and a sound sensor to tell it how noisy the atmosphere around is. Others may have only one or two of these.

Phase II – Classifying and analyzing the data

Sensors provide output in the form of values for particular properties of the context (e.g., location, temperature, movement, etc.). The next step is to use this information to determine the state of the environment as a whole, based on a model for context. The 'raw' information about the environment is combined to create higher-level information that, in rudimentary abstract form, expresses the state of the environment or user. For example, a device's sensors may be telling it that it is at home, the time is 3 a.m., the lights are off, the device is stationary and that there is very little ambient noise. During the Classification Phase, the device will combine this information to conclude that 'user is asleep'. On the basis of its current input, it would rule out 'user is on a bus', 'user is deep in conversation' and many other options.

This is a complex process, and many of the techniques required to effect it are still under development. One approach to this 'classification' process uses neural networks as a way of distilling raw information into statistically likely abstract states. This approach, modelled on our understanding of how the human brain works, is particularly powerful in that the states do not have to be predefined but will emerge during 'training' and become more accurate over time.

At this stage, the role of memory becomes important. If a device can remember that a given context tends to recur and then build an appropriate memory of reactions, we shall appreciate it as 'intelligent', as it implies an ability to learn, evaluate and learn from earlier events and mistakes.

Phase III — Interpreting the context and taking action

In essence, the device has so far used its 'senses' to perceive the environment, and based on this input and its memory, it has built a 'picture' of what it thinks the context is (i.e., what is going on around it). Now it needs to use this high-level knowledge to decide what, if anything, it should do.

One important thing that the device needs to work out is what the user wants most in the context it has perceived and analyzed. Only when it has decided that will it be able to take appropriate action. A number of models have been developed to explain human-computer interaction, and these can be adapted for our purposes. One very influential model is known as GOMS (where GOMS stands for Goals, Operators, Methods and Selection rules). [1] Under this approach, users are seen as information processors with perceptual, motor and cognitive subsystems. Users are assumed to act rationally, setting themselves the Goals of achieving certain states through the working of perceptual, motor and cognitive Operators. Various Methods can be used to achieve these goals, the choice of method being determined by Selection rules. Another significant approach is based on Activity Theory, [2] originating from Soviet psychological research done in the 1920s. This approach builds on the concept of 'unit of activity'. This is made up of one or more 'subjects' (the people engaged in an activity), 'objects' (an objective that motivates the subject(s) to engage in the activity), 'actions' (goal-directed processes that need to be followed in order to reach an object), and 'operations' (routinely processed tasks that constitute an action). Activity Theory differs from GOMS in that it does not describe each step in a user's activity in detail, and is thus able to cope with changes in the conditions under which an activity is carried out. Furthermore, Activity Theory, by defining the activity itself as the context, can combine elements internal to the user (e.g., the user's objectives and preferences), and elements external to the user (artifacts, other people and environmental settings).

Context-aware devices can use such models as these to describe and analyze what the user is likely to want to achieve in this context, and then apply rules (given or learned) to make a sensible decision about what to do. What is described elsewhere in this volume as computational intelligence will be applied to calculate the options and likely outcomes of any action taken.

Applications

HomeLab, Philips' feasibility and usability laboratory, contains a number of working context-aware devices. They are not only able to determine the proximity of people and other devices, but can also identify users, reacting appropriately by installing the user's personal settings, so the device will operate in the way preferred by the user.

One of these devices is a personalized remote control. Designed for use in the home, it can function as a telephone and a control device, and incorporates a display. It has a number of sensors (infrared, front light, back light and touch) and a microphone. Applying a contextual model, it can decide whether it is in someone's pocket, in someone's hand, just lying around or moving. It can also hear whether the environment is noisy or quiet, and determine which TV set or display is nearby. Its behaviour depends on the context. If it receives an SMS (text) message, for instance, it will give a loud signal if it decides it is in a pocket. If it is in someone's hand, the signal will be much quieter. If it is 'lying around', the signal will start quietly and gradually get louder. What is displayed on the screen will also depend on the context.

Philips Research has also developed a jacket that uses integrated strain sensors to determine whether the wearer is walking, writing or shaking hands.

The development of context-aware mobile phones has received much attention. In addition to standard call services, these context-aware phones can provide personalized services tailored not only to the users themselves, but also tailored to the situation in which they find themselves at any given moment. The services are therefore offered to the people who are most likely to want them precisely when they are most likely to want them.

1   S.K. Card, T.P. Moran and A. Newell, *The Psychology of Human-Computer Interaction* (Hilsdale NJ, Erlbaum, 1983)
2   B.A. Narsil, *Context and Consciousness* (Cambridge MA, MIT Press, 1996)

4.7 UBIQUITOUS COMMUNICATION

Fred Snijders

No-one knows precisely what the communication needs and technologies of the Ambient Intelligence home will be in a decade or two from now, but we can make a calculated guess. The ultimate dream is that the Ambient Intelligence home will be packed with exciting yet unobtrusive gadgets, such as digital bathroom mirrors, virtual fish tanks, electronic paintings, and electronic wallpaper that adjusts to the mood of the occupants, who will also be communicating within the home. This will take a few years to materialize. But a reasonably safe prediction is that the Ambient Intelligence concept in the home will start with dozens of displays and interaction devices through which users will communicate with the outside world in order to access entertainment and information services. Although there will be a great deal of communication among the devices in the home itself, the bulk of the information exchange taking place will be with the outside world. The key technology in this communication will be 'broadband' connectivity, opening the way for unlimited access to value-added services, anytime and anywhere, both inside and outside the Ambient Intelligence home. Although 'broadband' has a well-defined technical meaning, it is now often used to refer to a two-way link between two or more users, or between a user (or user device) and a supplier of some form of infotainment services, where that two-way link is capable of supporting full-motion, interactive, real-time multimedia applications. It is in this sense that we shall use it here.

From service provider to user

The networked home of the future will consist of clusters of embedded devices communicating seamlessly through wires or, increasingly, through wireless technology. This in-home network will probably be linked to the outside world through a 'residential gateway'. This gateway will provide security functions and form an interface between the home network technology and the technology used in the external broadband access networks. This interface will be needed to allow the technologies of both the inside and outside networks to evolve each at its own pace. Ultimately, the gateway may become a home server, controlling all appliances and providing storage for all digital content in the home.

Just as today we connect to our Internet Provider or cable TV provider to receive their services, our future residential gateway will connect to a Service Point of Presence (SPOP), where a service provider collects input from the Internet, telephone and audio-visual core networks and adds other services. Although it is difficult to predict in detail what a typical service package will be like, it is likely to include a range of multimedia infotainment services, such as 'delay TV', profile-driven networked Personal Video Recording, recommender functions, On-Demand audio and video, networked multi-user games and information retrieval services. In addition, there may be home control, home management and healthcare services that enable remote management of technical aspects of the Ambient Intelligence environment and monitoring of the well-being of those living in the home.

Not all multimedia content will come into the home from external service providers. Some will originate within the home itself and be sent from it. People will like to share their personal multimedia content with others outside the home, for example, and are likely to be communicating with others via end-to-end video, using touch-sensitive screens.

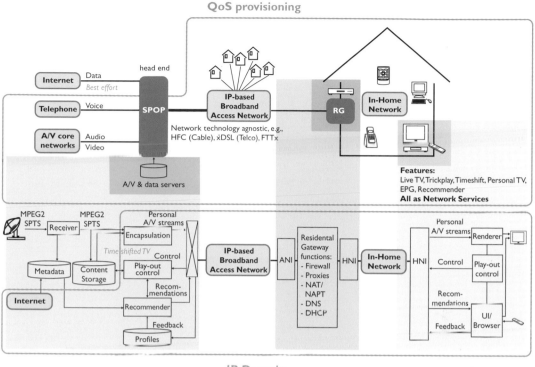

QoS provisioning

Internet — Data / *Best effort*

head end

Telephone — Voice

A/V core networks — Audio / Video

SPOP

IP-based Broadband Access Network

Network technology agnostic, e.g., HFC (Cable), xDSL (Telco), FTTx

A/V & data servers

RG

In-Home Network

Features:
Live TV, Trickplay, Timeshift, Personal TV, EPG, Recommender
All as Network Services

MPEG2 SPTS — Receiver — MPEG2 SPTS

Personal A/V streams

Encapsulation

Time shifted TV Control

Metadata — Content Storage — Play-out control

Recommendations

Internet — Recommender

Feedback

Profiles

IP-based Broadband Access Network

ANI

Residential Gateway functions:
- Firewall
- Proxies
- NAT/ NAPT
- DNS
- DHCP

HNI

In-Home Network

HNI

Personal A/V streams — Renderer

Control — Play-out control

Recommendations

Feedback

UI/ Browser

IP Domain

FIG. 1
Service delivery model
to the Ambient
Intelligence home

Delivering personalized services

The personalization of services, which goes hand-in-hand with the concept of Ambient Intelligence, will impose major requirements on the broadband network technology being used, both in the outdoor part ('access network') and the indoor part of the broadband communication chain.

Current broadband networks (such as those used for cable TV) are based on a 'broadcast', or 'push', model: the total content offering is broadcast and the user makes a selection at the end-device (e.g., when we choose a channel on our TV set). If cable TV networks are to support the large-scale deployment of personalized multimedia streams that will be required for the Ambient Intelligence home, they will need to be upgraded. Fortunately, recent studies by the Philips' Video Over IP Task Force have shown that this can be done at a reasonable cost per home. Meanwhile, cable TV networks are already delivering some personalized streams (e.g., data and digital interactive on-demand video), using a technique whereby the digital signal 'mimics' an analog TV channel. Cable operators are increasingly providing fast Internet access and voice (i.e., telephone) services, in this way offering a complete range of 'always on' telecommunication and entertainment services.

Other evolving broadband networks using DSL technology (gradually being deployed by telephone companies) have insufficient bandwidth to support multiple video streams, since they generally aim to make use of the current wiring infrastructure. This means that DSL technology is unable to support a 'broadcast' model. To be able to compete with the cable companies as Ambient Intelligence service providers, the telephone companies want to deliver video services, too. They are hoping to achieve this by removing bottlenecks in their existing networks, thus freeing up bandwidth that they can use for transmitting 'bandwidth-hungry' services such as high-speed Internet access, digital on-demand services and even some form of broadcast video.

Which of these two technologies is likely to become the delivery technology of choice? Or will some new technology arise that can offer unlimited bandwidth? Given the enormous investments that have already been made in the current infrastructures, widespread deployment of some new technology is unlikely – and it is in any case arguable whether subscribers will actually need (and be prepared to pay for) unlimited bandwidth. It is more likely that several broadband network technologies will exist alongside each other, and that the home may connect to several networks simultaneously. Service providers may even offer the same services through several different broadband infrastructures. Under this model (known as 'service unbundling'), the services themselves will have to be made independent of the technologies used to transport them.

Video communication – the home as source of high bit rate content

From 'push' to 'pull'

To solve the bandwidth dilemma for personalized digital streams in broadband networks, we will need to evolve from a 'push' model into a 'pull' model for delivery of our infotainment needs. We have seen already that in a 'push' model, all available information is sent to all homes, irrespective of their individual needs. Current TV broadcasting, for example, operates on this principle of 'one-to-many'. In a 'pull' model, however, only the information actually needed at a given moment is sent to the individual home. This means that the selection of programmes or content no longer 'physically' takes place in the end-device, in the user's home, but has become part of the network infrastructure (e.g., at the SPOP). The end-device 'tells' the SPOP what programmes or content should be sent and the SPOP dynamically composes a personalized digital stream for each individual home. This stream may consist of a number of audio-video streams, and some high-speed data and voice streams for delivery to the home. The 'pull' system obviously allows for a much more economical use of bandwidth in parts of the network where bandwidth is scarce ('the last mile'). It will also allow SPOPs and other network operators to guarantee, through careful dynamic management of the streams, that the bandwidth necessary for particular services will be available to a given user for as long as that service is required: these guarantees are known as 'Quality of Service (QoS) provisioning'.

Bandwidth limitations in the last mile can also be tackled by improving video compression technology. This would make it possible to either transmit the same content at even lower speeds, transmit more content at the same speed, or improve the quality of the video stream. Currently, it is possible to transmit 4-5 high-quality video streams, 2 high-speed data streams and some telephony all together at a bit rate of some 20 megabits per second. This bit rate can be carried as an individual stream to each home by most of the current or near-future broadband networks. This mode of delivery (known as 'the thin-pipe-to-the-home concept') will be an essential part of the personalized delivery of multimedia content to the networked home.

Needless to say, changing from a 'push' to a 'pull' model will create a paradigm shift in our way of thinking about overall audio-visual service delivery models. It will require a one-to-one relationship (and mutual dependency) between the service provider and the end-user, plus billing mechanisms based on the individual use of services. In addition, the architecture of the audio-visual end-devices will need to change radically. Currently, functionalities are integrated within audio-visual devices (such as TV sets and hi-fi equipment). They – and other functions, such as communication functions – will need to be distributed instead, and will rely heavily on external networked service providers for their operation. The consumer electronics industry has to start thinking 'out of the box'.

In-home networking

A prerequisite for the Ambient Intelligence home will be a versatile and transparent in-home network with communication that is 'ubiquitous'(i.e., always available), but non-intrusive. Some homes already have networks, usually linking several PCs for the purposes of sharing peripherals and broadband Internet access. This development is being reinforced by the increasing networking of consumer electronics equipment (e.g., in-home cinema applications) and the advent of non-PC devices, such as Internet radios and Internet TVs. Such non-PC devices depend heavily on the notion of connectivity, anytime anywhere, via an in-home network. It is predicted that, within the next 5-7 years, the majority of devices connected to the Internet will in fact be such non-PC devices.

Home networking presents some tough challenges. A home network will have to transport signals of different kinds (audio, video, data, control, etc.), each of which imposes different requirements on the availability and responsiveness of the network. Since people will come to depend on their home network for running their home, it will need to be highly reliable and manageable. It should also be easy to install, with device detection and identification mechanisms (an enhanced version of Universal Plug and Play, for instance), so that new elements can be added without hassle. Connectivity solutions will have to be worked out for legacy devices (i.e., equipment acquired earlier). The network will have to be capable of being maintained by non-experts (unless maintenance is provided by an external remote management service). And finally, since they will grow organically, home networks will need to be self-organizing.

Ideally, ease of installation would imply either use of the existing wiring in the home (for electricity, telephone, etc.) or of wireless technologies. Unfortunately, neither option lends itself to providing high-quality real-time audio and video streams. Both methods are subject to disruption and suffer from bandwidth limitations, although the latter can be solved by limiting the bandwidth of incoming streams to a bare minimum (the 'thin pipe to the home' mentioned above), leaving room for additional in-home communication between the devices themselves.

In-home standards

Various standards for in-home networks are currently under discussion. One possibility is IEEE1394. This is an international standard for a low-cost digital interface, integrating entertainment, communication and computing products in a single consumer media network. It can operate over copper, fibre and coaxial cable at speeds that provide adequate bandwidth

CONNECTED
PLANET

CAMP
AND MADS

OPEN TOOLS

ICD+

NEW
NOMADS

for in-home and peer-to-peer communication (up to 400 megabits per second, with enhancements of up to 3200 megabits per second currently being studied).

Wireless versions of IEEE1394 have also been demonstrated, but they are slower. Work on wireless in-home networks has tended to focus on the use or adaptation of wireless LAN (Local Area Network) technology, such as the IEEE802.11 standard (up to 52 megabits per second). However, current versions of this standard are not well-suited for real-time communication of video sources. Hiperlan/2, a European proposal for a wireless LAN standard, has somewhat better characteristics than IEEE802.11, but is not widely supported by the industry.

We are convinced that a special standard for in-home network technology for Ambient Intelligence will need to be developed. It will need to provide the following features:

- Seamless integration of real-time audio/video and 'bursty' data traffic (with Quality of Service provisioning)
- Segmentation of the in-home network into small clusters so that frequencies can easily be re-used
- High availability and reliability, even when products that may cause interference are close at hand
- Plug-and-play features
- High data security

Such a network could be based on a hierarchical network, possibly with a wired backbone (e.g., of polymer fibre) and wireless picocells at high radio frequencies, or broadband infrared connections within a room. Interference such as multipath fading could be combated by using multi-antennae techniques and advanced coding schemes. The radio base stations in the room could be simplified by using fibre radio technology and optical signal processing. Use of higher radio frequencies (e.g., 17 GHz) would make it easier to confine the radio spectrum to a single room, thereby making it possible to use the same radio spectrum again in adjacent rooms or homes. They would also make higher bandwidth available, and make it possible to offload local traffic within a picocell (i.e., a room-sized area covered by the wireless network). The European WIND-FLEX project is an early example of this approach to in-home networks.

Convergence

If, as predicted, multimedia services enter the home via multiple broadband networks using different network technologies, some sort of integration or convergence layer will be needed to integrate the various streams in a seamless fashion, both at the SPOP and in the home. The use of the Internet Protocol (IP) as a convergence layer is currently being studied, and considerable progress has been made in the IP streaming of high-quality audio and video: the mapping of these IP mechanisms onto the existing cable, DSL and fibre access networks has already been worked out in some detail. Note that video over IP delivery where the SPOP does the encapsulation of video into IP is completely different from the current low-quality video streaming experienced over the Internet. The SPOP and access network operators provide Quality of Service guarantees for IP-encapsulated video and audio streams.

The advantage of IP over alternative transport packaging mechanisms is that IP and the IP-related Ethernet transport technologies are mainstream technologies in the PC domain. This guarantees a powerful 'back wind' for the consumer electronics industry from the PC industry, with low prices and widespread support as a result. IP traffic is also easy to route within the access and in-home networks, thus providing the necessary hooks and handles for network segmentation both inside and outside the home. Data is already entering the home in IP format, and new access networks can be implemented cost-effectively using gigabit Ethernet technology.

Telecommunications companies are currently deploying the first optical Ethernet networks in access networks as an alternative to DSL in 'greenfield' situations, but, at this rate, it will take many years for a substantial level of deployment to be achieved. Also, for in-home networks the use of 1000Base-T or 100Base-T technology is a cheap and versatile way of integrating data, control and video appliances into a single network concept. The 100 megabits per second version can be used on a radio carrier for wireless in-home connectivity. A lot of research still remains to be done, particularly on quality of service provisioning, but IP-based networking of audio, video and data holds all the winning cards and looks set to become the preferred technology for the transport of signals within the Ambient Intelligence home.

CONNECTED
PLANET

CAMP
AND MADS

OPEN TOOLS

ICD+

NEW
NOMADS

COMMUNE, INTEGRATE, TRUST

How might Ambient Intelligence systems enhance our quality of life within our communities? Will they make us more social? How could they help us find a healthy balance, integrating the different parts of our lives? And will we be willing to place our trust in these systems?

5.1 COMMUNITY, MEMORY AND AMBIENT INTELLIGENCE

Anton Andrews, Mark Hartevelt

Winston Churchill once remarked that 'we shape our buildings, and afterwards our buildings shape us'. The same can be said of the cities, towns and neighbourhoods in which we live and form communities. These physical places are meaningful to us because they embody our history, allow us to express our identities and help us achieve a sense of belonging and community. In the last few decades, however, we have been faced with developments such as the increasing density of urban populations, information overload, anonymous living patterns and the effects of globalization and commuting. Many of our residential, recreational and work environments are consequently witness to the loss of a sense of community and of meaningful collective memory. One of the challenges in the face of such change is to create sustainable communities by providing suitable informal mechanisms for awareness and knowledge sharing.

Information is exchanged constantly in any community, not just within a network of family, friends and neighbours, but also between members of the community who don't personally know each other. Whereas our individual relationships with information transform it into knowledge, our relationships with each other bring that knowledge to life in the community.[1] It is especially in this light that technology has often failed to provide a true solution, keeping people apart at the ends of sterile communication channels, rather than bringing them together in their local environment. Too often the mechanisms for information exchange and communication in the community are divorced from the physical environment. To quote the architect Norman Foster, 'the future of our cities is linked to our ability to handle physical communication'.[2]

As part of the inquiry into the qualities of living in environments enabled by Ambient Intelligence, we are therefore exploring how to enhance the informal communication that occurs within communities and how to promote social sustainability. What could the effects of Ambient Intelligence be on patterns of neighbourhood behaviour? How could it reconstitute the relationships between people and information in a community?

New communities, old principles

During the last three decades, technology has introduced an accelerating increase in connectivity:[3] we can communicate with relatives and organizations more often, in more ways and with ever-richer content. The dazzling speed with which mobile phones have become a part of our lives has surprised many, and the availability of e-mail in most western households is almost de rigueur. Networks allow us to easily book holidays or conduct financial transactions anywhere, at any time, and 'going on holiday' no longer implies isolation from those back home.

This increased connectivity influences the way people, organizations and society organize themselves. Friends stay in touch across continents, family ties survive dispersion and cosmopolitan networks of friends replace local village communities. Companies increasingly run harmonized projects across continents, and governments facilitate business development and knowledge exchange across nations. The greater efficiency in the travel and logistics industries facilitates increasing mobility and globalization.[4] Society fundamentally changes and new communities emerge.

Thanks to the growth in connectivity, we are able to maintain more relations, but perhaps at the cost of depth. We have more information available, but probably at the cost of simplicity. We have a larger audience to express ourselves to, but often at the cost of real dialogue.

In the light of the Ambient Intelligence vision, we need to ask what happens to communities when 'home' becomes less localized, 'goodbye' less rigorous and relations more wired. Will our new communities cater to our basic need for emotional growth and growing valuable relations? Will they support us in establishing a satisfactory role in society? Will they provide a sufficient and sustainable framework for personal and collective growth?

Every mature and healthy community shares a few basic principles, irrespective of culture, scale or enabling media:[5] community members need mechanisms for representing themselves (identity) and for building up their reputation (reward and recognition). A community needs its own territory within which people can adopt specific habits and rituals. Community members need a way to express their shared values and keep their collective memory. This collective intelligence is the main embodiment of the community's culture, which in turn is the foundation of that community.

Traditionally, these basic principles have worked through age-old mechanisms. Typical examples include the seating plan of the local village church reflecting the churchgoers' reputation, or the tight network of relations within a local community that facilitates quick dissemination of its members' visions and ideas, or the role of elderly people as 'repositories', keeping alive a collective memory of community life.

One can question to what extent these basic community principles are fully addressed now that connectivity and mobility have grown so strongly and that we rely so heavily on technologies that are in fact still in their infancy.[6] For example, although the mobile phone can connect people at almost any time and place, that connection differs drastically from a real encounter in emotional richness and completeness of knowledge exchange. Moreover, it is typically geared towards bilateral encounters and does not support any group dynamics. Similarly, the so-called 'networked collaborative work environments' raise expectations but do not enable colleagues to manage the extent of their encounters with others, to share impulsive ideas or exchange informal experiences and references in a rich way.

In general, current connectivity and information technologies provide thin and rigid communication streams, and focus mainly on supporting formal processes and on handling formal information. But how can community support systems make the family chitchat in front of the TV meaningful for a son living abroad? How can the informal stream of wild ideas generated at the coffee corner efficiently become integrated in the multinational company's innovation process? How do locals at the bar become aware that old Mrs Taylor at 21 Church Street has become immobile and would appreciate the odd visitor?

The importance of collective intelligence has been acknowledged throughout our history. In the 10th century, the Islamic mysticists Al Farabi and Avicenna described it as a prototype shared intellect, a unique entity common to the entire human race.[7] Similarly, Pierre Teilhard described the surface of the earth as an 'organizing web' allowing ideas to encounter one another, generating social energy.[8] More recently, knowledge management has become a 'hot' issue. Could the distributed and adaptive networks of intelligent devices proposed by Ambient Intelligence support such a collective intelligence?

To really support the coherence, dynamics, culture and growth of new communities, we need to get closer to the members' daily lives, to integrate in the streams of informal information. We need to empower natural acts of social exchange, to integrate with those physical circumstances which lend themselves to social exchange, and to make community memory tangible and available. Making systems that fully support new communities in this sense is an almost unexplored area that requires a dedicated approach.

Anticipating social connections

Our premise is that it is preferable to build on existing social connections within the community, levering on the unique identity and subjectivity inherent to them, rather than trying to impose new ones. For this reason, we have focused on enabling the flow and abundance of grassroots content. For example, when looking for a restaurant on the Internet, one is typically presented with standardized, factual information about prices, location and luxury level. It may be informationally richer and far more interesting to circulate local and personal comments on the restaurant or on other local issues, potentially leading to contact with the author.

Activities like these are not necessarily related to 'intentional' communication, but are part of a wider sociological matrix that, once linked, can lead to new connections between people, places and information within the community. Informal community knowledge is built into the fabric of the community and reflected 'incidentally' across its entirety. Because these incidental communication activities occur spontaneously and without much planning, they need to occur within the natural flow of daily activities. Discovering, browsing, accessing and contributing to such community content should be intuitive and part of our normal routines.

Community dynamics

Community spaces tend to be defined by a large number of unplanned and fairly unregulated overlapping social activities and cultural processes. Whilst institutional processes and information tend to be temporally stable and predictable, grassroots activities and information are less stable, and give rise to the constantly emerging and dynamically changing structure which is the living community.

Over time, people, places, events and information become connected across the community. Natural societal networks are formed: depending on local activities and concerns, their links fluctuate, thickening and thinning over time. Information accumulating within the community is constantly reprioritized and redistributed by natural processes, settling in different parts of the 'network', intensifying or becoming redundant and fading from view.

A living memory

A community is held together by its memory of these dynamic, unpredictable processes, and they determine how people feel about a neighbourhood, how desirable it is to live there, and whether or not it is safe to walk alone on the streets at night. A community, be it a business, a hotel or a neighbourhood, is therefore a time-sensitive, organically networked entity with many dynamically acting components. The flows and densities of people, places, events and information forming it undergo constant flux and change.

A community's ability to cope with such change depends largely on its internal awareness or collective intelligence. Communities which are self-aware and sensitive to their past are able to respond rapidly and positively to change and to grow under such conditions. It is therefore important for the sustainability of a community that its members be able to express their concerns, skills and knowledge to each other in an open way and that this information remains accessible, building a 'living memory' of the community over the years.

Starting points

This understanding of community dynamics and memory can be condensed into three key starting points for the creation of ambient intelligent solutions:

Memory

First, collective, evolving memory should be tangibly present. Memory provides the community with coherence and a frame of reference. A knowledge exchange system must convey a sense of the community's memory and allow contribution to it in order to build on the richness and experience of its heritage.

Community as database

Second, we propose that the most relevant, vital knowledge is in people's heads, not in databases, and that knowledge exchange systems should provide intelligent references to the people holding this knowledge, rather than to 'cold' databased information.

Territory as interface

Third, we believe that people shouldn't have to sit at a computer in order to get information, but should be able to access the system in natural locations during their everyday routines. Community members should be able to easily access, share and exchange relevant community knowledge in meaningful locations using natural, habitual gestures.

Design approach

Ambient Intelligence frames a vision in which memory can be mapped back into the physical community in a meaningful and interactive way. Embedded, ubiquitous and responsive systems could, given the right qualities, help us interpret and preserve the richness and complexity of our local cultures and assist us in capturing, sharing and exploring our collective memory and experience. To this end, we have begun developing a design approach towards creating

A New Sense of Place

Ezio Manzini

Ezio Manzini
Professor at the Polytechnic
of Milan and author

Over the next few decades, we will have to learn to live better, consuming less and regenerating the context-quality of our lives, the quality of the places we are given to live in, both physically and socially. On these grounds, Ambient Intelligence can seek, and maybe find, a sense – or rather, a sense fitting to its potential.

Vision

Imagine a new sense of place emerging. A highly connected place, where each person, if they so desire, can carry on their activities with access to the best services, facilities, and every type of information. A socializing place where the new neighbourhood networks are elective communities of people who choose when and how to cooperate. A bottom-up place, linked in a network with other places, where whatever can be decided and put into action on a local scale is enlarged to its maximum potential.

Possibilities

This scenario, the multi-local society scenario, does not represent the dominant tendency today. However, it is not an impossible scenario, and various signals indicate its potential feasibility. But this is not all. It is also consistent with the nature of Ambient Intelligence: a technology that, by definition, refers to a place, takes root there and expands its potential. A technology which explicitly presents itself as a prosthesis of places, and so binds its promise of wellbeing to the quality of the environment where it is applied.

Proposition

It is a question of promoting this new sense of place. Of generating extended places where the new prostheses of Ambient Intelligence facilitate and support the activities and services of a multi-cultural society. In so doing, they favour the emergence of sustainable lifestyles, the localized yet cosmopolitan lifestyles which such extended places – (truly) intelligent environments – will be able to foster.

knowledge exchange systems which are informal, interactive and a natural part of the local environment and daily routines.

This approach has grown and matured during the course of several connected community projects. The first large-scale research project conducted in this area was Living Memory (LiMe), a European Commission-sponsored research project targeting a residential community. Since then, we have continued to extensively develop this and other subsequent real-world projects. This hands-on involvement has resulted in the development of a set of basic design principles and methodologies which allow such systems to be built in the real world.

Community system principles

Our design approach is informed by a number of structural and behavioural principles that translate the thoughts described so far into a way of conceiving and building ambient intelligent knowledge management systems:

The system should be embedded in accepted community practices

People shouldn't have to go out of their way to interface with the system, and its use should be meaningful, simple and part of the flow of daily activities. It should offer intelligently contextualized, relevant information depending on time, place and people. It should allow the easy browsing and creation of rich content and mechanisms for capturing and sharing it.

The system should offer a relevant mix of institutional and grassroots content

The system should offer a mix of the more 'official' institutional content and vibrant but unpredictable grassroots content, allowing each to feed off and stimulate the other. The correct balance of this mix will depend on the nature of the community application.

The system should be flexible, adaptive and evolving

A living community is in constant flux, so any system catering to its informal nature needs to be open, flexible and adaptive. The system should welcome diverse interface and interaction mechanisms, including unforeseen additions during its lifecycle. The system architecture should be responsive and evolutionary, allowing the emergence of distribution patterns in information flow which meaningfully reflect shifting community dynamics and interests over time.

Community involvement

Ambient Intelligence is about meaningful technology for people. No two communities are the same, and the design of an embedded connected community solution must be tailored to the specific needs and requirements of the community in question. This requires an ethnographic community analysis on many levels, and close collaboration and co-creation with the members of that community. Beyond this, ongoing feedback after the implementation of the solution is required to help it fuse and mature with the community it is embedded in.

For example, during the research and prototype development phases of the LiMe project in Edinburgh, the project team chose a specific community, an area, as a test group. Working with on-site ethnographic experts from Queen Margaret University College, the project was able to maintain a sustained dialogue with local users throughout the project, helping find solutions truly relevant to their local community. The initial prototypes were then iteratively installed and tested in various locations in Edinburgh. This process met with an overwhelmingly positive response, and the intensive participation and feedback of the user group has been invaluable in ensuring the development of relevant, accessible and meaningful solutions.

Prototyping: experience and time

User involvement and co-creation in the design and construction of embedded connected community systems can be taken to a certain point with traditional methods such as discussion workshops and user observation. However, to truly test the impact of such a system on the community and to gain a real understanding of its suitability and experiential qualities over time, we have realized that a more experiential and tangible form of partnership with the end-users is necessary.

To this end, the use of 'experiential prototypes' is invaluable. These prototypes are a hybrid of a technical prototype and a design model in that they strongly convey the intended tangible user experience, are interactive and perceived to be fully functional. In other words, they are as much a test of 'look and feel' as they are of functionality. The challenges of designing augmented community environments are more easily resolved by the immediate and compelling nature of a direct hands-on experience with such working prototypes.

In the Pl@net project at Philips Design, not only the individual interfaces but also the time-based system behaviours have been designed and functionally prototyped. This has allowed us to experiment with the observed relationships between people, interfaces and content in real time, in turn allowing us to tune and customize the properties of the system to match the behaviours of the community.

Implications

This chapter has presented an approach for addressing new communities with a set of community principles and solutions informed by Ambient Intelligence. We have referred to the LiMe and Pl@net prototypes, fully functional community systems that utilize informal information and foster the community's collective memory. They do so by pervasively integrating in social environments with interfaces that connect to social actions. The integration is achieved not only by using embedded interfaces, but also by using a responsive architecture to route and redistribute the growing pool of information over the years in a way which reflects the changing interests, behaviours and needs of the community. These prototypes sketch solutions for our near future.

However, the design principles we have developed for the connected communities of tomorrow can equally be applied to today's immediate context. Company intranets tend to be used as a means for information dissemination, as a resource of company knowledge and management guidelines and as one-way broadcasting systems. Nevertheless, the same technologies can be used to promote knowledge exchange between employees, to facilitate collaboration over distance, to increase employee awareness of corporate developments, to initiate dialogue with the company, articulate company culture and foster company coherence. The introduction of simple but clever grassroots publishing functionalities, flexible reference facilities and effective identity and reputation mechanisms can turn today's intranets into 'living' systems that can effectively increase operational efficiency and employee loyalty.

1   I. Nonaka and H. Takeuchi, 'The Knowledge-creating Company', *Harvard Business Review on Knowledge Management*
    (Boston, Harvard Business School Press, 1995)
2   Taken from the exhibition entitled 'Norman Foster: Architecture is About People', Museum für angewandte Kunst
    (Cologne, 25 October-30 December 2001)
3   F. Hesselbein, M. Goldsmith, R. Beckhard and R. Schubert (eds), *The Community of the Future* (San Francisco, Jossey-Bass Publishers, 1998)
4   J. Hagel and A.G. Armstrong, *Net Gain: Expanding Markets through Virtual Communities* (Boston, Harvard Business School Press, 1997)
5   F. Hesselbein et al., op. cit.
6   J. Preece, *Online Communities: Designing Usability, Supporting Sociability* (New York, John Wiley & Sons, 2001)
7   I.R. Netton, 'Al Farabi', *Islamic Philosophy*, vol. 3, *The Routledge Encyclopedia of Philosophy*, ed. E. Craig (London, Routledge, 1998), 554-558
8   P. Teilhard de Chardin, *The Phenomenon of Man* (New York, Harper and Row, 1961)

5.2 AMBIENT ENVIRONMENTS

Lira Nikolovska

What is 'Ambient'?

The word 'Ambient' refers to atmosphere, environment, feel, setting, mood and character. If what matters is not technology itself, but its relationship to us, then what is the role of technology in the space around us? How will the various interpretations of 'Ambient', coupled with technology, manifest themselves in our environment? And how will ambient technologies influence our perception, experiences and behaviour in different scales or kinds of environments?

Scale

Scale is one of the key issues in architecture, particularly in relation to time. How is a city or a building perceived from afar? And how is it experienced when one is approaching or entering it? The French architect Jean Nouvel states that 'scale is always a function of the proximity to the object, and the object should provide a specific scale for each one of those experiences through the sequence'.[1] Scale depends on the sequence of arrival, the quality of the matter and the nature of the elements that enter the composition; and these elements exist regardless of technology.

Nouvel's Lyon Opera House is an interesting example of how technology (in particular, interactions with light) adds to the experience of a building when perceived from inside or from far away. The lighting of the building is carefully choreographed and indicates the nature of the activities within the space. The building's 'skin' acts as a membrane that communicates information to the external world and can be perceived in a number of different scales according to the proximity to the object.

Programme

We inhabit, on a regular or temporary basis, a variety of built structures and spaces: airports, metro stations, theatres, museums, temples, hospitals, educational institutions, recreational centres and parks, streets, markets, squares, parking facilities… Each of these spaces has a distinct 'programme', a set of requirements (functional and related to the size of the space) based on the kinds of activities that take place in them. Airports, hospitals and theatres have a clear division between public and staff spaces, and our presence is of a visitor, staff member, or passer-by. The needs of those who inhabit these spaces also vary. How will ambient technology augment or alter the nature of interactions with and in these spaces? How will the programme of the space change? What kinds of new user needs will emerge? How will the behaviour of the users alter the programme?

As indicated by Marc Weiser[2], at least 40 microprocessors can be found in any middle-class home in the USA today. These microprocessors are embedded in alarm clocks, microwave ovens, stereo and TV systems, kitchen appliances, children's toys, etc. Weiser argues that these microprocessors do not qualify as ubiquitous computing, because they are mainly used individually and hidden in 'old-style' devices like toasters and clocks. Networking together millions of information sources with hundreds of information delivery systems enables technology for Ambient Intelligence.

Computing power increases if we are at the airport, train station, or even in our car.

Even if we connect and link this computing power to the Internet to provide access to a variety of services, how will the use of these spaces and the user nature of the interactions in them evolve? The technology doesn't need to be visible, but how will the spaces themselves evolve? What will the interactions and experiences of the users of these spaces be?

Our built environments, regardless of the scale or nature of the building, are no longer 'independent' of content and the activities of those who inhabit them. Constantly updated travel schedules, layered news banners on ticker-tapes, wall-size audio-video announcements or personalized, context-aware instant news on mobile devices continually add to the experience of physical spaces. The programme of the buildings is changing as technology enables different ways of living and working. Banks are one example of evolving spaces; these institutions increasingly offer online services to customers, to the extent that contact with a real person is no longer free of charge. Plane travel has also been strongly impacted by technology: travellers book e-tickets online and check in themselves. The spaces we 'visit' no longer need to be either purely physical or wholly abstract, but can be 'augmented' spaces, providing access to information and the ability to navigate through content. The boundaries between the physical and the virtual are blurring.

Metamorphosis

Spaces change. Our homes or office desk spaces relocate or reorganize according to tasks, activities and the number of occupants. Architects have addressed the need for altering space in the past. Gerrit Rietveld's Schröder house, built in Utrecht in 1925, is not made up of walls that create spaces linked to one another; instead, it comprises a number of components which can enclose a space or be pushed away to create a single, open space. The same space can be a number of independent living units, or one large open space. This home offers the flexibility needed by the homes of today.

The Philips Design project 'La Casa Prossima Futura' raises the question of the polycentric home. As new types of products and services are increasingly available and present in people's homes, the concept of living with separate areas assigned to separate tasks or functionalities (kitchen, bedroom, bathroom, living room, etc.) is challenged.[3] Although contemporary domestic architecture still closely follows the traditional model of mono-functional areas, it is apparent that an additional matrix is overlaid on top, consisting of leisure, social and work activities. The home has become polycentric and the rooms have become multi-functional.

Changes can occur on the level of the membrane of the building. The façade of Nouvel's Institute of the Arab World is an example of the active membrane of a building. The façade is constructed of solar-activated mechanical diaphragms that operate like camera lenses and control the amount of light in the building. Possibly, the opposite could happen, i.e., the lenses could receive input from the patterns of visitors' behaviour and modify or control the amount of light from the building to the outside, as with the Lyon Opera House. Alternatively, these lenses could have a whole set of behavioural attributes linked to the building's temporal community of visitors, or communities outside its immediate physical setting.

The Blur Building by American architects Diller + Scofidio, built for the Swiss Expo 2002, is an example in which the actual structure appears and disappears. The architects created a 100-meter-wide cloud that hovers over Lake Neuchâtel in Switzerland. The structure is based on a concept structure by Buckminster Fuller, with the addition of a system of mist sprinklers that gather water from the lake and create a cloud. The user profiles of the visitors and the 'braincoats' they wear in the space are used to communicate with the computer network of the cloud and to 'negotiate' its visibility. This example points to a multitude of alternative appearances and configurations of spaces influenced by the users of the space. It also raises the issue of whether a building is ever finished or is in a constant flux or redefinition of spaces.

Motion

Buildings have traditionally been associated with stability and permanence. This association has been questioned in examples of mobile spaces such as Aldo Rossi's Teatro del Mondo (a theatre-boat that travelled the Adriatic, built for the Venice Biennale in 1979) and a number of Archigram projects such as Ron Herron's Walking City.[4]

People themselves are also increasingly mobile, commuting daily to work, taking business trips across continents, staying in hotel rooms or airports. Dutch architect Rem Koolhaas proposed a vision of a new kind of city: an island airport in the north of the Netherlands that provides both an airport hub and accommodation for frequent travellers. Another example

Blur

Blur is an architecture of atmosphere. Its lightweight tensegrity structure measures 100m wide by 65m deep and 25m high. Its primary building material is one indigenous to the site, water. Water is pumped from the lake, filtered, and shot as a fine mist through a dense array of high-pressure mist nozzles. The resulting fog mass changes from season to season, from day to day, hour to hour, and minute to minute in a continuous dynamic display of natural versus man-made forces.

Diller + Scofidio

Architects

Social radar

Typically, vision dominates our behavior in public space and establishes the basis of social relations. We use vision to assess identity; a quick glimpse of another person allows us to identify their gender, age, race and social class. Normally, this visual framework precedes any social interaction. Within the cloud, however, such rapid visual identification is not possible. The foggy atmosphere, combined with visitors in identical raincoats, produces a condition of anonymity. It will be difficult to distinguish a 25-year-old Japanese fashion model from a 13-year-old Indian boy or a 70-year-old Russian grandmother.

The blush

As the visitor in Blur is deprived of the clues typically used to gauge both the physical environment and social relations within, the media project compensates with a social communication system that extends the body's natural system of perception. A prosthetic skin in the form of a raincoat, equipped with a sixth sense, allows each visitor to navigate the cloud and interact with other visitors without speech. This new form of 'social radar' produces a condition of anonymous intimacy. As the

on a much smaller scale is the work of the awg_AllesWirdGut group. This group of Viennese architects developed the turnOn project, a visionary housing experiment that proposes an all-in-one combination of housing and the automobile industry into a new experimental lifestyle. These concepts are visions of technology-augmented spaces, and allude to prior work by Archigram in the 1960s. [5]

Perhaps the ambient spaces of the future are ones that move and morph based on user needs, desires and activities, as well as contexts? As Kari Jormakka puts it, 'The most obvious way to move away from architecture as representation is to make architecture and other parts of the built environment really move'. [6]

human skin is a sensory organ that picks up and also broadcasts involuntary reactions beyond an individual's control, such as blushing from embarrassment or goose bumps from the cold, can't this prosthetic skin do the same?

All visitors to Blur are given a questionnaire when they enter. Answers to the questions will be used to produce a response profile for each visitor that is continually added to a database. Each visitor is also given a 'braincoat', a smart raincoat with embedded technologies in its skin. These technologies include an imprint of the visitor's response profile that enables the coats to communicate with one another once the visitors reach the media platform. The basis for this communication is the cumulative database. This multi-dimensional statistical matrix comprises a data cloud that complements the fog cloud.

The braincoats have the capacity to display three types of responses. First, a visual response. As visitors pass each other on the Blur platform, their coats can compare character profiles and change color indicating their degree of affinity, much like an involuntary blush. When stimulated, the chest panel of the translucent braincoat displays a diffused colored light that glows in the fog. The coat functions like a sophisticated Lovegetty, a matchmaking device popular with Japanese teenagers. The color range is coded so that a shift toward cool blue-green represents antipathy and a shift toward warm red, affinity. The degree of color shift intensifies in proportion to the strength of the match.

The coat can also render an acoustic response. With knowledge of visitors' profiles, the communication network can identify visitors that have the highest affinity and assign each visitor a statistical match. An acoustic pulse, like a sonar pinging, sounds from a speaker embedded in each coat. The pulse is audible only to the wearer. Like sonar, as matched visitors approach one another the steady pulse accelerates, reaching a peak when they are very near. Slow or rapid, the sound pulse constantly identifies the relative location of this statistical match. Each visitor may choose how to navigate with this social sonar by either avoiding encounter, or tracking his/her match, or by remaining indifferent.

There is also a tactile response. Occasionally, visitors in Blur may have a 100% affinity. To register this rare occurrence, a third response system is integrated into the coat. A small vibrating pad, modelled after the vibrating motor of a pager is located in the rear pockets of the braincoat. When two perfectly matched visitors encounter one another in the fog, the motors send a vibration through the coat, mimicking the tingle of excitement that comes with physical attraction.

(This project was to be made in collaboration with IDEO of Palo Alto. It was never realized because of the loss of our sponsor, a telecommunications company, after a corporate takeover.)

Transparency

The social impact of imbedded computers may be analogous to two other technologies that have become ubiquitous. The first is writing, which is found everywhere from clothes labels to billboards. The second is electricity, which surges invisibly through the walls of every home, office, and car. Writing and electricity become so commonplace, so unremarkable, that we forget their huge impact on everyday life.[7]

Mark Weiser and John Seely Brown

Weiser has pointed out that there is no less technology involved in a comfortable pair of shoes, a fine writing pen, or delivering the New York Times on a Sunday morning, than there is in a home PC. Why then are the presence and anticipated behaviours related to the PC or to some electronic devices so enraging, when the shoes, pen or paper round are so calming? Weiser stresses that the difference is in how these technologies engage our attention, the 'calm' ones moving continually from the centre to the periphery of our attention, the others requiring constant presence in the centre.

The same is true of our built environment. Imagine smart houses and interfaces that monitor our every move, develop user profiles based on our behaviours and consequently change the behaviour of the space. They might link all the devices in the house to one another, and start recommending content or activities while anticipating our desires. Or they might connect the members of our household to many other users with similar interests and start bombarding them with the appropriate (albeit privacy-secured) information. Perhaps calmer, smaller interventions are needed, ones that are based on real needs and have the potential to provide improvements. How about a smart wall that is able to discretely change the lighting conditions of the room when it notices a child is asleep, dims the sound in the space if one starts speaking on the phone or cleans itself. This is not about less technology as much as it is about technology that is non-intrusive and embedded in our daily lives, at home, on the road or at work.

1 J. Nouvel, Jean Nouvel 1987-1998 (Madrid, Croquis Editorial, 2000)
2 M. Weiser and J. Seely Brown, The Coming Age of Calm Technology (Xerox PARC, 5 October 1996)
3 Philips Design, La Casa Prossima Futura (Royal Philips Electronics, 1999), 11
4 P. Cook (ed.), Archigram (New York, Princeton Architectural Press, 1999)
5 M. Brayer and B. Simonot (eds), Archilab's Future House: Radical Experiments in Living Space (London, Thames and Hudson, 2002)
6 K. Jormakka, Flying Dutchman: Motion in Architecture (Basle, Birkhauser, 2002), 63
7 Weiser and Seely Brown, op. cit.

5.3 COMPOUNDING WORK AND LIFE

Pete Matthews, Lesh Parameswaran

Work-life

While the content and nature of people's work across the globe is as varied and diverse as the ways in which they lead their lives, for many, and particularly for knowledge-based workers, the boundary between work and other aspects of life is blurring.

Work-time

The traditional time constructs of 'working 9 to 5', 'Monday to Friday' and the '40-hour-week' are increasingly irrelevant. Recent figures from the UK's Department for Education and Employment state that '19% of employees worked in workplaces operating 24 hours per day, seven days a week', 'one in eight employees worked both Saturday and Sunday', and approximately 'one in seven fathers were working 60 or more hours a week'.[1]

Work-place

Not only is when we choose or are required to work changing, but where we work is also being redefined. The fact that the laptop segment of the PC market is faster growing than its desktop counterpart indicates a need for more flexible and portable work solutions. Such trends are not hard to spot; we need only look to briefcase and luggage manufacturers to see how this is reflected in their new ranges. New language is replacing the old. 'Flex-work', 'tele-work' and 'home-working' are becoming familiar terms reflecting the new mix.

Work-life-balance

Flexible working arrangements reflect a drive to support people in better combining or 'balancing' their jobs with their other personal responsibilities and ambitions. Creating such equilibrium can benefit both employers and employees in terms of productivity and wellbeing. While flexible ways of working can certainly contribute to better balance, simply taking a laptop home to work is not enough in itself. There is no single or universally applicable solution to providing work-life-balance; contributing factors are embedded in organizational cultures and within our own personal attitudes and priorities. It is clear that a combination of practical, motivational and spatial measures all contribute to balancing the work-life equation. Creating balance is as much about changing mindsets as it is about changing office layouts and locations and introducing new technologies.

Work-life-culture

Perhaps a shift in the underlying 'logic' of work culture is required. Typically, work centres upon the 'logic of production'. Here, the focus is upon deliverables and the planning of tasks; efficient problem-solving is paramount. Following this logic leaves us little time to process experiences, and can potentially limit innovation. An alternative is a culture that values 'developmental logic'. Thought, reflection, collaboration, sharing and rest are encouraged. These aspects are fundamental to balance.

Work-life-technology

The decoupling of work, location and time, resulting in the merging of work and life, has partly been enabled by new technologies. Networked infrastructures, increased storage capacity and miniaturization have all played a role. It is now easy to take work home or work around the clock. Interconnected and ubiquitous technologies can be applied to meld disparate elements of these lifestyles and help make a manageable whole. This is particularly true for nomadic workers, whose lifestyle elements may be distributed globally as well as locally. But just because it is possible, is it really desirable to totally fuse our working life with our personal, domestic lives? Flexible technologies do not necessarily lead directly to balanced solutions.

Work-life-intelligence

Technology can certainly enable us to work where and when we choose, to be efficient, to share, to connect – and much more besides. But for more balanced solutions, we need to manage and use technology in a more intelligent manner, or indeed to develop more intelligent technologies. Responsive, adaptive and personalized environments can be used to support the changing needs of today's workers as they try to balance their lives. Developmental work logic values the ability to 'switch off' mentally and physically. It is during these moments of disconnection that reflection, thoughts, rest and sometimes innovation occur. In this case, it is the absence of technology that enables us.

Work-life-challenge

Three broad themes have been identified; each with associated research questions:

Switching and switching off	For many, multitasking and multiple roles are a fact of working life, particularly in an age of project-based work and freelancing. How can the switching between tasks, and switching off, digitally, mentally and physically, be better supported?
Nomadic worker	How can the flow of work between different people and places (the office, home, hotel, airplane, etc.) be smoothed, facilitated and sometimes frozen?
Tools and spaces	Which new tools will be required for future work, and how will the notion of the 'work surface' change?

Philips is creating a rich mix of concepts, some addressing a particular issue of imbalance while others are a response to new trends in the workplace. Viewed together, the concepts combine to form a more balanced system of working.

Work-life-system

Work-life-balance could be regarded as a privilege, and certainly must appear so to the unemployed or disadvantaged. Yet we cannot deny that ways of working are changing and that work is no longer done in an isolated, compartmentalized fashion. New tools and services are needed that not only accept the natural imbalances that we enjoy in life, but also allow us greater choice in those moments of imbalance. It is less about providing balance '24/7' than about providing choice and tools to create balance from imbalance as and when we choose.

Work-life-balance and Ambient Intelligence

As people go about their working lives and family lives today, they experience new locations, environments, activities and priorities. The blurred boundaries between life and work generate a dynamically changing set of emotional, functional, practical, physiological, physical and psychological needs and desires. The technologies and culture of Ambient Intelligence can be applied to this dynamic context to help people meet their changing needs and strive to create a harmonious relationship with places, environments and, most importantly, the people in their lives. Responsive, adaptive and personalized environments can be used to support the changing needs of today's workers as they try to balance their lives.

1   UK Department for Education and Employment, *Work-Life Balance 2000 Baseline Survey*

5.4 LIFE 21 – MOBILE COMMUNITIES

MOBILE PEER-TO-PEER NETWORKS: ENHANCING SOCIAL AND AMBIENT INTERACTION

Martin Elixmann

Interagio, ergo sum

For many of us, life is interaction. Most of us interact faster, more often and with more people than ever before – our peers, clients, friends, family, colleagues and others. Everyday we experience personal, face-to-face interaction as something that is vital for us and for our relationships. It is in personal interaction that we dedicate most of our attention and time, discussing our concerns, developing plans, coordinating actions, exchanging information, and experiencing others and ourselves. Successful interaction relies on our perception of expectations around us, and how we reveal our own expectations: the better we understand people and their expectations, the more effectively we can interact with them.

Communities can be defined by the interactions of their participants. We all want to belong to several communities, to which we need or want to contribute effectively. The better our 'clubs', the better we feel about ourselves. Forming communities and keeping them alive by active participation is seen as a highly valued social capability.

New interaction technology can heavily influence existing communities, or even be instrumental in forming completely new ones. Online communities are a recent example of a completely new form enabled by the Internet. There are now a countless and varied number of online communities purely defined by interaction. The next wave of new communities could be mobile communities technically enabled by peer-to-peer networks between personal mobile devices. The world is increasingly 'mobile *ad hoc*': personal mobile devices with wireless connectivity will soon become as ubiquitous as wristwatches are today, and most people will carry some form of personal mobile device most of the time.

The ability to easily set up *ad hoc*, short-range wireless networks between mobile devices with plenty of storage, CPU power and communication bandwidth will enable new patterns of social interaction between like-minded people. Together with our friends, families, colleagues or business partners, we will interact as mobile communities. We will be able to exchange personal information on the spot or conduct peer-to-peer trading without involving service providers. Many social relationships will gain a new dimension as peer-to-peer networks enhance personal perception and cognition through the ability to digitally identify people, record encounters and remind peers of others and other facts and events.

Mobile peer-to-peer connectivity (MP2P) can 'upgrade' existing communities with a fixed place of interaction to mobile communities in which interaction can take place anywhere. An example of an 'upgraded community' might be a group of professionals rendered more effective and efficient as file sharing, calendar synchronization and instant meeting scheduling become possible 'by remote'. MP2P can also facilitate the formation of new mobile communities on the basis of social needs that cannot otherwise be met. Consumer communities could use MP2P to enhance their interaction by exchanging information, or music and video material of mutual interest. Children could get together in real-life (or even virtually) to exchange and interactively play games. MP2P might enable the formation of a new community by helping physically or cognitively impaired individuals to come together in the same way for assistance and to overcome social isolation. They could be equipped with 'JustWear&Care' technology that continuously monitors vital signs of life and lets the environment perceive how to interact with them accordingly. In this way personal healthcare could become a part of community interaction.

These developments will bring about a new sociology of mobile communities. How will this enhanced social interaction create new roles, expectations, experiences and rituals in personal interaction? How will it create a feeling of being better involved, of a more active life, of more autonomy and choice? If MP2P is widely adopted, we can expect mobile communities to become the norm rather than the exception, and these questions will all need to be addressed.

This MP2P connectivity, based on matching expectations, could also enable a new paradigm of mobile intelligent ambience, facilitating new *ad hoc* uses such as:

- Internet access and downloading at home and on the move
- Seamless in-home connectivity between digital cameras, camcorders, television sets, PCs or digital video recorders
- *Ad hoc* connectivity on the move between portable devices such as mobile phones, PDAs and audio players
- Local push/pull access to short-range radio services from mobile phones and PDAs
- Connectivity for personal area networking at home and on the move
- Personal health monitoring in hospitals, at home and on the move
- Personalized driving
- Consumer-to-consumer business around digital content of any kind
- Digital kiosk services

Consumers expect MP2P connectivity to be 'JustPlay' connectivity, so that they need not be aware of the networking or discovery aspects of interaction but can concentrate fully on its peer-to-peer aspect. They also expect MP2P technology to include wearable electronics, preferably integrated into fashionable clothing ('JustWear'), or even to be 'implantable' (if this is possible with only minimally 'invasive' techniques), so that they can use it anywhere and anytime, in the most convenient way, without even noticing it. Obviously, MP2P must also address and solve human concerns regarding security and privacy of interaction and concerns about growing dependence on MP2P technology.

Ultimately, MP2P will not only enhance our interactions but also our cognition: all of the entities around us will describe themselves the moment we look at them. With 'JustKnow' glasses on, we will be able to read the names of people and things as we approach them.

Digital perception: the conceptual model: *Esse est percipi*

The fundamental concept enabling this form of MP2P is digital perception. Digital perception means that an aura of 'interaction expectations' surrounds people and interactive devices. Other people and devices are able to perceive this aura as they approach, by means of short-range radio technology, smart discovery software and matching algorithms. Mutual digital perception can then lead to a 'matching' interaction. This matching interaction can enable, support, guide or even define how people experience their personal interaction.

In the world of digital perception, entities only exist for others if they can be perceived, and perception requires those entities to expose their own interaction expectations. This is a very powerful concept that could radically change social behaviour and social networking, and could redefine our ideas of trust and privacy.

Although the basic idea of digital perception seems strikingly simple, defining a conceptual model that makes it useful in reality is far from easy. Such a model is needed if the issues around digital perception are to be constructively addressed and if the technical solution is to be usable (i.e., if it is to show predictable behaviour for all intended scenarios).

CONNECTED
PLANET

CAMP
AND MADS

LIME
AND PL@NET

Conceptual model

The cornerstone of the conceptual model is the notion of a 'peer' (not only a physical device, but also the user behind this device). Figure 1 illustrates the anatomy of a peer. A peer is characterized by a profile, which expresses his interest in certain topics. A topic is related to an interaction expectation. For example, the profile of peer 1 in Figure 1 indicates that he is interested in the topic 'music', and that his interaction expectation concerning music is to chat about it. Topics can be organized in a topic hierarchy (e.g., sharing MP3 files is subordinate to Peer 1's interest in chatting about music). Interest in a general topic can lead to a subsequent interaction relationship concerning a more specific topic, e.g., a chat about music may result in sharing some MP3 files. Equally, interest in a specific topic can lead to an interaction on a more general topic.

FIG. 1
The anatomy of a peer

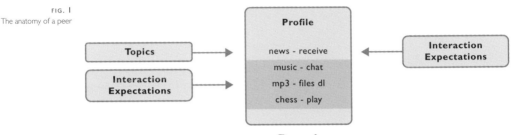

Two peers coming into proximity can perceive each other. As depicted in Figure 2, the process of perception is initiated by the mutual exposure and discovery of each peer's profile. Matching the profiles may then lead to the identification of common topics and interaction expectations. For example, in Figure 2, both peers recognize that they have a common interest in chatting about music and sharing MP3 files. An interaction relationship is possible if there is a perception of a common topic and if the interaction expectations of the peers for this topic match (e.g., chatting about music or sharing MP3 files). However, the mutual perception may be filtered, despite proximity and common topics, due to some context conditions. In the context of a business meeting, for instance, two users may not be willing to chat about music, regardless of their principal interest in this topic.

FIG. 2
Perception and
interaction

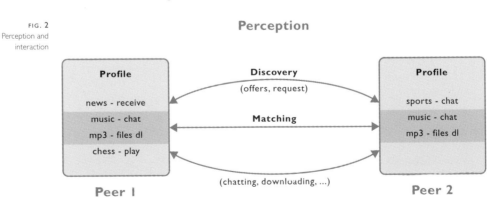

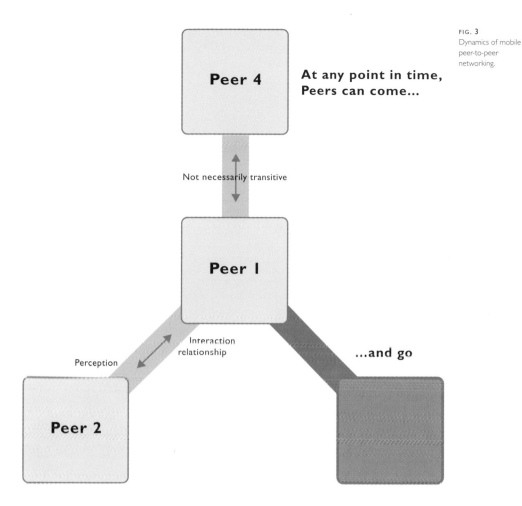

FIG. 3
Dynamics of mobile
peer-to-peer
networking.

A peer may perceive and interact with several other peers at the same time, although the perception and interaction relationship is not necessarily transitive, as illustrated in Figure 3. Both peer 2 and peer 4 are perceived by peer 1, but they do not perceive each other (either because they are not close enough to each other, or because they do not have a common interest). At any point in time, new perceptions can be added to a peer's current perception, or a peer may lose the perception of another peer, in which case no further interaction with that peer is possible.

Creating value: interaction-ware

Mobile communities will rely on a new, emerging type of system, known as mobile *ad hoc* systems (MADS). These systems are highly dynamic and self-organizing, and enable spontaneous, proximity-aware face-to-face interactions between individuals and with the environment. They are highly decentralized, and so are independent of a dedicated communication and computing infrastructure: they rely solely on the capabilities of mobile devices.

Mobile *ad hoc* systems present new challenges in design, as they must be based on layers of abstraction in interactivity. At the networking layer, appropriate wireless technologies must be chosen, such as wireless local area networks (WLAN) of the IEEE 802.11 standard, Bluetooth or ZigBee, or even a combination of these. Moreover, whichever technology or combination of technologies is chosen, it will exhibit performance weaknesses and functional

CONNECTED
PLANET

CAMP
AND MADS

LIME
AND PL@NET

NEW
NOMADS

gaps, both with respect to *ad hoc* networking and typical MP2P use-cases, so that extra measures will be needed to compensate for these. If several wireless technologies are used, a wireless access layer needs to be there to support interoperability and roaming. The network layer interface should be based on the Internet Protocol (IP).

At the middleware layer, functionality is needed for device and service discovery in dynamic networks. The Universal Plug and Play (UPnP) middleware platform provides much of the functionality needed, and is likely to become an industry standard. However, UPnP was not designed for wireless *ad hoc* networks, either in terms of its operational model or in terms of the bandwidth it consumes. For wireless networks, an optimized wireless UPnP (WUPnP) version comes into play that is more closely linked to the MP2P networking layer. Additional challenges to be addressed include audio and video streaming applications and content scouting.

The application layer provides the entities and protocols needed to realize the conceptual model of digital perception and peer-to-peer interaction, represented as an application programming interface (MADS-API) at the application interface. As part of this model, the MP2P interaction privacy concept needs to be defined and implemented in such a way that users experience and control the level of openness, security and trust they expect in any given situation.

At the user interface, many interesting issues arise. How should the rich and powerful conceptual model appear to the user, given the constraints of limited interface bandwidth (e.g., due to the small screens of mobile devices and of limited user attention when on the move)? One way might be via an 'opportunity scout', an intuitive screen-based interface for

mobile devices, capturing the key ideas of MP2P interaction. However, having to look at a screen while meeting face-to-face may not be the only or ultimate solution of enhanced peer-to-peer interaction. Multimodal interfaces using all of the human senses could further enhance interaction, helping to reduce the levels of attention and distraction in MP2P interaction. They could also enable further miniaturization of personal devices.

The concept of mobile peer-to-peer systems not only enables new paradigms of social interaction, but it also currently seems to be the most challenging area of software system technology. This is because these systems require new constructions at all layers of the software stack, in order to support the fully autonomous mode of operation expected. The concept also implies networking performance and wearability requirements that have not been met before.

The challenge: ubiquity

The success of any notion of connectivity ultimately depends on its widespread use. There are three key success factors in making MP2P connectivity a ubiquitous feature. The first requirement is 'JustPlay': the user should be able to simply do whatever it is that they want to do, be it to copy a friend's videotape, download an Internet schedule on the bus, or give a presentation to a customer. The second factor is 'PlugIn': product manufacturers must be able to readily apply MP2P connectivity as a concept, and embed the technology in their products. The third factor is low cost. MP2P must be able to be built into as many products as possible, and therefore must not be prohibitively expensive.

A fourth factor, the speed of implementation and time to market, is also critical. At the time of writing, the Philips MADS project is running at full steam.

CONNECTED
PLANET

CAMP
AND MADS

LIME
AND PL@NET

NEW
NOMADS

5.5 TRUST IN AMBIENT INTELLIGENCE

Jean-Paul Linnartz

In Ambient Intelligence space, intelligence is pervasive and unobtrusive. It is embedded in the surrounding environment, sensitive to the presence of those in it and supporting their activities. This new space, which encompasses both the physical and virtual worlds, is shared by people, physical entities and their agents, and is characterized by extensive interaction between humans and systems. To work well and be of value, many of the functions and services provided by Ambient Intelligence will need to enjoy the user's full trust and confidence, making security, dependability and privacy major issues.

Where do the security risks lie in an Ambient Intelligence setting?

Textbooks on security list four fundamental cryptographic principles: confidentiality, authentication, integrity and non-repudiation. Traditionally, researchers have addressed these aspects in 'Alice and Bob' scenarios, whereby Alice wants to communicate to Bob, while Eve intercepts the message and possibly modifies it. Yet Ambient Intelligence requires a more sophisticated model. In this space, people and organizations will participate in many parallel, overlapping, interleaved and evolving one-to-one, one-to-many and many-to-many relationships. Some of these will be brief, established *ad hoc* and instantaneously, while others may be longer, but active only intermittently.

In any context, establishing trust requires a prolonged relationship. The rich interactions foreseen in Ambient Intelligence spaces involve a variety of contacts, each with its trust and risk profile. Security issues in this context become increasingly complex, due to:

- The number of devices and processes interacting simultaneously
- The mobility of users and devices (*ad hoc* networking and intermittently available connections are more vulnerable than static ones)
- The heterogeneity of devices and processes
- The complexity of the interaction (e.g., mobile agents will be performing functions on devices 'somewhere' in the network)

Traditionally, computer security has been approached in terms of the Open Systems Interconnection (OSI) model, based on client services and relationships that were fixed and bilateral. However, given the growing number of interactions, it is unlikely that we shall be able to treat security in an Ambient Intelligence space as simply a question of an amalgamation of many one-to-one interactions. Moreover, such an approach would fail to adequately model the specific threats associated with the participation of multiple, partly trusted and possibly colluding players. The parties involved certainly cannot be captured by an 'Alice and Bob' scenario, as any such scenario must include the following:

- The user and the user's family
- Visitors
- Device and infrastructure manufacturers
- Financial institutions
- Communication services providers
- Content providers
- Public services, utilities and the government
- Employers (as teleworking becomes increasingly prevalent).

Additional threats are posed not only by anonymous hackers (either within radio range of the home or from afar), but also by quasi-trusted parties with a legitimate reason to interact with the space. For example, without the user's approval, service providers and e-commerce companies may gather user profiles to target advertising; one company's software may intentionally interfere with that of other vendors; and operating systems (whether open or closed source) may contain functions that conflict with the user's privacy.

Home radio station – a scenario

The following scenario, featuring a personal home radio station called Ambient Intelligence Music (AIM), illustrates some of the security issues discussed above and outlines some possible approaches to solutions.

AIM plays songs from Han's personal music collection, using information about his current preferences. To do this, AIM gathers information about Han over time, observing and tracking him in various moods.

Han wants to keep full control over the use of information about his preferences to ensure that it is used only by AIM and other trusted applications. Misuse (e.g., by direct marketing companies) must be prevented, so his profile will need to be kept confidential.

Nevertheless, Han would like to be notified about new releases, and he may want to buy those he likes.

More precisely, Han wants to buy songs (or rather the right to play them) downloaded from the Internet. This requires anonymous transactions and database searches. In Han's home, the content is stored securely to prevent Han from giving illegal copies to his friends.

At breakfast-time, AIM connects to a server on the Internet to download newsflashes and up-to-date reports on the Far East stock markets for those companies for which he has or wants to buy stocks. For this purpose, AIM is allowed to access information about Han's financial portfolio.

Under what conditions will applications developed by different companies or operated by different service providers be allowed to exchange such data? Presumably, an automatic mechanism will be needed to configure the system so that it will allow some applications to access each other's data and functions, while preventing exchanges between others.

AIM anticipates the preferences of Han's close friend Tom, who pays Han a visit one evening.

In principle, Tom could let his PDA transmit his profile, and AIM could analyze it to find commonalities, or to identify songs that one of the two has never heard before. But a completely free and open profile exchange would be unacceptable from a privacy point of view. One solution might be that a Trusted Third Party (TTP) could analyze both Tom's and Han's profiles, only revealing commonly acceptable conclusions; although whether an interesting business model could be found for such a TTP is questionable. It is possible that future advances in secure multi-party computing may allow profiles to be matched without revealing unnecessary details.

AIM establishes that Han has never seen a video clip on Tom's favourites list, called Hot Beat, and it also establishes that Han will probably like the song.

PHENOM

WWICE

PML

MIME

CAMP
AND MADS

SPICE

OPEN TOOLS

LIME
AND PL@NET

Since AIM sees that Tom is at Han's place, it can retrieve the digital rights for a single play of Hot Beat.

AIM shows the clip in Han's home.

An unsolved copyright issue is whether it is possible to prevent Han from capturing the clip and making an illegal copy.

Han likes Hot Beat and decides to buy the song.

After an online transaction with the copyright owner, AIM receives the digital rights to unlock the clip for Han.

Han's home is aware of the mood Han and Tom are in and fine-tunes AIM's play list for the rest of the evening.

The home becomes aware of the residents' moods through sensors (including cameras and microphones). Without security measures, this activity would give rise to opportunities for hackers and intruders: the data from the sensors must be kept confidential to prevent the 14-year-old next door from eavesdropping on Han's home. And Han needs to be able to trust the sensor itself (i.e., it must be authenticated, the data must be time-stamped and the integrity of its data checked).

This scenario sketches some of the challenges for the future security architecture of Ambient Intelligence space. Today, we can already see a number of developments that begin to shape this architecture, or at least define boundary conditions for it. These include a secure operating system (e.g., Microsoft's Palladium) and secure hardware for personal computers, the extensive use of SIM cards in mobile phone applications, the security restrictions dictated by copy protection (e.g., in DVD players), and the legal requirement to protect the user's privacy. We will now elaborate on the last two of these aspects, and then extend the discussion towards a more generic solution, which may come in form of a newly defined 'trust model'. Based on this, our challenge will be to distribute cryptographic functionality and roles over various devices.

Content protection

Entertainment content (music, movies, games) delivered by today's technology already play an important part in people's lives. But with Ambient Intelligence, the experience of 'content consumption' will be enriched and integrated, with content being actively managed, stored and retrieved by agents operating on behalf of their human 'owners', to support the interactions between people. Consequently, issues of content protection and Digital Rights Management (DRM) will loom large, and the techniques used to deal with them will be a determining factor in shaping the security architecture of Ambient Intelligence.

Hollywood studios have built their empires on the business model of selling a physical medium (e.g., a CD or a DVD) with content. This model has been under attack by technical innovations from at least three sides:

- Increased bandwidth (broadband Internet access is rapidly becoming available in many housholds)
- Increased storage capacity (CD-R and other disc formats have become available, and a typical computer hard disk now stores tens of gigabytes)
- Increased compression efficiency (MP3 audio and MPEG 4 video that reduce file size while

maintaining acceptable image and sound quality are accelerating the growth in content exchange and storage)

With the advent of DVD, content protection has changed fundamentally. Digital content is released only in protected form, and only to devices that can authenticate themselves and comply with copy-protection rules. Moreover, revocation mechanisms can deny compromised devices access to content. This has set the stage for a world of compliant digital devices that will not release digital content to any non-compliant device. Although copy tools for DVD have since emerged, the manufacturing of non-compliant devices is still largely under control.

'Digital watermarking' will refine the security model, as it prevents circumvention via an analog representation. In fact, the strengths and weaknesses of watermarks versus encryption are largely orthogonal. Press reactions to Secure Digital Music Initiative (SDMI) audio were unfavourable because of its lack of user-friendliness, its disregard of 'fair use', and the limitations on content-handling functions (even where fully legal). New systems offer fewer features at a higher price. Nonetheless, this model is dominating the discussion about new standards and systems. Digital rights management will increasingly become an issue as the usage model is extended beyond the traditional Copy Once, Copy No More, or Copy Freely statuses of content.

The recent 'Your content, anytime, anywhere' vision assumes that electronic systems provide access to content wherever the user is. High bandwidth communication networks, portable storage and caching in intelligent networks together provide a seamless continuation of the user's experience, regardless of fluctuations in the network and the quality of service. This is a move towards user-friendliness, compared to the restrictive nature of many early DRM implementations. As a stepping-stone, the concept of an Authorized Domain has been proposed. This would allow the secure but unconstrained flow of content within the confines of a given user's environment. The technical implementation is currently under discussion, as is the legal question of how far an Authorized Domain might extend beyond the home, and whether it is associated with an individual, a family or household (whatever the definition of these might be in this new context).

Within an Ambient Intelligence space, these concepts would need to allow for the processing of such securely packaged content, combined with personal usage rights and privacy-protected user-profiling metadata. In this context, privacy becomes essential.

Privacy

But what is privacy? A useful definition is 'the right to exercise control over the use of information about oneself'. In current software and hardware products, measures to protect the user's privacy are rapidly increasing. In wireless networks, radio signals are generally encrypted to protect the user from unauthorized eavesdroppers. But the user's privacy concerns are much wider. Browsing behaviour, URLs visited, telephone numbers dialled, the locations of base stations connecting to their mobile phone, the titles of music and videos played on a PC, the software installed on that PC – all these reveal a wealth of information about the user. In fact, consumers are becoming increasingly proactive in protecting themselves by installing special software on their computers, for example. Many Web-connected PCs not only have a virus scanner and firewall installed, but also anonymous browsing and 'anti-spyware' programs to deactivate software that collects data and reports these to the software provider. Privacy on the Internet is increasingly a matter of concern. In an Ambient Intelligence context, the issue may well be even more complex, because the anonymity that is often sought in cyberspace does not lend itself to the development of many rich new experiences.

In many societies, ancient and modern, a long-standing relationship of trust between merchant and customer has been seen as highly beneficial to both parties and to the general stability of society. The equivalent of this relationship in Ambient Intelligence is not yet well understood.

PHENOM

WWICE

PML

MIME

CAMP
AND MADS

SPICE

OPEN TOOLS

LIME
AND PL@NET

Moreover, who will pay for privacy? What is its value to manufacturers? Besides their legal obligations, their reputation and brand name are two important motivations for them. But making such a long-term investment is at odds with ever more stringent time-to-market requirements. The situation in the software field is even more problematic. The growth in the number of 'spyware' programs is largely influenced by the user's increasing desire for free software. In their search for a viable business model, certain companies have experimented with a model whereby users surrender their privacy in return for a product.

'Traitors' are a problem, and researchers are now looking into how they can be traced. The delivery of user-specific keys for broadcast or multicast content is a similar problem: the technology does not protect against illegal copying but does make it possible to trace consumers who misuse content. This evidently requires a redefinition of acceptable practices with regard to content protection and user privacy.

Trust model

At best, most potential users have a limited understanding of security. At worst, they distrust their services or products. A clear and appealing trust model may help users to overcome their fears regarding security in the context of Ambient Intelligence.

What is an appropriate trust model for Ambient Intelligence?

One approach could be a hierarchy of trust. This model resembles the solution adopted in Germany of making the organization receiving payment from the user responsible for all aspects of security. In the case of mobile phones, that organization would be the telecom operator. Under this scheme, for telephone gambling, for instance, responsibility for the security of the transactions would lie with the operator, rather than the gambling company. That would not mean to say, however, that the telecom operator would be liable for any fraud committed by the gambling company.

On the Internet, it is not always clear who is responsible or liable for security attacks, and legislation differs from country to country. It is difficult to blame your phone or cable operator – or even your Internet service provider – if your computer is attacked by a virus. In the PC world, the provider of the operating system (e.g., Microsoft) is seeking to become a key player in controlling the security of the environment. In PCs and consumer electronic devices that handle audio/video content, there is already strong competition between the various companies who offer solutions for protecting content: each sees this as an opportunity to gain control over the standards and licensing of devices and their environments. Although a trust hierarchy is appealing in that it is technologically straightforward, it is unlikely that the conflicting interests can be reconciled. Companies striving for control aim to position themselves high up in any trust hierarchy. Interoperable solutions, similar to those standardized in Open Platform Initiative for Multi-Party Access (OPIMA), can level the playing field, but that would not be in the interest of all market forces.

Security problems posed by different types of devices

The trust hierarchy needs to be reflected in the architecture of Ambient Intelligence space, but there are additional constraints, such as power consumption, that limit the freedom of choice in allocating cryptographic functions over the devices. The way in which the devices are powered is important. Some will be self-powered, absorbing energy from the environment, while others will use batteries or be mains-powered.

Self-powered devices

Self-powered devices are likely to include sensors and possibly also low-power actuators.

Their energy can be extracted from the environment, by absorbing light, for example, or from vibrations caused by air ventilation. Low power severely limits the application of known cryptographic algorithms and protocols.

Although users may prefer a bulk installation of self-powered devices (e.g., by 'painting electronics on the wall', or scattering them in the form of 'smart dust'), they will have to go through a process of identifying which sensors they trust and will admit to their personal environment. This identification of individual devices as 'friend or foe' is common practice with DECT cordless phones. During an initialization phase, the phone and base station are physically connected and initialized with a PIN code. The challenge is to make 'pour-authenticate-play' as user-friendly as 'plug-and-play' is supposed to be.

It is still a moot point, however, as to whether sensor authentication will provide sufficient protection. Replay attacks may still be feasible; and confidentiality may be required. We should not assume that every trusted sensor will remain unbreached. Furthermore, the system may need to rely on data from sensors or PDAs whose security risk profile is not fully known.

Battery-powered devices

Battery-powered devices need attention from their patron (probably their owner, as cautious users may distrust borrowed devices). Biometrics can play an important role in enabling a system to respond to individual people, and can complement a Public Key Infrastructure. But the use of biometrics to provide a security check on the authenticity of a person is not fully understood. In an Ambient Intelligence environment, all kinds of sensors will be continuously capturing the biometric data (faces, voices, fingerprints) of people who live within it, and the architecture of the combined in-home and external system will determine to what extent this data is protected. One solution may be to allow biometric data to be read only by personal devices, which are typically of this battery-powered class.

Mains-powered devices

Mains-powered devices will presumably be sufficiently stationary to form part of the infrastructure. Ambient Intelligence space will have no 'central administration', i.e., no single virtual machine to run all the applications, nor will there be one single trust (and trusted) infrastructure. Instead, there will be a number of compatible local infrastructures. Nodes in these infrastructures will be able to host a proxy server for mains-powered or battery-powered devices.

In MIT's Oxygen project[1], these variously powered devices are called E21s, H21s and N21s, referring to their role in the Environment, as 'Handy', or part of the Network in the 21st century. The H21s are handheld PDA-like devices, and are assumed to be anonymous: they can therefore be used by different people. A proxy running on a remote machine executes all security-sensitive operations. However, this would not seem to solve the privacy needs of consumers, as a malicious device owner could still tap signals directly from the sensors.

Conclusion

The best way to protect privacy and anonymity in the context of Ambient Intelligence is not yet fully understood, particularly because many functions within such a system depend on the system having a deep understanding of users' likes and dislikes – information that is likely to be highly sensitive and confidential. And, given the projected scenarios involving the use of entertainment content, privacy and copy protection will also pose challenges. In short, many questions remain to be answered.

1 http://oxygen.lcs.mit.edu

PHENOM

WWICE

PML

MIME

CAMP
AND MADS

SPICE

OPEN TOOLS

LIME
AND PL@NET

TRANSFORM, GROW, BECOME

Could Ambient Intelligence transform us as people? Could it help us to develop our full potential and make us more 'human'? How might it enable us to play a significant role in shaping an increasingly networked society? And how could our interactions through and with Ambient Intelligence systems become more meaningful, 'poetic' and imbued with 'stories' from our own imagination?

6.1 NETWORKS, SYSTEMS AND SOCIETY

Anton Andrews

From products to meshes

Design is in the process of losing its traditional muse, the perfected object, pure in the simplicity of its isolation. Ambient Intelligence reflects a shift in industry away from the traditional focus on designing and marketing individual, isolated products with predetermined functionalities, and towards the creation of flexible ensembles of networked devices and services. To quote Kevin Kelly, 'As we shape technology, it shapes us. We are connecting everything to everything, and so our entire culture is migrating to a "network culture" and a new network economics… The dynamic of our society… will increasingly obey the logic of networks'.[1]

Manuel de Landa draws attention to how the steady advance of input and sensing technologies and developments in software programming have resulted in the progression of the digital objects in our environment from being hardware-driven to software-driven, then data-driven and now event-driven.[2] Things are now capable of responding to occurrences around them, whether a simple mouse-click or a more complex change in situation. Identification technologies such as biometrics will soon allow secure access to personal content through almost any networked device. Products are using less application-specific hardware and more software, increasing their potential for adaptation and opening up new horizons for innovation.

These devices are currently still separate from the network. However, as faster network technologies emerge, the distinction between network and device begins to disappear. As SUN Microsystems put it, 'the network becomes the computer'. Information can be spread across this ensemble, and devices can form 'on-the-fly' alliances, using each other as stepping-stones to form peer-to-peer 'mesh networks'. The architectures of these systems are becoming sensitive to context, and in some cases the rules governing their workings could soon become dependent on the very content flowing through the system, making system behaviour emergent, adaptive and responsive.

Some of the tools we use daily, such as the mobile phone, already clearly reflect these trends, constituting product/service mixtures fused with complex back-end systems. At the next level of organization, these 'back-ends' are merging into increasingly complex mega-systems. These developments can all have significant cultural impact. Where, in all of this complexity, can we find a focus which will allow us to shape these developments in a meaningful and humane way? How can we describe the emerging context of the digitally networked world?

New descriptive models

Describing this new context requires a new language. It is no longer sufficient to use a purely sociological description, or to rely on technical descriptions of networks or on a description of objects or user-interactions with objects. A full description needs to overlay networks of objects, technical networks and sociocultural networks, merging everything into one multidimensional web of relationships. In this picture, human beings, objects (both 'dumb' and connected digital objects) and environments are all 'actors', acting upon and with each other and establishing or ending relationships over time.

This network has no final or definitive state, but is in a constant state of growth, decay and flux. Various contemporary philosophers have already attempted to define this kind of fluid, organic network concept. Bruno Latour coined the term 'actor-network',[3] and Deleuze and Guattari refer to 'the rhizome'.[4] Beyond these descriptive approaches, the dynamics of such an actor-network can be characterized in terms of its relationships.

The dynamics of the networked context

If the environment within which Ambient Intelligence is emerging consists of networks, then our tools' ability to offer us meaningful services will lie in their ability to correlate with the informational environment and with each other. We will ourselves increasingly relate to our tools both as individual products and as parts of larger connected systems.

This emerging networked context can be broadly divided into three main sets of relationships and their interplay over time: the immediate relationships between people and products, the ecological relationships between products and products, and the systemic interactions between larger technical, economical and social networks of products and people. These sets overlap and mingle.

Immediate context	Ecological context	Systemic context
	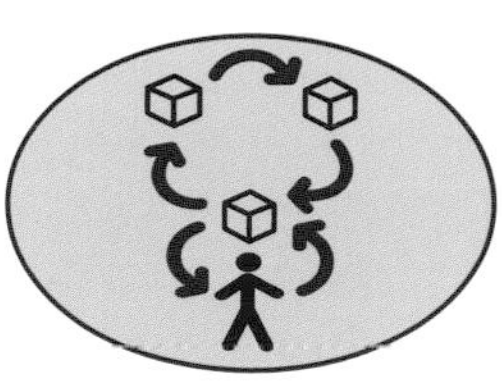	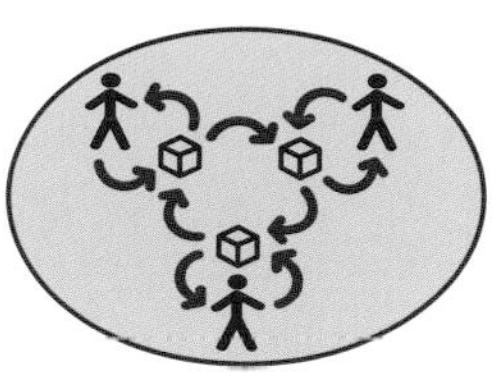
Immediate relationships between people and digital products or services	Internal relationships between the digital products in a system	Relationships between larger networks (technical and sociocultural) of products and people

FIG. 1
Three contexts

The immediate context

The first set of relationships includes the immediate interactions that people have with products whilst using and operating them, and the relationships they have with each other in and through the mediating presence of products and environments. We can picture two people quietly talking to each other under the dome of a great mosque, or somebody smiling as their mobile phone heralds an incoming SMS with its customary tune.

The ecological context

The second set includes the interactions between networked products. These can be simple (e.g., between an infrared remote and a CD player), or more advanced (e.g., when two wireless devices find each other, 'shake hands' and exchange information). These different types of network relationships will display different behaviours, ranging from formalized, standardized and carefully planned to personalized and even chaotic or messy interactions.

The system context

This set provides a perspective from a greater distance onto the first two. It consists of the interactions between larger complex, adaptive systems such as ecosystems, cultures, markets or home networks. These include what Anders Michelsen describes as the 'context of genesis': the creation, production, marketing, consumption and recycling procedures and systems in our society.[5] An example of this is the interaction between a brand and its customer base. The collision between the Windows and Macintosh computing platforms is a clash of two such networks, with all the constituent products, services and people involved, and therefore with tangible consequences.

Intelligence

Examining the context of Ambient Intelligence through these three lenses helps clarify how the concept of a future of networked products will affect our lives. The greatest difference to our traditional context is in the density, immediacy, flexibility and adaptivity of networking allowed by digital technologies, and the gradual increase in intelligence in our environment. Beyond the implicit intelligence of the user, explicit 'intelligence' is creeping into our interactions with devices, the interactions between the devices, and the systems governing relationships between people, brands, communities, designers and public infrastructures (see Chapter 7.4, Intrinsic and Extrinsic Intelligence).

Architectural space itself is becoming informationally denser and interactive, collaborating with the people and objects in it and moving through it to form 'augmented space'. Examples already abound, from the Singapore traffic system which automatically deducts road tax from drivers, to Diller + Scofidio's Blur Building with its responsive raincoats and the Fresh Water Pavilion by Lars Spuybroek of NOX Architects at Neeltje Jans Waterland.[6]

Once these products and environments become more responsive and anticipatory and start learning from our habits, they change from passive objects to interdependent subjects, making decisions about their status and functionality in our absence without needing to be programmed. The objects themselves need not necessarily be particularly 'smart', as once large numbers of devices are hooked up to each other in networks, a high degree of the intelligence will reside in the interconnection patterns and behavioural protocols of this 'ecology of things'.

Whereas current networks are pre-structured and organized from the top down by large corporations, the trend is towards *ad hoc* networks which structure themselves, emerging spontaneously from the bottom up to form mesh networks ('meshworks'). Rather than being pre-planned, the new networks will form *ad hoc* in response to information looking for ways to route itself across the landscape and between groups of peers.

Network behaviours

Agent and object-based programming already allows the creation of networks which display organic behavioural properties such as emergence, growth, competition, symbiosis, autopoiesis and decay. As we make our machines and institutions more complex, we have to make them more biological in order to manage them.[7] These networked 'ecologies' of products, environments and services will be increasingly behaviour-driven. Rather than thinking of the ideal, isolated product, we can now think in terms of networked populations with behaviours and gene pools. These ecologies and systems will display emergent properties not held by any of their individual members alone, potentially leading to the ability to self-evaluate and evolve, forming and updating representations of the world they 'live' in.

The intelligence and technologies we introduce into this networked society are in a position to have a greater and more far-reaching effect on the dynamics and the nature of the relationships that constitute our reality than ever before. The aesthetics of our experience will no longer only be determined by our immediate interactions with the objects and spaces around us, but also by system-internal behaviours. Designers and industry can play a role in shaping the qualities of these relationships into meaningful and enriching solutions by managing the rules, qualities and ethics of the underlying interactions and system behaviours.

Qualities and ethics

The network society represents an increase in the complexity of control and organization. The things around us will soon be able to form alliances, exchange information, learn and anticipate, and play an active role in larger systems. This may often happen in unanticipated, unplanned ways, in response to the situation at hand. How can we hope to manage the dynamics of such a hyperactive, complicated community? How can we ensure these dynamics are ethically appropriate and qualitatively desirable?

Nichols and Schwartz's '5 Rs' model of interpersonal dynamics propose that rules, roles, relationships, realities and response patterns can be used to understand various aspects of relationships.[8] This model has been successfully applied to understand, and when necessary correct, the dynamics of family relationships. In the context of Ambient Intelligence, the five Rs can also be applied, not only to people, but to any 'actors' and the interactions between them.

Using the five Rs, designers and industry will need to extend their attention to the design of the rules governing product behaviours and response patterns. They will need to consciously shape the roles these products will play and the relationships they will allow in the ecological and systemic networked contexts and social realities they inform. This suggests a shift towards controlling fields of potential rather than supplying fixed outcomes. Instead of discrete products, the focus will be on collective dynamics and symbiosis.

The network paradigm will inherently have many implications for the issue of control. Where will the balance of control lie between the occupant of a connected home or the user of a networked product, and the company or service provider? Responsive and adaptive networks can allow end-users to wrest much control from corporations, but may also imply that the end-user will have to relinquish some control to the system itself. Will this be empowering or will we be gradually trapped in a network of decision-making that goes above our heads?

The issues of human trust and acceptance will be key to Ambient Intelligence. People are generally poor at dealing with distributed intelligence, preferring to attribute it to localized entities. Tarkovsky's film *Solaris* tells the story of interactions between people and a 'thinking' planet, in which the people are eventually unable to deal with the superiority, pervasiveness and intangibility of the planetary mind.[9] We tend to trust a system more if we are explicitly part of it and can clearly influence its behaviour. In other words, we require reassurance and desire the freedom to exercise choice and control.

Yet it is precisely this freedom which has allowed us to construct our current context. We wish to be omnipresent, aware and enabled in our actions, building faster transportation systems and better communication methods, yet in developed countries we cannot deal with the present information overload, or the complexity of having to organize so many simultaneous aspects of our globalized lives. Rather than access to everyone, everything, everywhere, all the time, we need meaningful access to relevant information and services at the right time. We need to ensure that Ambient Intelligence provides meaningful and appropriate solutions which provide simplicity and sustainability in an increasingly complex world.

At the same time, we want to improvise and move freely and creatively across situations and environments. Current technologies focus so much on the propagation and proliferation of media, and so little on the quality of 'flow' (see Chapter 3.4, Flow) and poetry during our daily routines and actions, that the cyber-artist Stelarc has commented that they are 'becoming better life support systems for our images than for our bodies'.[10] In this sense, flexibility is a quality which the 'brittle' mechanical and computerized solutions have until recently been lacking in, and to which the networked context responds well. How can industry strike the right balance between creating enabling solutions which are versatile yet provide a sense of stability and confidence? Heidegger wrote of 'worlding' or the sculpting of an object through prolonged use. Gradually, an uncomfortable new pair of shoes responds to how the wearer walks, becoming snug and indispensable. The qualities of memory and flexibility allow a tangible and intuitive response to our investment in the things around us.

Similarly, the quality of redundancy, an important part of biological networks, can inform our technological context. There is almost always a number of ways of doing something in the physical world, and our actions do not always have to be precise to achieve the desired result.

The current world of electronic objects requires absolute precision in control if we are to achieve any kind of result at all. Interactions in the networked context of Ambient Intelligence, however, could carry the quality of looseness or redundancy, resulting in a more forgiving relationship with technology.

Ambient Intelligence could provide us with security and awareness, but it could also easily lead to infringement of our personal privacy. Distributed intelligence will be able to make use of many inputs from the environment not even perceived by humans. The way in which different surveillance systems are being connected in big cities and the protocols governing their use are already having a large impact, both positive and negative, on the affected criminal and residential communities. In New York, websites now allow pedestrians to map routes across the city avoiding security cameras, and groups of mime artists perform provocatively in front of CCTV and web cameras. The transparency of such information will be a critical quality in the construction of a networked world.

Another quality affected by the onset of high-speed networking will be the sense of ownership. Once access through a network is fast enough, there will be no need to store content or functionality locally. Companies could make their applications available to each customer depending on personalized criteria, and we could pay for access rather than ownership. This would have a huge impact on the nature of the relationship between the provider, the customer and the service. However, if the borders between any two systems are unclear, having merged and inextricably fused, where does ownership of a system lie? 'Warchalking', for example, is a new subculture in London of white chalked signs on the pavement indicating free 'parasitic' access to the Internet through an unsuspecting company's wireless LAN network. In response, some companies have entered into the spirit and actively welcome such use.[11]

Empowering people

Ambient Intelligence proposes a future in which networked products and augmented spaces provide us with services, and in which the quality of experience from the point of view of the human is paramount (see Chapter 1.6, Experience Design). It proposes 'enabling' systems which make intelligent use of resources, respond appropriately to our needs and provide us

with meaningful information. The vision is closely linked to the idea of the experience economy, in which the goal is to guide customers through transformations.[12]

Since it has its roots in the pervasive, embedded paradigm of ubiquitous computing, it proposes a greater degree of immersion than traditional product paradigms.[13] The focus is on designing patterns of relationships over time in the immediate, ecological and systemic contexts. In this triple-context, we need to ensure that the way in which the services are delivered and the nature of the guided experiences are both ethically appropriate and qualitatively desirable.

Within Ambient Intelligence, people should be seen as 'protagonists' and co-creators rather than passive end-users or consumers. Ambient intelligent products and services should aim to provide innovative and enabling means for us to improvise and move freely and creatively across situations and environments. They should respond usefully to the effort we invest in them, be sensitive to our current needs and leave control firmly in our hands, enriching daily life and human interaction.

STREAMIUM

MIME

CONNECTED
PLANET

CAMP
AND MADS

HICS

OPEN TOOLS

LIME
AND PL@NET

1   K. Kelly, *New Rules for the New Economy* (USA, Penguin, 1999), 9ff.
2   M. De Landa, 'Meshworks, Hierarchies and Interfaces', *Surroundings Surrounded*, ed. Olafur Eliasson
    (Cambridge MA, MIT Press, 2001), 332ff.
3   B. Latour, 'Mixing Humans and Non-humans Together: The Sociology of a Door Closer', *Social Problems*, vol. 35, no. 3 (June 1988)
4   G. Deleuze and F. Guattari, *A Thousand Plateaus* (Minneapolis, University of Minnesota Press, 1987), 3ff
5   A. Michelsen, 'The Artificial Environment: Smart Design, Design Semantics and Designer Intelligence', *Surroundings Surrounded*, 398
6   D. Baum, 'The Ultimate Jam Session', *Wired* (9 November 2001); Diller + Scofidio, 'Blur Building', *Surroundings Surrounded*, 176;
    Nox Architects/Lars Spuybroek, Fresh Water Pavilion (Neeltje Jans Waterland, the Netherlands)
7   K. Kelly, *Out of Control: The New Biology of Machines* (Reading MA, Perseus Publishing, 1995)
8   M. Nichols and R. Schwartz, *Family Therapy: Concepts and Methods* (Boston, Allyn & Bacon, 1988)
9   *Solaris* (Director: A. Tarkovsky, Mosfilm, 1972)
10 http://www.stelarc.va.com.au
11 http://www.warchalking.org
12 B.J. Pine and J.H. Gilmore, *The Experience Economy* (Boston, Harvard Business School Press, 1999)
13 M. Weiser, 'The Computer for the Twenty-First Century', *Scientific American* (September 1991), 94-10;
    'Hot Topic: Ubiquitous computing', *IEEE Computer* (October 1993), 71-72

6.2 INTIMATE MEDIA

EMOTIONAL NEEDS AND AMBIENT INTELLIGENCE

John Cass, Lorna Goulden, Slava Kozlov

This chapter explores how people construct their history, identity, relationships and spaces to express themselves and to feel at home, both in their own homes and in the wider world. It investigates how Ambient Intelligence will enable people to enhance this and open up new possibilities for sharing stories, storing memories and enriching relationships.

The lost space of emotion in technology innovation

High-tech industry has concentrated on understanding the needs of the workplace from the perspective of productivity, and on creating new tools and technologies that enable organizations to manage their processes, information and communication more efficiently. This has been driven by the economic benefits of being able to respond faster to market changes and customer enquiries, of faster product development cycles, and so on. In this competitive world, businesses are willing to pay for incorporating new technologies and understand the benefits of applying new technologies early.

As people become familiar with the potential of new technologies in their workplaces, they find ways to re-use what they have encountered there and find benefits in other parts of their lives. Simultaneously, some of the providers of these new technologies are perceiving a demand for these technologies in the consumer market, and have started to re-engineer them to make them appropriate for the home.

Orienting new technologies to serve emotional goals

Companies typically expect the benefits from productivity-driven innovation to transfer naturally into the non-productivity domain. We can see this process in the migration of the PC from an office tool to a hub for home entertainment, or in the evolution of imaging technologies from broadcast equipment to the personal camcorder or digital camera.

However, in these cases, as in many others, the technology would benefit from being interpreted differently to make a very different type of application. In some cases, the technology itself could be completely re-thought. Research that addresses emotional needs from the start may lead to a very different technology. Technologies could then find their way through other applications into the workplace.

What are these emotional needs?

These needs are not functional or physiological but psychological and cultural. They are towards the top of Maslow's hierarchy of human needs.[1] They include the need to represent roots and heritage, to create a sense of belonging and connectedness and to demonstrate personal identity and achievement.

In essence, this is the human need to make sense of oneself and one's circumstances and to be able to communicate that sense of self to others. This need relates to understanding the past, living in the present and preparing for the future.

Building your self, an integrity of personality

As part of the ongoing development and understanding of their own personality, people constantly build expressions of their self, their beliefs and their loves. Many factors contribute to this fundamental process, including the human memory process, collections of objects and how they are assembled in a space, the importance of stories and how they are shared, and the nurturing of a web of relationships.

Memory – on storage and stories

A way of seeing is a way of not seeing, a way of remembering is a way of forgetting, too. If memory were only a kind of registration, a 'true' memory might be possible. But memory is a process of encoding information, storing information and strategically retrieving information, and there are social, psychological and historical influences at each point.[2]

Michael Schudson

Human memory and computer memory are very different. Computer memory aims to be a factual record, a system into which data can be entered, to be recovered at any time in an identical form. There should be no erosion and no interpretation. This is entirely in keeping with the heritage from which and for which these technologies were developed: accuracy in accountancy, legal bookkeeping and the storage and retrieval of business-sensitive information. In contrast, human memory is a process, and the act of remembering is one of interpretation. Based on elements of factual recall, a memory is constructed in the present to serve a current need; this may involve new interpretations of old knowledge to fit into a new scheme of understanding.

Narration is understood by modern human sciences as an essential activity that constructs and maintains the sense of self and identity of a person.[3] Or, as Sartre put it, 'Man is always a storyteller! He lives surrounded by his and others' myths. With them he sees everything in his life, no matter what befalls him. And he seeks to live his life as though he were telling it'. Memories are perishable, and need refreshing or retelling to keep them 'alive'. Depending on the memory and the mechanism storing it, this refreshing will need to be frequent or seldom. Digital systems refresh their memories millions of times a second by pulsing them with electricity to keep them intact. Memories stored in books are likewise refreshed when they are read and used by someone to pursue a new line of thought. The retelling of a story will reinforce its relevance, as well as enabling us to adjust its precise characteristics, to make it more relevant to the 'now' and especially to enable us to achieve the 'next'.

Our memory and the stories we create, share, retell and live are a powerful way in which we determine and express who we are.

Turning a house into a home

As an externalization of the memory process, people build and maintain complex collections of artifacts: books, images, letters, souvenirs, etc. The process of decorating the home with these collections makes the space one's own. Human knowledge is deeply contextual; it can be effectively triggered by spatial and/or temporal contexts of the original event, and by use of imagery. The process of creating and arranging space enables people to embed triggers to certain memories or stories into the environment around them.

These collections of objects are not merely owned by a person; very often they contribute to the creation of what researchers called 'extended self'.[4] Extended self is understood here as a network of meanings, attitudes and values distributed in the space and mediated by objects and ways of interacting with them. How space is arranged and objects are distributed through that space contributes to the deepening and representation of memory and personality. All 'external' forms of memory serve as an aid to human memory and as a transfer mechanism to other people, distant in either place or time. People use external triggers extensively to help them reconstruct a memory as accurately and vividly as possible.

FIG. I

Intimate Media collections are created and accessed from many places

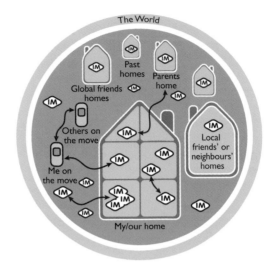

In their semiotic analysis of 'irreplaceable possessions',[5] researchers discovered that such possessions are highly efficient tools for story-telling activities and are explicitly or implicitly valued by people because of these capacities. Grayson and Shulman found that one of the major functions of 'irreplaceable possessions' is a 'verification' of the event. Such verification serves as a 'proof of the authenticity' of the fact that the person actually had the experience they're talking about.

It's not what you know, it's who you know

This process of understanding the self is also closely bound to the relationships that are nurtured by a person. In a cycle of self-reinforcement, people demonstrate their relationships through the collections of objects and photographs in their space and use the space itself to enhance relationships with visitors. The stories people tell about their history inevitably also revolve around the other actors in the history, other friends and relatives who have shared experiences in the past, are active in the present or have plans together for the future.

Feeling at home in the world

All of these activities, and others, contribute to a person's sense of feeling at home in the world. Achieving and maintaining this state is one of the powerful drivers of human activity. People actively create and nurture their framework of how they relate to the world and the people around them as a fundamental process.

We call this 'intimate media'

'Intimate media' describes the things that people create and collect to store and share their personal memories, interests and loves. Typical examples include photographs, photo albums, diaries, letters, souvenirs and music, although anything could be intimate media, depending on the meaning and value attributed to it. That meaning can relate to a person's past, their present or even potential futures.

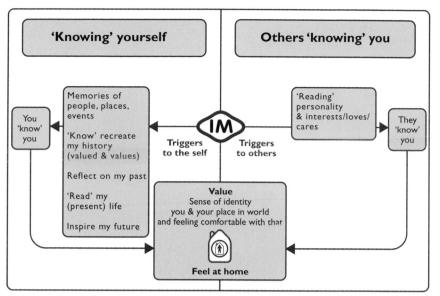

FIG. 2
Intimate Media is central
to a person's sense of
'feeling at home' in the
world

The deepest relationship people have with their material possessions is through associating them with experiences. The most mundane object can be imbued with emotional meaning. If you ask what someone would save from their home if it were on fire, most people mention something that has sentimental value, that connects directly to their understanding of themselves and their history or identity, such as a photograph collection. Generally, people do not attach such a high 'value' to the technology in their home (TV, stereo, etc.), although it might have 'cost' more.

Intimate media acts as a trigger to a memory process. Take a photograph, for instance. On the one hand, it is a pictorial record of a scene. But when the photograph is intimate media for someone, it carries much more information. It's the trigger for a whole range of emotions, stories and memories around that particular scene, also spiralling off into other scenes that happened around that time or involving those people, places or things. All of the senses contribute to this experience, from vision and hearing to touch, smell and taste.

Digital intimate media

To date, most of the material collected in this way has been physical. Letters are on paper, images are printed on photographic paper or held on the original negative, souvenirs are objects collected on shelves or mantelpieces. Increasingly, people are creating and collecting these materials as digital assets. Some of the most significant mediated interpersonal communications now happen by e-mail or SMS rather than by letter. Images are taken with digital cameras and camcorders and stored on CD-ROM or hard disks, and more often than not are never printed out (this has caused some museum curators to worry about the photographic record we are leaving for future generations).

What does this mean for the ways in which people create, manage and share their intimate media collections? How will people do this with their digital intimate media? Digital media is not available in the same way that the physical collections are; they will have to be presented to the 'real world' though translating technologies, such as a screen or loudspeakers. How will people be able to construct and arrange their living space with assets that are digital, stored remotely or accessed as a service and potentially short-lived?[6]

Bringing these assets into the virtual digital domain opens a range of new possibilities.

For one thing, they are not locked into a particular physical location, and can be simultaneously present in multiple locations, or shared over time in multiple locations. They can be copied and shared easily. They can also be animated, or 'given behaviour'. This means the intimate media asset can become active, can create connections to other assets or locations in which it could be presented, can interact with other data streams or sources. This extends the concept of object-oriented programming.

Ambient Intelligence can humanize technology

Traditional design skills enable us to create form languages that evoke an emotional response – the skilful use of curves, material and colour can bring a 'character' to an object which allows people to relate to it beyond appreciating its functional benefit. This approach has a humanizing influence on technology. Design is also bringing this sensitivity to bear in how objects work and how people can interact with them.

Designing within Ambient Intelligence enables a layer of extra richness to be constructed within the same 'space'. It allows a representation of that 'space' to be accessed remotely – to leak into other people's homes, to be carried with us as we move, to be around us in our workplaces…

Ambient Intelligence enriching human relationships

The increased availability of communication devices, especially mobile devices, is already changing how we treat our relationships. The ability to send a short message at almost any time enables people to 'pulse' their relationships, to maintain an almost constant low level of communication. As Ambient Intelligence becomes more prevalent, the possibilities for sharing communication 'on the fly' like this will become more diverse and enhanced. An example of this is in the Planet project concepts, where people are given an opportunity to share information with each other through public access terminals. This can lead to an increased involvement with a local community and the establishment of new relationships.

Ambient distribution

So far, it has not been possible to emulate how people construct the space they live in with digital tools, simply because access to the digital world has been through highly specialized and non-intuitive devices – computers, keyboards, screens. Nevertheless, there are examples of ways in which people create, nurture and share their personality in the purely virtual world. These include personal websites, web communities, web diaries,[7] and certain services like photo developers that create online photo albums. The popularity of these points to the desire to express and develop the self and relationships in the digital domain.

The nature of Ambient Intelligence is that the benefit of these digital services would be distributed in the real world, spread throughout the environment and available to be accessed from diverse places (not just the personal computer). This brings a web of connections and potential interactions within real space, where people are familiar with constructing their 'external selves'. The GlowTags concept from the MIME project is an example of this.[8]

Intelligent anticipation

A second quality of the distributed access to digital media and connectivity is the potential to nurture an 'intelligence' within that system. Within Ambient Intelligence, context and history will be shared between the diverse elements making up a person's collection of intimate media. Through a pattern-recognition and context-dependent filter, and particularly with nurture over time, connections of relevance to the owner will become established and active. The pattern of connections itself will become a piece of intimate media, in the same way that the arrangement of artifacts through the home does. This means that digital intimate media could become associated with real objects in the home, with distant objects or with other people's intimate media. It could lead to emerging patterns of media exposure or regeneration, for example, when an image of an old holiday spontaneously appears in a digital picture frame on its anniversary. The value of this type of intelligence is only complete when it leads to an evocation within the person, the arousal of an old memory or the sparking of a new thought.

Creating, collecting, browsing and sharing

Intimate media can be gathered from the most diverse locations. It could be something found or bought on holiday, the sounds from a particular place, a present made in someone else's home, or something received through the post. As important elements of our communication and collection become digital, the assets will be equally diverse – from SMS to e-mail, from digital images to MP3 files. In all of these cases, and others we don't yet know about, there will be many ways to capture and create the things that help us define ourselves. The importance of Ambient Intelligence is that we anticipate that all of these diverse things will eventually have to come together seamlessly and ubiquitously. Media should be effortlessly accepted and integrated from diverse sources.

Apart from the creation of individual assets, Ambient Intelligence will open up new possibilities for creating meaningful collections of intimate media. Through new interaction techniques, people will have more intuitive ways of categorizing and constructing relationships between the media they have collected. Simultaneously, more contextual information will be associated with the media collection at the time of creation and when reviewed, so the system will be able to make appropriate connections between relevant assets.

Having created and nurtured this collection, people will want to browse and review the contents. Again, this process will be transformed and made more natural as technologies enable more diverse, embedded ways of recalling and representing information. Categories of media will be called up through relevant context, using natural interactions in the home or on the move. Through interacting with other 'real' objects or with gesture or speech, layers of digitally stored information will add richness of memory and recall. Holding a souvenir from a holiday will call up images and sounds on a variety of displays.

Finally, the ability to transmit and copy digital information will make sharing intimate media a more dense and accessible experience. Ambient Intelligence will mean being able to share collections with friends and family remotely and at different times. We will be able to project a recent image into a digital picture frame in the home of a loved one, or browse the 'live diary' of a friend travelling somewhere exotic. When together, we will view 'albums' at home with visitors, using a range of displays, screens and sounds but also some enhanced traditional media like books and photographs, tagged so the system can recall the digital assets when required. While engaging in this shared recollection or storytelling experience, assets can be shared and transmitted between the collaborators, so that even the event of retelling a story supported by Ambient Intelligence becomes the beginning of another story…

1   A. Maslow, *Motivation and Personality* (New York, Longman, 1987)
2   M. Schudson, 'Dynamics of Distortion in Collective Memory', *Memory Distortion: How Minds, Brains, and Societies Reconstruct the Past*, ed. D. Schacter et al. (Cambridge MA, Harvard University Press, 1995), 346-364
3   L.P. Hinchman and S.K. Hinchman (eds), *Memory, Identity, Community: The Idea of Narrative in the Human Sciences* (Albany, Suny Press, 2001)
4   R.W. Belk, 'Possessions and the Extended Self', *Journal of Consumer Research*, vol. 15 (1988), 139-168
5   K. Grayson and D. Shulman, 'Indexicality and the Verification Function of Irreplaceable Possessions: A Semiotic Analysis', *Journal of Consumer Research*, vol. 27 (2000), 17-30
6   S. Brand, *The Clock of the Long Now* (London, Orion, 2000)
7   http://www.blogger.com and http://www.livejournal.com
8   L. Goulden, J. Cass and F. Rees, *MIME Concept Creation Report* (Philips Design, 2001)

6.3 POETIC INTERFACES

Fiona Rees, John Cass

...and I noticed the size of the revolution,
and the great promises of the machine, and I felt,
as I had read recently,
that there were poets who were trying to write poems
without words.[1]

Louis I. Kahn

Poetry within everyday life

Poetic interactions are by no means limited to the library, theatre or gallery. Experiences of emotional and aesthetic appeal can be found in many contexts within everyday life. When we listen to our favourite records, we feel the poetic effects of music and song. Similar poetic effects fuel the fun in watching a line of dominoes fall. Through its form, an inert kitchen utensil may tell a poem about the qualities of the food it helps to prepare.[2] In other situations, the everyday invites us to make poems for ourselves. Through the ritual of making coffee in a stovetop coffee pot, we create poetic effect through the qualities of process. In handling of chime balls, we create the poetic effects of weight and tempo to make space for spiritual thinking.

We may also make poetry to share, or share the making of poetry. In mixing a tape for a friend, we make a poem for another to read through listening. When we tell or hear a joke, the force that leads to laughter is poetic technique. And at a football match, both the crowd on the terrace and the team on the pitch together make stadium poetry, through the dialogue of chanting and play.

Interacting with the world in these ways has the potential to cause 'readers' to shift their perspective and to experience a richness of emotional or intellectual meaning that can persist long after the interaction has finished. When we talk about Poetic Interfaces, we are talking about bringing these qualities to our interactions with the digital world and Ambient Intelligence within everyday life.

Poetic Interface as a trait of Ambient Intelligence

In many of these examples, the everyday object plays the role of Poetic Interface, a tool for the making of poetry. As such, the industrial product addresses not only those needs concerning function and pleasure, but also those concerning beauty and spirituality. In its capacity to comprise numerous forms of industrial product, the Ambient Intelligence system may also adopt the Poetic Interface as a feature. The system can also act as mediator of poetic dialogue and emotional effect.

Poetic Interface versus robot poet

The Poetic Interface's capacity to create emotional value through the promotion of poetic dialogue stems largely from its role in relation to that dialogue. The key is mediation. Whilst some within the field of affective computing might favour the fantasy of the near-human computer, so 'advanced' in its understanding that it not only maps but mirrors human emotion, such a computer may prove less interesting in relation to poetic dialogue than the Poetic Interface. While the near-human computer could become a form of robot poet, expressing its near-emotional self to the world, the poetic tool, a thing to create poetry *with*, is perhaps a more desirable alternative in the domain of the social human.

Interacting with Poetic Interfaces, the user finds that the computer remains the tool and people the poets, the ones sharing emotional experience. Having 'acknowledged' its inferior social skills, the Ambient Intelligence system assumes the role of mediator rather than reader or owner of emotions. It acts upon its sophisticated understanding of people in a sophisticated manner. In reading what it is and what it cannot be in terms of addressing the emotional needs of humans, the system adopts the Poetic Interface and so is free to serve people in bringing their emotional selves to the fore.

In a system that 'understands' self as complex-technical and people as complex-emotional, and 'knows' it is different from people and should act accordingly, Poetic Interfaces can assist the system in acting on that knowledge for the good of the user.

Poetic Interfaces and the emotional needs of users

In trying to establish the potential emotional value of the Poetic Interface as part of such a system, we must begin to explore the following questions: how might various forms of Poetic Interface be created and used to support poetic experience? What could be the roles of designers and end-users within these processes and what specific emotional benefits might result? In adressing these questions, let us first sketch a model of production and consumption for Poetic Interfaces. We will then explore the relationship between the use of certain poetic techniques in the design of Poetic Interfaces, the resulting qualities and effects and the consequent emotional value.

The production and consumption of Poetic Interfaces

Practices such as poetry therapy are able to describe (and practise) the means by which they make '...intentional use of poetry...for healing and personal growth' in schools, hospitals and nursing homes.[3] But what are the similar processes to be applied to the wider everyday world of Ambient Intelligence experience? A possible model for the production and consumption of Poetic Interfaces stands as follows.

In designing for poetic experience, the industrial designer forges two types of tools to make poetry: 'words' and 'poems'. 'Words' are system components that hold poetic potential. 'Poems' are more complete interfaces built from 'words' by designers using poetic techniques.

These two forms have different recipients. The words or components are received by designer/makers, craftspeople who use their own choice of poetic techniques to forge the words into a different kind of poem or interface.

The poems or interfaces are received by the end-user, who will read the poems or interact with the interfaces within a variety of contexts. In many cases, the poems will not only be poetic in use, but also be used to create experiential poetry for others.

Poetic causes and effects

One thread running through these poetic processes is the sequence of poetic causes and effects. Poems are forged using poetic techniques, which put poetic qualities in place within the poem. In turn, these qualities create certain poetic effects for the reader. Finally, the reader's acknowledgement of these effects creates a shift in perspective, a rush of feeling or richness of emotional meaning. Let's now explore how poetic cause and effect might fulfil emotional needs through ambient intelligent experience.

Speed and soul power

In *Six Memos for the Next Millennium*,[4] Calvino writes about how, through the characteristics of economy, poetry may develop the quality of 'quickness'. He goes on to describe how this speed, or rhythmic rush of ideas, 'elevates and fortifies the soul' through energy and excitement. In today's everyday objects, we can see poetic economy in the post-modern pieces of Alessi,[5] and Ralph Ball's Naked Light collection.[6] The designer uses metaphor and the reader's knowledge of past and present icons within material culture to trigger a buzz of simultaneous, linked ideas about form and function. Through swift semiotics, the object relays a multitude of associated meanings. Following the grapple with the object's semiotics, the listening to the riddle or the well-told joke is the crescendo of pleasure found at the punch line.

Within the world of Ambient Intelligence, quickness is a prominent quality, but how it comes about should perhaps have more to do with economy and rhythm than is common today, if that speed is to give power rather than drain it from the system user. But how is the designer of the networked system to economize? With its potential for global connectivity, can the system's form or behaviour be likened to any poem but the epic? Must the rush of speed be brought to the user by alternative means?

With speed already such a dominant quality of the Ambient Intelligence experience, it may be more interesting to the user to provide value through slowness. Pleasure can be drawn from many forms of speed. The Philips LiMe and Nebula systems provide value in slowness through the Poetic Interface.

Speed and the Poetic Interfaces of LiMe and Nebula

LiMe's calm, green flow of knowledge passes slowly across the table in its wide, U-shaped channel. The low-key nature of the flow and its gentle form and rhythm contribute to creating a place of calm. In engaging with this poem, the user may be helped into its rhythm, put in the

Ambient Happiness?
Dunne & Raby

Beneath the glossy surface of official design lurks a dark and strange world driven by real human needs. A place where electronic objects co-star in a noir thriller, working with like-minded individuals to escape normalisation and to ensure that even a totally manufactured environment has room for obsession, adventure and transgression

Anthony Dunne
& Fiona Raby
*partners in the design
practice Dunne & Raby*

One example is the man in Australia who married his TV. During the ceremony, he placed a gold wedding ring on top of the TV set and one on his finger. He even promised to 'love, honour and obey' the product. One day it just occurred to him that his TV was the best companion he had ever had – he watched up to ten hours a day. It is easy to criticise someone who watches so much TV, but in many ways this form of happiness shows what might be in store for the rest of us as society becomes even more comfortable with electronic mediation. Though it is not necessarily a good thing, some people clearly find the company of electronic products more satisfying than that of people. These individuals are not rejecting other people because of technology; they have found happiness with technology instead. Before the advent of television and the web, they might have been lonely.

Maybe these obsessive behaviours provide glimpses of a future where electronic products have been fully assimilated into everyday culture and our psyche. They are cautionary tales; they push our relationship with the medium of electronic technology to the limit. We don't think that design can ever fully anticipate the richness of this unofficial world and neither should it. But it can draw inspiration from it and develop new design approaches and roles so that as our new environment of 'Ambient Intelligence' evolves, there is still scope for rich and complex human pleasure.

right frame of mind for casual browsing and chatting, the activities the table was built to promote.

In Nebula, an interactive projection system designed to enrich the experience of going to bed, sleeping and waking up, the projection sits still to span the expanse of the bedroom ceiling. Its illuminated imagery creeps silently and slowly, creating new space – sky space as breathing space or outer space as exploratory space. Drawn into a 'hypnotic' gaze, the reader of this poem of time and space stares into or through the image, seeing beyond. Image space turns into the space of dreams.

Weight and freedom of mind

Calvino describes how our sensing the qualities of lightness can create a certain freedom of mind. He suggests that through the use of form, the writing itself, abstraction in description and visual imagery, the poet creates lightness for himself and the user. Calvino points to this quality as a tool with which to work against 'the weight, the inertia, the opacity of the world'. In the recognition, acknowledgement and feeling of lightness, a person can change their image of the world, look at it from a different perspective and thus without 'escaping into dreams or into the irrational' find a mental means to 'fly', bringing moments of uplift to everyday life.[7]

The incorporation of software goes some way in providing lightness to Ambient Intelligence systems. But is it a lightness that brings about a sense of freedom? Lightness of form might bring about a sense of physical freedom. Note our newfound ability to carry so many of our Ambient Intelligence tools in one PDA or mobile phone. However, the weight of connectivity, services and information that accompany such light forms might inhibit mental freedom to the extent that a sense of freedom disappears altogether.

We must ask ourselves how the physical and virtual forms of Ambient Intelligence systems might be kept light. How might the form or behaviour of such systems create in the user a lightness of mind and spirit? The Philips MIME Glow Tag system begins to show us how.

Weight and the Poetic Interfaces of MIME

MIME's small, transparent Glow Tags hold lightness even before glowing. Through their form, these tiny wireless computers are physical and yet barely there. They sit quietly on the periphery of perception. In glowing, their small, soft light may slowly pulse but by no means demands attention. As the tag gently awakens the viewer's memory, no alarm bell rings. There is a shared lack of urgency in the trigger's glow and the viewer's mental response. Lightness is maintained.

Poetic Interfaces and the practical needs of users

In adopting a Poetic Interface, the Ambient Intelligence system may support many forms of positive emotional experience. But the value to the user may not stop here: the Poetic Interface may further support users in helping them to recognize the system's potential and limitations. This recognition is important, because ever more aspects of the seemingly familiar everyday world are changing in behaviour and function, due to Ambient Intelligence augmentation. In this world, users need a tool with which to read and understand these new capabilities, so that they can remain active within and responsive to their everyday world. The Poetic Interface could be one such tool.

Poetic Interface as sign

In working at or beyond the flesh and skin of the Ambient Intelligence system, the interface brings 'early signs', enabling the user to begin reading the qualities and capabilities of the wider system through their first impressions. In the case of the Poetic Interface, the form and behaviour of such early signs could be defined through the designer's use of metaphor, simile and

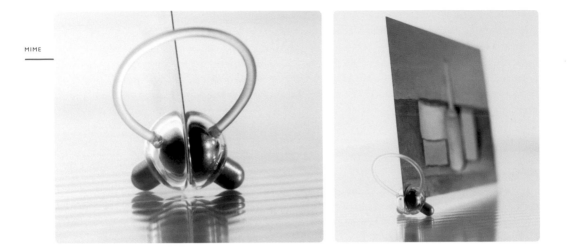

familiar object icons, past and present. The interface reveals the potential functionality of the system through the meta-language of poetics.

Flesh, skin and sign

Nearly half a century ago, in *Mythologies*, Barthes explored the notion of flesh and skin as sign.[8] Manzini recognized the relevance of skin as sign in relation to electronic objects more than ten years ago.[9] The poetic skin-sign is already a well-used tool within many realms of communication, particularly advertising. In a recent advert for Persil Antibacterial Liquid, the Persil bottle is replaced by a cleaning sponge and its lid by that of a perfume bottle. The caption reads 'New Persil Antibacterial. Smells like heaven. Works like hell'. While we might choose to avoid such a crude use of metaphor and simile, we might still find potential in the method. And despite the arguable benefits of the wastepaper basket as the icon for digital trash, we might, within the Ambient Intelligence world of tomorrow, expect to move far beyond the onscreen image as prime poetic sign.

Poetic Interface as map or manual

In its potential to be moving, static or both, and physical, virtual or both, the Poetic Interface of the Ambient Intelligence system creates the potential for highly sophisticated poetics. Such poetics are already under exploration within Philips. Nebula's physical bedside 'pocket', strange in location but familiar in form, invites the system's pebbles to be kept inside. In acting on this invitation, the user activates a change of projected image on the ceiling. In such cases, the physical aspects of interface become, to some extent, the system's user manual. 'How to' instructions are revealed through the intuitive actions of play. As manual, the interface is also a map, helping the user to negotiate a domain of unfamiliar character but exciting secrets.

Poetic Interfaces towards wise relationships

The culture of Ambient Intelligence is about applying and giving form to Ambient Intelligence tecnologies in order to create solutions which embody intelligent, harmonious relationships between people, products and environments over time.[10]

Stefano Marzano

Poetic Interfaces bring poetic forms, behaviours and functions to the system. In doing so, they provide both practical and emotional benefits to the user. This facilitates the creation of harmonious, intelligent and ultimately wise relationships.

From a practical point of view, supporting users in promoting their recognition of the system's potential and limitations within any one context allows them to maintain an understanding of their newly developing world as it unfolds before them. It also provides emotional benefits in enabling users to gain a better understanding of the self and of other people and perspectives within society. This allows them to refresh their consciousness through feeling and seeing the world in a different way.

To be or not to be...

We have quite some way to go in fully exploiting the poetic potential of Ambient Intelligence systems. The tools of production for the Poetic Interface are largely in place and the end-user benefits clear. But to write a poem demands a certain attitude towards the potential of the tool you write with. To make the creative leap between being given a pen and writing a poem requires an instinct for expression and the opportunity offered by the tool to be perceived and grasped. The industrial designer, craftsperson and end-user must be willing to nurture and wield such an instinct if the Poetic Interface is to fulfil its true potential in making the Ambient Intelligence landscape a beautiful place to be.

CDS

'Ceiling poems'

1 M. Bell and L. Lerup, *Louis Kahn: Conversations with Students* (New York, Princeton Architectural Press, 1998)
2 A. Alessi, *The Dream Factory* (Milan, Electa, 2000)
3 The National Association for Poetry Therapy, http://www.ncata.com/poetry
4 I. Calvino, *Six Memos for the Next Millennium* (Cambridge MA, Harvard University Press, 1996), 3-29
5 Alessi, 107-119
6 R. Ball, Naked Light Collection (1997/98)
7 Calvino, 4, 7
8 R. Barthes, *Mythologies* (London, Vintage Books, 1993)
9 E. Manzini, 'Objects and their Skin', *The Plastic Age*, ed. P. Sparke (London, Victoria & Albert Museum, 1990), 115-127
10 S. Marzano, *The Ambient Intelligence Definition* (Philips Design, 2002), 1

6.4 NARRATIVE AND LEARNING

Job Rutgers

Stories surround us

In childhood we learn fairy tales and myths. As we grow up, we read short stories, novels, history and biography. The Bible and Torah are huge collections of narratives. Plays tell stories as do film, television shows, comic books, paintings, dance and many other cultural phenomena.

Much of our conversations are taken up with stories, even newspaper articles are called stories - and when we ask for an explanation of something, we may say; what's the story? We cannot escape even by going to sleep, since we often experience our dreams as little narratives, and we recall and re-tell our dreams in the shape of stories.[1]

David Bordwell and Kristin Thompson

As we understand the world around us through narratives, we are able to relate to ideas, socialize, express ourselves and organize our lifes. Narrative seems to be a key element of how we structure our lives and helps to define the fabric of everyday life. As our world moves from the Industrial age to the Knowledge age, this fabric is changing.[2] In this knowledge age, our society will be diffused with ambient intelligent 'knowledge tools' and systems.

For Ambient Intelligence to be successful, it must be woven carefully into this fabric of invisible relationships among people, objects and experiences. It must provide people with the tools and systems that blend into their everyday lives while delivering intelligence in our distributed knowledge infrastructure.

Learning society

Within the knowledge society, we become knowledge workers and citizens who continuously need to improve their skills and knowledge. Learning will not be limited to schools or universities, but will become a permanent process. 'Lifelong learning' is the slogan used by

POGO

the European Commission to spread this message.[3] For every level of society – individuals, social groups, companies – learning is becoming both permanent and intrinsic.

As a result, we need to address a number of important questions. What are the current and future implications of lifelong learning? How can narrative inform the design of learning tools and systems? What are the general learning needs of corporations and large organizations? And what is the relationship between narrative and content?

Learning organizations

Nowadays, companies are becoming increasingly knowledge-based, both in their products and their processes. The success or failure of companies will depend on the speed and strategy of reshaping their inner structure from industrial machines into knowledge powerhouses.

The roadmap towards Ambient Intelligence will transform Philips from a producer of 'black boxes' to a knowledge powerhouse, developing technology solutions that will be near invisible. To be a successful shaper in this fast changing, knowledge intensive high-tech landscape, Philips and other companies will need to become adaptive learning organizations.

What is a learning organization?

A learning organization is good at absorbing, sharing, integrating and creating knowledge: absorbing information and knowledge to maximize awareness, and sharing information and knowledge to fully leverage what is already known. Moreover, it must be able to integrate existing knowledge and to create new knowledge in response to emerging trends. The whole organization needs to be engaged in developing foresight with regard to emerging opportunities, and swiftly building knowledge and skills to address these opportunities. An organization that can do this is truly a learning organization.

Beyond knowledge management

The question of how best to manage knowledge, a company's most valuable asset, is not new. An entire service industry promising to deliver knowledge management solutions has blossomed. Many books and articles have been published and countless presentations have been made.

The first generation knowledge management systems aimed to capture all tacit knowledge into large databases. These strategies proved to be little more than mechanical solutions and have passed away silently. The current generation is based on the insight that knowledge is essentially something that resides within people and cannot be extracted and codified. The emphasis in knowledge-sharing solutions is thus to enable 'smart connectivity' between the thousands of employees. 'Intelligent agents', 'concept mining' and 'smart databases' are the key terms in the solutions now available.

These 'sharing solutions' allow people to create, share and publish their own stories and questions. In a way, these platforms can be regarded as a new kind of newspaper in which the content is created dynamically by its members. The format of the 'old' newspaper has been re-interpreted as a model for knowledge sharing.

The content that populates these solutions has many narrative characteristics. Best practices, for instance, are nothing more than a story about how to do certain things best, to share with other people who may encounter a similar situation in another place or time.

Some solutions currently being developed go even further as they take narrative as structuring principle. As David Snowden puts it, "In third generation knowledge management systems we recognize that people always know more than they can say, and will always say more than they can write down".[4] The solutions in development use oral storytelling databases that apply archetypes as the algorithms to create intelligent indices.

PHENOM

PML

MIME

TOONS

POGO

OPEN TOOLS

LIME
AND PL@NET

Scenarios for design

In order to design and develop such large-scale knowledge management applications, a huge body of information about many different users is collected. Each user has their own 'story'. Usually, when designing an interactive product, the use of a design scenario is helpful to contextualize 'real world' information about the situation in which the product is used, the space in which it is used, user characteristics, etc. How can we use storytelling or scenarios for the design of such complex systems for thousands of users?

Network scenarios

Storytelling in modern film provides an inspiration with regard to the issue of multiple users and system complexity. A useful metaphor can be found in *Short Cuts*,[5] Robert Altman's mosaic of interwoven story elements. The film is made up of many stories, all situated in Los Angeles, and many story 'threads' connected within one narrative framework. If we drew lines on a roadmap of LA linking the various story locations, we would probably find a network of crossing storylines.

With some creative adaptation, this narrative structure can be used to adapt current design scenario-building techniques into network scenarios. In network scenarios, different user scenarios are developed based on interviews and an analysis of the users' needs, roles and character traits. This methodology will become increasingly important as large-scale ambient intelligent systems will enter our homes and connect us to a seamless web of intelligently delivered content and services.

Much more to learn

Companies must transform into learning organizations and must use new 'e-enabled' structures that help them to create a backbone for sharing, integrating and creating new knowledge. Many of these systems currently in development make use of insights into narrative structures, or are built with narrative-based design tools. More generally, an in-depth knowledge of narrative structures is required, both for the understanding of larger complex systems and for the development of complex systems.

The domain of modern film and literature offers many more examples and models of narrative structures that give us an understanding and inspiration for the design of embedded ambient intelligent systems.

Learning environments

I would say that the moment an object appears in a narrative, it is charged with a special force and becomes like the pole of a magnetic field, a knot in the network of invisible relationships.[6]

Italo Calvino

People's everyday lives are characterized by their activities – shopping, relaxing, learning, talking and so on. As simple as these activities may seem, to describe, define and understand them in such a way that Ambient Intelligence could be embedded into them is far more complex. As an example, the way young children learn is a process that may look simple at first glance: a teacher stands in front of a blackboard, before a class of children sitting at desks, telling them about the animal kingdom, or history, and so on. But if we look more closely at this learning process, a far more complex model emerges.

Children and storytelling

Children talk and tell stories to communicate, to express themselves and to construct models of the world they experience. They project their fantasy world onto inanimate objects such

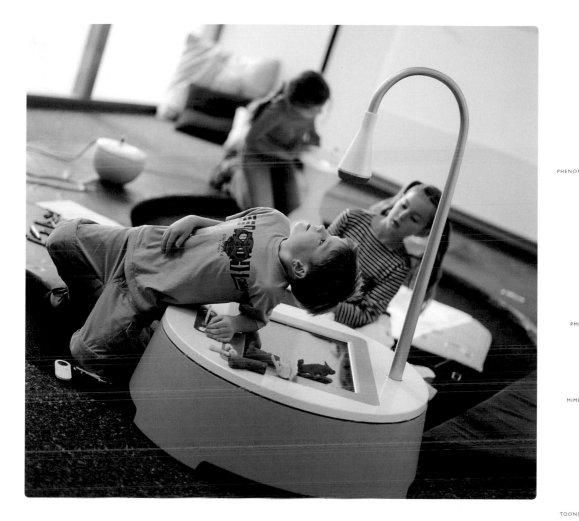

PHENOM

PML

MIME

TOONS

POGO

OPEN TOOLS

LIME
AND PL@NET

as toys in order to act out and engage in relationships. Early learning is driven by the children's needs to explore their world by engaging with artifacts and people.

These experiences are proactively contextualized by the child in the form of storytelling with imaginary others, often facilitated by the use of inanimate objects as surrogate people within an environment. This process is further stimulated and supported by the use of stories read by parents and teachers.

The computer and storytelling

The introduction of computing and interactive media into the classroom in the late 1980s promised to enrich this learning process. But the benefits that it brought have had little to do with telling stories. While computers may help children with such analytical skills as calculation, they seldom stimulate their imagination and rarely help them to be creative.

The computer as exists today offers few opportunities for children to go beyond button-pushing and mouse-clicking. This is the problem of existing software, as expressed by Resnick, Bruckman and Martin: 'By learning to play the piano, you can become a creator (not just a consumer) of music, expressing yourself musically in ever-more complex ways. In the field of technology there has been too much emphasis on the equivalent of stereos and CDs and not enough emphasis on computational pianos'.[7]

Behind storytelling

Through storytelling, children learn to express themselves and make sense of the outside world. Through collaboration in building stories, children can negotiate interpretations with others in order to achieve more consciousness rather than unanimity.[8] The activity of collaborative storytelling is an essential part of the child's learning process. The seamless and continuous psychological process of making a story can be broken down, not in the children's mind, but in the focus of an articulated pedagogical activity.

The 'cycle of creative imagination'[9], a process describing how a child experiences the external world, forms impressions, assembles them in a new way and shares this production with others, offers a model for understanding children's narrative activities in the classroom. Narrative activities at school include all of these phases, often in linear sequences, sometimes with small loops or repetition, and sometimes with a leap.

This model has been used to focus, contextualize and articulate the development of Ambient Intelligence solutions such as Pogo in the classroom. The narrative activity model has enabled developers to imagine the operation of intelligent tools in the classroom, using information about the spatial distributions of activities, the artifacts used, the role played by the teacher and the social relationships of the children.

The future of narrative learning environments

The concept of the child as an active participant in the learning process (and not as a passive recipient of knowledge) is the first step in a transformation of learning as we know it. In time, school will be the nucleus of a learning experience that expands from the playground to the home and into the public domain. Ambient Intelligence tools and systems will enable the child to be part of a consistent and experiential learning experience that is intelligent, social and human in its essence.

Content: the elementary particle

Over the past few years, the term 'content' has become an abstraction in the high-tech world, repeated all too often, like a kind of mantra, losing its meaning in endless management presentations and advertisements. Content has been one of the big promises of the World Wide Web glossy magazines promised access to all content in a veritable universe of information. What was often overlooked was that what many people really wanted was to exchange a simple message or chat.

Interactive television, the long-held dream of a story influenced by its audience, has also failed to date. The thrill of a good story is often that its author has crafted an emotional rollercoaster very carefully – the fact you don't know what is about to happen is what makes it fun. This simple knowledge has been suspended in the interactive TV debate.

The day after

The old 'new economy' dream of interactivity seems like a nightmare in retrospect. Huge sums have been spent in the development of a new entertainment paradigm, involving the viewer in an 'immersive, interactive experience' which has not really materialized. In the post-'new economy' era, narrative formats like the 'open newspaper' and the narrative-structured site-specific intelligent tools described earlier will be more successful models as they enable us to become content producers rather than just passive receptors. The mass individual production, distribution and sharing of content will follow the peer-to-peer distribution model, like Gnutella and Napster. The systems that need to deliver personalized, tailored and timely content will require enormous intelligence.

Story DNA

Through the development of ambient intelligent systems, a large nerve system will evolve, embedded in the world like the veins in a body. Not surprisingly, what will flow through these veins is content, created by people. Again, this content must be personalized, tailored and timely.

The recognition, indexing and concept-mining algorithms needed to deliver this intelligence are all based on an in-depth knowledge of the structure of this content. For example, one of the key findings in recent research is that American television is very easy to 'smart-index' through its repeatable and frequency of advertisement blocks. The same research shows that this is not the case in Europe or Asia, where content genres and TV programming followed a culturally different logic.[10]

It will be the understanding of content in its smallest 'particles' or characteristics that will enable the development of a large-scale ambient intelligent landscape that is a prerequisite for the lifelong-learning society.

A good story

All the interactivity and intelligence that may soon come to us will not change the fact that there is little, if anything, better than a good novel, movie or comic to become immersed in an imaginary world carefully crafted by an author. The product of our imagination is something no machine or system can replace. This reminds us that ultimately the world of Ambient Intelligence is essentially human, crafted by ourselves. As Stefano Marzano points out, 'Ambient Intelligence is more than just a question of embedding technology into objects. It involves human culture in its broadest sense: universal desires; complex social relationships; different value systems; individual likes and dislikes; the sustainability of economic and natural ecosystems; and codes of ethics, conduct and communication, both in civil society and in business'.[11]

The Ambient Intelligence that will surround us in future must embody, incorporate and transcend our stories, as these express our needs and most fundamental and intimate desires. If the 'story' of Ambient Intelligence comes to pass, we may ultimately live in the world as we imagine it to be.

PHENOM

PML

MIME

TOONS

POGO

OPEN TOOLS

LIME
AND PL@NET

1 D. Bordwell and K. Thompson, *Film Art: An Introduction* (New York, McGraw Hill, 1997), 89

2 J. Green, *The Transformation to the Knowledge Age* (Philips Design)

3 European Commission, *The eLearning Action Plan: Designing Tomorrow's Education* (28 March 2001)

4 D. Snowden, 'Narrative Patterns: Uses of Story in the Third Age of Knowledge Management', *Journal of Information and Knowledge Management* (2002)

5 *Short Cuts* (Robert Altman, 1993)

6 I. Calvino, *Six Memos for the Next Millennium* (Cambridge MA, Harvard University Press, 1996)

7 M. Resnick, A. Bruckman and F. Martin, 'Pianos Not Stereos: Creating Computational Construction Kits', *Interactions*, vol. 3, no. 6 (1996)

8 F. Decortis, P. Marti, C. Moderini, A. Rizzo and J. Rutgers, 'Disappearing Computer, Emerging Creativity: An Educational Environment for Cooperative Story Building', to be published in *Interacting with Computers*

9 L. Vygotsky, *Mind in Society: The Development of Higher Psychological Processes* (Cambridge MA, Harvard University Press, 1978)

10 R.S. Jasinchi, *A Framework for the Representation and Integration of Multimedia Content and Context Information* (seminar paper given to the Department of Electrical and Computer Engineering at Carnegie Mellon University, 29 April 2002)

11 S. Marzano, *The Culture of Ambient Intelligence*, speech given at the opening of the Philips Homelab (2002)

PARTNER, BRAND, CREATE

How might Ambient Intelligence redefine the business landscape?
What impact might it have on consumers and organizations,
on marketing, branding and design practices? And most importantly
– can Ambient Intelligence contribute to the development of a
sustainable society?

7.1 THE SUSTAINABILITY OF AMBIENT INTELLIGENCE

Simona Rocchi

From clean and green to the triple bottom line

The meaning of 'sustainability' or 'sustainable development' has changed over the years. In the past, to many people, 'sustainable' has been virtually interchangeable with 'green', 'ecological' or 'environmentally friendly'. Today, the term has increasingly assumed socio-economic connotations. It encompasses not only environmental issues, but also questions of social equity and economic viability. To be merely eco-efficient, by optimizing the processes and the products of traditional growth-oriented industrial models, is a necessary but insufficient condition for satisfying the needs and wants of an exponentially increasing global population. More attention must be paid to new production and consumption patterns, addressing both the supply and demand sides of the economy. To quote the World Business Council for Sustainable Development, 'Sustainability implies a system of production and consumption able to assure a greater equity, quality of life and environmental well-being today and for future generations'.[1] These are (almost) the three Ps of the triple bottom line: people, planet and profitability.

A new market-competitive landscape

'Hard' environmental and socio-economic factors (e.g., material consumption, pollution, loss of biodiversity, population growth, diffusion of ICT, globalization and inequality) are changing the competitive landscape for corporations. Sustainability is becoming a new point of entry into the market for companies and for brands that wish to be competitive in the coming years.

Some enterprises have already embraced sustainability as a framework for driving development, increasing shareholder value and stakeholder satisfaction, and protecting and enhancing brand reputation.[2] Accordingly, they have started to look for new approaches to innovation that go beyond 'technology push' and 'market pull' to address these two issues in respect of the environmental and sociocultural contexts in which they operate. They have started to look for innovative solutions capable of drastically reducing the use of current environmental resources, while increasing the added value for users and feeding new business revenue streams.

Responsible choices to improve people's lives

Considering sustainability as a challenge to ensure people's quality of life now and in the future, and as an opportunity to generate both wealth and brand reputation in the business process, the following questions must be raised in relation to the Ambient Intelligence vision. Is our company able to generate sustainable value in the framework of Ambient Intelligence? If so, how far can Ambient Intelligence enable the creation of a sustainable society? And in which way? For whom? Let's try to outline some possible answers here.

Going beyond a risk-reduction approach, we have started to look at sustainability as a creative process of change, which aims to generate strategic directions, scenarios and solutions ensuring profit for the business, value to society, quality to the environment and meaning for the individual. In this perspective, we adopt a particular process [Fig. 1]. We use our 'human focus' research, tracking new and emerging longer-term personal and social values (e.g., ethics, balance, responsibility, belonging) in line with more sustainable patterns of consumption, combining them with potential environmentally friendly technologies (e.g., upgradeable and updateable digital platforms, solar and human power technologies) and new business strategies (e.g., sharing, leasing, access to digital services). Our ultimate ambition is to create innovative solutions capable of increasingly contributing to the triple bottom line, indicating to the business new sustainable routes in a shift from a 'possible' to a 'preferable' future. In the words of Stefano Marzano, 'Philips, adopting a human focus and embracing personal and social values as well as new technologies to create new sustainable innovation and business models, can bring us into a preferable future'.[3]

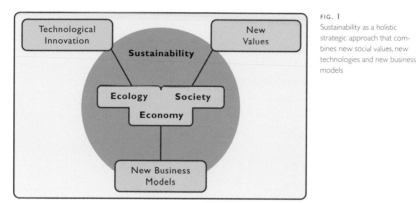

FIG. I
Sustainability as a holistic strategic approach that combines new social values, new technologies and new business models

In this attempt, we are guided by our digital vision of the world. Through the use of relevant, meaningful and responsible technology for people, we can propose solutions for a better life. Through the use of environmentally, socially and economically responsible technology for society, we can also propose solutions for a better world. In the transition period in which we are currently living, moving from the Industrial to the Knowledge and Service Age, the digital wave increases the opportunities for the dematerialization of production and consumption models of high energy and materials use, and for the democratization of society. Through Ambient Intelligence, we can explore these opportunities at the levels of product and system innovation.

Product innovation
Responsible technology can generate new 'intelligent devices' of increased eco-efficiency (saving energy and materials), improved life-cycle cost (guaranteeing economic affordability) and higher customization (respecting the diversity of socio-cultural needs) compared to current market solutions.

System innovation
Responsible technology can also enhance the 'intelligence' of current socio-economic systems in order to support their 'sustainability performance' through the reconfiguration of manufacturing, marketing, distribution and use. Ambient Intelligence solutions do not necessarily imply the development of new high-tech devices, but they can propose a different use (or re-use) of the available devices, optimizing the materials-energy-information flows of the context in which they are located and operate.

System innovation, even if more complex to implement, appears the most promising approach, since it better stimulates social changes able to embrace more sustainable lifestyles and ways of consumption. We can think of using Philips' core technological competences (storage, connectivity and display) to facilitate the reorganization of the relations between global and local stakeholders in the provision of solutions that may be placed in communities or public spaces for common use (increasing the number of people served while containing the amount of hardware introduced into the market). This can be applied either to developed, or (even more) to less developed economies. Indeed, it is probably through considering the combination of low-tech and high-tech components that we can aim to satisfy, in a more sustainable manner, the needs of the 4 billion people representing the new emerging market of the 'have-nots'.

Our unique approach for a sustainable business and brand

Until now, 'Let's make things better.' has guided us in our ongoing commitment to look for new ways of improving people's lives by designing and producing everyday products that are both affordable and user-friendly. Today, we have the chance to enrich our brand promise with sustainable values capable of embodying and interpreting the new, emerging spirit of the times. In pursuing this, we have elaborated our unique approach towards sustainability. A holistic approach focusing on environmental, social and personal aspects is able to encapsulate the new search for well-being in today's society.

Sustainble vision — Enviromental — Social — Personal — Economical — Current reality

Ambient Intelligence and environmental aspects: dematerialization and virtualization

Current western societies are characterized by many devices and applications that are sub-optimal from an environmental perspective. Many devices duplicate at least some of the same functions (e.g., televisions, projectors, stereos, radios, stoves, microwaves, toasters, etc.). Many are energy-inefficient (they consume more energy than is strictly needed for the functional result, and energy losses are usually dissipated as heat, etc.). Consumer behaviour is diffuse and unsustainable (devices are used in a non-rational way, and are replaced due to technological obsolescence or outdated style).

This context, however, is changing. The convergence of digital technology and information and communication technology is offering alternatives to address people's needs and wants. The miniaturization of components and the diffusion of digital services are stimulating a dematerialization of our artificial habitat. Many stand-alone products are being reduced in volume and are assuming an unobtrusive appearance. Many functions are now offered through the Web (e.g., telebanking, telecommuting, e-commerce), reducing the mobility required of people and the impact of their transportation activities on a local scale. And ownership of products is steadily being replaced by access to product-service solutions.[4]

Within this trend, Ambient Intelligence offers us the chance to provide digital solutions able to support people in their daily activities more effectively and with a lower environmental impact. Taking the potentialities of display, storage and connectivity into account, 'Philips can digitally provide functionalities and benefits whilst decreasing material output'.[5]

Since 1995, we have started to outline some scenarios in this direction in our strategic projects.[6] Thanks to the diffusion of digital networking, we have broken down the traditional distinction between physical products and intangible services to envision Internet-based product-service combinations that pave the way for lightweight interfaces, increased portability and upgradeability. We have taken the issue of dematerialization into account in these projects, using a roadmap that goes from the miniaturization of devices (reducing weight and size) to the integration of product functions (combining different electronic stand-alone devices in multifunctional applications) or their virtualization (replacing hardware by online services).

Today, a 'living' result of this exploration is represented by Nexperia, a series of Silicon System Platforms (SSPs) that can adapt to different application areas. With Nexperia, all the key hardware and software components inside a digital television, for example, are put on a single chip that can be upgraded as soon as new services become available. The ultimate benefit for the user is to avoid the cost of buying a new television, and for the environment, to avoid the disposal of a device that still works.

Taking our research one step further, our devices can eventually disappear, maximizing material savings. Microchips, online connections and digital services allow technology to become increasingly embedded and invisible, enabling us to exploit the integration of different product functions into our furniture and even our clothes.

Ambient Intelligence and social aspects: cohesion and sharing

Current social issues under discussion relate to a broad spectrum of different aspects: human rights, discrimination, education, equality, inter-generation equity, the gap between the haves and the have-nots... Until recently, Philips' commitment to social issues has focused mainly on internal questions, such as health, safety and employment conditions. By revitalizing our social commitment and enriching our current 'caring' attitude, we can go beyond that. We can aspire to the initiation of a programme capable of supporting community spirit on a local scale, and of bridging the have/have-not divide on a global scale. 'Philips can provide assistance and support by establishing more caring cultural relationships and by sharing knowledge'.[8]

More specifically, looking at the short-term time frame and considering the capabilities of our digital technologies, Philips' engagement in social issues is oriented to address the following aspects. Internally, Philips supports the building of our business community by facilitating the exchange of information. Externally, we focus on the support of local communities, digitally supporting social cohesion among people. Accordingly, we focus on a deep understanding of local needs and aspirations, supporting the consolidation of cultural relationships and the sharing of knowledge in an Ambient Intelligence environment.

In this regard, we can mention the example of the Philips Yellow Pages: a people-oriented expert system that allows for locating people, sharing knowledge and open questions. In other words, we can refer to our internal virtual network where Philips' employees come together to support and consult each other in their daily business.

For external solutions, we can point to one of our richest scenarios, the Living Memory project (LiMe). LiMe is an EC-funded research project that proposes a scenario of knowledge exchange and mutual help within the local community to improve the quality of social relationships within it. To do this, LiMe provides intuitive networking interfaces at a common point of digital access embedded in public spaces. These points of digital access offer community members new opportunities to share goods (e.g., gardening tools), skills and knowledge (e.g., after-school help in mathematics) and time (e.g., for babysitting) – opportunities that communities often fail to take. The social value of this project lies in the way of using Internet-based solutions. Indeed, networking technology does not have to be used necessarily to 'go global', nor to replace physical relationships with virtual relationships, but to support information-transfer across territories and to connect people, perhaps turning electronic contacts into face-to-face relationships.[9]

Ambient Intelligence and personal aspects:
empowerment and co-creation

Not only is the environment suffering, but individuals are also burning out from an overload on their time and energy. The desire is to be empowered, not overpowered. From this perspective, the concept of quality of life starts to go beyond the traditional equation of personal wellbeing with a good income (especially in western societies) to encompass such concerns as self-actualization, self-fulfilment, balance, responsibility, meanings and beliefs.[10]

Our constant human-focused technological innovation can respond to this new emerging and evolving mindscape. So far, Philips has only partially covered the personal sustainability dimension by designing 'ease-of-use' devices to simplify people's lives. We now have an opportunity to move from standard user-friendly devices to co-created product-service mixes in cooperation with the stakeholders and the user. This will enable the holistic personal well-being of individuals: in other words, it represents a shift in values from material fulfilment to sensorial experience and personal satisfaction through empowerment.

The Pronto universal remote control, which allows a broad customization of its interface directly by the user, is one product that partly represents this approach. Pronto can be considered as one of the first Philips commercial solutions in which users have been involved during the process of product development, giving continuous input (on their specific needs) and feedback (testing the product), contributing to the definition of the final solution.

NEBULA

Users become active
players

Nebula, a more futuristic concept, is another example in which the user participates, even if only in the ultimate phase, in the co-creation of the value of the final solution.[11] Designed for the home environment, it attempts to offer a new ritual for waking up in the morning. To do this, Nebula replaces the traditional sound of an alarm clock with a diffused light system capable of creating an atmosphere in the bedroom that encourages and enhances relaxation, reflection and intimacy. In this scenario, users become active players. They are empowered in the co-creation of the final interface. They can select the content to be used (sounds and visuals) or, eventually, add their own content.

The next challenge: from mass customization to local diversity

So far, our exploratory route towards sustainability has delivered solutions and studies which have sometimes emphasized the environmental dimension over the social or the personal, or vice versa. However, all these aspects have to be balanced.

In this attempt, we need to question how a global company can provide better solutions with respect to a quality of life that emerges from specific socio-cultural human values and physical local conditions. In the search for relevant answers, we believe that Ambient Intelligence can open many new doors. Our next challenge is to think in terms of flexible technological and organizational platforms that can be customized, or rather 'contextualized' on a local scale with regard to the optimal use of local human and environmental resources and available infrastructures.

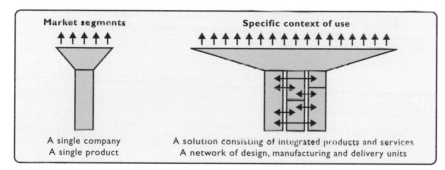

FIG. 3
From mass customization to local diversity

As a starting point for this investigation, Philips is currently participating in an EC-funded project called Highly Customerized Solutions (HiCS) to create sustainable product-service systems for specific local lifestyles and conditions. Within this project, Philips is experimenting with new methods to involve the users and local stakeholders in a process of value-co-creation of the final solutions suitable to specific contexts. This experiment can be considered a first step in the shift from mass customization to a new socio-economic trend: local diversity.

1   World Business Council for Sustainable Development (WBCSD), *Sustainability Through the Market: A Business-based Approach to Sustainable Consumption and Production* (Geneva, 1999)
2   S. Hart, 'The Bottom of the Pyramid', *Tomorrow Magazine* (January/February 2001)
3   S. Marzano, internal communication (Philips Design, 2000)
4   J. Rifkin, *The Age of Access: How the Shift from Ownership to Access is Transforming Capitalism* (London, Penguin Books, 2000)
5   Philips Design, *Philips Sustainable Brand Vision* (project commissioned by Philips Global Brand Management, Eindhoven, 2001)
6   Philips Design, *Vision of the Future* (Blaricum, V+K Publishing, 1996)
7   Philips Global Brand Management, *Philips Brand Book* (Eindhoven, Lecturis, 2002)
8   *Philips Sustainable Brand Vision*
9   J. Wilsdon (ed.), *Digital Futures: Living in a Dot.com World* (London, Earthscan, 2001)
10 Philips Design, 'Social Survey', *Building a Better Future: Innovation, Technology and Sustainable Development* (Geneva, WBCSD, 2000)
11 Philips Design, *Smart Connections: An interrogation to capture the meaning from Ambient Intelligence to Ambient Culture* (Eindhoven, Royal Philips Electronics, 2001)

I-PRONTO

HOMELAB

HICS

OPEN TOOLS

LIME
AND PL@NET

NEW
NOMADS

7.2 ACCLIMATIZING TO AMBIENT INTELLIGENCE

Laura Taylor, Cees Jan Mol

In exploring new directions such as Ambient Intelligence, it is important to remember that innovation and change will always be assessed in the context of cultural values, traditions and the spirit of the times. How can we work towards acclimatizing people to innovation? In this chapter, we discuss the importance of timing for innovation in general, and what it could mean for Ambient Intelligence. We ask whether people are ready for Ambient Intelligence and discuss how to accelerate their acceptance. Finally, we look at the organizational impact of a new paradigm and what can be done to manage it.

The importance of timing for innovation

Timing is a critical success factor in implementing the Ambient Intelligence vision and creating successful businesses based on that vision. To time introductions better, a new perspective on adoption processes and communication is required.

Traditionally, scientists and engineers quickly become aware of new technologies and try them out in demos and prototypes. On the basis of scientific ethics and an eagerness to make a given technology function properly, communities of technology experts share insights without looking deeply at the business implications. At this early stage, what is created is intellectual property (patents), and what is respected is intellectual ownership.

It can take many years before these new technologies come to the mass market in a way that is accepted by the public. It took the Compact Disc approximately 20 years to become the preferred format for storing music and video content. E-mail, which began as an exchange of simple text messages between members of a scientific community in the 1980s, did not become *de facto* in offices until the mid-1990s, and its use is still growing in the domestic environment. Although products for a personal communications network were prototyped more than 10 years ago, mobile phones have only recently become an integral part of how we communicate.

FIG. 1
The gap between internal awareness and societal readiness for a new technology[1]

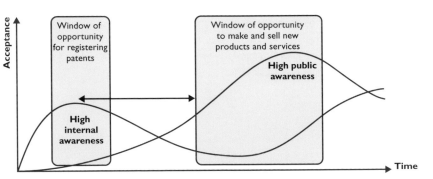

Figure 1 illustrates the acceptance gap between the specialists who understand a new technology at a very early stage and the public, who decide whether to accept it. This gap between internal awareness and societal readiness is a typical problem for technology companies.

This begs the question 'Do we want to close the gap?' Do we want to speed up the acceptance of new technologies? What is wrong with just waiting until people are ready? Traditional thinking suggests that if you wait until the public is ready, the market will be a mass market and its business models will be clear. However, doubts have been raised about whether the traditional mass-market approach is appropriate for new, more systems-based value propositions. In any case, waiting imposes the problem of having to assess which moment is the right one for a massive market introduction. It is better to try to manage the gap.

The problem with the acceptance gap and the uncertainty of timing is that momentum is lost and management loses faith; investments are diverted, teams disbanded, and competencies disappear. Opportunities vanish into a sort of Bermuda Triangle. Another problem is that if market introduction is not timed correctly, not only will the window to recoup investment be missed, but also the ability to make a profit even at a later stage may completely disappear. When the evolution of an entirely new consumer electronics paradigm is involved, such as Ambient Intelligence, these risks are even greater, since the new technological competencies that have to be built up represent both intellectual ownership with a potential high return on investment and high-risk investments.

There is another factor that makes the acceptance gap an issue. It has been suggested that the speed with which new technological waves are introduced is increasing, as shown in Figure 2. If this is indeed the case, it could be argued that Ambient Intelligence may emerge earlier than expected through a faster introduction of new technologies and their convergence.

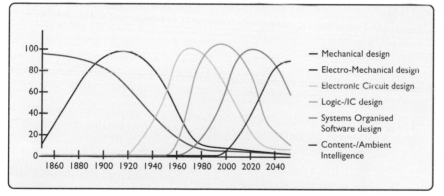

FIG. 2
Relative adoption
of technology[2]

Timing market introduction has always been a problem; it becomes even more so with the advent of Ambient Intelligence. The competences built up in technology companies represent both a bigger opportunity for profit and a bigger possibility of losses. Investments in a new paradigm are much higher-risk than investments into technologies for well-established markets. If new technology waves are adopted by society with increasing speed, this raises the stakes and the urgency.

Are people ready for Ambient Intelligence?

We believe that people are ready for the ultimate benefits of Ambient Intelligence, but the real question is how much effort and money they will be willing to invest to get these benefits, and in what form they will be prepared to accept Ambient Intelligence. The key to people's uptake will be in the execution, i.e., how the benefits are proposed and delivered, and by which companies. Because these propositions will undoubtedly reflect a break with conventions, people will weigh the propositions against the level of effort, change and cost demanded from them in exchange for benefits.

At present, we cannot tell how the benefits of Ambient Intelligence functionalities and services will be perceived. Many of the Ambient Intelligence solutions will be immaterial and embedded, without a perceived presence in terms of weight or size, so their benefits will have to be very clear. Designing, marketing and branding the benefits of Ambient Intelligence will be a huge challenge in the coming decade.

If the Ambient Intelligence vision is driven solely by technological improvements and possibilities, it risks missing opportunities to capitalize on technological breakthroughs because of an inability to overcome the acceptance gap. As Marshall McLuhan observed, the content of the new medium is the old medium. For example, the first TV broadcasts were in effect televised radio shows. The first Web content was text, and the Web is still made up of hypertext. Ambient Intelligence, as an entirely new paradigm for the consumer electronics industry, faces the same initial difficulties as the car, introduced to consumers as a horseless carriage: it may be misperceived in terms of old technology. McLuhan calls this 'rearviewmirrorism'.

New patterns of use

In fact, Ambient Intelligence involves new technological breakthroughs that demand new patterns of use. Since some of the technological breakthroughs are now known, while new business models are yet to emerge, the technologies can already be explored to minimize the barriers to acceptance and use. For example, the benefits of technological breakthroughs must be meaningful within existing anthropological frameworks. If they are not, the benefits have to be improved to a level where people want to make the changes required. As Mike Koenig of Andersen Windows put it, 'You need to get permission from the consumer to change the anthropology'.

Within a new paradigm, it is impossible to know in advance what consumers will want to buy without testing this. Interaction designers and people researchers are currently exploring meaningful propositions, using test situations such as the Philips HomeLab to monitor results and identify improvements.

New business models

Ambient Intelligence's ultimate business models will not be the ones within which early efforts will be introduced. It is likely that the professional world will adopt Ambient Intelligence early. In the case of mobile phones, only business people bought the earliest, bulky models. Consumers did not buy phones; they bought unlimited contact with friends at any given moment. When it becomes technically possible for the phone to evolve into a handheld control device for ambient information access in a personalized fashion, its benefits will be quite different, as will its business model. As we cannot tell how the real benefits of Ambient Intelligence functionalities and services will be perceived, its business models are largely unknown, although much research is being done into who will want such solutions and at what cost.

Accelerating adoption by bridging the acceptance gap

When risks of technology introductions become greater, as with Ambient Intelligence, it becomes increasingly necessary to manage adoption processes better. Theoretically, this means switching from a traditional view of adoption as a linear diffusion process, to seeing it as a joint realization process.[4] John Dewey's definition of communication as 'the establishment of cooperation in any activity in which there are partners and in which the activity of each is modified and regulated by partnership' enables such an approach.[5]

The solution lies in seeing the acceptance gap as an opportunity to transfer momentum from one community of inventors/consumers ('technologists') to another community of users/improvers ('consumers'), and to establish forms of cooperation between the two.

By placing people's needs at the centre, we bridge the acceptance gap in three ways, in a Strategic Innovation Service pioneered by Philips Design. First, through 'user need exploration', we create rough overviews of timing and assess how long it will take for a solution to shift from being a cutting-edge manifestation of a trend to being widely accepted. These rough timeframes enable attempts to manage the momentum of internal awareness, by clarifying a framework from decision-making to driving business strategy and investments in different technologies.

Second, through 'experience creation', we make technology more meaningful for people by designing the consumer's total experience, including the interaction and the context of use. This requires us to come up with a proposition for how the new technology will be used in a logical way that is 'backwards-compatible' with current devices from a technological perspective and with established ways of doing things from a practical perspective. By giving people a real experience of the new technology, its benefits can become real and tangible.

Third, we bridge the acceptance gap through 'future exploration'. In order to generate broader social acceptance for a solution, we try to plant 'memories of the future', using public presentations of visionary projects that illustrate possible future applications through realistic means (e.g., videos, simulations, working prototypes, etc.). This helps to give people an understanding of, and familiarity with, technology that is yet to come. In 2002, Philips opened up its Corporate Research Exhibition (CRE) to strategic customers. Established 50 years ago, the CRE traditionally served the purpose of enabling networking across the research laboratories spread around the globe. Today, the CRE is becoming an opportunity for dialogue with strategic partners to capitalize jointly on new opportunities.

Through these three steps we create anticipation by creating attractive propositions that have a sustainable place in people's lives. If this is done successfully, it can result in a third window of opportunity, as shown in Figure 3. This is the opportunity for leadership and brand equity to be built by creating experiences through communications.

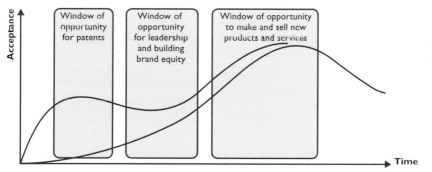

FIG. 3
Additional window of opportunity resulting from managing the awareness gap[6]

What Philips considers vital is the acknowledgement that the really new content of the medium can only be created when the new medium is used. Going back to the McLuhan example, we believe that there was no way to predict what would be broadcast on television until people realized there was no added value in merely filming radio broadcasts. The significance of the car only started to emerge when its horsepower increased well beyond what real horses could provide. The real application of wireless technologies like Zigbee, wearable electronics, real-time content tagging, face recognition, speech recognition and increased processing power will only become clear when products and applications begin to emerge on the markets. Only then will people be able to see what the benefits of these new products and their applications can be.

I-PRONTO

STREAMIUM

CDS

Q4 PLUGGED

HICS

LIME
AND PL@NET

ICD+

Q4 PLUGGED

Managing the organizational impact of a new paradigm

In addition to managing the market's acceptance, we also have to manage the acceptance of people within the organization. Benedict Anderson argues that after any revolution, the body of the old state awaits the hand of its new ruler.[7] For Ambient Intelligence, the revolution is yet to come. In simple terms, beyond the technological community developing a radically new technology to perfection, their organizational surroundings need to come to terms with its impact.

Here, too, the Strategic Innovation Service can play a role, even though it was not designed specifically for this purpose. Exploring user needs enables an organization to picture the people it intends to target. Experience creation, enabling new technologies to be modelled according to people's expectations and behavioural patterns, also helps to educate people inside the organization. The exploration of the future is a great way to revitalize an organization and focus it on the future.

The challenge is not only to bridge the acceptance gap between the inventors/consumers and the users/improvers, but also the acceptance gap within the organization between the inventors/consumers (technologists, designers, marketers) and their management. This is especially important in times like these, when managers have to make decisions increasingly quickly, on the basis of new criteria rather than established routines.

Philips has taken some initial steps in this direction. At the highest levels of the organization, a 'one Philips' ideology is being advocated, focusing the key Philips technologies of storage, connectivity and displays towards the vision of Ambient Intelligence, to be realized by 2020. Obvious next steps include 'one Philips' project teams, communicating the lessons learnt throughout the organization to increase the momentum within Philips.

The realization that the acceptance gap can be bridged in dialogues with both the market-place and internal decision-makers allows a number of practices to become increasingly orchestrated. Because of the more established ground on which the design and technology marketing efforts rest, new ways to turn new technologies into real experiences can be more easily realized. What is more difficult is the adoption of improvements to constitute real dialogue between inventors/consumers (technologists, designers and marketers) and managers whose responsibilities traditionally do not include investing in a revolution. However, Philips has already taken some steps towards creating the right environment for this.

Conclusion

The earliest consumer electronics paradigm was that of the 'empty world'. People lived in a home, lit by a light bulb. Gradually, Philips helped bring the world to people, through audio and then through video technologies. The modern household, with a number of radios and TVs, has not changed much since the 1950s. For decades, mass-marketing practices functioned perfectly, positioning mass communication as a linear transmission model in which people were simply presented with an option that they would gladly accept (or were unable to resist). Adoption was also a linear process, one of diffusion via communication-as-transmission.

Ambient Intelligence recognizes that the world is no longer empty. The adoption ratio of radios and televisions lies well above one per household across most of modernized society. There is no need for more TVs, radios, remotes or even light bulbs. These are not what people want, but what they already have.

Ambient Intelligence represents an entirely new paradigm for the consumer electronics industry. We believe that this opens up new opportunities to renew perspectives on innovation and to centre it on momentum management and experience creation. What we have tried to make clear is that, particularly in technology companies, innovation and communication are increasingly inextricably linked on the route to success. The acceptance gaps between inventors/consumers and users/improvers, and between revolutionaries and managers, need to be bridged. This can only be done by exploring the new; and the new can only be explored by creating it. Ambient Intelligence will only happen if we make it happen.

1 Output of discussions during a joint project between Philips Lighting, Philips Design and Philips Research
2 Henk DeVries, Direct Communication, Philips Semiconductors.
3 M. McLuhan and Q. Fiore, *The Medium is the Massage* (New York, Bantam, 1967)
4 E.M. Rogers, *Diffusion of Innovation* (New York, Free Press, 1995)
5 J. Dewey, *Experience and Nature* (New York, Dover, 1958), 179
6 Philips Design
7 B. Anderson, *Imagined Communities* (London, Verso, 1991)

I-PRONTO

STREAMIUM

CDS

Q4 PLUGGED

HICS

LIME
AND PL@NET

ICD+

7.3 THE QUESTION OF DESIGN

Steven Kyffin

If we were able to take as the finest allegory of simulation the Borges tale where the cartographers of the Empire draw up a map so detailed that it ends up exactly covering the territory... then this fable has come full circle for us, and now has nothing but the discrete charm of second order simulacra... It is the generation by models of a real without origin or reality... [1]

Jean Baudrillard

Revising the role of design

As the immaterial world becomes increasingly important, design must reinterpret its role in the context of Ambient Intelligence. Design has long been the mediator between the natural, artificial and commercial worlds, concerning itself with the interdependencies of people, habitats, technology and commerce, while simultaneously exploring its own meaning, purpose and future. As our post-electronic information culture reaches a new level of maturity, a period of questioning begins; with emergent answers that only time will prove to be appropriate or valuable.

How will design make sense of an ambient intelligent world? Through experimentation, exploration and testing of the opportunities and territories of expression presented by the mix of emerging technologies and cultural development. These new opportunities reveal themselves between the physical, the digital and the linguistic domains on the one hand, and, on the other, the swirling relationships generated by the continuous flux of multiple identities becoming one.

A changing discipline

As a commercial discipline, design was born into a world whose corporate attributes included the production of stand-alone products and services, a world in which differentiation was achieved through innovation and brand communications culminating in large and complex brand architectures. Design must now respond to an economic model which supports the provision of converged and connected solutions, combining products and services to suit individual needs. Here, differentiation is achieved by providing the right customer experience. Traditionally, design was exploited to create or reinforce product distinctiveness; now, distinction is created through the declaration of values, aligning all an enterprise's activities on many levels. The results place design in a position to extract and embrace true customer insights gained across all points of contact.

Once the province of craftspeople, design subsequently interpreted the world of mass manufacture and then mass personalization. Eventually, it will concern itself with the design of the immaterial as well as the purely material. The previous manifestations of design were concerned with the physical realm, in which we could easily identify the designer. The new challenges we face concern the non-physical (the idea, the meaning, the content, the other) and the changing identity of the notion of 'designer', which now also includes the owner, the user, the participant and others. All the stakeholders are not only involved, but are also essential contributors to the future sustainability of our world. This is taking place within a society which demands greater intelligence from products and services, and is changing its abilities through demographic shifts, communications systems, healthcare and travel. This society is becoming sensitive to the needs of and responsibilities for the local environment, enabling people to organize how they create things and the resources they use in the process. Design has become one of the fundamental disciplines of our time.

Reinterpreting the world?

As designers, we no longer design merely 'stuff'; instead, we are increasingly becoming proactive builders of our respective cultures. We must therefore respond to and understand a cultural platform rather than a merely technological one. By responding to and participating in this cultural platform, we will enrich the cultural qualities of human experience and expression at an artistic rather than a purely functional level.

In giving social significance to and deriving meaning from new materials and technologies, design has always concerned itself with the relationship between the world of ideas and the material world through which those ideas are expressed. Over the coming decades, immense technological advances and our need to express and respond to more abstract ideas and behavioural possibilities, provided by the increased use of computers and the 'information' explosion they bring, mean that the once familiar linear, problem-solving and creative processes inherited from the physical, representational world of mechanics and electronic 'black boxes' will limit our ability to respond. We must seek out new creative processes to interpret and represent these emerging technologies and cultural values.

It is clear when we think of architecture, a particularly mature discipline, that the best work is produced by architects with their own scale of values, which are, of course, different from those of the property developer. If the architect shares the values of the developer, he or she will produce 'property developer architecture' rather than works of value. How then can we expect good design to come from designers who share the values of the industrialist, whose only responsibility is to make a return on shareholder capital?

Design must therefore set about reinterpreting the language and values – the mindset – of the emerging world. This is not only because the new advanced technologies demand a broader and more abstract approach, but also because the emergence of such challenges to the established orders as new forms of socio-political, economic and environmental awareness, sustainability and the current major geopolitical changes, are demanding a complete rethink of innovation, production, marketing and delivery throughout the industrial value chain.

It will not be enough for design to provide only competent technical or problem-solving services. As industries worldwide are rethinking their strategies, we must be able to respond and offer the vision and leadership that will shape the product-system-service mix of the 21st century. Design is now charged with unravelling the complexities of digital convergence to reveal 'moments of being', to provide relevant and timely content, and to offer freedom from the potential overloads of the information and knowledge ages.

Not only are we designing the new material aspects of objects, bearing in mind the changing nature of materials at a chemical and physical level, but we are also creating and mediating new levels of relationships, behaviours and the revitalizing of qualities lost over time. These relationships are between our selves and the things we make, and between individual people and between groups of peoples, mediated by those things. We must also begin to consider emerging relationships between the individual things themselves and, most interestingly, the relationships and behaviours between the different networks of things (see Chapter 6.1, Networks, Systems and Society).

Meaningful mediation over time?

As we have now seen, the role of design is to provide meaningful mediation: we see that the objects of mediation, such as the screen or the telephone, have ceased to be the barrier between people and now provide the links between people and the information which surrounds us through a landscape of systemized devices – the hosts of our experience. However it is not difficult to see that very soon a world full of interconnected systematised objects feeding information to everyone all of the time in an unfettered manner will result in technological chaos.

PML

MIMI

POGO

HICS

OPEN TOOLS

LIME
AND PL@NET

Once the society begins its take-off for superindustrialisation, this 'anything goes' policy becomes wholly and hazardously inadequate. Apart from the increased power and scope of technology, the options multiply as well. Advanced technology helps create overchoice with respect to available goods, cultural products, (information) subcults and lifestyles. At the same time overchoice comes to characterise the technology itself.

Faced for the first item with technological overchoice, the society must now select its machines (objects), processes, techniques and systems in groups and clusters, instead of one at a time. It must choose the way as the individual chooses his lifestyle. It must make super-decisions about its future.[2]

Alvin Toffler

This limitless technological possibility within any one object or system faces the designer with three fundamental areas of consideration: (1) the basic role or function of a thing or system and its overall identity; (2) the framework for the behavioural rules of exploration and discovery through use and over time, as these will change the thing or system towards new and enriched roles supporting the user's creative fantasies; and (3) the definition of the behavioural boundaries (or field of liberty) by installing certain development or evolutionary parameters.

As designers, we are therefore moving from a time of hands-on creation of a thing (an archetype) to one in which the initial idea or functional purpose is supported by the potential for becoming something defined and in fact designed and changed as we use it (see Chapter 3.1, Deep Customization). This 'potential for growth' obviously stems from the original and will follow a path informed by its own embedded cultural histories. Thus, the established archetype of form, function and meaning is enabled by its own potential series of 'futures', leading to a widening of the spectrum of user experiences over time. We are coming to a time when no designer, engineer or architect will be able to know the whole system as it grows in all its detail. Although at any time, any piece could be examined, we are creating these pieces fragment by fragment, while still needing to maintain responsibility for the conceptual and increasingly immaterial whole.

New material culture?

A culture built on technological immateriality is emerging, supported by an overloaded, complex and accelerated material world. In this context we must consider how it is possible to give cultural weight and permanence to this plethora of technological applications, banal products and the resulting confusing aesthetic pollution?

The new technologies have led to a redefinition of the concept of 'object'. Those objects, which exist only inside the computer are referred to as 'virtual', and for the time being it is still impossible to give them a physical presence, because there are not yet any materials that conform to their forms. However, these objects do live within the realms of another physicality, a host, so to speak. It is the seamless integration or convergence of the two levels of existence that design needs to begin to reconcile. It is almost possible to make objects halfway between solids and computer-defined surfaces: sponge-like entities which, despite their ill-defined identity, have some level of existence.

In a world of computer-generated multi-modal content and multi-dimensional forms, it is possible for the user to control and transform these into other forms, and to set up behavioural procedures in an almost autonomous way, without the slightest break in continuity. We are seeing that particular interactive mechanisms enable the user to begin to create and develop these 'objects' as they are being used. In this way, not only does the design process affect the nature of the object and system over time, but the creative process is now also directly in the hands of the user, the receiver of the technology, rather than only those of the producer. The user becomes co-producer, building on the possibilities offered by the raw material. So, not only are we beginning the redefine the nature of raw material but also the manner and by whom it is refined and modelled for future use.

Where will design reside?

The consequences of this for design are significant. The question we face is this: in whose hands and minds is the design process to be found: the producers or the consumers of these emerging technologies?

While we consider the role of the designer in this new design process, we must remember that the reality of how we actually use an object or system of objects remains the focus of the designer's attention and should be unaffected by the enabling software systems involved. In fact, the designer and the software capabilities together provide a multitude of possible journeys or activities and routes for development. The designer provides the conditions which shape the interpretation of the system's 'offer', and consequently its meaning. The physical-virtual objects and content elements within and hosting the system are now therefore in an endless state of becoming, caused both by the conditions set up in the initiating design process and by the developing design process acted out by the users over time.

PML

OPEN TOOLS

HIHL

POGO

It is as if these technologies and design processes are again fulfilling the Bauhaus ideals of seeing the object beyond its single physical nature, as part of a vast signifying system of elements that are mutually referential, like words in a language. Perhaps communications theory and linguistics can be used as the referential systems to conceptualize content elements, function, objects and systemic network configurations.

HICS

OPEN TOOLS

The responsibilities of design

Faced with this endless and connected systemic possibility, design's new purpose should therefore be to select, reinforce and give cultural value to a reduced number of technically

LIME
AND PL@NET

feasible opportunities. First, we should focus on reinterpreting the semiotic environment and research the aesthetic-linguistic offering of this 'new materiality' or 'aesthetics of the immaterial'; and second, we should study the emerging nature of the socio-cultural values to which these technologies may respond. To the first, we need to develop languages of material representation that signify the multiplicity of the emerging socio-cultural conditions and for the second we need to identify the new qualities of life to which we can turn our attention and find the significant technologies and advance them within a system of cultural reference.

While exploring how we respond to criteria of quality rather than quantity, we continuously question whether it is still enough for the designer to propose complete (or closed) solutions in such a rapidly changing and complex world. Or would we rather provide the system elements or tools which, when engaged, adapt and emerge with the collaborative behaviour of the user groups, such that their significance and meaning is found through use in a particular experience cycle, rather than as a universal given, pre-formed and predefined as in the past?

Creativity: design and science

Within their creative processes, artists and designers need to switch between and combine many different modes of communication, media, analogies and manufacture. This synthetic approach to creativity and finding ideas requires great flexibility, but it has the benefit of providing the creative process with many tools as the designer gains a better understanding of the project in question. A scientist, on the other hand, applies an analytical approach and is often fluent in a specialism, but can sometimes be constrained by this fluency. Hence, scientists are forced to exclude and eliminate options. Scientists look for and use information. Designers look for and use experience. In this respect, designers are divergent thinkers, whilst scientists are convergent thinkers. A fuller understanding and the exploitation of the inter-dependencies of these two apparently conflicting processes, as presented in this hypothesis, could not only revolutionize the research and exploration of art and science, but also the manner in which engineering and art lead creative innovation within the business development process.

The scientist's background of scientific training is actually very broad in comparison with the specialism that probably encompasses the solution to a given problem. From science, the scientist moves to Chemistry, for instance, and then to the sub-discipline Catalysis, and so on, until the scientific solution is complete. Hence, as time progresses, scientists become more focused, enabling them to exclude certain options, so that the solution can be better defined. However the designer's approach appears very different. Designers focus on their experience of certain fields. From this experience, they explore a number of solution propositions and representations. Consequently, they arrive at a position where a number of solutions are viable and the technological and socio-cultural understanding is high.

The paradox we face is that the designer's path is a complete and intrinsically explorative journey of which the chosen solution is an incremental part, whereas the scientist's path is a journey, ideally as short as possible, during which the solution is the only target and the journey only an inevitable period of development needed to reach it. Both are fruitful, but both are insufficient alone.

New paradigms and processes

Unless we develop and implement alternate design paradigms and creative processes that transcend the existing ones, the natural evolution of the old creative order will be nothing more than a product of the existing process and will therefore be subject to the same flaws and inadequacies as when it responded to the purely mechanical and physical worlds.

Throughout design history, we have been reminded that design was born out of the need to compensate for the absence of art in the forms of industrially produced products. Today, the objects of commercial output are often increasingly immaterial. In the past, it was always material that constrained the representation of ideas. This is no longer the case. With the onset of the immateriality of the output, the medium is now becoming just as important as the idea itself. The representation of our ideas is increasingly occurring through dynamic modes of representation enabled by digital media rather than through the traditional, static semiotic codes. In an ambient intelligent world, responsive and adaptive technologies will simulate and process our reality, feeding it back to us in a constant cycle. As we edit this loop, and as these technologies become embedded in our environment, the distinction between reality and simulation will disappear.

In this context, today's explosive technological changes, coupled with the rapid rate of socio-cultural development, have driven and increased demand for design *per se*. As a result, the responsibilities of design are becoming greater. The changes in modes of visualization and representation effected by digital and eventually ambient intelligent technologies are so great that we have begun to question whether the prevailing notions of communication, consumption and of the meaning of the sign need to be completely re-examined.

The argument is still open as to whether we can conclude that the material and representational possibilities offered by these technologies will only cause decline and confusion within the languages of social significance, or whether they will in fact make it possible for us to realize all our idealized visions in their wonderful simultaneous complexity. Now that almost everything seems possible technologically, we are left asking: what ought we to do? How, as designers, do we drive, interpret and represent the significance of this technological possibility in our cultural lives? This is a great responsibility.

PML

HIML

POGO

HICS

OPEN TOOLS

LIME
AND PL@NET

1   J. Baudrillard, *Selected Writings*, ed. M. Poster (Stanford, Stanford University Press, 1988)
2   A. Toffler, *Future Shock* (New York, Bantam Books, 1970)

7.4 INTRINSIC AND EXTRINSIC INTELLIGENCE

Damian Mycroft

For a list of all the ways technology has failed to improve the quality of life, please press three.

Alice Kahn

When Edison invented the telephone in 1875, it was intended for short messages; no one envisaged that it would be used for conversations. Strangely, the evolution of the telephone into portable wireless devices has come full circle: mobile phone operators report their biggest profits from the runaway success of short text messages. This is just one example of what happens in technology development. Designers and developers imagine how technology can best be used by people, and create product offerings with a set of functions which, in theory, is ideally suited to their needs. When there is some flexibility in how the product can be used, users adapt and change the intended function to suit their requirements better, or to reflect more accurately their socio-cultural aspirations and context.

Clearly, a product whose functionality is 'hardwired', such as a steam iron, offers little opportunity for users to subsume the original functional intent. The user must combine these simpler, more direct product offerings and gather such functional objects around them to best serve their individual needs. Indeed, people have become skilled at arranging, combining, 'jury rigging' and generally bastardizing the intentions of product developers to suit their own ends.

As products have become more interactive, using software to keep their offerings ahead of the competition in an investment-effective way, the user's input to such systems has increased, and the possible permutations of adaptation and customization have grown at a rate that equals Moore's law. Some firms use this adaptation to drive their innovation process. Palm has encouraged a 'market pull' development of new applications for their platform by promoting open architecture and business models. This gradually changes the product archetype of a PDA from organization to connectedness.[1] Palm's strategy, based on keeping 'the simple things simple and the complex things possible', as Director of Software Solutions Ray Combs put it, has balanced a clear product message (whereby purchasers can relate easily to the way the Palm will fit into their lives) with a flexible benefit potential that allows the Palm to grow and adapt with use.

FIG. 1

	Hardwired products	Software products
Features	Specific functions	Flexible benefits
Message	Dedicated solution	Personalized support

Fixed-function products versus software-based products

There are clear business benefits to building flexible software solutions rather than traditional hardwired products. Mass customization has often been touted as an escape from the commodity trap, defending added value by building core competences and outsourcing non-core activities. The strategy of companies such as Palm has been to outsource the customization of products to the end-user. This also helps to build a bond between user and product, and eventually (when the user/product relationship runs smoothly from 'first love' to 'marriage') builds brand loyalty.

For the developers and marketers of such products, there are at least two major areas of difficulty in reaping these benefits. First, where should the developers put their efforts, and where should they draw the line and leave the rest to the user; how can the company best leverage its partnerships and strengths in the market and its overview of technology trends to provide an optimized platform for users to build on? Second, how can marketers communicate the benefits and uniqueness of their offering when it is fundamentally an open tool?

On the one hand, it can be argued that people need some 'hooks', well-recognized attributes, in order to understand, relate to and eventually buy a product. On the other, it seems clear that companies need to find ways for technologies and systems to better support the needs, priorities and lifestyles of individuals.

The intelligence in the system
Where is the intelligence?

On the spectrum ranging from fixed products offering dedicated solutions to flexible platforms offering ultimate flexibility, the answer probably lies somewhere in the middle. However, there is a strong case for increasing the level of intelligence in the system as a whole, not only to provide people with customized solutions, but also to ensure the creative flow which consumers have always had to go through, linking the artifacts surrounding them into systems with meaning and utility, is simple and effective.

With traditional, fixed-function products, the intelligence of the user has taken centre stage in linking and ordering discrete functionalities. From the range of tools used by early man to the average kitchen today, the way that objects are used, stored, shared, adapted and misused speaks volumes about the adaptability and inventiveness of everyday people. The system intelligence can be found in the user in these cases, rather than in the smart networking of technology.

To leverage the user's intelligence, discrete product offerings from a company could therefore build on a commonality of affordances (the black rubber that says 'grip me' in OXO products, or the yellow highlights that say 'hit me' on Stanley products), or the synergies of combining products from a single brand (Sony's memory stick). Alternatively, they could build on more emotional elements, where the combination of a range of the same product offerings enhances the owners' status, as with couture and automotive brands.

Of course, it is also quite common for systems to pass information between each other to adapt to the needs of users. Computer preference settings, Internet cookies and even the smooth handover of address-book information to the telephone mode of a new-generation PDA attest to the possibilities of making tomorrow's experience of technology easier and more enjoyable.

So, Ambient Intelligence, as a concept whereby technologies and product offerings are smartly interconnected to the benefit of a particular user, can be found either in the technology system or in the broader technology-user environment. These different interpretations or aspects of Ambient Intelligence could be called 'intrinsic intelligence' and 'extrinsic intelligence', as summarized in Figure 2.

FIG. 2

Extrinsic intelligence	Intrinsic intelligence
Hardwired products	Software products
Dedicated solution	Personalized support
Flexibility, adaptation and customization are effected by the user (e.g., Leatherman tool)	Flexibility, adaptation and customization are a system parameter (e.g., iPronto)
Expression of known technology and affordances	Application of sophisticated technology and profiling
Leverage intelligence of the user	Leverage intelligence of the technology

What is the benefit?

The benefit of increasing the system intelligence, either within the technological system or by leveraging the user's intelligence, is to better support the needs, priorities and lifestyles of individuals. As individuals, we have rational, functional needs to accomplish particular tasks. We also have emotional needs for self-actualization, self-expression, belonging and a host of 'softer' factors. The increased level of intelligence in the system can provide advantages on both levels.

FIG. 3

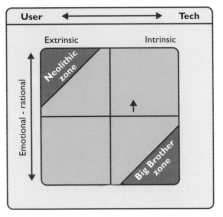

Extrinsic Ambient Intelligence

Emotional benefits

The user's ability to gather and 'connect' products so as to derive emotional benefits is the lifeblood of many western companies. These include brand-led companies such as Nike: the collection of a range of Nike products, and their integration into a consumer's life, builds a statement about that person's values and identity. Of course, the user chooses to collect the items; but their choice is supported by the consistency of the brand message communicated by Nike, which provides the 'glue' linking otherwise disparate products, from clothing to watches and, more recently, to audio products co-developed with Philips. Indeed, design theorists are realizing that the role of the designer is evolving from a focus on designing the end result to a broader definition of design for the experience and interrelationship between people, mediated by objects and organizations.[2]

Functional benefits

When the linking between functional elements of a product or system is in the control of the user, it is important to limit the resulting technical complexity. In the development of the iPronto product for Philips Remote Control Systems, this was certainly the case. Early concepts, in which the intelligence and adaptation to user behaviour was inherent to the product's workings, implied a huge overhead of time and complexity for the software development team. Implementing such concepts also calls for highly intimate joint ventures and the alignment of standards with partners in the value chain, such as service and database providers.

Focus group testing with end-users also revealed a deep-seated mistrust of adaptive products. Consumers questioned in the US felt that a system that tracked their preferences (and especially an Internet-enabled system), posed a risk to personal privacy. The promise that technology could adapt to user behaviour without the intervention of people was not trusted.

The path that was followed in developing the iPronto was to enable the user to adapt the functionality of the product as far as possible, by providing a user interface to use the various applications of the product together in a highly customizable manner. The core applications, i.e., EPG (electronic programme guide), remote control and browser could be arranged on the same screen together, and the set-up of each could be configured by the user and stored on the device. This would allow the user to 'create' a product for movie information, for instance, by setting one browser window to pull up the Internet movie database, and setting the EPG to alert the user about movies coming up tonight on TV. The remote control window would feature movie channels such as Fox, and a second browser window would give updated information on movie times at the local multiplex.

In this case, the intrinsic intelligence is simply a link to a 'Smart Box Management' server, where new services akin to the EPG can be found and downloaded to further enhance the experience.

Carrying Nothing, Interacting Much

Kevin Kelly

Kevin Kelly

Co-founder of Wired magazine, author & member of Global Business Networks

My goal in life is to carry nothing, and to interact much. I want my environment to be smarter than I am, so that I in turn will appear smarter than I really am.

Right now, humans and living things are social beings adrift in a sea of inert materials. What I'd like to be is a human adrift in a sea of social materials. My daily travels should cross an ecology of machines, all alive in their interactions with me and each other. Our built environment should be wild with diversity and adaptation.

Rather than introducing more predictability into our lives, this ambient living technology should introduce more adventure into our lives. Imagine if our toaster remembered who we were, and had a message from our refrigerator about the availability of bread, and was updated with the most recent smarts via the Webmaster, and was repaired by itself, and kept track of my calories, and was in communication with all the other toasters in the world to better itself — why, the world of machines would be liberated at last!

And when my machines are happy, I am happy.

I-PRONTO

Intrinsic Ambient Intelligence

Companies should be sensitive to the issues of trust and acceptance highlighted by the i-Pronto case; related intelligence built into products and systems. They also need to explore how consumers can be made to understand the immediate benefit of purchasing a product with intrinsic intelligence; this understanding is traditionally afforded by clear functions hardwired into the fabric of a product. PDAs are good examples of how the convergence of traditional functions into single products provides functional benefits of greater convenience and accessibility to the ever-increasing quantities of digital information and media surrounding us.

The computing power of such small devices with fairly well-known functionalities such as diary, address book, picture storage, cellular telephony, and limited Web browsing in the case of GPRS, CDMA and other third-generation platforms, makes it possible to transfer relevant data from one application set to another in a relatively smart way.[3]

Whether this is intelligence in the same way that the Turing standard would like to see computers evolve is questionable. One could argue that for functional system intelligence to truly serve the needs of specific users, the emotional aspects of those needs must also be taken into account. While the possibility of systems offering emotional advantages to users is intriguing, we should question what personal details our products may one day discuss among themselves! To quote Glover Ferguson, 'Someday, objects will have wide-ranging and deep conversations with other objects, and their silent form of commerce will be the rule'.[4]

Building new value and new experience

There is a clear opportunity for companies such as Philips to leverage the commonality and compatibility of their products' functions and affordances to increase the role that the user can play in enhancing products. From a branding perspective, the sharing of cultural values between people can also be enhanced by system intelligence.

Ambient Intelligence can be seen as a bridge; a way of connecting the main corporate value drivers of branding and of technology. If we can sensitively synergize the intelligence of the system with the inventiveness of the user, perhaps we can foresee the ultimate marriage of technology and branding, in which the potential for personal expression is realized by a working partnership between consumer and producer – a partnership in which data networks support the need for self-expression.

I-PRONTO

WWICE

STREAMIUM

OPEN TOOLS

1   E. Schonfeld, 'Beating Bill', *Business 2.0* (June 2002)
2   L. Alben, 'Navigating a Sea Change', *Design Management Journal* (Spring 2002), 47
3   A. Marcus and E. Chen, 'Designing the PDA of the Future', *Interactions* (January 2002), 34
4   G. Ferguson, 'Have Your Objects Call My Objects', *Harvard Business Review* (June 2002), 138

7.5 THE NEW BUSINESS LANDSCAPE

Neil Gridley

Our business landscape seems to have changed more rapidly in recent years than ever before. The main drivers of this change include socio-cultural trends (see Chapter 1.1, Thinking the Future), developments in information communication technologies (especially the Internet), digital technologies, democratization, the deregulation of markets, and advances in manufacturing and supply chain management. These factors have led to a number of trends in the increasingly globalized and networked economy.

The networked information and knowledge economy

The above-mentioned drivers have created a more connected world. As a result, business structures are changing, moving away from monolithic, vertical, homogenized institutions towards extremely decentralized, distributed, heterogeneous and flattened organizations – in other words, networks.

A fundamental implication of these changes is a shift in power and value. Both of these can be leveraged through a network of associates in the less tangible marketplace, resulting in smaller and 'lighter' companies. Linux is an interesting example of power through collaboration and co-creation, using a network infrastructure. As Kevin Kelly argues, 'In the networked economy the power of price control moves away from the retailer toward the consumer'.[1] There are signs that a new organizational power is emerging; 'collections of consumers [or customers] with enough combined clout to influence economic direction', to quote Stan Davis and Christopher Meyer.[2]

In this new arena, business models often become more complex and exchanges can be multi-purpose. Money is not necessarily the sole mediator of exchange. The traditional model of buying and selling gives way as economic, informational and emotional tangibles and intangibles are exchanged in many ways and forms.

Value chains are breaking up to reveal 'value Webs' with considerably lower transaction costs, creating a 'reversed' economy in which value lies in abundance, not scarcity. The 'fax effect' comes into play: one fax machine is worth nothing alone, but in a network its value is proportional to the size and relevance of that network.

Convergence through partnerships

Within this networked economy, it is increasingly difficult for companies to provide all of a complex product/system alone. To provide these product/systems within an intelligent network support structure, collaborations are becoming essential and more complex. Businesses are increasingly coming together in partnerships to ensure their survival, sometimes in 'coopetition', and in new business models to create and establish platforms, network standards and mass-market dominance (e.g., VHS, CD, DVD, MPEG, Windows, Java, Linux, Bluetooth, etc.). We can now see several examples of more open systems and strategic architectures that can be adapted and upgraded.

Businesses are also partnering for other reasons – in reaction to converging digital technologies, to add value and innovate by sharing ingredients or providing product/service combinations, and to gain access to new distribution channels. The traditional demarcation between B2C (business-to-consumer) and B2B (business-to-business) enterprises is fading as each finds new markets and business models. It is becoming increasingly hard to determine exactly where one business starts and another ends.

Adaptivity, personalization and co-creation

Business models are shifting to more complex multi-directional exchanges between stakeholders, and in order to receive more personalized solutions, consumers play an increasing role in their design and delivery. The boundaries between customer and provider become blurred, and other roles in the process, such as design, production, supply and marketing, will have to be re-thought.

Today, it is difficult to buy a new car without selecting from a large number of variable options and creating a potentially unique vehicle made to order. Volkswagen uses platform modules to develop its cars, even across brands. Nike enables customers to build their own sports shoes, and Philips offers the iPronto remote control, software-customizable on a number of levels. Nokia became market leader by offering hardware- and software-customizable phones, and Motorola is now planning to challenge this leadership with the 'Motomorph', a personalized phone concept based around a skeleton of hardware.[3] Amazon.com uses available technology to gather personal preferences and information to constantly offer more personally relevant selections and even anticipate likely interests. By paying readers book vouchers for book reviews, used to inform product selection, Amazon is using networks to build multi-way exchanges of economic, informational and emotional value.

Within this trend, 'anytime access' (i.e., making services available to customers when it suits them) is allowing people to be more flexible in managing their lives, particularly for banking, shopping, helpdesks and Internet businesses.

From experiences to transformations

The focus of business is shifting from being product-oriented to being customer-oriented, often by combining products and services to suit customer needs. In developed countries, services already account for 65 to 80% of GDP. This statistic includes the provision of experiences and guiding transformations, which Pine and Gilmore argue are actually distinct categories higher up in 'the progression of economic value'.[4]

Providing experiences is now seen as a key element in building a brand. Across all industries, marketers are refocusing their efforts in this area; half of the world's largest brands are differentiating themselves increasingly through customer experience.[5]

Taking this customer focus to another level, enterprises are moving towards the business of guiding transformations, in which the customer, who aspires to change, is the product, and time plays a key role. Consultancy is a large area of B2B business that is mainly focused on the principle of guiding transformations (although often only delivering a theoretical map). Counsellors and companies like Weight Watchers are relying on this principle in the consumer market. The customer's role in the offering is essential to guiding transformations. Whereas an experience may be memorable and attract the customer to return, guiding a transformation guarantees customer loyalty over a longer period. Transformations are truly personalized to the customer and rely on co-creation.

Challenging commoditization through innovation

More rapid advances in technology, reduced development cycles, improved supply chain management and cheaper global sourcing are accelerating commoditization. Moore's Law still holds true. Businesses now have to anticipate this commoditization and respond on multiple levels, by saving costs, by adding value and by innovating. Saving or managing costs is standard procedure and implicit. Adding value usually involves the constant reorganization and search for product/service differentiation through features.

I-PRONTO

STREAMIUM

Q4 PLUGGED

HICS

OPEN TOOLS

ICD+

Innovation used to mean creating different or completely new product types; but as it becomes increasingly easy to rapidly copy product types, its meaning has evolved. Innovation now often relates to process and knowledge, and not products. As Michael Porter argues, 'a good strategy is concerned with the structural evolution of industry and the firm's own unique position within that industry'.[6] Often, the business models that change a market and possible even reshape an industry are the most successful.

Business competency focus and mega-corporations

In the past, owning and managing the whole supply chain has been a source of business expansion and value-maximization. In a more global networked world, 'companies that grow by selling capabilities they excel at as separate businesses create new sources of competitive advantage',[7] sometimes outsourcing non-core capabilities. (i.e., manufacturing, assembly, logistics, process control, branding, design, finance, etc). In the case of customization, this outsourcing is to the customer.

The finance industry has faced deregulation, and now businesses such as supermarkets and care companies are exploiting their existing customer base and leveraging their financial and marketing competencies to offer credit cards or loans.

The obvious problems in managing an increasing number of complex relationships and partnerships across industries may also lead to an increasing divide in the global market between niche players and entirely new entities which Prabhu Guptara calls 'mega-corporations',[8] which build a chain across industries and can supply a range of cross-sector products and services.

Business loyalty and reassurance

As the Internet and 'infomediaries' provide access to more and more comparative information, consumers become increasingly sophisticated in their shopping behaviour. Switching brands becomes more tempting, and businesses are therefore keen to develop ways to retain loyalty to their company and brand. 'Loyalty schemes' providing customers with bonuses and discounts in return for repeat business and information are prevalent, as in the airline and supermarket industries. Some business partnerships and business models provide discounted or even free products in return for service or network contract buy-in.

It also becomes important for brands to be honest and to communicate real and 'liveable' values. Communicating aspirational values or a cause that drives the brand is becoming commonplace in many consumer markets and this is spreading to B2B markets.[9] The next level could be building a relationship over time based on shared values – co-creating the brand.

Globalization, localization and regulation of business

In today's global market, companies must source inputs, capital and labour globally, and finding new emerging markets in global locations is commonplace. At the same time, the unique critical mass of skill, expertise, suppliers and local institutions make certain locations the innovation centre in a particular business.

In the global village, new organizations, networks and technologies can enable local to global and global to local supply, providing the benefits of capabilities and knowledge from any location. Potentially combining these through global/local partnerships can create more culturally relevant and appropriate solutions. The HiCS project is one attempt to meet this goal.

In reference to the rush of capital into China that affected the value of the Thai baht and influenced the Asian 'crash', Guptara points out that globalization can make us vulnerable to parts of the world we don't know about. There is perhaps an emerging role for governments in regulating the speed and impact of market forces and building more intelligence and sustainability into the system.

Sustainable business

The term 'sustainable' now encompasses what are commonly known as the three Ps: people, profitability and planet. Due to growing pressure from media, consumers, governments and non-governmental organizations, responsible businesses are reporting this 'triple bottom line'. 'Corporate citizenship', the idea that business has a broader societal responsibility, is strengthening with the development of the global economy.

Business must look for solutions that are beneficial in terms of the environment, society and profit. We must shift from thinking of sustainability as a problem to seeing it as an opportunity for innovation, new revenue streams, employee motivation and brand equity. Business has to move from 'end-of-pipe solutions' and 'green products' to new business models based on offering functions and benefits instead of just products; access rather than ownership.

Some companies are already experimenting with these models. Electrolux is supplying 'pay-per-wash' services to 7000 people on a Swedish island. The machine is supplied at installation cost and customers pay according to an itemized bill. At the heart of the initiative is new technology connecting the machine to a central database via smart energy meters in every home.

Ambient intelligent business

Ambient Intelligence has the potential to address each of these trends. In providing personalized, adaptable and pervasive solutions, it will create benefits that are directly relevant to consumers. It also has the potential to support more sustainable solutions and the power to access, through individual, community and global networking, the best and most appropriate information, knowledge and wisdom – in other words, intelligence.

New business models lie in multi-directional economic, informational and emotional transactions through open systems. The co-creation of content, system and brand can develop relationships and revenue streams over longer periods of time that guide transformations and assist in meaningful and relevant solutions.

Perhaps Ambient Intelligence can be applied not only to user/system and system/system relationships but also to the relationships that evolve to supply Ambient Intelligence systems; the combining of stakeholders such as users, businesses, governments and brands.

1 K. Kelly, New Rules for the New Economy: 10 Ways the Network Economy is Changing Everything (London, Viking, 1998)
2 S. Davis and C. Meyer, Blur: The Speed of Change in the Connected Economy (Oxford, Capstone Publishing, 1999)
3 Motorola, 'Motomorph', Brand Republic (25 July 2002)
4 B.J. Pine and J.H. Gilmore, The Experience Economy (Boston, Harvard Business School Press, 1999)
5 Marketing Leadership Council, Report from the Front: Implications of Brand Strategy Shifts on the CMO Mandate (2002)
6 R. Gowan (ed.), Rethinking the Future (London, Nicholas Brealey Publishing, 1996)
7 B. Willen, G. Jonk, N. Bishop and J. Aurik, Rebuilding the Corporate Genome: Unlocking the Real Value of your Business (John Wiley & Sons, 2002)
8 P. Guptara, Life, Work and Careers in the 21st Century (UK, Career Innovation Research Group, 1999)
9 A.T. Steinle, Living in the Electrosphere (UPM-Kymmene Fine Paper, 2000)
10 J. Andriof and M. McIntosh, Corporate Citizenship: what is it and how to assess it? (Warwick Business School, Greenleaf Publishing Ltd, 2001)

7.6 TOWARDS THE LIVING BRAND

THE FOURTH AGE OF BRANDING

August de los Reyes

Divergence and simplicity

As any physicist can tell you, the law of entropy states that in a closed system the amount of chaos increases over time. But what does this principle have to do with brand relationships and Ambient Intelligence? Branding consultants Al and Laura Ries propose the inherent quality of entropy – divergence – as the main thrust of one of their many immutable laws of branding.[1] In nature, things diverge: for example, new species are generally born from a single species, not from the combination of two separate ones. There are several thousand varieties of dogs and several thousand kinds of cats, but no 'dogcats' or 'catdogs'. In talking about the future of products and technology, many mistakenly sing the praises of convergence, whereas in reality technologies also tend to diverge. The telephone has given us mobile phones, wall phones, speakerphones, satellite phones, and so forth; the car has given us sports cars, station wagons, pick-up trucks, buses, tractor-trailers, and vans. However, just because something is possible does not necessarily mean that it is practical: as noted by Ries and Ries, past attempts to develop a mainstream amphibious vehicle have resulted in an apparatus that 'floats like a car and drives like a boat'. And where are all those flying cars?

Ambient Intelligence will bring about a great paradigm shift in branding, a 'fourth age' of branding, if you will. In order to understand the possibilities and potential of brand relationships in Ambient Intelligence, we must keep the principles of divergence and simplicity in mind while exploring the evolutionary paths causing this shift: the paths of the product, the brand and the consumer.

The first age of branding

In the 19th century, you could go to a store and ask for sugar, and it would be measured out of a big barrel into a parcel for you to take home. If you wanted a hammer, you were given a hammer – the one sort of hammer that the store owner happened to stock at the time. Then, with the introduction of mass production, consumers were suddenly given a choice of sugar, hammers and many other commodities. Suddenly, manufacturers had to distinguish themselves from the competition. They had to provide the consumer with reasons to choose their product over those of their competitors. Usually, this distinction was driven by one of two things: the invention of a new technology or a statement of consistent quality associated with that maker. In the case of new technology, invention itself was the clear distinguishing factor, but in the case of the statement of quality, the distinction took the form of the trademark, and so the brand was born. One could say that the brand as trademark was the first age of branding.

The second age

So what was the second age of branding? As more and more choices became available to consumers, even the notions of distinct qualities among products began to blur. To further distinguish one brand from another, companies found themselves applying traits to the brands they maintained. These traits tended to be whatever consumers aspired to be. Depending on a given consumer's aspirations, they could purchase the 'right' set of products, from cars to drinks. These aspirations were further buttressed by the use of celebrities to personify brands. In the late 1940s, the notion of a corporate personality was born, and the use of aspirational values continued for the next 40 years.

I-PRONTO

OPEN TOOLS

STREAMIUM

CDS

Q4 PLUGGED

OPEN TOOLS

ICD+

The third age

Then, in 1988,[2] Philip Morris bought Kraft Foods for $12 billion. On paper, Kraft was only worth $2 billion; what accounted for the other $10 billion was simply the name 'Kraft'. In other words, the brand name was worth many times more than the actual buildings, factories and other forms of physical equity. This sent a clear message to the many markets of the world, and a sort of branding frenzy began. Advertising appeared in public restrooms; whole neighbourhoods became branded spaces; television shows advertised on stickers on fruit at the grocers; concert tickets included perfume testing strips; and so forth.

On 2 April 1993 (a date known in branding circles as 'Marlboro Friday'), Marlboro announced that it would slash its prices 20%, and increase promotional outlays to compete with the so-called bargain brands. This move on the part of the owners of the longest-running advertising campaign in history, 'the Marlboro Man', was astonishing, communicating a message that perhaps brands no longer mattered; perhaps consumers purchased primarily on the basis of price. On that same day, the stock prices of all major household brands dropped, with Philips Morris shares plunging 23%.

As the recession of the 1990s began to dissipate, it became clear that the power of the brand was not dead, but had taken on a new form. Companies which flourished during this period of brand-blindness (e.g., Apple, Calvin Klein, Nike and Starbucks) shared a common element in their approach, an approach which characterizes the third age of branding. These companies had ingrained their brand vision into every aspect of their corporate being. They created their own symbols and languages – their own traditions – all in the name of supporting their brand. What they created were semiotic belief systems. And so we arrive at the current, popular definition of brand: an idea by which people live.

Going back to the law of entropy, several variations of this brand-as-belief-system have appeared in this third age of branding, from the idea of 'lovemarks',[3] espoused by Kevin Roberts, CEO of Saatchi & Saatchi, to cause-related marketing, whereby a brand wraps itself in the trappings of some social cause close to the hearts of its stakeholders. Another interesting and significant development in third-age branding was the *Cluetrain Manifesto*,[4] which stressed the importance of maintaining a dialogue with the consumer. With the introduction of interactive media, maintaining a constant stakeholder dialogue became not only possible, but also practical.

The first five axioms of the Manifesto argue the following: (1) markets are conversations; (2) markets consist of human beings, not demographic sectors; (3) conversations among human beings sound human; they are conducted in a human voice; (4) whether delivering information, opinions, perspectives, dissenting arguments or humorous asides, the human voice is typically open, natural and uncontrived; and (5) people recognize each other as such from the sound of this voice.

Branding in Ambient Intelligence

This continuing dialogue in brand relationships only becomes richer and more human in the culture of Ambient Intelligence. The authors of *Cluetrain* recognized the possibility of bilateral conversation between brand and stakeholder, a conversation prompted by the advent of the Internet. In Ambient Intelligence, such conversations increase exponentially: dialogues between brand, stakeholder, product, environment and behaviour all become possible. The wealth of possibilities also increases for brand relationships themselves, including product-to-product and even environment-to-environment relationships. However, let's not forget: simply because something is possible does not make it practical.

Ensuring the practicality of any brand effort in Ambient Intelligence means safeguarding the human qualities in any given system. But should these qualities come from the system itself? Is instilling these properties even possible? Possible, yes, but from a branding perspective, largely impractical. In *The New Marketing Manifesto*,[5] John Grant paraphrases R. Buckminster Fuller in pointing out that people cannot be taught new ways of thinking, but can only be provided with the tools as if they were thinking in the new manner.

ICD+

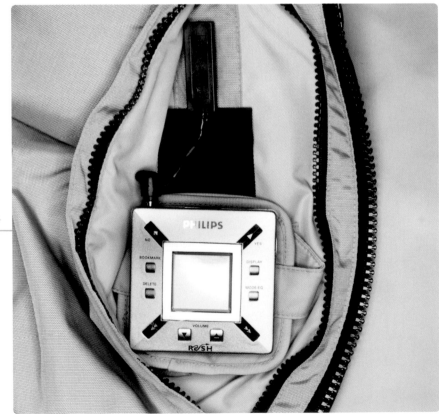

What does this mean for the designers of ambient intelligent systems and for the crafters of the brands behind them? In Chapter 7.3, The Question of Design, Steven Kyffin points out that in Ambient Intelligence, the identity of the designer will grow to include the owner, the user and all other stakeholders in the brand experience. Even the creation of the brand itself must involve the entire range of participants in varying degrees. While designers are providing tools for thinking in a new manner, 'branders' must shift from developing and communicating brands as belief systems towards providing practical and human responses in the emerging brand manifestations of Ambient Intelligence.

The fourth age

This shift will herald the fourth age of branding. Brands will transcend belief systems and become living ideas that are transformed by people, while they transform people's lives. For the developers of brands, an interesting challenge arises: how does one manage living ideas? As third-age branding strategies have diverged into manifold value systems, in the fourth age, a brand will be able to enrich the lives of its stakeholders in meaningful and human ways, and in as many ways as there are stakeholders. Ambient Intelligence will make this fourth age possible and – we hope – practical.

I-PRONTO

STREAMIUM

CDS

Q4 PLUGGED

OPEN TOOLS

ICD+

1   A. Ries and L. Ries, *The 22 Immutable Laws of Branding* (New York, HarperCollins, 1998)
2   N. Klein, *No Logo* (London, HarperCollins, 2000)
3   http://www.lovemarks.com
4   C. Locke and R. Levine, *The Cluetrain Manifesto: The End of Business as Usual* (Cambridge MA, Perseus Books, 2000)
5   J. Grant, *The New Marketing Manifesto* (London, Orion, 1999)

7.7 AMBIENT INTELLIGENCE AND THE CLIMATE FOR BRANDING

Reon Brand, Marco Bevolo

Societal foundations

The unfolding postmodern idiom in technologically advanced societies has already created a foundation for deploying solutions based on the Ambient Intelligence vision. Whereas in 'westernized' countries societal values used to be based on rationalism, objectivity, Newtonian perspectives on science, productivity, materialism and the ideal of linear progress towards a utopian world of material abundance, this has changed substantially since World War II. Postmodern ideals have shifted from the ideas of industriousness and material ownership towards the acceptance of subjective ambiguity, access, playfulness, experience and the resurgence of metaphysical aspects such as emotions, spirituality and the rediscovery of meaning.

As we consider this shift in societal values, it becomes clear that many of our technology-based foundations and logistics are still deeply rooted in the modernist idiom. The challenge for companies in the context of Ambient Intelligence is to understand that they cannot simply rely on creativity and technological possibility to successfully deliver ambient intelligent solutions. They first need to understand the socio-cultural context. .

Society and technology: an ambivalent relationship

Many studies have demonstrated that modernism, despite its unparalleled technological and economical progress, is not a sustainable path for society and the environment. The negative side-effects of modernism include alienation between humankind and nature, growing social inequality and dissociation from technology.

Trailing his fingers along the edge of an incomprehensible computer bank he reached out and pressed an invitingly large red button on a nearby panel. The panel lit up with the words 'Please do not press this button again.'

The Hitchhiker's Guide to the Galaxy

The challenge for players delivering Ambient Intelligence solutions will be to influence and renegotiate the contract between technology and society by providing access to more seamless solutions in a sustainable, meaningful, culturally relevant and socially ethical way.

Today, technology has already become pervasive in so-called 'advanced' societies. Most of our productive hours are spent interacting with a plethora of devices acquired in the hope that they will simplify our lives and help us to cope, perform and relax better. Instead, they rudely interrupt us and demand our attention. In creating a climate in which Ambient Intelligence will flourish, the challenge is to turn this around, so that technology begins to dynamically learn about us and adapt to us. Ambient Intelligence has probably the most potential to restore society's faith in the role of technology and put us back on a more human-focused, sustainable pathway. The question is how high-tech companies and their brands can proactively contribute to achieving this.

Getting the fundamentals right

First, we must consider Ambient Intelligence from a much wider perspective than just the new functionality that it will bring to people. We have to think of how it must be shaped to comply with our value systems, daily rhythms and personal desires, our temporal, cultural and societal contexts. None of the fundamental aspects necessary to achieve this vision should be taken for granted; each intermediate step needs to be based on a deeper understanding of human values and aspirations. Even a definition of what intelligence is becomes a crucial starting point in truly living up to this vision.

The concept of intelligence in western society is still based on the IQ system developed around 1900. This system primarily gives an indication of our spatial, logical and verbal capabilities. It misses a number of important areas that make up our total intelligence, such as emotional, intuitive and spiritual intelligence. We tend to value that part of intelligence that makes good computers, but overlook the part that makes us uniquely and completely human. It is now widely accepted that in our global and networked era, emotional intelligence (EQ) and even spiritual intelligence (SQ) are as important as IQ, if not more. For Ambient Intelligence solutions to enable our lives to be more meaningful and balanced, we have to understand, envision and develop intelligent interaction on all of these levels.

How to know what people will value

To understand what people will value in future, we cannot simply ask them now. We must gain insight into the deeper dynamics of a culture or society by understanding its underlying mechanisms, values, history, relationships and aspirations. We need to understand the latent global values that are emerging in different societies and cultures.

Through a combination of global and regional research, it is possible to identify a number of key human needs for the future. We can envision a future in which people will increasingly need affordable access to technology that meets personal preferences, cultural context and societal values. Connectivity will be key, but will have to be delivered with true respect for social norms and protocol. Increasing awareness and concern about the privacy and security of personal information will require effective and simple solutions. In our information overloaded society, people will need to manage their access to knowledge and information more effectively and intuitively. We will increasingly look beyond mere functionality, in search of rich, memorable, multi-sensorial experiences. Finally, people will increasingly look for meaning and balance, in search of greater harmony. Understanding such emerging values and needs, and having insight into their momentum and cultural nuances forms a solid foundation for Ambient Intelligence.

A paradigm change in branding

Brands aiming to succeed in this environment will have to focus on two levels to expose their audiences to the total brand experience. On a micro-level, brands will have to engage in a direct interaction, and on the macro-level, they will have to inspire people about their belief systems while co-creating the shared philosophies and the new ways necessary to enliven the Ambient Intelligence proposition in a meaningful way.

The hours are good… but now you come to mention it, most of the actual minutes are pretty lousy.[1]
The Hitchhiker's Guide to the Galaxy

Micro-level

At the micro-level are the moments when people experience technology. We must make this micro-interaction as seamless and as enticing as possible. There is a great need for 'smart' technology that can reduce the complexity and mundanity of our micro-tasks. An important consideration is how to develop the potential and ability to personalize the brand relationship

ICD+

with individuals. The first 'smart software' examples are available on the Internet, but we are still far from making these interactions emotionally intelligent, highly personalized and believable.

The micro-level will represent the front line of the battle for brand presence in the Ambient Intelligence arena. While Ambient Intelligence will simplify the user experience, it will introduce a new level of complexity in brand management. If part of the vision is for objects to disappear into the surroundings, how will brands manifest themselves? A further dilution of brand presence comes about as companies increasingly have to cooperate and deliver co-branded, multi-branded or ingredient-branded solutions. In future, it may even become difficult for brands to choose their co-brand partners, as users will increasingly have the power to concoct their own brand mixes to create the solutions they need. Brands that do not mix well will be left out of the cocktail. In such a confusing kaleidoscope of brand pollution, it will become harder for brands to make a lasting impact and achieve a distinctive, memorable positioning.

But there will need to be more to branding than micro-branding. People will demand more than entertaining distraction, convenience and performance from brands. To think it is enough for Ambient Intelligence to take care of our chores and be a personalized assistant may be to miss a substantial part of what the vision has to offer. In the long term, we are all looking for what makes our lives meaningful.

Macro-level
The great Spanish cellist and humanist Pablo Casals once said that the capacity to care is what gives life its deepest meaning and significance. On the macro-level, a brand should

demonstrate in authentic ways that it understands and cares about the values and needs of its customers. It needs strategies to move from initial awareness towards inspiring its customers to form relevant long-term relationships and to share ownership. Successful macro-level branding turns customers into ambassadors and (dare we suggest) disciples.

It will become more important than ever for brands to find new effective ways to communicate and share their core beliefs effectively with all their stakeholders. Many brands today are still very marketing- and product-focused, and most of their customers recognize them only through their products and logo. With the dematerialization of tangible products, a shift of focus in brand communication clearly has to follow.

One interesting way to build a brand on the macro-level will be to actively and intimately involve stakeholders in the development, deployment and evolution of its vision. Take the evolution of the computer programming language Linux, which has almost become a religion for some. This is because Linux is literally co-created by a community of people. Each of these stakeholders has contributed a small amount of intellectual DNA to shape and evolve both the brand narrative and the product specifications, to the benefit of all. Although in this example the 'congregation' is mainly an elitist group of programmers, the principle remains very interesting. Current Philips responses to such societal stimuli include the i-Pronto universal remote control and the Nexperia Silicon System Platform. These are both examples of open-architecture technology empowering users to co-create solutions according to their specific needs.

The power of the iPronto lies in its 'open tool' approach and is found in the daily interactions between fans engaged in Web communities. Here the product is co-defined in its software possibilities by people who enjoy the co-creation of a platform of their own. This makes it a winning proposition beyond its technical qualities, because it plays a special role as the social engine of a highly involved community. The brand shines in the absence of any overpowering branding techniques. The Nexperia platform is a so-called 'future-proof', open software/hardware architecture, positioned on the chip market as a cutting-edge 'architecture of flexibility'. This means that manufacturers, service providers and content developers can rely on a new level of versatility for developing uniquely customized propositions. This potentially translates into the kernel of a cross-category business-to-business community, co-designing a range of versatile benefits. Nexperia has the quality of an open tool because co-creative cooperation is embedded in the fundamentals of its proposition.

Conclusion

Can we empower and inspire our audiences to buy into the principle of becoming co-owners through co-design? Can we engage people in a dialogue to develop applications of their own for the benefit of all? Achieving this would clearly create the ideal climate to embed the brand at a deeper level of societal presence. To prepare for the future context of Ambient Intelligence, companies aiming to be relevant as a brand will have to engage in soul-searching, finding those unique paths and propositions that lead to a dynamic, inspirational personality based on authentic principles and a socially relevant, culturally shared vision.

1   D. Adams, *The Hitchhiker's Guide to the Galaxy* (New York, Harmony Books, 1979)

7.8 MARKETING AND BRANDING FOR SUCCESS
HOW A GENTLE TECHNOLOGY REVOLUTION WILL IMPACT MARKETING MODELS AND PRACTICES

Marco Bevolo, Cees Jan Mol

A rebirth of marketing

The Ambient Intelligence vision paints a picture of a future in which people will be empowered by meaningfully interactive environments, and benefits will be available on demand. We will be able to invest both operationally and emotionally in our tools and environments, moulding them to our needs. Hyper-customization might even end alienation: because the act of purchasing will be fragmented in a myriad of micro-transactions, the sense of alienation embedded in decision-making when significant consumer budgets are at stake will be replaced by a permanent sense of relief.

This will ostensibly be the 'apotheosis' of 'transitive design', as described by Clino Castelli.[1] The transitional relationship between man and artifact will be expanded to all of our environments, from the home to the office and from public spaces to connected wearables. Should this vision become the daily reality of 2020, Ambient Intelligence can be expected to revolutionize marketing by delivering new models exclusively focused on 'pulling' through highly personalized contact points, instead of 'pushing' through traditional media as in traditional models.

Ambient Intelligence will have an impact on more than just devices. Media content will increasingly be articulated through innovative formats, from static, passive-fruition models to engaging, co-created entertainment. In a number of recent experiences, semiotic rules have been stretched beyond narrative conventions. One example of this is the cross-media success story of the cult movie, *The Blair Witch Project*. In the near future, we can even expect media-channelled content to incorporate 'software features', becoming increasingly HTML-like. Old rules will slowly cease to be valid, and the classic set of tools in an organization's marketing mix will no longer be effective. From taglines to electronic tagging, retail and marketing communication will blur in immanent, dynamic brand narratives.

Al and Laura Ries predict the end of advertising and the rise of PR.[2] Is viral marketing the future of marketing? Defined by Faith Popcorn as 'the Holy Grail of Internet marketing',[3] this tool leverages the oldest and yet most complex channel – word of mouth – magnified by electronic facilitation. The social construction of reality will increasingly embed a commercial presence, implying not only huge marketing opportunities, but also worrying ethical risks.

The marketing value of technology architectures

The Ambient Intelligence high-tech artifact goes beyond the stereotypical paradigm of the 'black box with a logo': its essence is the 'engine' of those invisible architectures underpinning omnipresent content and enabling us to experience it. This will imply a shift from classic marketing to a new design ability to motivate people to 'pull' experience from the system interfaces at any moment. The Living Memory (LiMe) project and its follow-up, Pl@net, are perfect examples of such a shift. Aiming to understand how technology could enable social bonding, LiMe included an ethnographic study defining the working mechanisms of collective memory in European towns. The results were translated into a sophisticated technological architecture, encompassing intellectual property management tools and proprietary software. This translation is exactly how the technology architecture can evolve and migrate into the artifact enabling the generation and circulation of cultural meaning. If we consider marketing as a technique to motivate people to engage in transactions through the micro-branding and communication of potential benefits in a culturally meaningful way, this opens a whole new territory to explore.

The cultural value attached to the Linux brand, for example, is both the result and the basis of its unique positioning. The Linux open source architecture is both a technical blueprint and a cultural statement. The 'open source operating system' positioning is in the very essence of how the system was designed, managed and distributed from its early days, as a student project. The marketing proposition stems from and is one with the technology/architecture. This can be expected in future Ambient Intelligence success stories. Technology architectures will be the necessary (although invisible) platforms governing the circulation of content, its delivery formats, and ultimately enabling the generation of shared meaning.

Visions for a new marketing foundation

In the Ambient Intelligence context, high-tech companies will focus on empowering and servicing end-users through integrated systems. Applications will provide the necessary differentiation, and will be powered by technology/architectures. The marketing management function will be fundamentally redefined. Marketing will have to interface with technology portfolio management at early stages of the business creation process. In summary, technology portfolio management will be the basis of all marketing strategies. The new 'marketing kernel' will lie in the core of the high-tech enterprise. The positioning of invisible artifacts and interfaces will become unified.

The entire value chain will essentially be redesigned. From an organizational perspective, we can envision a new synthesis of corporate bodies that today operate in separation. Brand management will be key in providing dynamic identity to a shared and vital company narrative, a necessary *raison d'être*. The power of this narrative will unfold through viral marketing techniques, both internally and externally.

Process quality management will be required to facilitate and validate the integrity of a new, complex and fuzzy value chain. Quality approaches such as the European Foundation for Quality Management, deployed within Philips as BEST (Business Excellence through Speed and Teamwork) will develop into a natural, organic toolkit to support daily operational practices.

From technology pillars to experience solutions

The Ambient Intelligence vision is based on Philips' ability to deliver high-tech excellence in its three key domains – displays, connectivity and storage – together with a unique insight into human needs. Displays (the interface between users and digital content and services), connectivity (the enabler of seamless, pervasive and omnipresent access) and storage (the ability to allocate, relocate and manipulate digital content) are key to pursuing an ambient intelligent future. But other relevant technology assets (e.g., power management) are equally indispensable, offering huge opportunities for truly sustainable applications. Sensing capabilities enable physical environments to digitally detect and proactively react. Processing hardware and software provide fundamental functions, and research into materials and the identification of shared standards are mission-critical areas. Nevertheless, excelling in each pillar is not enough to be a winner in the world of Ambient Intelligence.

In Chapter 7.11 Competitive Cooperation, Karin Daly explores new business partnerships necessary in the context of Ambient Intelligence. In synthesis, cross-category partners will join forces to co-deliver experiences re-affirming their positioning. Business players will not need mere technologies, neither at the mainstream, component level, nor at the level of consortia of co-designed open architectures. Instead, business players will need application-focused toolkits, complete in their technical features, bringing meaningful technology to audiences at the right time. This will result in more integrated value chain management, avoiding the risk of dividing the portfolio between star technologies (those with a 'wow' effect, but which are not feasible in isolation) and mainstream technologies (less exciting but necessary to enable Ambient Intelligence). With the Ambient Intelligence vision as a reference point, we can sketch an experience toolkit solutions portfolio. This would be clustered, for example, in pillars enabling content management and context awareness in the appropriate 'smart' fashion. Interfacing and interconnecting could both be enabled in a seamless manner by further potential application toolkits. Reassurance about privacy and digital safety could be another crucial area in which high-tech companies could think up new supportive solutions. Software, consulting skills and the ability to envision the future will be necessary ingredients. This would be one way to leverage existing assets, integrating the efforts of scientists, designers, marketers, managers and engineers through the filter of what business partners and end-users actually need.

Revolutionizing customer relationship management

The growing number of products, standards, services, players in the market and their separate positions in the value chain will cause current business models to become unmanageably complex. This complexity might be successfully tamed in two ways: through a 'pre-fab' approach and through a new partnership behaviour. The pre-fab approach, consisting of producing smaller parts intended to fit into a bigger architecture, has been trickling down successfully in the semiconductors industry. This is the world of Silicon System Platforms and Nexperia. This approach increases uncertainty in the initial adoption phase when potential partners evaluate the specific architecture. Once the architecture has been decided, virtual integration can be expected to strengthen the relationship further into a true, structural partnership.

The management of these new relationships is the next Client Relation Management (CRM) challenge on the radar. The Hollywood studio model still seems to hold valid as a reference, with cultural entrepreneurs like Robert Redford starring in management essays. 'Momentum management', the ability to maintain complex relationships over time and at the appropriate level of intensity, will be crucial. Key account management will be a critical, digitally enabled core capability for high-tech enterprises. This new approach to CRM will itself be enabled by 'always-on' digital tools informed by the Ambient Intelligence vision, as depicted in the PI@net project. Partners will exchange value beyond financial terms, leading to a shift from Internet, intranet and extranet virtual facilities towards '24/7/365' 'anynet' networks. Web domains will no longer be seen as separated entities, and all 'whatever-nets' will offer access points to knowledge exchange and transaction opportunities. Shared ownership of elements added to the network will be perceived as a shift towards a better dialogue rather than as intrusions. With new media connecting people across vast distances, cultural understanding will be increasingly important.

A new ethical positioning for new marketing practice

An integrated system approach will allow us to look at the whole enterprise from a totally new perspective. Branding becomes the carrier of the company vision in its effort to connect the user, the business partners and the company audiences. Marketing and viral communication opportunities are available (and actually unavoidable) all across the value chain, from R&D to waste management. In the wider context of Ambient Intelligence, marketing could aim to be both one of the facilitating functions and a means of supporting the company's long-term vision.

For Philips, marketing can only be strongly related to a new ethic of being, doing and performing. From the early days of the 'Let's make things better.' strategic principle, the need for a strong drive towards a more sustainable world has permeated Philips. Ambient Intelligence is just a door opening on new possibilities. In Chapter 7.1 The Sustainability of Ambient Intelligence, Simona Rocchi explores the theme of how companies can shift the focus of business to the 3 Ps of People, Planet and Performance, in search of a higher sustainability standard. In the journey to Ambient Intelligence, marketing will hopefully evolve to provide the necessary tactical tools and strategic practices to achieve this goal.

1   C.T. Castelli, *Transitive Design* (Milan, Electa, 2000)
2   A. Ries and L. Ries, *The Fall of Advertising and the Rise of PR* (New York, HarperCollins Business, 2002)
3   F. Popcorn and A. Hanft, *Dictionary of the Future* (New York, Hyperion, 2001)

7.9 SELLING WEARABLES

Clive van Heerden

Expanding into a new area of business: a case study

Ambient Intelligence will require companies to form partnerships with companies active in unfamiliar fields. As everything in our environment becomes 'smart', makers of 'traditional' products (many of which, like tables and chairs, have arguably not seen any really radical renewal for centuries) will increasingly be moving into unfamiliar territory and working with electronics companies. And, of course, this necessity and unfamiliarity will apply just as strongly to the electronics companies. What sort of problems will they come up against? What benefits can they look forward to? How will they work together? Over the past few years, Philips has been making exploratory moves towards the fashion and clothing industry to develop 'wearables', clothing in which electronic devices and circuits are integrated. Just a few of the issues we encountered are described below.

Protection – and the lack of it

Leadership in the electronics industry is largely based on the successful protection of innovative intellectual property, specifically technologies and processes. Philips, for example, owns some 60,000 patents, fiercely defending them when necessary. Copying is deemed to be unacceptable within the industry. Within the textile industry (and related fields such as fashion and home, car and airliner interiors and furnishings), a completely different ethos exists. Although leaders in this field invest huge sums in developing complex fibres, which are then processed into yarns for specific applications in woven and knitted textiles, the industry is driven by quickly capitalizing on new innovations. Copying is accepted as a way of life: by making only slight modifications in composition or structure, companies can copy functionality without infringing any patents or copyrights. Even major brands engage in this practice, and it hardly seems to affect business relations between 'copier' and 'copiee'. In fact, it is impossible to keep ahead in the industry unless you engage in perpetual innovation and change.

One of the very few companies that have managed to secure technical leadership through material innovation and defend their technologies by legal means is Gore, with its Gore-tex technology. But during the five years of the patent, many other textile companies were already busy developing cheaper, more efficient versions of the same technology to flood the market the minute it was legally possible.

This means that as electronics and textiles move closer together we will need to find ways of achieving a return on the investment made in developing and manufacturing soft electronic components. New common parameters of acceptable practice will need to be defined. Inevitably, new yarns and fabric constructions will need to be patented, but applying the protections common in electronic manufacturing to this new domain will be a challenge.

Different cycles, different speeds

The two industries differ considerably, too, when it comes to the complexity of their manufacturing and distribution processes. Current electronics displays and MP3 players are not made on looms or knitting machines, and the technology of embedding electronics into fabric is new territory for consumer electronics companies. The rate of innovation and the structure of the product cycles in the textile industry also differ dramatically from those in the consumer electronics industry. A consumer electronics company may bring out a new phone once a year, with a typical production cycle of three years. The textile industry,

by contrast, produces new product lines two to four times a year; and today, thanks to offshore production, many companies manage to have 'modified' copies of designer clothes in the stores before the designers themselves have the originals out of their own workshops. The two industries will need to find a modus vivendi that accommodates or resolves the different speeds of their markets.

Partnering

Partnerships will be needed at many levels – R&D, procurement, manufacturing and distribution. Industry leaders, forming a 'soft technology consortium' will need to be involved at each stage of the process. These parties will include companies that are either already working with conductive textiles or who are capable of making the transition between the worlds of 'hard' and 'soft'. In practice, these consortiums are likely to be very fluid. Membership may vary depending on the stage of the development process and on the type of product involved.

Finding a natural fit between companies (i.e., where they have complementary core activities and a common interest in expanding into new product territory) will involve matching business cultures and combining brands in innovative ways. Market opportunities are based on brand credibility and established penetration, so the partners also need to be compatible on this score. It is in this light that one can view Philips' recent alliance with Nike, in the field of personal audio and infotainment. On the broader front, a company like Philips in fact needs two kinds of partner: high-volume partners (such as Nike), with the power to establish new markets and with enormous credibility in large markets; and small, niche leadership brands that will enable them, by association, to cross over into previously uncharted territory.

Changing consumer perceptions

How will consumers react to the idea of wearables? What will they think when they read the washing instructions? After all, we have learned from childhood that water and electricity don't mix; and the idea of washing your personal audio or mobile phone is on a par with the urban myths of little old ladies putting cats in microwave ovens to dry. In other words, people will need to get used to seeing a brand name like Philips in unusual places. Washing is only one novel aspect: we shall be partnering with companies who deal with all the stages in the life of a garment – from polymers to fabric-finishing processes, from the washing basket to the wardrobe. Creating a natural association between the Philips brand and products that are currently the preserve of apparel or textile brands will involve the gradual education of consumers to accept our presence through association.

The process

The areas in which wearables and intelligent fibres are most likely to be adopted first include apparel, automotive interiors, home furnishings and interiors, workstations and medical monitoring. At Philips we have assembled a team of scientists and engineers and fashion and textile designers to work on the basic technologies involved in the 'soft-hard merger' and develop preliminary concepts. It was their work which resulted in the New Nomads concepts and ultimately developed into the Philips-Levi's collaboration for ICD+.

To identify new joint business opportunities, we combine insights from our partners' knowledge of their market, technology forecasts and the analysis of sociocultural trends. On the basis of these trends, we work out what people's concerns, interests and lifestyles will be like in a few years' time. Our technology forecasts indicate what technologies will be available then, and our partners' market knowledge indicates what will be commercially viable or a gap in the market. This narrows the field down, and within that field we develop concepts that combine different technical functionalities to meet projected social and personal needs. These are then filtered down to one, which becomes a 'beacon' project with which we test the water.

Creating a beacon like this allows us to work backwards and identify achievable product materializations in shorter timeframes. Suppose our beacon objective is to integrate a flexible display into many different types of clothing during the coming decade; and suppose, too, that we know that the best technical solution will not be ready for five or six years. What we can do in the meantime is identify different technical solutions as temporary 'placeholders' until such time as the preferred technology is available. In this way, we can produce solutions that will grow new markets, facilitate consumer acceptance and encourage product familiarity – all before the arrival of the technology itself.

Revenues

'Fashion dictates' – whatever fashion decrees, we do. Certainly, the fashion business is very effective in making consumers want ever-changing styles, regardless of price. With luxury price points determined by consumer desire rather than manufacturing cost, the clothing, textile and fashion industries can command margins that other sectors can only view with envy. By contrast, the electronics industry is faced with perpetual price erosion. It is obvious, therefore, that combining soft, electronic 'componentry' with clothing offers the electronics industry the promise of greater returns, and demonstrates that co-developing the required materials, operating systems and setting the industry standards can have strategic importance and lead to benefits along the whole product chain.

In addition, by combining electronic functionalities with apparel, we can create systems involving several products, which can lead to potentially enormous follow-on sales. For instance, an electronic device that will work with several items of clothing will generate more revenue than a single-item device. And if services are linked in as well, then the potential return is even greater.

Learning curve

We will shortly witness a great upheaval in the manufacturing industry: all sorts of 'traditional' products will start hosting Ambient Intelligence and join with others in an intricate network, not only within the home, but outside it, too. Companies will learn to work with partners from other, quite unfamiliar, fields. Differences in industrial and corporate cultures and processes, differences in market understanding, differences in pricing and positioning — all these (and more) will need to be resolved. Philips and its partners to date have taken the first steps in the process. It is a sharp learning curve for all, but the effort is worth the reward: new business opportunities that promise to enhance people's lives significantly.

7.10 A NEW CULTURE OF MARKETING

RETHINKING THE BUSINESS BETWEEN CUSTOMER AND BUSINESS

Marco Bevolo, Reon Brand

The end of consumers, the rise of users

Within the new marketing paradigm of Ambient Intelligence, 'targeting consumers' will become an outdated concept. Marketing will need to be redefined, as consumers as we know them cease to exist. The increasing focus on information will blur the distinction between cultural and commercial consumption, and because holistic, ongoing relationships will be the only option for companies, tactics and strategies will merge in the management of long-term dialogues.

This does not imply a world of unexciting, fluid quietness, almost boring in its perfect 'user-centred' implementation. On the contrary, the human factor might be the crucial asset in a potential revival of what Stephen Brown calls 'retro marketing',[1] perfectly suitable for viral marketing success. Stimulating users to tell others about things, generating and managing networks of 'buzz', and playing on the whole spectrum of human emotions will be key.

Nevertheless, difficulties may lie in how to present the general Ambient Intelligence proposition to consumers. Closing the gap between innovators, early adopters and the necessary mainstream audiences (what the Chiat/Day agency defined as: 'the rest of us' in a highly memorable advertising campaign for Apple in the late 1970s) will be no easy task. This is because Ambient Intelligence implies a fundamentally different consumption model, asking customers and consumers to invest heavily, both emotionally and financially, in new domestic infrastructures, new product service mixes and ultimately totally new brand belief systems. This is a much bigger step than moving from VHS to DVD; it is closer to switching from horse-drawn carriages to 'horsepower' trucks. How can high-tech companies and business players at large facilitate this complex transition?

A viable approach might be to first prove the benefits of the Ambient Intelligence proposition in the context of public buildings and spaces. This would expose the benefits to a wide and diverse group of people, while minimizing the investment required from them. It could also offer governments, institutions and corporations the opportunity to brand themselves by adhering to the exciting Ambient Intelligence proposition.

This approach has worked before. In the 1950s, in Italy, the telephone was an exclusive 'high-tech application' and was not affordable to the masses. People were nevertheless exposed to its advantages in their offices and in public environments. This extensive presence ultimately determined the acceptance of the technology: after a few years of making phone calls at the office, people simply adopted the device as a necessary commodity in their home environment. The chasm was crossed.[2] Similarly, Ambient Intelligence business operators will have to focus on culturally meaningful applications, not only because of a natural desire to give intangible technology tangible benefits, but also because of the magnitude of the consumer marketing challenge for Ambient Intelligence.

Partnerships

Partnerships with real estate companies, building management operators and governmental agencies might be key in a first phase, when early adopters will increasingly play the role of evangelists for Ambient Intelligence as a philosophy and as a source of benefits. In parallel, major cross-category brands might introduce ambient intelligent solutions in their portfolios, acting as portals to more early adopters, and leveraging and re-affirming their premium positioning. From this foothold, 'early majority' consumers will start to buy into the Ambient Intelligence proposition. The branding of the technology solutions provider should enable the necessary continuity from endorsing the 'portal brands' in the first phase to offering the newly connected interfaces and software updates. The molecular approach to the growing complexity of brand architectures, as proposed by Hill and Lederer, will prove to be one of the possible tools required to manage the vertigo of brand extension potential.[3] Addressing the end-user through highly innovative, newly co-branded solutions may lead to completely new business models.

Semiotics applied to marketing: the key to new simplicity

The semiotician C.S. Peirce[4] drew a distinction between 'type' and 'token' that may be of use in this new approach to marketing. A semantic 'token' is socially built and related to its form by a number of necessary (but not objectively determined) links. A 'type' exists in abstract as the ideal, Platonic model derived from the semantic recurrence of all 'tokens'. In traditional marketing, the logo on the object works as a 'token', designed to represent the synthesis of the brand positioning. It has to be culturally relevant, memorable and distinctive across all media to generate the necessary awareness and reactions. In the distributed, augmented space of Ambient Intelligence, brands will be manifested by anticipatory avatars, omnipresent 'types' offering users the constant power to translate them into preferred, concrete 'tokens'. Users will proactively shape the relationship with the provider within, behind and beyond the avatar, resulting in the explosion of 'distinction', the individual differentiating factor of our current social systems of taste, lifestyle and their symbolic expression, as analysed by Pierre Bourdieu. One day in 2020, the explosion of individual 'distinction' will remind us of the current data explosion. Looking back in amused fulfilment, we will be charmed by memories of the age of keyboards, consumers and old marketing conventions

I-PRONTO

STREAMIUM

Q4 PLUGGED

HICS

OPEN TOOLS

ICD+

1   S. Brown, 'Torment Your Customers', Harvard Business Review (October 2001)
2   G.A. Moore, Crossing the Chasm (New York, Harper Perennial, 1991)
3   S. Hill and C. Lederer, The Infinite Asset (Boston, Harvard Business Press, 2001)
4   See G.P. Caprettini, Aspetti della Semiotica (Turin, Einaudi, 1980)

7.11 COMPETITIVE COOPERATION

WHY THE AMBIENT INTELLIGENT COMPANY MUST EMBRACE PARTNERSHIPS

Karin Daly

The ambitious mission of Ambient Intelligence is to create meaningful technologies that improve people's lives. It would be arrogant and unrealistic for any one company to think it can or should achieve that mission alone. The ubiquitous relationship with technology within Ambient Intelligence will call for business partnerships that go beyond simply embracing common standards and platforms. This will require us to understand the value that can be derived from combining and recombining assets from two or more entities, and translating the resulting value into consumer benefits and trust.

Ambient Intelligence will create the impetus for a movement towards partnerships, signalling a new definition of innovation and a new means for companies to create value, to become 'ambient intelligent companies'.

Historically, companies succeeded by focusing on and excelling at one thing, as in the oil, steel or artisanal industries. A generation later, the concept of synergy was in vogue, whereby conglomerates looked up and down the value chain and tried to own as much of it as possible: Ford owned a rubber-making facility for tyres, for example. Today, businesses look to downsizing and outsourcing: if you can't excel at a particular thing, buy it from someone else.[1,2] In the Ambient Intelligence future, we will re-think the concept of synergy; not within companies, but between them, in networks and partnerships.

This era will bring about a new way of doing business. Not only will we have to understand how people interact with each other, with objects and with technology, but we will also need to forge a new conception of how organizations must interact with each other in the creation of these partnerships and networks. The most successful technology companies will understand that the only way to be competitive is to be cooperative.

Brand trust

The premise and the promise of Ambient Intelligence (i.e., the seamless linking of devices and services in our environment) demands partnerships and strong networking between companies. Consumers and customers simply will not tolerate anything less than a turnkey approach, and will want to work only with companies they trust to accomplish this complex technological requirement.

In a report in June 2002, Forrester Research warned that 'a single viewpoint of a consumer's entire technology portfolio and how the devices in that portfolio interconnect, must be shared by all concerned'.[3] The report argues that while open standards for interconnection are key as a starting point, the future of interconnected devices lies with partnerships between technology brands that bring complementary technology competence and – even more importantly – brand trust.

Technology companies that already have this trust, such as Philips, Sony and Siemens, must leverage it through co-branding partnerships that bring consumers the ambient intelligent interconnectivity they will demand.

Partnership benefits

Ambient intelligent companies will derive a variety of benefits from collaborating, including the following:

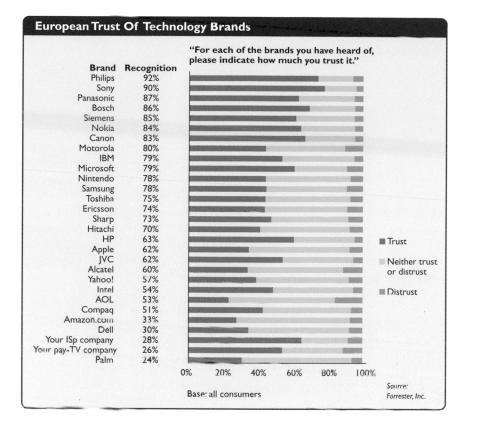

European Trust Of Technology Brands

"For each of the brands you have heard of, please indicate how much you trust it."

Brand	Recognition
Philips	92%
Sony	90%
Panasonic	87%
Bosch	86%
Siemens	85%
Nokia	84%
Canon	83%
Motorola	80%
IBM	79%
Microsoft	79%
Nintendo	78%
Samsung	78%
Toshiba	75%
Ericsson	74%
Sharp	73%
Hitachi	70%
HP	63%
Apple	62%
JVC	62%
Alcatel	60%
Yahoo!	57%
Intel	54%
AOL	53%
Compaq	51%
Amazon.com	33%
Dell	30%
Your ISp company	28%
Your pay-TV company	26%
Palm	24%

■ Trust
Neither trust or distrust
■ Distrust

0% 20% 40% 60% 80% 100%

Base: all consumers

Source: Forrester, Inc.

Leveraging the assets of all of the enterprise

Conglomerates in particular can benefit from the synergy that becoming an ambient intelligent company entails. This includes maximizing the use of intellectual property that currently might be unused, as well as invigorating collaboration between business units.[1]

Creating value by recombining assets

Partnerships can drive innovation (and vice versa), and create new avenues of growth for the ambient intelligent company.

Creating brand value for ingredients

Many of the component parts of Ambient Intelligence will be developed in networks, consortiums and partnerships. In the past, this might have been relegated to an anonymous OEM (Original Equipment Manufacturer) role. These crucial ingredients will demand to be branded, with resulting value creation.

Sharing risk in new markets

Like any technology revolution, Ambient Intelligence may stumble and fail a few times before it truly takes off. The ambient intelligent company recognizes that partnering can offset some of the financial and other risks inherent in making this transition.

A wider brand authority trajectory

If the partnership is between brands in different categories, it can extend the area that a brand is allowed to cover, providing the authority to enter new markets and pursue new targets.

I-PRONTO

STREAMIUM

Q4 PLUGGED

HICS

OPEN TOOLS

ICD+

B+B2C: a value-generating equation

Companies are traditionally classed as either B2C (business to consumer) or B2B (business to business). The new paradigm of partnerships that Ambient Intelligence brings could be referred to as B+B2C (business plus business to consumer). This new equation suggests that neither type of company alone could create the specific value and consumer proposition that the two (or more) of them could generate together. It allows for extension into new categories or segments that neither partner could access as effectively alone.

Examples of this burgeoning partnership equation already exist. Nike and Philips recently came together to leverage their expertise in technology and sport to develop sporting apparel that combines communications, connectivity and information to motivate athletic performance. Ericsson seems an early convert to the importance of technology partnerships, partnering with Sony to create SonyEricsson in order to access additional value in a difficult mobile phone market by combining their assets. Ericsson and Electrolux formed a joint venture in 1999 to develop the concept of the networked home; the Screenfridge was the first product in this area. Intel was also one of the first to recognize the value of partnerships and to leverage trust with the end consumer: partnerships are the lifeblood of Intel, and it has become even more vital to its partners through its strong relationships with various divisions (R&D, Marketing, etc.) within the partner organizations.

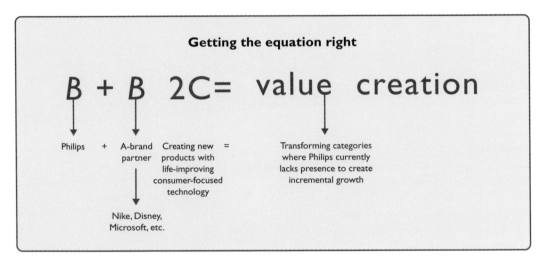

FIG. 2
Getting the equation right

Innovation and the art of recombination

The Ambient Intelligence company is fundamentally an innovative enterprise. Yet, like all companies, it may face obstacles to its ability to innovate and to generate growth. It is estimated that a 'normal' company utilizes only 5-15% of its intellectual capital. Under-utilized assets cause inefficiency, a 'brain drain' syndrome, and are at odds with the premise of sustainability. One method of fighting this problem is recombination.[4]

Innovation guru Gary Hamel talks of recombining resources to generate value, scrutinizing a company's assets, competencies and processes separately, and then combining and recombining them in different ways.[4] This can happen within firms, but is perhaps most effective as an innovation driver and new value creator if the exercise is done between companies and even industries.

Is your brand a key asset? What about your business model? Perhaps you have a tremendous amount of under-utilized intellectual property, or your customer service or logistics are highly regarded. Combining your resources with another's can be a tremendous source of new value creation and is crucial to the Ambient Intelligence company.

It seems many companies suffer from 'business unit blinders': once assigned to a business unit silo, people begin to perceive the overall business in a very limited way. Recombination allows you to look at your business with a 'the parts are greater than the whole' lens, and explore how you could combine current assets to develop benefit-driven, value-creating partnerships.

Companies that understand that innovation means recombining assets in new and value-generating way include Amgen, one of the most profitable firms in the Fortune 1000. Its core business is essentially hunting down technologies and sciences and repurposing them to sell to other players. Another example is Philips, which had long made coffee makers in a stagnating market. Douwe Egberts was looking for a new way to sell coffee with higher margins and increased loyalty. Putting two and two together in the hope of creating at least five, they partnered to create Senseo, a new kind of coffee maker that creates high-quality cups of coffee with a 'crema layer' and requires specially formulated coffee in high-margin custom-made pads. Customers in the Benelux test markets couldn't get enough; demand outstripped supply for both the appliance and the coffee pads.

Home Depot, a US DIY store, is a master at recombination. The company has partnered with Toys 'R' Us to create branded tool toys, with GE Capital to offer on-the-spot home improvement loans in-store, and with local handymen to provide assistance to customers who just don't have the time or skills to 'DIY'[4].

Getting to 'I do'

Successful partnerships in this new paradigm can come about in many ways: by identifying an unmet consumer need; validating a trend foreseen; creating technological intellectual property; recombining assets; or through brand strength and 'stretch'. Companies that have invested in understanding consumers, their relationship with technology, and future trends, will have an advantage in forging and steering partnerships in the ambient intelligent future.

Prenuptial screening

In this new age, firms that have found the keys to successful 'business dating and marriage' will be the ones that flourish. These relationships might last only as long as the joint project, or they could become almost marriage-like, and even produce entirely new companies and brands. The importance of a clear 'prenuptial agreement' and an exit strategy cannot be underestimated. The current rate of failure of joint ventures is far worse than the divorce rate: 7 out of 10 fail to meet the objectives of the partner companies and are disbanded. In an era of cooperation, the Ambient Intelligence company must look for new means of screening potential partners to ensure the marriage lasts.

I-PRONTO

STREAMIUM

Q4 PLUGGED

Q4 PLUGGED

Roomchair

HICS

OPEN TOOLS

ICD+

Philips uses a screening device that measures 'fit' from a strategic, operational, cultural, organizational, human and brand perspective. Both partners are rated on 14 measures within these areas to determine overall compatibility. Ambient Intelligence firms must conduct due diligence in vetting potential partners to ensure success, offset risk and maintain consumer trust.

When brands meet

The business of branding used to be easy. We burned our initials on a cow to show ownership, engraved our coat of arms on our shield to denote heritage, or stamped a symbol on pottery to denote its origin. But when boxes no longer exist, technology is embedded and invisible, and companies partner with others, how can a brand make itself known? How can a company receive credit for its contribution? How can multiple brands be combined in one concept?[5]

Branding will have to change, and new rules will have to be developed. There will be an interesting struggle to determine who will brand (and therefore control) the user interface: with technology disappearing and becoming distributed and embedded, both the user interface and system behaviours will determine the relationship with the user. Companies with significant expertise in this area are well-poised to have a strong and relevant brand in the Ambient Intelligence era.

I-PRONTO

Questions and considerations

Finding the right combination of assets and possible partners and leveraging the potential value this could create will be the hallmark of a successful Ambient Intelligence company. As we move forward, companies seeking to become players in the Ambient Intelligence world will have to face key issues:

Structure: What will an Ambient Intelligence company look like? How can it stay fluid enough to capitalize on partnerships without losing structure and governance? How can partnerships be designed for speed to market?

Culture:	How can we develop a culture of innovation and creativity and drive the cooperation necessary for Ambient Intelligence partnerships?
Knowledge transfer:	How can we take the knowledge embedded in our company, and convert the latent intellectual capital into value? How can this happen between companies?
Attractiveness:	What can we do to make our company attractive to the partners that will help us to gain advantage?
Values:	Does our company embrace the values necessary for Ambient Intelligence such as cooperation, sustainability and entrepreneurship?

Gary Hamel has asserted that in the last one hundred years of the 'age of progress', wealth has been a function of time, diligence and knowledge.[6] Now we look to wealth as a function of 'creativity, connectivity and courage' – words that also define an ambient intelligent company. The most important question remains: Are we ready?

I-PRONTO

STREAMIUM

Q4 PLUGGED

HICS

OPEN TOOLS

1 A. Campbell and M. Goold, *The Collaborative Enterprise* (Cambridge MA, Perseus Books, 1998)
2 J. Ridderstrale and K. Nordstrum, *Funky Business* (Stockholm, Bookhouse Publishing, 2000)
3 P. Jackson, 'Europe's Multidevice Brand Battle' (Forrester Research, June 2002)
4 G. Hamel, Innovation Academy (London, Gloucester Hotel, 24-25 April 2002)
5 G. Hankinson and P. Cowing, *The Reality of Global Brands* (Maidenhead, McGraw Hill, 1996)
6 G. Hamel, *Leading the Revolution* (Boston, Harvard Business School Press, 2000)

ICD+

FIRST STEPS

The issues, approaches and challenges addressed throughout this book are currently being explored in a number of practical projects led by Philips Design and Philips Research. These projects give life to some of the key ideas and principles behind Ambient Intelligence.

Within the boundaries of ethical considerations, these projects try to take account of people's fundamental motivations – what it is that makes us human – while responding to the interests and concerns of the various societies we live in. Ideally, concepts such as these should not only make our lives easier, but should also improve the very quality of our experience. By giving their concepts tangible form, designers and technologists can engage in a relevant and meaningful dialogue with future users, opinion leaders and experts to incorporate new insights and to adjust their course.

For the reader's convenience, each project has been given a particular colour. That colour appears in the margin of each page dealing with relevant technologies and techniques, and allows the reader to select topics of interest at a glance.

8.1 NEBULA

A VIRTUAL/PHYSICAL EXPERIENCE FOR BEDTIME

Noah's Ark was a Design Research & Development project that formed the first step towards establishing a Centre for Applied Experience Design Research at Philips Design. Over the course of 11 weeks, six designers worked together with seven students in three different teams. The teams' objectives were to research, design and produce something that would advance Philips Design's knowledge and understanding of experience design, and enhance their ability to communicate it. The teams explored three general areas: the virtual/physical, the sensorial and the spatial/environmental.

The purpose of Noah's Ark was not to define 'standard' experiences for people to have, but to design multi-sensory stimuli from which people could create their *own* meaningful experiences — either to enjoy alone, or to share with others. The focus was on people and on time in the context of the experience. Nebula, Garden and Aurora are thee concepts that emerged from the project.

Nebula is an interactive projection system designed to enrich the experience of going to bed, sleeping and waking up. It provides an intuitive and natural way of physically participating in a virtual experience, through simple body movements and gestures. The aim is to create an atmosphere in the bedroom that encourages and enhances rest, reflection, conversation, intimacy, imagination and play.

Nebula consists of a ceiling projector linked via the Internet to a database of content. Once you have selected the content for projection, you can manipulate it simply by adjusting your sleeping positions and interacting with your partner while in bed. For example, one algorithm in the system translates body positions and movements into moving imagery and text. Since the dynamics between individuals are random and unpredictable, the flow of content created by you and your partner will be unique and specific to you. In general, the ceiling projection becomes livelier as you become more active...

Pebbles

To select content, you place a smart 'pebble' into the bedside pocket. Each pebble represents a different topic or theme. For example, a 'cloud' pebble produces content related to clouds and the sky, while a 'poem' pebble produces content related to poetry and rhymes. The content also changes according to the time of day and the season. For example, a cloud pebble will trigger a dark sky when viewed at night, but produces a bright, blue sky during the day.

Alarm and time

Once the alarm clock is set, the system projects two dots onto opposite sides of the ceiling. During the night, the distance between the dots diminishes, visually illustrating the time remaining before the alarm goes off. If you wake up in the night, you can easily gauge time left till morning from the distance left between the two. When the dots collide, sound and images are combined to create an appropriate waking experience.

Message and drawings

You can also incorporate your own messages and drawings into the projections. Simply write a note or sketch something on a piece of paper and place it underneath the alarm clock. When the alarm goes off, a snapshot of the note or illustration will be projected.

Games

Pebbles can also contain games, such as ping-pong. These will only be revealed when you and your partner have assumed a particular combination of sleeping positions. Once the positions have been discovered and the game is revealed, you can activate the game at any time by holding the top section of the duvet cover. Pulling the duvet to the left or right controls the left and right movements in the game.

www.design.philips.com/smartconnections/nebula

8.2 GARDEN

A SENSORIAL EXPERIENCE FOR BUSY TRAVELLERS

Garden is a collective work of art created by and for public transport users as they travel the underground system. Each traveller (or 'tuber') is represented in the work as a virtual flower. As the flowers begin to grow and multiply, a whole community of otherwise anonymous travellers is depicted as a virtual garden. Day by day, the actions of the tubers cause the garden to grow, creating a shared experience.

Fluid

The landscape and flowers in the garden consist of pieces of information relevant to the underground environment: poetry, train schedules, advertisements and announcements all combine in a fluid, graphical manner to create the garden. This flow of information continues in other parts of the underground: corridors, escalators, platforms and carriages – all places where people can retrieve and experience it in different ways

From ordeal to experience

Travelling by public transport, whether as a commuter or as a tourist, can often be a daunting and somewhat unpleasant experience. You're often squashed together with a group of complete strangers, reducing what should be an enjoyable experience to an anonymous ordeal.

Alone – or together?

Garden capitalizes on this anonymity and tries to use it to build a community. It is a twofold attempt to stimulate a sense of self – a deeper sense of individuality and responsibility – and a sense of community – shared involvement in a project with other tubers. The idea is that change and growth in the garden will help to alleviate the repetitive routine and discomforts of public transport and make it once again a pleasant experience.

8.3 AURORA

A SPATIAL/ENVIRONMENTAL EXPERIENCE
TO LIGHT UP YOUR LIFE

Aurora is an interactive light surface for the home. It enables you to draw and erase with light over the entire surface of a wall. Aurora comes in rolls and can be fixed to the wall like wallpaper. A specially designed skirting board connects the strips electrically, creating a large interactive wall surface.

Tracing patterns in light

Use your finger as paintbrush: Aurora lights up wherever you touch it. Touch the same point again and the light will disappear. Draw a circle or loop and it will fill with light. At the end of each day, the wall will display the traces of light left behind by everyone who has interacted with it. The wall can be cleared by means of a reset button, located on the skirting board.

Creating a new home ambience

Aurora has considerable potential within the home. It can be used as a means of communication: just leave a light message scribbled on the wall. It can also be an endless source of fun and games: sketch with light, or play games, like Hangman or Noughts and Crosses. What if you want to read? You can vary the properties of the light, switching it from ambient lighting to direct lighting, even spotlighting. And for decorative effects, just play with the intensity and colour of the light. By using light of different colours with drawing or stencilling patterns, you can quickly create a new ambience in your home.

8.4 I-PRONTO

One of the cornerstones of Ambient Intelligence is the concept that products can adapt, communicating with other products to share functionalities, while becoming customized to the specific practical and emotional needs of the people who use them. This is perfectly illustrated by i-Pronto, which began as a remote control concept for a home entertainment system in the early 1990s. Today it is capable of 'communicating', adapting and evolving in new, unprecedented ways to suit people's wishes, needs and tastes even better.

Beyond stand-alone

The challenge with i-Pronto was to build in the intelligence that would allow it to change its functions as influenced by the user, and set up an ambient interconnection of functionality beyond the stand-alone product. The aim was to create a space where people would be able to use several entertainment-related consumer-electronic applications all at the same time. The core of i-Pronto is a 'dashboard'. This allows you to configure and combine the applications (electronic programme guide (EPG), Pronto remote control and browser). The resulting personalized 'layouts' are stored in the device.

These 'layouts' are effectively user-defined software products. To create a movie-information appliance, for instance, you can set one browser window to pull up the Internet movie

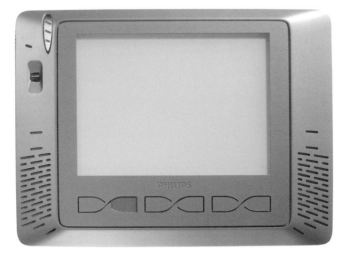

database, and set the EPG to alert you to movies coming up on TV tonight; the remote-control window can provide details of subscription movie channels; and a second browser window can give you up-to-date information about your local cinemas.

Ultimate customization

i-Pronto allows you to download new remote control functionalities, create sequences of commands to automatically run installation and start-up procedures, and create or configure graphics and icons to suit your tastes. Websites such as www.remotecentral.com host thousands of set-up files and even new applications made by users, which are shared among a growing community. Developments like this take i-Pronto's capability for achieving ultimate customization even further.

Building on the concept of the Pronto community, the i-Pronto is also linked by a back-end server to a database of i-Pronto updates (e.g., the EPG application), which also allows upgrading to new applications. But it is really the user's own intelligence that is at the centre of the experience, guiding and directing the functionality of the device using relatively simple and independent applications. i-Pronto is one of the first products to grow beyond hard-wired, stand-alone functionality to become a commercially viable enabler of a rich, personal and highly adaptive experience.

www.pronto.philips.com

8.5 HOMELAB

WHERE IT'S ALL ALREADY HAPPENING

Before Ambient Intelligence becomes an everyday reality, considerable research will be needed into its practical implementation in ordinary homes. What technical problems have to be overcome, and what objections from users need to be resolved? Philips has set up a special observation home, called HomeLab, in which multi-disciplinary teams of researchers can try out technologies in realistic settings and observe people using Ambient Intelligence in normal home surroundings.

The Home
The Home itself is a two-storey house with a living room, a kitchen, two bedrooms, a bathroom and a study. It looks like a normal family home. Only the small black domes in the ceilings concealing cameras and microphones give the game away.

The Lab
The Lab, next door, has two observation rooms from which researchers can watch what is going on in the Home via two-way mirrors and video cameras. The main one looks on to the living room, the other, upstairs, looks on to the bathroom, so that researchers can watch people shaving, drying their hair or cleaning their teeth. The two-way mirrors here can be turned into 'smart mirrors', which enable people to check the news, traffic situation or even their weight...

Here are just some of the problems that can be investigated in HomeLab.

Where are you?
Radio and ultrasound waves can locate us in ideal conditions. But in the home, furniture and people moving around complicate normal reflection and transmission.

Speak up!
We can talk to our Ambient Intelligence system. But echoes and background noise can prevent the system from hearing us clearly.

Are you pointing at me?
Video recognition of gestures is possible in good lighting conditions. But a door opening or closing, someone walking around, reflections from shiny surfaces and changing light conditions can all cause problems.

Mind your own wavelength
We will want our information or entertainment wherever we want in the home. Portable devices that can be used anywhere in the house require 'ad hoc' wireless networks. Quite likely, several systems on the same frequency band will be used. How do we solve problems of mutual interference or the influence of walls and ceilings?

You've got to hide your ... away
Ambient Intelligence technologies will be largely hidden. But many issues emerge when you try to hide everything away in practice. The Home has all the potentially problematic elements found in a real house (e.g., walls that block the infrared beam of a remote control), while the adjacent location of the Lab means that it is possible to simulate Ambient Intelligence applications in the Home next door, ahead of the time when sufficient miniaturization will have been achieved.

Quality of experience
How will people use their Ambient Intelligence? How will they use the interfaces? Which will they prefer? Will they want certain aspects of their Ambient Intelligence to be visible? The only way to answer these and the many more questions that will arise as Ambient Intelligence evolves is through iterative processes of testing, observation and refinement. HomeLab provides a unique environment that will allow us not only to examine individual issues but also to investigate people's overall experience of Ambient Intelligence – because ultimately it is the quality of that experience that will be the touchstone of success.

8.6 PHENOM

As the amount of information and entertainment we have access to increases, there is a rapidly growing need for intelligent systems that will help us find the right content instantly at any time or place. PHENOM explores how Perceptive Home Environments can help us easily find or browse through valuable personal memories, and enjoy sharing them with others.

View digital photos anywhere

We all make significant efforts to record our memories, increasingly in the form of digital photos. The PHENOM system aims to take the effort out of retrieving photos by facilitating easy access to them anywhere in the house. The photos (or other relevant data) are stored on the home server (PC hard disk or other storage device). This is wirelessly connected to a portable touch screen ('Sepia'), which we can, for instance, use to retrieve the photos while sitting comfortably on the couch in the living room.

Choose your screen

The interface of the Sepia has a continuously moving 'photo roll', showing thumbnails of the albums and photos stored on the server. The photos can be viewed on the Sepia using simple drag-and-drop gestures. Thanks to an in-home positioning system, the interface will also automatically show icons that indicate which screens (e.g., TV or photo frame) are available in the particular room we are in. We can then drag photos to these icons for immediate viewing on the relevant screen.

Natural associations

We can also get instant access to particular photos or photo albums by picking a relevant object in the room – say, a holiday souvenir – and placing it on a table or other surface that is fitted with a detection loop. Thanks to a small radio frequency identity tag attached to the object, the detection loop will allow its identity and location to be determined. An icon of the object then appears in the interface and also the photos associated with the object.

Showing and sharing

Besides providing a wireless interface to photos on a central storage device, the Sepia also has a storage buffer of its own. As a result, people can take a number of photos with them when they leave the house, or download photos from other Sepia owners, for instance. A special data management system called 'Memory Safe' is being developed to handle file conflicts that may emerge in such multi-user, multi-device systems (e.g., when copies on different devices are re-synchronized after having been renamed or otherwise modified).

Future versions of PHENOM will include a conversational interface that will allow less structured searching and new features that will make the memory-sharing experiences even richer.

www.project-phenom.info

8.7 WWICE

THE EXPERIENCE OF BEING CONNECTED

Ambient Intelligence is based on the concept of networks. Many people already access the enormous network known as the Internet from home, but they will soon also have their own in-house network. Then, in-home systems, driven by broadband always-on Internet, will offer consumers many exciting new opportunities. In a project called WWICE2, we examined how the goals of Ambient Intelligence could be furthered in this way, exploring new functions, new interaction concepts for those functions and the underlying system architectures required to implement them. The outcome is a working prototype currently installed in Philips Research's HomeLab.

Spaces – for meeting people

In the real world, people gather to interact socially at physical locations. Thanks to network technologies, we can now meet and share experiences 'virtually'. In WWICE2, the concept of virtual 'spaces' is designed to make this easier. In your space you can share things with other group members, adding content that they can access anywhere in the world. With real-time video-conferencing, you can also 'meet'. You can even undertake joint activities, combining synchronized experience of content with personal contact via video-conferencing.

A system for spaces

The WWICE2 system overcomes two key problems:

- Since people will be using many different devices (e.g., TVs, PDAs or Web tablets), the system needs to cope with this heterogeneity without bothering the user. If you choose to watch the news at 8 p.m., an Application Management subsystem selects the right source (e.g., satellite or the Internet), and starts the right application, depending on the decoders, bandwidth and interaction devices available. A User Interface subsystem arranges for the application to present its user interface in a device-independent way, so that you see it normally on the device of your choosing.

- Sharing information in your space with people outside your home essentially means others can access your system. You need to be sure only authorized people are 'allowed in'. To take account of this, proxies (similar to firewall proxies) check the access rights of anyone trying to enter.

Keep on moving

As we carry our portable devices around, we want to experience content in the best way available wherever we are (e.g., on the best screen nearest to us). We also want to enjoy the content without interruption. If you are listening to music on speakers in your living room, controlling it with your PDA, and you then go out to the car, you would like to continue listening. We therefore developed the concept of 'linking'. In our system, each room operates as a coherent set of devices, so that you can interact with the room as a whole. Bring a portable screen within viewing and listening distance of a stationary set of devices (e.g., a big screen and loudspeakers) and you will be asked whether you would like to view the same content on the big screen. If you say yes, the portable screen becomes part of that room's devices, and you can transfer activities from the screen to the set and vice versa, controlling everything from your portable device.

A system for linking

A system that enables linking will need to need to know which devices are within range of each other and who is near which device. Sensors, location technologies and video, in combination with context awareness sub-systems establish precise locations and identities.

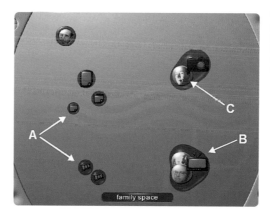

Your family space, showing some items of content (A), a shared activity (B), and another member engaged in an activity (C)

Watching a movie together in a friend's space

8.8 STREAMIUM

Streamium is the world's first micro hi-fi system that offers one-button access to personal digital audio content via broadband Internet. In providing a customizable service via the Web, with access to almost unlimited content, Streamium is one of the first products to prefigure the possibilities of ambient intelligent audio.

Online music services

Via broadband Internet access, the Streamium connects to the many online radio stations and premium digital music services launched by major content providers, including AOL Music, Andante, MP2.com, MUSICMATCH, Radio Free Virgin and iM Networks. This combination of content options allows consumers to choose their online music, either via personalized radio stations or via playlists of personally selected music, stored in a secure 'online jukebox' and then streamed to the system.

Connectivity

The device is connected to the home network in much the same manner as an additional PC, by plugging it in as an additional Ethernet connection to the home Internet Gateway or router. As such, not only can the device access and play the direct Internet radio feeds, but it can also access playlists and MP3 files located on PCs sharing the same network, thus providing networked storage.

The unit also includes a CD player to allow users to play CD, CD-R or CD-RW discs as well as CDs containing MP3 or mp3PRO formatted audio. On its large five-line LCD display, the Streamium continuously shows information about what the system is playing, with the artist name and song title displayed, regardless of whether the track is being streamed or being played back via a CD.

Personalization

Digital connectivity also enables the Streamium to receive additional services and features from Philips and its partner companies as and when they are offered. Users can manage their experience and personalize their music preferences through the online service my.Philips.com. Personalization options allow users to select preferred artists and styles. These are then streamed to the user, along with occasional new artists or tunes based on the user's set preferences.

Philips is currently adding identification technology to make the Streamium user-aware and propagate this in the local network. Finally, using UPnP middleware, Streamium will interact with portable infotainment devices to extend the experience beyond the home.

www.audio.philips. com/streamium/mci200.asp

8.9 EASY ACCESS AND LISY

ASK AND YOU SHALL RECEIVE, HUM AND YOU SHALL HEAR

Taming your music collection with Easy Access

Many people have extensive collections of music, and find it difficult to locate pieces exactly when they want them. Easy Access is a system designed to help them in a way that does not require any laborious cataloguing or physical searching on the part of the user.

Music, Maestro

You're in a nostalgic mood and want to hear one of your favourite Beatles songs. You know which one, so you simply say to your Ambient Intelligence system, 'Maestro! Lucy in the Sky with Diamonds, please'. The system 'wakes up', finds the song and plays it for you. It identifies you by analyzing your speech patterns, and retrieves your personal profile of preferences so that the settings are just as you like them. The system uses phoneme-based speech recognition to identify what you said, and since it 'knows' the contents of your collection, it is almost certain to 'hear' you correctly: it knows it can ignore 'ums' and 'ahs', for instance. The system will let you know how it is doing when looking for your choice by tones, synthesized speech, or graphics on your portable touchscreen.

It goes like this

Suppose you want to browse through your collection for another song. Just pick up your touchscreen and browse through the menus, tapping your choice each time. Of course, if your hands are wet or you're busy eating or reading, you can browse using voice control – just tell the touchscreen your choices. But what if you can't remember the name of the piece of music but you can remember how it goes? Just hum it to the system. Ignoring the key in which you hum the tune, the system will analyze the intervals, synthesize the melody and play it back to you to check that it has 'heard' you correctly. If it has, it will search for a song containing that melody and play it to you, starting at the point where the melody was found. If it's the right piece, you can either continue listening or tell the system to play it from the beginning.

Sounds like you

You can build up a profile of your likes and dislikes, which the system will then use to recommend new items for your collection. When asked, it will connect to a server on the Internet to find people with a profile that matches yours, who are likely to have the same taste in music. The system will identify pieces highly rated by your 'match' but not yet rated by you and suggest them to you. It can rank suggestions in order of closeness to your own tastes.

Taming your digital video and speech collection with LISy

We now have access to incredible amounts of speech and images, whether from the many TV channels now available to us, from the Internet, or from our own collections of recorded material. This is largely due to the greater network bandwidth we have available today, combined with increased storage capacity that consumer electronics products and computers offer us. Both bandwidth and storage capacity are growing exponentially. Personal Video Recorders, providing selective recording and hard-disk storage are already available, and in the very near future, we shall see mass-market hard-disk recorders that can store more than 100 hours of video.

So access to content is no longer an issue: the real bottleneck comes when we want to make a choice from among everything we have. How can we cut through all this material to find exactly what we want? The Living Room Information System, LISy for short, allows users to ask their system to provide whatever they want. It then searches in its archive – including TV broadcasts that are only minutes old – to find and display the material required.

Tell me all about...

You come home in the evening. You've just missed the news on TV, but you'd like an update – not everything, only the things that interest you. So you ask LISy 'What happened in the Musgrave case today?' The multiple microphones focus on you and pick up your words. The system's speech recognizer knows what you're talking about, because it has been monitoring broadcasts and has analyzed their content. The system's dialogue manager triggers the retrieval process and before you know it, the latest newscast on the Musgrave case is on the screen.

A clever librarian

How did it pick the right piece out of the stream of sound it has available? For a start, it knows how to segment a stream of audio into blocks that go together, not only by identifying potential breaks, but also by analyzing adjacent content for similarities and fitting fragments together to form a coherent story. The story is then analyzed semantically to establish its topic (e.g., Sports, News, Finance), and keywords (e.g., names of people, places and organizations) are identified to facilitate later searches. This information is stored along with the video and audio data in the database.

Just tell the touchscreen which song you'd like to hear, or scroll to see more

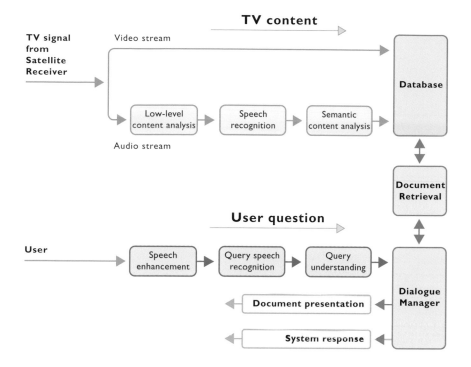

How the Living Room Information System works

BLUE MODULES:
The video input arrives at the system (e.g., from a TV broadcast). The video content is stored directly in the Database. The audio content is subjected to analysis, first roughly (in terms of coherent blocks, based on changing patterns of sound, for instance). The speech content is then recognized and on that basis the semantic content of the programmes is analyzed. This analysis is then stored with the video images in the Database and indexed.

GREEN MODULES:
The user asks the system for a particular piece of content. The user's speech is enhanced to eliminate distracting factors, such as hesitations and unnecessary words. Speech recognition technology then recognizes the words, after which the meaning is extracted and the request passed to the Dialogue Manager.

ORANGE MODULES:
The Dialogue Manager presents the query to the Document Retrieval unit, which finds the requested material in the Database and communicates this fact to the Dialogue Manager.

YELLOW MODULES:
The Dialogue Manager then presents the material to the user. If the material is not present, or if further details are required, the Dialogue Manager makes an appropriate response to the user.

8.10 PML

WHEN YOUR ROOM BECOMES YOUR BROWSER

Ambient Intelligence, with its network of cooperating devices, offers the promise of providing us with exciting new experiences in the home. Suppose, for instance, that while you are reading a book or watching a movie the whole room around you begins to reflect the imaginary scene?

Physical Markup Language

To make this possible, besides a physical infrastructure, you need standard descriptions and protocols that enable you to describe experiences and interpret them in terms of appropriate effects within the network of devices – rather like HTML encodes the features of the Web pages that our browser then interprets for us and presents on screen. The framework of rules would need to be flexible enough to cope with the variety and complexity of the real world and the personal attributes of the individuals undergoing the experience. For this purpose, Philips has developed a common language for describing experiences within an Ambient Intelligence environment: Physical Markup Language (PML).

Your room as browser

An Ambient Intelligence system can interpret a description in PML in such a way that the devices in its network can jointly use their individual capabilities to render that experience at a given location.

A PML EXPERIENCE

Little Red Riding Hood

Story retold and illustrated by Martine Sheppard

In effect, your whole room becomes a 'browser' that brings the experience to life. For example, PML-enabled lights add to the experience by getting brighter or dimmer, or changing colour. A PML-enabled hi-fi provides an appropriate soundscape. Almost any device can be PML-enabled: the possibilities are only limited by the imaginations of their manufacturers. Suppose a room is rendering an experience described as 'warm and sunny': the lights, the TV, the central heating, the electronically controlled blinds and (a little further into the future) even the ceiling, walls and floor coverings could all contribute to creating it.

All the better to thrill you with, my dear...

To illustrate the principle, we have developed a PML-enhanced storybook telling the story of Little Red Riding Hood. As you turn the pages of the book, the book knows exactly where you are in the story. The PML associated with the scene described on that page is communicated to the space around you. The many Ambient Intelligence devices in that space then use their capabilities collaboratively to transport you into the world of the story.

Little Red Riding Hood sets out for Granny's house, walking across some fields. The storybook shows a sunny blue sky, birds in the trees and Little Red Riding Hood happily humming away to herself. The PML representation associated with this page is transmitted to the room and describes the scene in much the same way. The lights then mimic daylight on a sunny day, the hi-fi locates a suitable birdsong soundtrack, and a gentle breeze wafts from a fan in the corner. Even Little Red Riding Hood's humming is heard from one of the speakers. But later, when she is deep in the forest, the wolf suddenly appears: the lights go down, you hear brooding music, and a cold draft catches the back of your neck. Suddenly a low growl shakes your chair, and a pair of wolf eyes peer out from the TV...

PML

8.11 CDS

FUTURE PROJECTIONS – NEXT STOP, REALITY

Projectors are no longer confined to cinemas, classrooms and offices, and they are no longer showing just films and images. They will soon form an integral part of our home experience as well. With the new generation of advanced multimedia projectors and Surround Vision™ technology, it is now possible to project crisp and colourful moving images onto almost any wall surface – walls, curtains, screens and furniture – in the full light of day.

With new applications and content specially designed to take advantage of these capabilities, we can transform our homes into a dynamic, engaging and interactive environment, one which we can change with the press of a button, a spoken word or even a gesture. A variety of new developments are likely to make projection systems the leading technology for creating visual experiences in the home. Taken to its full potential, projection will leave conventional TVs light-years behind. The alternative isn't TV, it's reality.

Surrounded

We are all used to using lighting and music to set the mood in a room. But in the home of the future, we will use projected images as well. Surround Vision™ will let us sit around the images – face-to-face with friends and family in a more relaxed situation – rather than in a row in front of the TV screen.

Dynamic Staging

Dynamic Staging creates a living room where the walls are constantly changing. Maybe you're looking out the windows of a spaceship. Or you're underwater among a shoal of fish. Or watching a 360° real-time video transmission from the top of the Roden Crater in Arizona as the sun slowly sets.

Well, hello!

We all know the world is getting smaller. Not only can we talk to someone anywhere or anytime, we can also see them, thanks to video telephony. But seeing someone on a small videophone display is not the same as seeing them in real life. Why not make video telephony life-size, using a projector? It will be our virtual window on the world. Whether we want to chat to our loved ones on the other side of the world, or catch up with our colleagues back in the office, a projector will make it seem like we're in the same room.

Reality Fusion

Reality Fusion games are blurring the line between the real and the unreal. Video games of the future will appear more lifelike than ever, as intelligent projectors show characters at different locations to create visual depth, much like characters on a theatre stage. Our imaginations will be the only limit, and we'll be able to express ourselves in ways we hadn't even dreamed of. The home will become a way to stimulate our imagination and support our creative behaviour.

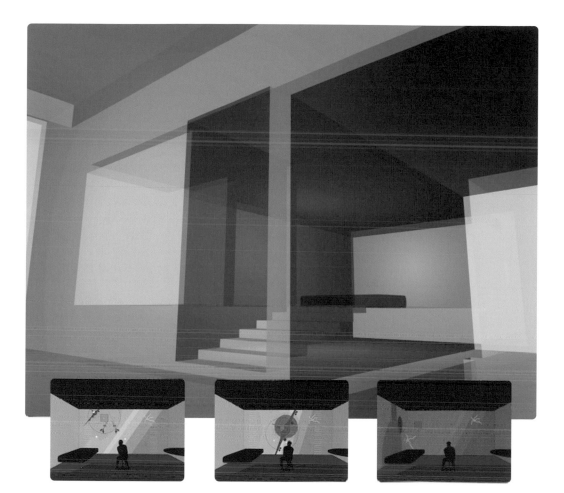

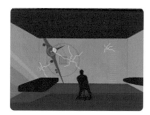

8.12 MIME

Everyone has their own ever-growing collection of 'intimate media' – photo albums, souvenirs, diaries, anything in fact that holds special meaning or value, relating to our past, present or future dreams. MIME explores how computer technology can help us experience our collections around the home more intensely. Instead of allowing our intimate media to disappear into the computer, as it moves deeper into our personal lives, MIME considers how artifacts and systems can help us get more out of the human experience of collecting, storing and sharing intimate media.

Glow Tags

Glow Tags trigger personal memories. Taking the form of bookmarks, clips, ribbons or sticky labels, for instance, they can be attached to intimate media anywhere in the home. They store a small amount of information relating to the 'story' behind the intimate media in question, such as dates, people's names or locations.

Glow Tags are actually tiny computers that listen in to information flows in the home. Whenever they notice a connection between a current event and the facts they store (such as an anniversary or a voice-mail from a certain person), they glow, gently reminding us of that link and triggering a memory.

The Living Scrapbook

The Living Scrapbook enhances the continuing delight many of us have in owning and interacting with paper, especially books. This scrapbook lives and grows. You can change, add to or annotate the content in the book itself using pen or pencil, sticking in pictures, or any other traditional means. These manually-made changes are then automatically added to the digital file containing all the contents to date, so that you always have a complete digital version of the scrapbook, which you can view or print out as you wish.

The Picture Ball

The Picture Ball makes it easy to capture and browse images any time you like – holiday snaps, pictures of small objects, tickets, drawings, or whatever. It can either be used in a casual, random way or in a more directed manner. The ball's weighting and bearings make it easy to spin; it will keep spinning after you've let go, gradually slowing down to stop on a single image.

Lonely Planet Listener

The Lonely Planet Listener revives personal memories of faraway places – the bells of an old church, the call to prayer in Istanbul, the dawn chorus on an African lake... These Listeners are simply microphones installed at selected places around the world. When travelling, you can collect access codes to local Listeners. They are linked to a transmitting service that relays the sounds they pick up (e.g., via the Internet) to a distribution service. You can then listen in on a browser, the telephone, or a dedicated Lonely Planet Radio, on which you can tune in to various Listeners around the world, as if you were tuning into a radio station.

www.design.philips.com/mime

Paul's holiday takes him first to Seville, on to Jerez da la Fronterra and Malaga, back to Seville and then home again

Paul opens the book to the page showing his stop at Malaga. He sees prints of the photos he took there and space to add things himself

Paul's brother Pete receives a copy of the printed book, complete with Paul's additions

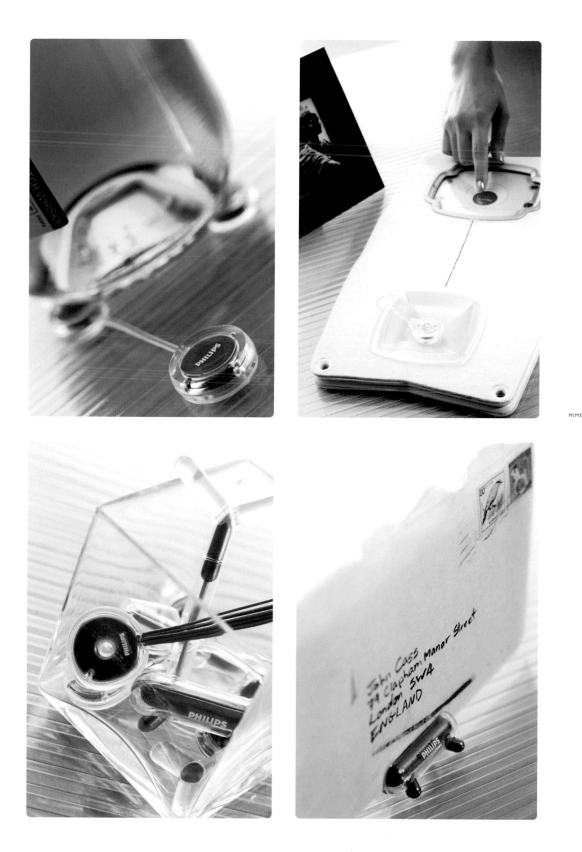

8.13 Q4 PLUGGED

Q4 Plugged (created in partnership with Felice Rossi) is an 'intelligent' couch designed with the connected home in mind. Its modular design allows its owner to create a wide variety of polyfunctional 'zones' for relaxation and socializing, ranging from a traditional-looking settee, to a chaise longue or self-contained 'work and play' area. A number of electronic entertainment features are integrated into Q4 Plugged, and it is also fully 'wired' so that it can be easily fitted with a variety of others.

Making your own connections

The basic elements of Q4 Plugged are four square seat-modules (140cm x 140cm), upholstered in an apparently 'buttoned', mattress-like style. Various armrests, backrests and table elements can be slotted into holes in these modules to form any configuration desired. Possibilities include a traditional couch with backrests along the length, armrests at each end and a table in the middle; a square couch with sitting options on various sides for central positioning

in a room; or a square lounging 'zone' totally enclosed on all sides with armrests or backrests.

All elements can be linked together not only physically but also electrically. One of the modules has a power lead to connect the whole to a nearby mains socket. The 'buttons' in the mattress tops are actually elasticized holes into which you can plug the various elements in the positions of your choice or make the necessary electrical connections.

Integrated intelligence

The armrests of Q4 Plugged provide functions as well as support. One is fitted with a music player (the control panel being 'embroidered' in the side of the armrest), another contains the loudspeakers, while the third is hollow for general storage purposes. The basic Q4 Plugged system is supplied with two table units, one in the form of a low tray, the other in the form of a higher table. A projector (for ceiling or wall projection), Web pad (screen and charging base) and 'table lamp' using light-emitting polymers are also available, so that you can personalize your Q4 Plugged to meet your needs and tastes exactly.

www.design.philips.com/smartconnections/94
www.design.philips.com/portfolio/visionary/roomchair.html

8.14 SMARTMIRROR

Through the ages, the mirror has always shown its two faces: reality and fantasy, technology and symbolism. It has been a practical grooming aid, a means of divination for Snow White's stepmother, the polished shield in which Perseus safely viewed the Medusa and, more recently, Harry Potter's Mirror of Erised.

The mirror is the oldest object made by mankind to give visual feedback and has been around for thousands of years. Its more modern counterpart, the television, has only been around for a few decades. Recent developments in flat displays, most notably plasma displays and liquid crystal displays, now open up the opportunity for another step in the evolution of mirrors, because we can make a mirror from a display or enhance a mirror with the functions of a display.

The classical mirror above a fireplace or in a bedroom may in fact be a TV. And in the bathroom, we can have an intelligent and interactive mirror, providing alternative or enlarged views of our face or body, coaching us to brush our teeth better, or helping us to lose weight. We can also save time in the morning by reading the news headlines while shaving. In the car, mirrors can become intelligent and proactive by warning us about things we can't see, such as cyclists in our blind spot or dangers at night. And, in leisure moments, our mirror can become our personal coach, teaching us to dance or improve our golf swing.

The ultimate 'intelligent mirror' is likely to consist of one or more displays and a mirror (of course), with cameras, microphones, computing power, storage, wireless sensors and appliances, plus a link to the outside world. We will interact with this mirror using touch control, voice control, person identification and gesture control, although the precise combination we will want remains to be seen. Today we use the metaphor of the desktop on our computer: what will be the appropriate metaphor for our interface with a mirror? (Certainly not a desktop!)

How will the mirror and display be combined?

One way that has already been explored is to place a display behind a semi-transparent mirror. Although this works, it is a compromise: it degrades the functionality of both the mirror and the display. The light falling on the mirror is only partially reflected, and some of the light transmitted by display is held back by the mirror. Recent developments in LCDs enable a much better performance, taking advantage of the fact that the light from an LCD is polarized. We use a special mirror that reflects all the light of one polarization and allows all the light of the opposite polarization to pass through. By aligning the mirror's polarization with that of the LCD screen behind the mirror, we achieve an excellent quality of reflection as well as allowing all the light from the LCD to pass through the mirror.

8.15 TOONS

EXPLORING FUN EXPERIENCES – TOON TOYS

Ambient Intelligence can enhance our experiences and make them more enjoyable. Implicitly, much of this book has discussed Ambient Intelligence in relation to adults. But what about children? Can Ambient Intelligence be applied to create enjoyable experiences for them, experiences that challenge their cognitive and physical abilities at an appropriate level, stimulate interaction and develop their natural curiosity?

As part of a project to develop toys to serve as input devices for an interactive TV show for 8-10-year-olds called TOONS, as well as a general device for playing games, three interactive electronic toys and games were developed. They each address a different range of motor skills. One requires fine motor skills (better developed in girls); another requires gross motor skills (better developed in boys); and the third requires both fine and gross motor skills, and was thus suitable for both girls and boys.

Stickysticks

Stickysticks is a game for two players. The game board resembles a chessboard, and there is a magnet positioned under each square. Each child has a magnetic stick, and they play by holding the stick over specific squares. This challenges their fine motor skills. They get feedback and 'feed-forward' through sound and magnetic force. The challenge is to make specific combinations of squares as quickly as possible without touching the board.

Twistyertouch

Twistyertouch is a large, soft cube (160 x 160cm). Attached to each visible surface is a cushion, which functions as a button. Children push, jump on, or hit the cushions, activities that

require gross motor skills. A sound tells them when they have activated the right cushion. The challenge is to hit all the right 'buttons' as quickly as possible, which encourages the children to cooperate.

Tunemein

The Tunemein is based on the Theremin, a musical instrument developed in 1919 by a Russian physicist, Lev Termen. Tunemein is an instrument consisting of a small base with a long aerial sticking out of it. Children produce tones by moving their hand towards the aerial. The closer they get, the louder the tone. The children need fine motor skills to make a very loud tone without touching the aerial. Different tones can be made by moving your hands along the aerial, an activity that requires gross motor skills. Each tone is linked to a specific action, which can only be completed when a certain volume is reached. Feedback and feed-forward information is provided through sounds and LEDs on the base of Tunemein. An extra challenge is provided by the fact that the positions of the tones on the aerial change occasionally!

The results show that the toys appear to be more difficult to use than the keyboard and mouse. But the children actually perceive the difficulty as a nice challenge and find the toys more fun to use than the keyboard and mouse.

Given the results of the study and the reactions of the children who participated, we believe that the heuristics that we adopted are a promising set of design guidelines to create tools, not just targeted at children, that will offer the user a fun and enjoyable experience.

More information about TOON toys can be found in:
M.A. Stienstra and H.C.M. Hoonhout, 'TOONS Toys: Interaction toys as a means to create a fun experience', Proceedings Interaction Design and Children (Maastricht, Shaker Publications, 2002) or contact jettie.hoonhout@philips.com

8.16 POGO

The introduction of computing and interactive media into classrooms in the late 1980s promised to enrich the learning process. But the benefits so far have been rather one-sided. While computers may help children with analytical skills such as calculation, they seldom stimulate the imagination. In fact, the world of multimedia tends to encourage passivity rather than enhance creativity. The challenge in the Pogo project was to design and develop an appropriate computer interaction for the classroom that would take the benefits of computer learning further into the realm of the imagination.

Interaction that encourages creativity and cooperation

The idea for Pogo came from storytelling. Children love to listen to stories and to tell them, too. In doing so, they express their fantasies, communicate with each other and create a picture of the world they experience every day. In doing all this, they do not merely explore the world they live in and its possibilities, they also learn about language, communication and dealing with other people – all key elements in the education and development of a well-rounded child. Pogo is a form of interaction that actually encourages creativity and cooperation with others: it provides children between the ages of four and eight with a set of tools that they can use to create stories collaboratively.

The only limit – your imagination

At first glance, you can't tell what Pogo is. Although the system is computer-based, the standard computer interface of keyboard, screen and mouse has been replaced with a far more intuitive one. A silver mat is surrounded by leather cushions and various tools, including a table with a built-in screen. The screen makes different noises when touched and, if you place an object on it and push a button, its picture is taken. This picture then appears on the table and can be added to by drawing with your fingertips in a wide variety of colours. The combination of table and screen makes it possible to create as many 'pictures' and 'characters' for your story as you want – the only limit is your imagination! There is even a small video camera to record moving images.

Really child's play

The interaction is so simple that when children start to play, it soon explains itself – there is almost no need for instruction. The Pogo story world is an interactive, computer-based creative world – a system that complements and enhances traditional learning processes.

More information about Pogo is available at
www.design.philips.com/portfolio/visionary/pogo.html

8.17 CONNECTED PLANET

The emerging consumer communications marketplace is characterized by the explosive growth and convergence of Internet-based services and mobile communications. As a result, people are acquiring unlimited access – anytime, anywhere – to information, entertainment and communication. How will we manage and organize this potential information overload? How will we keep control while keeping in touch? Philips Design and Philips Consumer Communications are exploring these challenges together in Connected Planet, a long-term, human-focused, strategic design project. These scenarios illustrate how this technology can be used to enhance the quality of our mobile lives.

Louise

A businessman finishes a phone call as he joins a meeting. Using voice control, he switches the device to 'Meeting' mode. It will now only 'ring' discreetly for high-priority communication, diverting all other calls. He takes notes, using his connected pen. During the meeting, a voice message from his daughter, Louise, is displayed as text on the display for discreet reading and replying.

Louise and a friend have similar devices. These devices not only give the girls direct 'contact' with their parents, but also allow them to do all sorts of other things. For example, through proximity sensing, they are invited to a group game on a train. Later, Louise and her voice recognition password are 'recognized' by her front door. A Home Hub, aware of her arrival, lights up the house while informing her parents that she is safely home.

Tom

Fourteen year old Tom receives new messages stored on his Home Hub. He listens to a music message through wireless earphones. In his bedroom, he amplifies the music by plugging the earphones into the Boombox. Later, he receives a phone call from his Gran. The music automatically becomes quieter.

Gran is on a train. Browsing through a magazine, she scans in a restaurant advertisement. The phone number is 'recognized' by her device and highlighted for her to call. She requests a reservation for that evening and receives a map showing the location. Arriving at the busy train station, Gran phones her daughter, and they use a location service to find each other.

Han

Han returns to his Hong Kong office after his morning run. His device has been tracking his performance and analyzes his progress on the desktop computer. With the device in 'Holiday' mode he arranges his communications accordingly by diverting calls, leaving notification of his absence, etc. He downloads his itinerary, tickets, maps and other travel information from the Internet.

Later, on the plane, he connects to a safe on-board network. He buys a Chinese-French voice translation service and tries it out on the passenger next to him. Once in Paris, he is led to the Eiffel Tower by map information and a location service, where he uses his device to take a photograph and send it to friends back home. A proximity sensor on his device enables him to receive an advertisement offering a ride to the top of the Tower. He takes another picture from the top of the tower and adds a voice comment to it.

www.design.philips.com/portfolio/visionary/connected.html

8.18 CAMP AND MADS

CONNECTIVITY IN CONTEXT

The CAMP (Context Aware Mobile Phones) and MADS (Mobile *ad hoc* Distributed Systems) projects are exploring how to provide location- and context-sensitive information and services and *ad hoc* mobile peer-to-peer applications enabled by short-range RF technology.

Technology: getting the opportunities across

The local environment strongly influences people's behaviour: a circle with a radius of 10 metres around them forms the basic context in which they operate.

Many mobile phones and other consumer and computing devices are now equipped with short-range wireless capabilities (e.g., Bluetooth). CAMP and MADS use these short-range transmission protocols as a medium for exchanging interaction opportunities and proposing ('pushing') location-based services and information to customers.

Interesting innovations include the modification of the Bluetooth standard to make it more appropriate for quick access, 'insecure' public transactions and short-range broadcast capabilities.

Software and processing: filtering the right opportunities

CAMP and MADS are developing a software architecture to process all the possible interaction and information opportunities a user might receive from other users or devices in the vicinity or from a particular place. The architecture supports the generic functions required to enable new application paradigms called 'Digital Perception' and 'JustPlay!'.

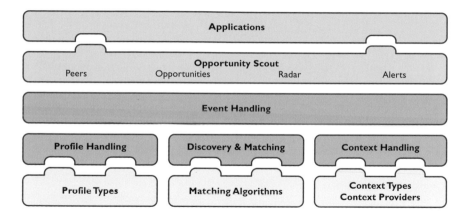

The major components of this architecture are:

- Profile-handling, i.e., discovering and remembering what the user is interested in and what the infrastructure is capable of. Profile data is largely static, although different subsets may become more important in certain contexts.
- Context-handling, i.e., managing a set of dynamic properties that describes the current situation of a mobile device and its user. Relevant context properties include location, time, time schedules, environment, user situation and device properties. One of the key challenges is to develop an open, universal 'context description format' that allows various sources of context data to be integrated into the platform.
- Opportunity discovery, i.e., announcing offers from the mobile device (and its user) to other devices and discovering offers from other devices.
- Matching and negotiation, i.e., bringing all the information together. Matching determines how relevant opportunities found as a result of Opportunity Discovery are to the user's profile and current context.
- Event-handling, i.e., informing applications and users about occurrences of interest such as relevant opportunities or context changes.
- Applications, e.g., as developed by third parties for specific purposes and making use of the data from the event-handling layer.

- User interface: presenting the opportunities to people.
  Finally, CAMP and MADS are concerned with how people will actually use Digital Perception and JustPlay! applications. We have experimented with a range of novel interfaces for presenting contextual opportunities and managing profile details, and have also conducted concept trials in a shopping mall. Reactions were generally enthusiastic. The preferred service examples were practical tools, such as mall guides or travel news, and social tools such as signals of friends' proximity or located messages. Even specific advertisements were considered enjoyable.

  Several other application prototypes have been built for ranging from wireless projectors, over content kiosks to mobile peer-to-peer entertainment applications.

More information is available online at www.justplay-technologies.com and www.wi-adhoc.de

THE ESSENTIAL REFERENCES FOR CAMP ARE:

Caswell, D., Debaty, P. (2000). Creating Web Representations for Places, in Lecture Notes in Computer Science #1927, Springer-Verlag, 115-126; also http://www.cooltown.hp.com/

Schmandt, C., Marmasse, N., Marti, S., Sawhney, N., Wheeler, S.(2000). Everywhere Messaging, IBM Systems Jnl., 39, 3&4, 660-677

Rankin, P. (2001). Context-Aware Mobile Phones: The difference between pull and push, Restoring the importance of place', HCII 2001 Conference Proceedings, Lawrence Erlbaum Associates, Aug 5-10, New Orleans

8.19 SPICE

JUST SAY WHAT YOU WANT AND I'LL DO IT

In an Ambient Intelligence home, we will be interacting with many interconnected devices. If we had to interact with them all in the way we interact with most electronic devices today (special commands, complex procedures, lengthy menu structures), we would soon end up in despair. In normal interactions with other people, we use words and gestures to indicate what we want: why can't we communicate in the same way with our Ambient Intelligence system?

SPICE

Philips Research has developed a conversational user interface, currently in prototype, called SPICE (Speech Interfaces for Consumer Electronics). This allows you to find out what programmes are on TV, program the VCR and control your TV set, either by speaking to it naturally, pointing on a handheld touch screen, or both. The system displays the requested information on the touch screen. An animated face, representing the 'personality' of the system, shows the present status of the interaction and makes the interaction more 'alive'.

SPICE lets you:
- Say what you want in your own words, without having to remember specific commands or be limited to a predefined menu structure. You can combine several steps in one utterance ('Any good dramas on BBC1 tonight?').
- Go directly to the information you want, rather than proceeding one step at a time (e.g., first Genre, then Artist, then Album); or scrolling through long lists.
- Provide only vague information: SPICE can make correct identifications from non-specific information ('The second James Bond film'), and will ask when it needs further clarification.
- Choose the most suitable modality: speech if your hands are full; touch if you don't want to disturb others; pointing if selecting from a list; speaking if you're describing a movie. You can also speak and point at the same time ('Give me more information on this one').

Finally, SPICE can guide you through a complex task (such as programming the VCR), offer viewing suggestions based on your preferences, and help with problems.

User: 'Any children's programmes on this afternoon?'
SPICE   Displays all programmes in the Kids genre for this afternoon.

User: 'When is *Gone with the Wind* on?'
SPICE   Searches for this movie and displays viewing details:
        '*Gone with the Wind* is on BBC1 next Friday at 8pm'

User: 'Is there a James Bond movie on this week?'
SPICE: Failing to detect a unique movie title in the user's words, SPICE assumes that 'James Bond movie' refers to a movie and searches the textual descriptions of all movies in the database showing this week for 'James Bond'.

SPICE: '*Golden Eye* is on Friday at nine on Sky Movie'.
User: 'Give me more information on this one'
        (taps an item in the programme list on the touch-screen display).

SPICE   Combines the spoken instruction ('give information') with the pointing input (identifying the item) and displays the information required.
User: 'Record the movie tonight'.
SPICE: 'There are several movies on tonight. Do you know the channel or the title of the movie you want to record?'

User: 'It's on HBO'.
SPICE: 'OK, I'll record *Titanic* on HBO for you tonight at 8.30'

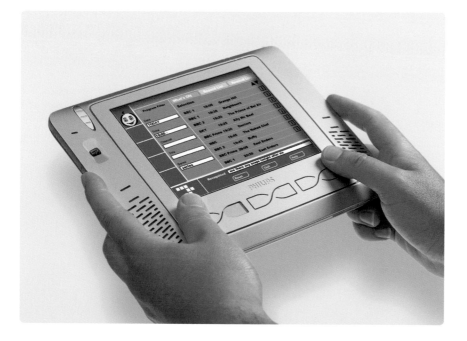

8.20 HICS

HIGHLY CUSTOMIZED AND CONTEXTUALIZED SOLUTIONS

Ambient Intelligence systems will provide a high degree of customization. How will businesses need to change in order to be able to deliver this in a context of increasing complexity? What new routes can they explore in identifying and satisfying these needs?

European project

To find answers to such questions, as part of its Competitive and Sustainable Growth Programme project, the European Community is funding a research project called Highly Customized and Contextualized Solutions (HiCS). Four research institutes, four companies (including Philips) and a consumer organization are taking part.

   The aim is to find industrialized, context-specific and sustainable solutions that companies can develop in partnership with consumers and other global and local stakeholders. Such solutions will go beyond traditional market segmentation (e.g., by sex, age, nationality and income) to consider people's physical, socio-cultural and personal contexts. They will also go beyond stand-alone products, developing highly customized 'intelligent' product-service systems.

Solution-Oriented Partnerships

The project explores these ideas within the concept of the Solution-Oriented Partnership (SOP), a customer-driven network in which partners collaborate in the design, manufacturing and delivery of systems that are economically viable and both socially and environmentally sustainable.

   This approach involves three basic activities:
* establishing global/local partnerships that can develop and deliver solutions
* identifying relevant contexts where consumers have specific needs and wishes
* defining a flexible technological and organizational platform with both global and local aspects.

	Explore	Develop	Explore	Develop
Partners	Platform Promoters	Platform Promoters	Tentative SOP	SOP
Context	Context of Use	Meta-Context of Use	Tentative Specific Contexts of Use	Final Specific Contexts of Use
Solutions	First Solution Ideas	Platform Solution Elements	Tentative HiCS	HiCS

The project applies this approach to the situation of people whose access to food is limited. Examples of such people include senior citizens living at home but unable to prepare their own meals, individuals who need to follow a strict diet for medical reasons, and people who need to eat at places where there are no cooking facilities. In each case, the same partners are involved: the customer, the food provider, the food preparer and the deliverer, plus possibly a medical service provider and a financial service provider. However, the providers' roles will vary from context to context, as the customers' needs and circumstances vary. The aim is therefore to develop generic technological and organizational platforms that can be customized – or rather, contextualized – on a local scale, using local people, environments and infrastructures, while at the same time being able to integrate the contributions of the various global partners.

Results so far

So far we have gained substantial understanding of the latent and unsatisfied needs and wants of people whose access to food is limited in selected contexts (e.g., homes, community centres and commercial centres), amassed knowledge concerning the food value-chain in Europe (e.g., delivery, preparation and consumption), and developed and tested an integrated method for bringing scientists, designers and users together to co-develop information and ideas for solutions that can address the complexities of people's lives at a given time and place. Perhaps most importantly, we have also identified a number of competitive ways of working within the digital networking service economy. In this way, we can begin to see emerging the general outlines of a viable business context in which Ambient Intelligence services involving many different parties can be developed and implemented.

The approach adopted in the HiCS project involves an iterative cycle of exploration and development at the levels of Partners, Context and Solutions (becoming increasingly specific, from left to right).

Using our research tools, users became co-researchers. Through their photographs, diaries and drawings, they provided HiCS researchers with many insights into their everyday activities relating to food, analyzing their problems and developing solutions to them with us.

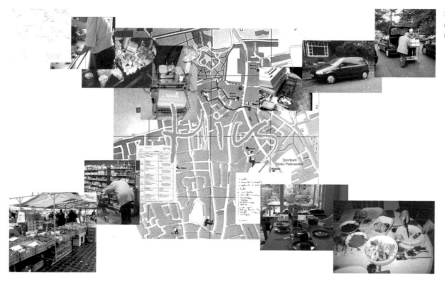

Source:
Milan Polytechnic,
HiCs Project 2001

HICS

8.21 OPEN TOOLS
DEEP CUSTOMIZATION IN PRACTICE

Over the next few years, even more professionals will be 'hypermobile', working and living in several locations. How can Ambient Intelligence help them navigate their way through this complexity while they maintain a healthy balance? Open Tools is a project that explores how deeply customizable, responsive and embedded products and services could provide an answer. These 'tools' are 'open' in that they are initially relatively 'undefined' and 'open-ended': users can largely specify and develop the functionalities of these tools as they wish, and the tools evolve over time, adapting and shaping themselves to the user's habits and needs, and becoming increasingly specialized. The project explored the impact such tools would have on users, on current mass-customization paradigms and on the brand-customer relationship.

Personal 'service units'

Open tools are 'service units', physical products connected to larger systems giving you easy access to functionality, services and content, as well as to other products and peripherals. Containing a range of latent functionalities, bounded by a set of rules, they allow you to negotiate and unfold their potential in your own way and at your own pace. An open tool will 'remember' how you have used it before, and use this memory to decide how best to link into your own pool of digital functionalities, data and services. The tools' system architecture allows them to link to digital resources, to each other and to other devices in meaningful ways.

OpenDesk, OpenFrame, OpenMirror

Three examples of open tools and a system rationale have been conceived, relating to the needs of professionals in work, mobility and well-being: the OpenDesk, the OpenFrame and the OpenMirror. They have been 'tested' against a six-month scenario, to show how they can evolve and become appropriately specialized and personalized. The two examples shown here, the OpenDesk and the OpenFrame, provide highly versatile and personalizable service portals for a new-media professional. Both have a biometric reader for personalized access, allowing data and functionality to be stored remotely and shared between these and other devices.

OpenDesk

The OpenDesk offers a work surface for the manipulation of digital media. The touch-sensitive display forming the surface allows you to access content and functionality from various work and domestic domains, and to navigate, organize and view these in a personalized way. The desk is open to software and is able to connect with other devices and open tools to extend its capabilities.

OpenFrame

The OpenFrame is a versatile mobile device which gives you easy constant access to customized digital resources and services while on the move. Physically it is empty, with no central display of its own. Instead, the touch-sensitive frame can host several peripheral, paper-thin bi-stable e-ink screens. Once loaded in the frame, these screens can be removed and even tiled. You can extend the OpenFrame with input and display devices of your choice. It is held together by the wrap, a fashion accessory that comes in diverse styles and has various technologies embedded within it.

More information about OpenTools can be found at www.design.philips.com/opentools

Connecting the community

With the fragmentation of society and the rise of virtual communities, there is a danger that important geographically-based social ties may become loosened by default. It might be thought that Ambient Intelligence, which enhances communication and socializing at a distance, might accelerate this development. But in fact it can be a vital factor in retaining and even strengthening local geographically-based communities. Two Philips projects – Living Memory (or LiMe for short) and Pl@net – explore how, rather than replacing geographic communities with digital ones, we can enhance neighbourhood cohesiveness with a 'living, digital reflection' of the collective consciousness. They aim to discover what might constitute appropriate, human-focused mechanisms for knowledge exchange in real communities, essentially using Ambient Intelligence to bring people closer together.

LiMe

Within any community there are everyday meeting-places and crossing points, such as cafés, bus stops and public buildings. These are ideal locations for people to access and share local

community knowledge in a casual and natural way. If there are appropriate interfaces at such locations, people can add a digital dimension to their community interactions without having to formally sit down at a computer at home or work.

A community in Edinburgh was chosen to be 'co-creators' of such a networked local community and to act as a test-bed for ideas. In an integrated programme of lab and field user testing, the team identified the typical things people do in the community, as well as where and when they do them. On the basis of this information, they were able to profile the community's natural knowledge exchange processes and pinpoint those locations (e.g., the local pub or café) where a LiMe interface should be set up. Then, with intensive participation and feedback from the community, appropriate interface prototypes were designed, installed, tested and repeatedly refined.

The result was a series of networked interfaces that would provide the community with seamless access from any of them to a pool of community information generated by themselves – local people and local institutions – ranging from 'help wanted' signs and flyers found on local notice boards to local cinema advertisements. People would be able to browse, access, share and create multimedia content in these everyday locations and then store that content on personal 'tokens', small coin-sized tags containing a chip.

LiMe, which was sponsored by the European Commission, was carried out from 1997-2000 by a consortium led by Philips Design.

More information about LiMe is available at www.design.philips.com/lime

Pl@net

Pl@net takes the ideas developed in LiMe further to provide richer, more personalized access mechanisms, enhanced system intelligence and improved connectivity.

Instead of downloading and storing information on tokens (as in LiMe), in the system envisaged in Pl@net, you use a personal, Bluetooth-enabled mobile phone. To store items of interest, simply *drag them onto to your phone*. Your phone learns your personal preferences and rearranges the data stream at each community location accordingly. In that way, you are immediately presented with the sort of information you are interested in.

Pl@net is community-driven: its pool of content and its interfaces are constantly being reconstructed in line with how people use them. As people enter content into the system, an intelligent, adaptive context engine learns from what people do where and when, so that it can dynamically filter content and redistribute it to the appropriate local terminals, according to context.

To fine-tune this system, a community simulator was developed to model how people behave in relation to such a system and how content flows through it. Pl@net enables real places to act as natural filters of information, making this system (unlike the Internet) sensitive to both geographical and social context. The information you come across on the Pl@net display while sitting in a coffee house, for instance, will be very different to the content mix you will find at a bus stop or kiosk, in the office or on your PDA. In Pl@net, the physical location of the screen becomes as much part of the interface as the screen itself.

Philips Design is currently looking at additional ways Pl@net can be exploited to serve the needs of public communities (where growth has led to anonymity), business communities (in which good knowledge exchange is vital), and temporary communities, such those at vacation resorts (where visitors lack recent local knowledge).

More information about Pl@net is available at www.design.philips.com/planet.

lcd+ (created in partnership with Levi's) was the first step towards the realization of Philips' Wearable Electronics vision, originally presented at Philips Design's *Vision of the Future* exhibition (1995). Inspired by the 'nomadic' lifestyle that was just beginning to emerge, it featured concepts such as multimedia T-shirts that enabled the wearer to download and listen to music on solid-state chips while on the move, and ski jackets with built-in GPS positioning and communication functions.

Technology on the go

The lcd+ range consists of four jackets designed for young professionals – active, modern and always on the move. The garments allow mobile communications via GSM phone (activated by voice-dialling through a microphone integrated in the collar), and music entertainment (from an MP3 player). The hardware is invisible and activated by remote control that not only allows automatic switching between the two, but provides new types of functionalities as well.

For example, you can listen to music through the ear-gear embedded in the collar, and also let someone else hear it directly on the phone. Thanks to the remote control, the MP3 function also stops automatically when a call comes through. The cut and positioning of the pockets, the housing of the microphone and the earphones, the interface on the remote control – all are designed to fit the lifestyle proposition and function of the garment, and to make it as easy and natural to use as possible.

Textile – the new, 'human' interface

lcd+ is at the forefront of a vision in which conductive fibres, flexible displays, fabric antennas, flexible interconnect and textile sensing will make it possible to create Ambient Intelligence solutions wherever textiles are used: in clothes, carpets, wallpaper, upholstered furniture, soft furnishings, car interiors and more. This development will enhance a new type of 'intelligence interface' between people and technology – soft rather than hard, human-centred rather than machine-centred, natural rather than complicated.

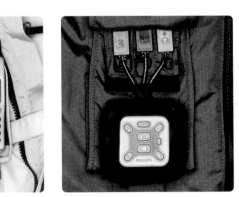
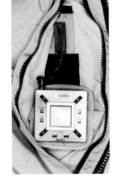

ICD+

Ambient Intelligence is not limited to the home. On the move, we want to enjoy the same sort of connectivity and digital support that we have at home – but without bulky equipment. It therefore makes perfect sense to start integrating Ambient Intelligence into our clothes.

Wearable electronics

Building upon Philips Design's initial exploration of wearable electronics as part of the *Vision of the Future* project in the late 1990s, Philips recently initiated a fresh approach to the future of lifestyle and fashion by bringing together a multi-disciplinary team of designers, scientists and engineers to explore the integration of technology into clothing.

Conductive textiles

A key challenge was to integrate an electronic infrastructure, to which intelligent objects could be attached, into clothing. This meant that we first needed to develop conductive textiles that could serve as soft 'componentry'. These textiles would enable data, power and audio to be conveyed around a garment through a body area network.

Assembling your identity

How people might engage with a body area network? To find out, we looked at the ritual of dress – how, by combining personal and cultural aesthetic preferences, people create a personal identity through their dress. New Nomads took this 'assembly' metaphor and extended it to cover the way people might assemble their electronic functionalities to create a truly personal portable electronic environment.

New Nomads

The result was the New Nomads, 'an exploration of wearable electronics'. The project looked at a spectrum of sub-cultures in which early adoption of wearable solutions was likely, from clubbers and active sportspeople to urban commuters and gamers. To show how their ideas might work out in practice, the team developed a number of concepts that demonstrate the 'ambient' relationship between products, apparel, furniture and the environments we live in.

Relaxation wear
Conductive threads can now be woven into clothing to help people 'de-stress' by gently and continuously inducing bodily relaxation. This cream kimono has a conductive embroidered spine at the back which disperses an electrostatic charge via the fibres in the lining, creating a soothing, tingling sensation.

Workwear
The shift from 'portable' to 'wearable' will inevitably affect workwear. In their work, flight attendants, hospital staff and maintenance workers all use electronic aids that can be integrated into their clothing for safety and efficiency.

Streetwear
This audio jacket is an expressive item of streetwear for young people, providing them with personal downloadable sound entertainment on the move. All the integrated audio devices can be controlled via a simple control panel, located on the sleeve for easy access. On the back of the jacket there is an electroluminescent digital display serving as an embedded spectrum analyzer. The emitted light pulsates at the frequencies of the music.

Kidswear
Providing peace of mind for parents and fun for kids, this coat uses phone and camera technology to pinpoint children's locations. It also allows kids to play exciting outdoor games. Cartoon character badges with identity chips can be attached to the coat. Other children see these characters on their own screens as monsters or animals. Playing together, the children can weave the actions of on-screen characters into their games.

Sportswear
High-performance sportswear can incorporate
embedded technologies that combine audio
features with body-monitoring. Integrated
biometric sensors that can monitor pulse,
blood pressure, body temperature, respiration
and other vital signs, analyzing and displaying
data to guide sportspeople during training.

AUTHORS

Stefano Marzano, Emile Aarts, Josephine Green, Karen Reddering, Liesbeth Scholten, Slava Kozlov, Christina Lindsay, Boris de Ruyter, Lorna Goulden, Paul McGroary, Marion Verbücken, Geert Depovere, Toon Holtslag, Ronald Aarts, Carel-Jan van Driel, Albert Comberg, Radu Jasinschi, Jan Nesvadba, René Collier, Eric Thelen, Stefan P. Grabowski, Hans Nikol, Marcel Pelgrom, Raf Roovers, Henk Jan Bergveld, Jef van Meerbergen, David P.L. Simons, Rob T. Udink, Warner ten Kate, Herman ter Horst, Anton Andrews, Monica Bueno, John Cass, Jan Korst, Wim Verhaegh, Eelco Dijkstra, Willem Jonker, Hans van Gageldonk, Paul Thursfield, Evita Stoop, Neil Bird, Clive van Heerden, Philippa Wagner, Jack Mama, Nancy Tilbury, Paul Gough, Henk van Houten, Wouter Leibbrandt, Fred Snijders, Mark Hartevelt, Lira Nikolovska, Peter Matthews, Lesh Parameswaran, Martin Elixmann, Jean-Paul Linnartz, Fiona Rees, Job Rutgers, Simona Rocchi, Laura Taylor, Cees Jan Mol, Steven Kyffin, Damian Mycroft, Neil Gridley, August de los Reyes, Reon Brand, Marco Bevolo, Karin Daly, Evert van Loenen, Vic Teeven, Nick de Jong, Esko Dijk, Elise van den Hoven, Yuechen Qian, Dario Teixeira, Mark Verberkt, Gerard Hollemans, Dietrich Klakow, David Eves, Richard Cole, Joost Horsten, Mark Lazeroms, Marcelle Stienstra, Jettie Hoonhout, Paul Rankin, Henning Maass, Andreas Kellner, Erno Langendijk, Rob Wubben, Marc op de Beeck, Ralph Braspenning

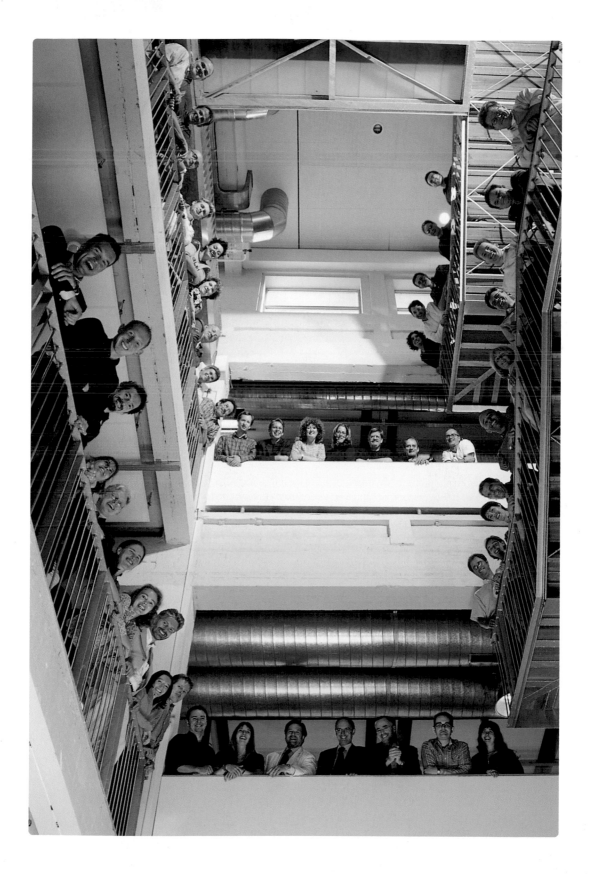

The New Everyday
Edited by Emile Aarts & Stefano Marzano

Content coordination
Anton Andrews, John Cass

Design
Ally Cane, Willem Kars, Anthony King, Anne Stas,
Christel van der Sterren, Paul van Vorstenbos

Editorial support
Baxter Associates

Project management
Bas Wouters

Production
André Senden, Vincent Vliegen

External experts
Elizabeth Diller, Tony Dunne, Ernst Homburg, Kevin Kelly, Dick van
Lente, Erkki Liikanen, Ezio Manzini, Fiona Raby, Ricardo Scofidio,
Egbert-Jan Sol

Lithography by Neroc Eindhoven B.V., The Netherlands
Printed by Lecturis B.V., Eindhoven, The Netherlands

British Library Catalogue in Publication Data
A catalogue record for this book is available from the British Library

Published by 010 Publishers, Rotterdam, The Netherlands
www.010publishers.nl

ISBN 90-6450-502-0